Asian Conflict of Laws

Asian Conflict of Laws

East and South East Asia

Edited By

Alejandro Carballo Leyda

Wolters Kluwer
Law & Business

Published by:
Kluwer Law International
PO Box 316
2400 AH Alphen aan den Rijn
The Netherlands
Website: www.kluwerlaw.com

Sold and distributed in North, Central and South America by:
Aspen Publishers, Inc.
7201 McKinney Circle
Frederick, MD 21704
United States of America
Email: customer.service@aspenpublishers.com

Sold and distributed in all other countries by:
Turpin Distribution Services Ltd
Stratton Business Park
Pegasus Drive, Biggleswade
Bedfordshire SG18 8TQ
United Kingdom
Email: kluwerlaw@turpin-distribution.com

Printed on acid-free paper.

ISBN 978-90-411-4756-1

Printed and Bound by CPI Group (UK) Ltd, Croydon, CR0 4YY.

List of Editor and Contributors

Elizabeth H. Aguiling-Pangalangan, Professor, College of Law, University of the Philippines

Ferry Artionang, Associate, Commercial Dispute Resolution, Hadiputranto, Hadinoto & Partners

Alejandro Carballo Leyda, Former Senior Associate at Cuatrecasas, Gonçalves Pereira. Observer Member to the working groups on the UNIDROIT Principles of International Commercial Contracts (3rd edition) and the Hague Conference Principles on Choice of Law in international contracts

Alan Gibb, Barrister, Professional Consultant, The Chinese University of Hong Kong (CUHK)

Reno Hirdarisvita, Associate, Commercial Dispute Resolution, Hadiputranto, Hadinoto & Partners

Yao-Ming Hsu, Associate Professor, College of Law, National Cheng-Chi University

Konrad Hull, Partner, VNA Legal

Naoki Iguchi, Partner, Nagashima Ohno & Tsunematsu

Naoko Kamimura, Special Counsel, Nagashima Ohno & Tsunematsu

Sae Youn Kim, Partner and Vice-Chair of the International Dispute Resolution Practice, Yulchon

Sy Nae Kim, Associate at Yulchon

Harish Kumar, Partner, Rajah & Tann Singapore LLP

Young Seok Lee, Partner and Chair of the International Dispute Resolution Practice, Yulchon

Miguel de Lemos, Legal Consultant, Timor-Leste

Wenwen Liang, Lecturer, School of Law, Research Institute of International Law, Wuhan University

Jorge Menezes, Partner at Legal Macau and Private Notary in Macau

Richard Morris, Director of the Postgraduate Certificate in Laws, The Chinese University of Hong Kong (CUHK)

Effendy Othman, Partner, Zaid Ibrahim & Co (a member of ZICOlaw)

Munkhselenge Purevdorjiin, Lecturer at School of Foreign Service, National University of Mongolia

Hendronoto Soesabdo, Partner, Commercial Dispute Resolution, Hadiputranto, Hadinoto & Partners

Vanina Sucharitkul, Attorney at Herbert Smith Freehills (Thailand) Limited

Chinnawat Thongpackdee, Partner, Herbert Smith Freehills (Thailand) Limited

Jonathan Toh, Senior Associate, Rajah & Tann Singapore LLP

Nguyen Thi Xuan Trinh, Partner, VNA Legal

Yongping Xiao, Professor of Law, School of Law, Research Institute of International Law, Wuhan University

Summary of Contents

Table of Contents

CHAPTER 7
Malaysia
Effendy Othman 129

Preface

This work was inspired by my experience advising European companies doing business in Asia and by two panels I chaired on Asian conflicts of laws; the first, in 2009 at the initial biennial conference of the Asian Society of International Law in Tokyo and the second, in 2011 at the ILA Asia Pacific Conference in Taipei. The panels prompted the debate on the usefulness of a regional instrument for the mutual recognition of judicial decisions in civil and commercial matters, and the need for coordinated efforts in harmonising private international law rules in the region.

In fact, the risks of litigation rank high amongst the deterrents to trade. A regional instrument for the recognition of judicial decisions, together with harmonised rules of conflict of laws could promote greater legal certainty and improve the commercial transactions both within the region and with other areas of the world.

However, a better access to, and understanding of, the different private international law frameworks in the region is needed before evaluating the feasibility of such harmonisation efforts. Indeed, even though similar proposals have been made already in the 1990s and despite the recent wide-ranging reform of the private international law rules in several Asian countries (Korea, Japan, China…), there is no comprehensive overview of the approach to Private International Law in the region.

The book seeks to support future regional efforts of private international law experts to continue deeper comparative analyses, as well as to increase the knowledge of non-Asian companies on the specific frameworks regulating international litigation and enforcement of foreign decisions in the region. The challenging task, which involved local specialists with particular expertise in private international law and international litigation, was initially limited to East and South East Asia, where there are closer economic and cooperation links.

Regretfully, not all countries are covered since in a few cases it was difficult to find experienced contributors available in the relevant jurisdiction and there were not enough published materials for a deep study. Yet, most of the jurisdictions are dealt with in the book showing the diversity of legal approaches to private international law in East and South East Asia.

Thanks to all the contributors for their support and great work. Thanks also to Kluwer Law International, in particular to Eleanor Taylor, for believing in the project and bearing with me during the editing of the book.

Alejandro Carballo Leyda
April 2015

CHAPTER 1

Mainland China

Yongping Xiao & Wenwen Liang[*]

§1.01 CODIFICATION OF PRIVATE INTERNATIONAL LAW AND RELEVANCE OF CASE LAW

[A] Codification and Case Law

From the foundation of the People's Republic of China (PRC) until the opening-up policy, the planned economy and the close-door policy left limited room for private international law. Civil and commercial disputes only occurred regularly after China started the reform and opening-up policy. Civil and commercial disputes have arisen significantly ever since. The total number of cases with a foreign element (Hong Kong, Macau, and Taiwan included) dealt with by the Chinese courts from 1979 to 2001 is 23,340. From 2001 to 2005, the number rose to 63,765. In 2009, alone, the number of foreign-related cases was 11,470 (in addition to 6,631 cases related to Hong Kong, 3,953 to Taiwan, and 329 to Macau).[1]

The Law Applicable to Foreign-Related Civil Relations Act (the Act) was adopted on 28 October 2010 and took effect as of 1 April 2011. It is a milestone in the codification of Chinese private international law since previously the private international law rules were dispersed in various acts, regulations, and judicial interpretations. Inconsistency and conflicts between the rules occurred frequently. To cure the defects of such fragmentation, the Act was adopted as a joint effort of the legislature,

* Yongping Xiao, Professor of Law, School of Law, Research Institute of International Law, Wuhan University. Wenwen Liang, Lecturer, School of Law, Research Institute of International Law, Wuhan University.

1. Huang Jin, *The Making and Improving the Chinese Act on the Applicable Law to Foreign-Related Civil Relations*, Tribune of Political Science and Law 3, 4 (2011).

judicature, and academia – including a Model Law on PIL presented by the Chinese Society of Private International Law in 2007.[2]

The Act makes the most significant relationship principle a supplementary principle to be applied when the Act is silent about the applicable law to a foreign-related civil relation (Article 2). It also gives a prominent role to the party autonomy principle (Article 3), which shows the openness of the legislature – although a liberal interpretation of this rule would ruin the purpose of the Act since parties can evade the otherwise applicable rules. In addition, the Act innovatively adopts the habitual residence as the connecting factor in personal law matters. Finally, the Act shows the protection of weak parties either by designating the law of the place of the weak party or expressly designating the law most in favour of the weak party.[3]

However, the Act has three shortcomings. First, it is a partial codification only touching choice of law rules for civil relations. Second, it is vague on its priority with regard to competing rules on the same matter by simply stating that special rules in other law apply prior to this Act (the issue lies in what is a special rule and the level of the rule maker). Third, the Act's pursuit of concise and simply wording may make it difficult to apply by the courts.[4]

In order to address the shortcomings of the Act, the Supreme People's Court adopted the Interpretation of Selected Issues of the Law Applicable to Foreign-Related Civil Relations (I) (the Interpretation) on the general part of the Act.[5] The Interpretation clarified that the Act is retrospective, since it has a bearing on parties' substantive rights; the Act prevails in marriage, tort, and succession, but surrenders in matters of negotiable instruments, maritime, civil aviation, and intellectual property law.[6] Rules of the Act and the Interpretation will be dealt with in specific parts.

Procedural matters, however, remain scattered mainly in the Civil Procedure Act – as amended in 2012; the 1996 Arbitration Act; the 1999 Special Maritime Procedure Act; the 2002 Provisions of the Supreme People's Court on Some Issues Concerning the Jurisdiction of Civil and Commercial Cases Involving Foreign Elements FASHI [2002] No. 5; the 1991 Supreme People's Court Provisions on the Procedures regarding the Application for Foreign Divorce Judgments by Chinese Nationals FM [1991] No. 21; and the Ministry of Justice, Supreme People's Court and Ministry of Foreign Affairs Notice on Implementing the Hague Service Convention SFT [1992] No. 093.

China is not a case law country. Judges are only competent in applying the law rather than creating the law. The purpose is to respect the integrity of the law. However, the pursuit of simplicity of Chinese legislations gives rise to discrepancy in the application of the rules by the courts. It is widely recognised that courts are granted

2. *Model Law of Chinese Private International Law* (Legal Press, 1999). For the process, see *Ibid.*, at 9-11; Chen Weizuo, *Modernization of Chinese Private International Law: The Achievements and Shortcomings of The Law Applicable to Foreign-Related Civil Relations Act*, Tsinghua Law Review 97, 98-99 (2011).
3. Articles 25, 29, 30, 43, 45, 46 of the Act.
4. Xiao Yongping, *Milestone in Codifying the Chinese Private International Law*, Legal Forum 44, 48 (2011).
5. It was adopted on 10 Dec. 2012 and took effect as of 7 Jan. 2013.
6. Articles 2 and 51 of the Act; Interpretation rule 3.

the authority to exercise their discretion in appropriate circumstances. The Supreme People's Court has published guidance cases in the official gazette which serve as de facto guidance for lower courts.[7] Where the law is silent, cases play a role of reference to the courts. The interpretations can be summaries of court practices, or replies to lower courts' enquiries in individual cases, or general rules to fill the gap of legislations. Those general rules are systemic, codified rules of law raising a challenge to their formal status under constitutional law: how a judiciary legislates in a non-case law country.[8] Despite the challenge to the formal status of the Supreme People's Court's published guidance cases and interpretations, they serve as current law.

[B] Multilateral Conventions Providing Uniform Substantive Law and/or International Jurisdictional Rules

The Chinese constitution is silent on the application of international conventions in China. Nevertheless, in principle, international conventions on private law matters in force in China prevail over competing rules of municipal Chinese law.[9] This is achieved in two ways: either (i) municipal Chinese law provides that relevant matters follow treaties or conventions,[10] or (ii) municipal Chinese law provides that treaties or conventions prevail over competing rules of municipal Chinese law.[11]

China is a party to the UN Convention on Contracts for the International Sale of Goods (CISG), the 1929/1999 Conventions for the International Carriage of Goods by Air, the 1969 International Convention on Civil Liability for Oil Pollution Damage and the Convention on International Interest in Mobile Equipment (together with its Aircraft Protocol). Some of the international conventions regarding sea transport are applicable only to the Special Administrative Region (SAR) of Hong Kong and Macao. China is a party to fourteen multilateral treaties administered by the World Intellectual Property Organization (WIPO).[12]

§1.02 JURISDICTION OF LOCAL COURTS IN FOREIGN-RELATED CASES

In relation to civil litigation involving foreign elements, the main legislation is the Civil Procedure Act - both general and special provisions - which was amended in 2007 and 2012. Provisions on civil procedures can also be found in the 1982 Constitution Act and the Special Maritime Procedure Act. The Supreme People's Court interpretations

7. Liu Xiangshu, *Doctrines and Cases as Sources of Law*, Journal of Chinese People's Public Security University 38, 41-42 (2002).
8. Yuan Mingsheng, *Legislature-Like Supreme People's Court Interpretations*, Studies in Law and Business 3, 3 (2003); Chen Chunlong, *Status and Function of Supreme People's Court Interpretations*, China Legal Science 24 (2003); Cao Shibing, *Legal Status of Supreme People's Court Judgments and Interpretations*, China Legal Science 175 (2006).
9. Xiao Yongping, *Conflict of Laws from a Jurisprudence Perspective* (Higher Education Press 2008), at 346.
10. For example, Succession Act, Article 36(3).
11. For example, Civil Procedure Act, Article 260.
12. http://www.wipo.int/treaties/en/ShowResults.jsp?country_id = 38C.

and answers regarding the Civil Procedure Act and other relevant acts also serve as guidance for judges in the application of law.

Civil cases with a foreign element are cases (i) where one or both parties are foreigners, stateless persons, foreign enterprises or organisations; or (ii) facts which establish, change, or terminate the civil legal relationship between the parties occur abroad, or the subject matter of litigation is located abroad.[13]

[A] Grounds for Jurisdiction

The general rules are jurisdiction by tlevel, territorial jurisdiction, exclusive jurisdiction, and choice of court by the parties.

[1] General

[a] Jurisdiction by Level

Regarding the international civil jurisdiction of Chinese courts,[14] Intermediate people's courts have jurisdiction over major cases of the first instance involving an international factor.[15] Major cases involving an international factor are defined as those cases where the disputed money is more than RBM 10 million, or the facts are very complicated, or more than one party is residing abroad.[16]

There are special rules on the jurisdiction on disputes with foreign elements relating to contractual or tort disputes; letter of credit disputes; application for revocation, recognition and enforcement of international arbitral awards; application for deciding the validity of arbitral clauses; and application for recognition, enforcement or avoidance of foreign civil and commercial judgments and rulings.[17] Jurisdiction of first instance over these disputes are allocated to courts of economic development zones approved by the State Council; intermediate people's courts of capital cities of provinces, autonomous regions, municipalities directly under the central government; intermediate people's courts of special economic zones and cities with separate state plans; other intermediate people's courts designated by the Supreme People's Courts; and high people's courts.[18]

13. Supreme People's Court Opinion on Selected Issues in Applying the Civil Procedure Act (Civil Procedure Act Opinion) rule 304 and Interpretation rule 1.
14. In general, see Du Xinli (ed.), *International Civil Litigation and Commercial Arbitration* (China University of Political Sciences and Law Press 2005), at 66-87.
15. Civil Procedure Act, Article 18.
16. Civil Procedure Act, Opinion rule 1.
17. Provisions of the Supreme People's Court on Some Issues Concerning the Jurisdiction of Civil and Commercial Cases Involving Foreign Elements FS [2002] No. 5, Article 3.
18. *Ibid.*, Article 1.

[b] Territorial Jurisdiction

The Chinese system follows the general principle of territorial jurisdiction (Civil Procedure Act Articles 21-22). As a principle, the court of the domicile or the habitual residence of the defendant has jurisdiction. Where a defendant's domicile is inappropriate or unavailable, the court of the domicile of plaintiff has jurisdiction over cases on personal relations against the defendant who resides abroad; cases on personal relations against defendant who is missing or declared missing; and cases against defendants who are detained.

In addition to the defendant's domicile, the Civil Procedure Act (Articles 23-29) grants jurisdiction to the courts of the place of conclusion of a contract in contract disputes; of the insured subject matter in insurance disputes; of payment in negotiable instruments disputes; of domicile of a company in company law disputes; of departure or destination in transport disputes; of tort in tort disputes; of the accident or the first stop after accident in transport accident disputes.

In disputes regarding contractual or proprietary rights, where the defendant has no domicile in China but the place of performance of the contract is in China, the property is in China or the defendant has attachable property in China, the court of the place of the signature or conclusion of contract, or the place of subject matter, or the place of attachable property of the defendant, or the place of tortious act, or the place of the domicile of the representative of the defendant, have jurisdiction.[19] For example: in a dispute over sales between Libyan and Chinese parties where they did not choose a competent court, the intermediate court of Guangzhou ascertained that a Guangzhou district court was competent on the basis that the Libyan party had a representative office in Guangzhou and the place of conclusion of contract was in Guangzhou.[20]

In maritime tort disputes, the doctrine of territorial jurisdiction is also the general principle:

- *Civil Procedure Act*, Articles 30-32: Courts of the place of collision, the first stop after accident, and the place of detainment of the injuring ship.
- *Special Maritime Procedure Act*, Articles 6(1)-(7): the place of tort or the place of flagship have jurisdiction in addition to general jurisdiction rules on tort; in maritime transport disputes, courts of the transfer port have jurisdiction alongside courts of place of departure or destination or defendant's domicile; in charter disputes, courts of the place of delivery, return, or registry of ships, or defendant's domicile have jurisdiction; in maritime insurance disputes, courts of the place of the insured, the place of accident, or the defendant's domicile have jurisdiction; in crew labour disputes, courts of the plaintiff's domicile, the place of conclusion of contract, the place of boarding or off-boarding of the crew, or the defendant's domicile have jurisdiction; in maritime guaranty disputes, courts of the place of collateral or the defendant's

19. Civil Procedure Act, Article 265.
20. *Libyan North Sea Trading Co. Ltd. v. He Tiping* (Guangzhou Intermediate People's Court) (final), (2010) 穗中法民四终字第49号.

domicile have jurisdiction; in ship pledge disputes, courts of the place of registry also have jurisdiction; in disputes over property rights in ships, courts of the place of the ship, the place of registry of the ship or the defendant's domicile have jurisdiction.

[2] Submitted to Jurisdiction

According to the Civil Procedure Act, in case of defendant's failure to object to the jurisdiction of a court, the defendant shall be deemed to have accepted the court's jurisdictional competence.

[3] Exclusive Jurisdiction

The CPL expressly authorises Chinese courts to exercise exclusive jurisdiction over certain civil actions. Disputes over immovables, port operations, and succession in China are subject exclusively to the jurisdiction of the courts of the place where immovables are located, the place of the port, and the place of domicile of the deceased at the time of death or the place of the estate, respectively.[21] Maritime pollution cases and maritime exploitation contracts are subject to the exclusive jurisdiction of the courts of the place of pollution and place of exploitation respectively.[22] Chinese courts also have the exclusive jurisdiction over performance of the contracts of Chinese-foreign equity joint ventures, Chinese-foreign contractual joint ventures, or Chinese-foreign cooperative exploration and development of the natural resources in China.[23] Finally, it is worth mentioning that a Chinese court is always competent (though not exclusively) over divorce proceedings between two Chinese parties even if one party has obtained a foreign nationality or lives abroad.[24]

[B] Exclusion of Jurisdiction

[1] Immunity

[a] Sovereign Immunity

Legislation on state immunity is scarce. An act on the immunity of property of foreign central banks from compulsory judicial measures conferring immunity on foreign central banks was issued in 2005.[25] In addition, a Supreme People's court notice listed foreign states alongside foreign diplomats who enjoy diplomatic immunity and ruled that courts should not accept jurisdiction before approval by competent high courts or

21. Civil Procedure Act, Article 33.
22. Special Maritime Procedure Act Article 7.
23. Civil Procedure Act, Article 266.
24. Civil Procedure Act, Opinion rules 13, 14, 15, 16.
25. 2005 Immunity of the Property of Foreign Central Banks from Compulsory Judicial Measures Act.

the Supreme People's Court.[26] China has insisted on absolute immunity until recent signs of shift to relative immunity (such as the signature of the 2004 United Nations Convention on Jurisdictional Immunities of States and Their Property).

China's current position on absolute immunity can be summarised as follows: (i) sovereign immunity of States and their property is a principle of international law based on the principle of sovereign equality of all States; (ii) all acts of a State or on its behalf should be absolutely immune from foreign jurisdictions, unless the State voluntarily and explicitly waives its immunity; (iii) state-owned enterprises with independent legal personality should not enjoy immunity; (iv) disputes on state immunity should be resolved through negotiation and international agreements and treaties; (v) if a foreign State infringes upon the sovereign immunity of China and its property, China will take counter-measures.[27] In *Russell Jackson v. The People's Republic of China*,[28] when the government was sued by US bond holders, China asserted absolute immunity from jurisdiction and enforcement measures before the US court. The judgment was overruled.

In *FG Hemisphere Associates LLC [HK] v. Democratic Republic of the Congo*,[29] Energoinvest (a Yugoslav company) entered into financing contracts with the Democratic Republic of the Congo (DRC), which incorporated ICC arbitration clauses. The DRC defaulted on its repayment obligation and ICC arbitral tribunals rendered awards in favour of Energoinvest. Energoinvest transferred its interest in the awards to FG Hemisphere Associates (a Hong Kong company). FG obtained an ex parte enforcement order in the Hong Kong Court of First Instance. The DRC resisted enforcement, claiming sovereign immunity. The Hong Kong court applied for the opinion of the PRC central government. It was confirmed that China has always insisted on the absolute immunity from jurisdiction and enforcement of a foreign state and its property; China has never applied relative immunity; Chinese courts have never been competent or have ever exercised jurisdiction over a foreign state or foreign government or its property; meanwhile, China will never submit to a foreign court over an action against China, or the Chinese government or its property.[30]

The attachment to the principle of absolute immunity is said to be rooted in the state-owned economy until the 1990s and the political humiliation by the western countries until 1949. The changed economic structure of more private economy and more Chinese companies dealing with foreign states abroad calls for a shift to the state immunity issue.[31] In fact, China has signed the 2004 United Nations Convention on Jurisdictional Immunities of States and Their Property (UN Immunity Convention).

26. Notice of the Supreme People's Court on the Relevant Issues concerning the People's Courts to Accept Civil Cases Involving Privilege and Immunity F [2007] No. 69.
27. Dahai Qi, *State Immunity, China and Its Shifting Position*, Chinese JIL, 307 (2008).
28. 550 F. Supp. 869 (N.D. Ala. 1982), 22 Int'l Legal Materials 75.
29. CACV 373/2008 & CACV 43/2009, affirming *FG Hemisphere Associates LLC [HK] v. Democratic Republic of the Congo* HCMP 928/2008.
30. Office of the Commissioner of the Ministry of Foreign Affairs of the PRC in the Hong Kong SAR, Letter to the Hong Kong High Court, quoted from Dong Likun and Zhang Shudian, *Hong Kong Special Administration Court Has No Jurisdiction over Act of State Cases*, Tribune of Political Science and Law 80, 87 (2012).
31. Qi Dahai, *supra* n. 27.

Although it has not entered into force yet, China's signature reveals its potential recognition of a limitation to the principle of absolute immunity.

[b] Diplomatic and Consular Immunity

China is a party to the 1961 Vienna Convention on Diplomatic Relations and the 1969 Vienna Convention on Consular Relations. China has also passed domestic legislation: the 1986 Diplomatic Privileges and Immunities Regulations and the 1990 Consular Privileges and Immunities Regulations.

[c] Other Immunities

China is a party to the 1961 Convention on the Privileges and Immunities of the United Nations and the 1947 Convention on the Privileges and Immunities of the Specialised Agencies.

[2] Forum Agreements in Favour of Foreign Courts

Subject to the provisions on exclusive jurisdiction, parties to a contractual or property dispute may choose, in writing, a foreign court with real connections with the dispute.[32] Such connection can be the domicile of the defendant, the place of performance of contract, the place of conclusion of contract, the place of signature of contract, the domicile of the plaintiff, the place of the subject matter, or other place with material connection with the dispute.[33] The only exception to the requirement of connection refers to maritime disputes in favour of Chinese courts: where foreign parties choose in writing a Chinese court as the competent one, the chosen Chinese court has jurisdiction even if there is no connection of the court with the parties or disputes.[34]

If the choice of court clause is valid, a Chinese court shall refrain from exercising jurisdiction.

A choice of court clause is invalid if there is no connection between the court and the dispute or the parties. For example: in a dispute on copyright transfer of an internet game, the parties were domiciled in South Korea and China, the conclusion and performance of the contract were in China, the parties chose Chinese law as the governing law to any dispute and Singapore as the competent jurisdiction. It was held that the choice of court clause was invalid, and the Chinese court was competent, since Singapore had no material connection with the dispute or the parties.[35]

32. Civil Procedure Act, Article 34; Civil Procedure Act, Opinion rule 305.
33. Civil Procedure Act, Article 34.
34. Special Maritime Procedure Act, Article 8.
35. *Shandong Jufeng Internet Company Ltd. v. South Korea Mgame and Tianjin Fengyun Internet Technology Company Ltd.* (Supreme People's Court) (final), (2009) 民三终字第4号.

[3] Arbitration Clause

A court will not accept a case if there is a valid arbitration agreement between the parties or an award rendered by a foreign arbitration body, unless the arbitration agreement is found invalid.[36] In particular, for disputes over trade, transport, and maritime with a foreign element, parties to a valid arbitration agreement are prohibited from commencing court proceedings.[37]

[C] Non-exercise of Jurisdiction

[1] Forum Non Conveniens

Although the Civil Procedure Act is silent on the principle of forum non conveniens, a specific Supreme People's Court interpretation seems to reject it.[38] According to it, a people's court shall neither delay nor decline exercising judicial power over the case under its statutory jurisdiction unless all parties are foreign enterprises involved in a dispute with no practical connection with China (in which case, it may advise the parties to choose alternative courts in other countries).

It is, however, expressly established in another interpretation of the Supreme People's Court that Chinese courts have the discretion not to exercise jurisdiction if all the following conditions are met:[39] (i) a defendant raises the issue of forum non conveniens; (ii) a Chinese court involved has jurisdiction under Chinese law; (iii) there is no choice of a Chinese court; (iv) there is no exclusive jurisdiction of Chinese courts; (v) no interest of Chinese parties is involved; (vi) the main facts occurred outside China and the applicable law is not Chinese law (all of which involves major difficulties in fact-finding and application of law); and (vii) there is a competent court with much more ease to hear the case.

Following similar criteria, some courts have exercised discretion to dismiss cases on the basis of forum non conveniens,[40] where defendants raised the issue on the basis that no Chinese court was chosen by the parties, the case was outside the exclusive jurisdiction of Chinese courts, no interest of Chinese parties was involved, major facts occurred in South Korea, South Korean law was the applicable law, and all parties were domiciled in South Korea. It was held that the Chinese court was not a proper court because of the factors despite the parties having property in China.

Similarly, in a dispute over a loan agreement between two Hong Kong companies with a non-exclusive choice of Hong Kong courts, it was held that the Hong Kong court (not the Mainland court) was the convenient court. The case was dismissed since both

36. Arbitration Act, Article 5; Civil Procedure Act, Article 259.
37. Civil Procedure Act, Article 271.
38. Civil Procedure Act, Opinion rule 306.
39. Supreme People's Court Summary of 2nd National Conference on Hearing Foreign-Related Commercial and Maritime Cases FF [2005] 26.
40. *Seoul Industrial Company v. Yuyan Paint Company*, Jiangsu Provincial Supreme People's Court (final), (2010) 苏商外终字第0027号; *Dahao Chemical Company v. Yuyan Paint Company*, Jiangsu Provincial Supreme People's Court (final), (2010) 苏商外终字第0053号.

parties were Hong Kong companies, the place of conclusion and performance of contract was in Hong Kong, and Hong Kong law was chosen by the parties as the governing law.[41] In another case, the Chinese court dismissed the case invoking forum non conveniens since both parties were US-registered companies, US was chosen as the competent court, major facts occurred in the US, no interest of Chinese parties was involved and the applicable law was US law.[42]

Sometimes the principle of facilitating parties and courts (Article 2 of the Civil Procedure Act) was relied on for dismissal where the court found inconvenient factors similar to the seven conditions test.[43] In many cases courts reject the forum non conveniens submission. For example, where companies in control of both parties were registered in mainland China, major facts occurred in mainland China, and the applicable law chosen by the parties was Chinese law, but the case was not in the exclusive jurisdiction of a mainland China court, no mainland China court was chosen by the parties, parties were not domiciled in mainland China, and the subject matter (shares in the Hong Kong company) was subject to mandatory rules on share transfers in Hong Kong.[44]

[2] Lis alibi pendens

A foreign *lis pendens* is not a bar to the exercise of jurisdiction. A Chinese court is allowed to accept a case if one party starts litigation in a competent foreign court while the other party litigates in the competent Chinese court; and a Chinese court can refuse to enforce the judgment rendered by the foreign court on the same matter, unless there are binding bilateral or multilateral treaties.[45]

Where one party is a resident of China and the other party is a resident abroad, a Chinese court is competent over divorce proceedings commenced by either party.[46] This principle has been applied by the courts to hold their competence where one party argues for the Chinese court to dismiss the case on the basis that there is an ongoing proceeding on the same matter between the same parties in a foreign court. The basis is that a Chinese court is competent regardless of whether other courts are competent, are hearing the case, or have rendered judgments[47] (in one case the court held that a

41. *The Sumitomo Bank Limited v. Xinhua Real Estate*, SPC (final), (1999) 经终字第194号.
42. *Baron Motorcycles INC v. Awell Logistics Group, Inc.*, Ningbo Maritime Court (first instance), (2008) 甬海法商初字第277号, affirmed Zhejiang High People's Court (final), (2009) 浙辖终字第81号.
43. *Green Techelectronics Limited v. Smar Techelectronic Company Limited*, Shanghai 1st Intermediate People's Court (first instance), (2009) 沪一中民五(商)初字第51号, affirmed Shanghai High People's Court (final), (2009) 沪高民四(商)终字第59号.
44. *Yao Mingfen v. Hong Kong Investments Group Limited*, Fujian High People's Court (final), (2011) 闽民终字第208号.
45. Civil Procedure Act, Opinion rule 306.
46. Civil Procedure Act, Opinion rule 15.
47. *Kwok & Yih Law Firm v. Xiamen Huayang Color Printing Company*, Fujian Xiamen Intermediate Court (first instance); *Ma Jingyi v. Symantec Corporation*, Shanghai High People's Court (final), (2011) 沪高民三(知)终字第88号.

Chinese court will entertain a case regardless of an ongoing foreign proceeding unless the foreign court has exclusive jurisdiction).[48]

§1.03 APPLICABLE LAW

Characterisation in Chinese courts prior to the adoption of the Act was uncertain. In a famous case, *China Technology Import Company v. Swiss Industrial Resources Company*,[49] parties to a sales contract submitted disputes arising out of the contract to arbitration. The Chinese party claimed that the Swiss party committed fraud and tort, while the Swiss party argued that the arbitration clause was binding. The Chinese court held that it was a tort dispute, the arbitration clause was excluded, and the Chinese court had jurisdiction. Currently, Article 8 of the Act states that characterisation follows the law of the forum. This solution has been criticised for being out of date and rigid.[50]

[A] Choice of Law

[1] Express Stipulation

Party autonomy – the freedom to choose the law applicable to the civil relations with a foreign element according to the law – is expressly singled out in the Act both as a general principle[51] and in provisions regarding specific relations. The general provision has been subject to criticism, since it seems to allow parties unlimited freedom to choose the applicable law despite otherwise applicable conflict of laws rules.[52] The broad interpretation is hardly persuasive since the party autonomy in the choice of law derives from the freedom of contract in substantive law, which is not universal in every branch of law. Article 3 of the Act should be interpreted as emphasising the extension of party autonomy into more branches of law that are expressly indicated in the Act. The Interpretation has cured this point. The choice of law clause concluded between the parties without express provision of law is invalid.[53]

Where there is no limitation on the law to be chosen, the choice of a neutral law which has no connection with the parties or the dispute is allowed. Courts should not support the submission that a choice of law clause is invalid from the mere fact that the chosen law has no connection with the dispute or the parties.[54] This is a response to the

48. *Piao Shanggen v. Tian Linzhen*, Shandong Qingdao Intermediate People's Court (first instance), (2005) 青民四初字第23号.
49. Supreme People's Court Gazette, 26-28 (1989).
50. Tu Guangjian, *Interpreting the Law Applicable to Foreign-Related Civil Relations Act 2010*, Present day Law Science 11, 15 (2011).
51. Article 3 of the Act.
52. SPC press conference brief for the Interpretation http://www.court.gov.cn/xwzx/jdjd/sdjd/201301/t20130106_181593.htm accessed on 1 Feb. 2013.
53. Interpretation rule 6.
54. Interpretation rule 7.

erroneous court practice of finding invalid the choice of the law of a neutral jurisdiction. This also reaffirms the principle of previous Supreme People's Court interpretation.[55]

Parties can choose or change the applicable law by explicit agreement before the closing of the hearing of first instance.[56] The law is silent on implied choice. Nevertheless, if parties during the proceedings refer to the law of the same country and make no challenge, the courts may find that the parties have made a choice of law.[57] This follows the previous Supreme People's Court interpretation[58] and confirms the court practice. In a dispute over a share transfer agreement it was held that the parties agreed to apply Chinese law during the hearing and Chinese law was applied under Article 3 of the Act.[59] Similarly, Chinese law will be applied if one party invokes it, whilst the other party makes no challenge before the Chinese court.

According to the Act, parties can choose the law applicable to contracts,[60] arbitral agreements,[61] unjust enrichment and voluntary service,[62] and in the transfer or license of intellectual property rights.[63] After a tort has occurred, parties can choose the applicable law;[64] though in case of an intellectual property tort, the choice is limited to the law of the forum.[65] Parties can also choose the law applicable to express agency and to trusts;[66] with respect to rights in rem over movables;[67] and the law applicable to trusts.[68] In consumer contracts, a consumer can choose the law of the place of provision of products or provision of services.[69]

In family law matters, parties can choose the law applicable to matrimonial property out of the law of the habitual residence or nationality of either party.[70] In consensual divorces, parties can choose the applicable law out of the law of the place of the habitual residence or nationality of either party.[71]

The extension of party autonomy is said to be based on the freedom of parties to dispose of their civil law rights in marriage and family, successions, rights in rem,

55. Supreme People's Court Provisions on Selected Issues in the Application of Law in Hearing Foreign-Related Civil or Commercial Contracts FS [2007] No. 14 rule 4(1); Brief.
56. Interpretation rule 8.
57. Interpretation rule 8.
58. Brief; Supreme People's Court Provisions on Selected Issues in the Application of Law in Hearing Foreign-Related Civil or Commercial Contracts FS [2007] No. 14 rule 4.
59. *Cai Yangcai v. Lin Shengxiong*, Jiangsu High People's Court (final), (2012) 苏商外终字第0008号.
60. Article 41 of the Act.
61. Article 18 of the Act.
62. Article 47 of the Act.
63. Article 49 of the Act.
64. Article 44 of the Act.
65. Article 50 of the Act.
66. Article 16 of the Act.
67. Article 37 of the Act.
68. Article 17 of the Act.
69. Article 42 of the Act.
70. Article 24 of the Act.
71. Article 26 of the Act.

obligations, and intellectual property, and the international trends of the expansion of party autonomy in private international law.[72]

The expansion of party autonomy is subject to a general public policy limitation. Public policy excludes the application of foreign law under the conflicts rule where the latter is likely to impair Chinese public policy.[73] However, public policy should be invoked only in exceptional cases and be kept within proper limits; otherwise the aim of the conflict of laws will be frustrated. It is generally recognised that only where some fundamental principle of justice and good morals may be violated, a court can reject the application of foreign law.[74] To resort to public policy too often would diminish its value.[75]

[2] Implied Choice

The law is silent on implied choice of law.

[B] Other Cases

[1] Civil Subjects

Civil capacities and competence of natural persons, declaration of missing or death of natural persons, and personality rights are governed by the law of the place of the habitual residence of the person.[76] Civil capacities and competence, shareholders' rights... of legal persons and its branches are governed by the law of the place of registration of legal persons.[77] The law of the principal place of business may be applicable if different from the place of registration.

Agency is governed by the law of the place where the agent acts. However, the agent-principal relation is governed by the law where agency is created. Parties to an express agency can choose the applicable law.[78]

If the parties do not choose the law applicable to trust, the law of the place where the trust assets were located or where the trust relationship was established is applicable.

72. Report on the Act (Draft) and Main Issues, available at http://www.npc.gov.cn/huiyi/cwh/1116/2010-08/28/content_1593162.htm (accessed 1 Apr. 2015); Huang Jin, *supra* n. 1, at 11.
73. Report on the Act (Draft) and Main Issues, http://www.npc.gov.cn/huiyi/cwh/1116/2010-08/28/content_1593162.htm (accessed 1 Apr. 2015).
74. For example Lord Collins *et al.*, *Dicey, Morris and Collins on the Conflict of Laws* (14th ed., Sweet & Maxwell 2006) at [5-003].
75. See Liang Wenwen, *The Applicable Law to Rights in Rem under the Act on the Law Applicable to Foreign-Related Civil Relations of the People's Republic of China*, in Andrea Bonomi et al. (eds), *Yearbook of Private International Law* (Sellier European Law Publishers 2013), 353.
76. Articles 11, 12, 13, 15 of the Act.
77. Article 14 of the Act.
78. Article 16 of the Act.

[2] Marriage and Family Law Matters

Substantive conditions of marriage, such as capacity to marry and consent to marry, are governed by the law of the common habitual residence of the parties; if parties have no common habitual residence, the law of the country of the common nationality of the parties applies; if parties have no common nationality, the law of the place of celebration applies if it is also the place of the habitual residence or nationality of a party.[79] A marriage is formally valid if any of the following laws is observed: the law of the place of celebration, the law of the place of the habitual residence or the law of the nationality of a party.[80] The relaxation on formality shows the support to validate marriages. The most significant relationship principle fills the gap if none of the rules is applicable. The provisions cover the substantive and formal conditions of foreign-related marriages, which are a significant progress compared to the previous approach that marriage between a Chinese and a foreigner is governed by the law of the place of celebration,[81] and foreigners in China may marry under the law of China.[82]

Personal relations between spouses are governed by the law of the place of common habitual residence; if parties have no common residence, the law of the place of common nationality applies.[83] Property relations between spouses are governed by the law chosen by the parties which can be the law of the habitual residence or the law of the nationality of a party or the law of the place of the majority of property. If there is no such choice, the law of the common habitual residence of the parties applies; if parties have no common habitual residence, the law of the place of the common nationality of the parties applies.[84] This provision fails to make an exception for the law of the place where immovable is located. The most significant relationship principle fills the gap if none of the rule is applicable.

Divorce by agreement is governed by the law chosen by the parties. Parties can only choose the law of the habitual residence or nationality of a party. If parties have made no choice the law of the place of the common habitual residence applies; if parties have no common habitual residence, the law of the common nationality applies; if parties have no common nationality, the law of the place of the authority dealing with divorce proceedings applies.[85] Divorce by litigation is governed by the law of the forum.[86] The most significant relationship principle fills the gap if none of the rules is applicable. The new approach distinguishes the divorce by agreement and divorce by litigation, which is different from the previous provision that divorce is governed by the law of the forum.[87]

79. Article 21 of the Act.
80. Article 22 of the Act.
81. General Principles of Civil Law, Article 147.
82. Ministry of Civil Affairs Responses to Foreign-Related Issues in Marriage Registration [1983] M 133.
83. Article 23 of the Act.
84. Article 24 of the Act.
85. Article 26 of the Act.
86. Article 27 of the Act.
87. General Principles of Civil Law, Article 147.

Personal and property relations between parents and children are governed by the law of the place of the common habitual residence of the parties; if parties have no common habitual residence, the law which is most in favour of the weak party, out of the place of the habitual residence or nationality of a party, applies.[88]

Adoption is governed in substance and form by the law of the place of the habitual residence of the adopter and the law of the place of the habitual residence of the adopted. The validity and effect of adoption is governed by the law of the place of the habitual residence of the adopter at the time of adoption. Revocation of adoption is governed by the law of the place of the habitual residence of the adopted or the law of the forum.[89] Adoption in China is governed by Chinese law.[90]

Maintenance obligations are governed by the law which is most in favour of the maintenance obligee out of the law of the place of the habitual residence, the law of the nationality of a party, or the law of the place of the majority of the relevant property.[91]

Custody is governed by the law which is most in favour of the party under custody, out of the law of the place of the habitual residence and the law of the nationality of a party.[92] There is a fundamental shift from the previous approach under which the law of the nationality of the person under custody applies, and Chinese law applies if the person under custody is domiciled in China.[93]

In summary in these matters, the habitual residence of the parties is a major connecting factor; party autonomy is adopted; the principle of favouring the weak party is also adopted; and the most significant relationship principle applies as gap filling.[94]

[3] Succession

Intestate succession is governed by the law of the habitual residence of the deceased person at the time of death except in case of immovables (which are governed by the law of the place of their location).[95]

In testamentary succession, the form of a will is valid if it complies with any of the following: the law of the place of the habitual residence or the law of the nationality of the deceased at the time the will is made or at the time of death, or the law of the place where the will is made.[96] The validity of a will is governed by the law of the place of the habitual residence or the law of the nationality of the deceased at the time the will is made or at the time of death.[97] Administration of estate is governed by the law of the

88. Article 25 of the Act.
89. Article 28 of the Act.
90. 1998 Adoption Act Article 21.
91. Article 29 of the Act.
92. Article 30 of the Act.
93. Civil Law, Opinion rule 190.
94. Guo Yujun, *Choice of Law in Marriage and Family Law Matters in The Law Applicable to Foreign-Related Civil Relations Act*, Tribune of Political Sciences and Law 21, 25 (2011).
95. Article 31 of the Act.
96. Article 32 of the Act.
97. Article 33 of the Act.

place the estate is located.[98] Allocation of estate with no successor is governed by the law of the place where the estate is located at the time of death of the deceased.[99]

There are more connecting factors which largely rely on the last domicile of the deceased.[100]

[4] Rights In Rem

Rights in rem to immovables are governed by the law of the place where the immovable is located.[101] Land, building, and fixtures on land are immovables.[102]

Failing choice of law by the parties, rights in rem to movables are governed by the law of the place where the movable is located at the time the facts occur.[103] This is a major deviation from the *lex situs* rule for rights in rem to both immovables and movables. The basis is that parties have the freedom to dispose of their rights in rem and the situs of movables change making the *lex situs* rule untenable. The extension of party autonomy has been criticised for failing to consider the impact of such choice over third parties and the mandatory nature of property law. This rule has not been applied in reported cases.

Failing choice of law by the parties, the law of the place of destination applies to rights in rem to goods in transit.[104] This rule reveals the expansion of the party autonomy. The unlimited scope of choice leads to criticism that interests of third parties may be harmed.

Securities are governed by the law of the place where rights can be enforced or the law with the most significant relationship with the securities.[105] Roughly speaking, bearer certificated securities can be enforced where the certificates are located, registered certificated securities can be enforced where the register is located, and dematerialised securities can be enforced where the central register is located.

Pledge of intangible rights is governed by the law of the place where pledge is established.[106] A charge over intangible rights can be established by registration with a competent authority.[107] The law of the place of the competent authority applies.

[5] Contractual Obligations

If parties fail to choose the law applicable to their contract, the applicable law is the law of the habitual residence of the party whose obligation is most characteristic of the

98. Article 34 of the Act.
99. Article 35 of the Act.
100. General Principles of Civil Law, Article 149; Succession Act, Article 36.
101. Article 36 of the Act.
102. Civil Law Opinion rule 186.
103. Article 37 of the Act.
104. Article 38 of the Act.
105. Article 39 of the Act.
106. Article 40 of the Act.
107. Rights in Rem Act, Articles 224, 226, 227, 228.

contract or the law determined under the most significant relationship principle.[108] It is in dispute whether the characteristic performance doctrine prevails over or is equal to the most significant relationship principle. There is no guidance on what obligation is characteristic of a contract or on what constitutes the most significant relationship to a dispute.

Nevertheless, given the change of the Act with the previous approach, the characteristic performance doctrine seems to prevail over the most significant relationship principle. Characteristic performance may follow the abolished Supreme People's Court interpretation before any new standard is given.

In the Supreme People's Court interpretation,[109] which has been abolished for discrepancy with the Act,[110] the characteristic obligation is a test of the most significant relationship.[111] A comprehensive consideration of all connecting factors is required in determining what constitutes the most significant relationship. The most significant relationship with a contract is examined under the test of the inherent characteristic of the contract. For international sales contracts, the place of characteristic performance is the place of domicile of the seller on conclusion of the contract. Where the buyer's place of domicile is the place of negotiation and conclusion of the contract or the place of delivery, the place of characteristic performance is the buyer's place of domicile. For processing contracts, the place of characteristic performance is the processing party's domicile; for equipment supply contracts, it is the place of installation; for real estate sales, rent or mortgage contracts, it is the place of the real estate; for movable leasing contracts, it is the place of lessor's domicile; for contracts regarding charges over chattel, it is the place of chargee's domicile; for loan contracts, it is the place of the lender's domicile; for gift contracts, it is the place of the donor's domicile; for insurance contracts, it is the place of insurer's domicile; for financial leasing, it is the place of the lessee's domicile; for construction contracts, it is the place of the construction; for warehousing contracts, it is the place of the bailee's domicile; for surety contracts, it is the place of the guarantor's domicile; for the issuance, sale, or transfer of bonds, it is the place of issue, the place of sale, and the place of registration respectively; for auction contracts, it is the place of auction; for brokerage contracts, it is the place of the broker's domicile. If a contract apparently has a closer relationship with another country, the law of the other country applies.

In practice, courts tend to blur the most significant relationship principle and the characteristic performance doctrine by referring to both. A court lists the connections such as place of conclusion, performance of contract, or place of the subject matter,

108. Article 41 of the Act; General Principles of Civil Law, Article 145. See Liang Wenwen, *supra* n. 75.
109. Rules of the SPC on the Relevant Issues concerning the Application of Law in Hearing Foreign-Related Contractual Dispute Cases in Civil and Commercial Matters, FS [2007] No. 14 rule 5.
110. SPC Decision to Abolish Judicial Interpretations or Quasi Judicial Interpretations issued from 1 Jul. 1997 to 31 Dec. 2011 (10th time), FS [2013] No. 7.
111. Rules of the SPC on the Relevant Issues concerning the Application of Law in Hearing Foreign-Related Contractual Dispute Cases in Civil and Commercial Matters, FS [2007] No. 14, rule 5.

refers to the article and determines the applicable law, without specifying the characteristic performance or the most significant relationship principle.[112] Or a court lists the place of the domicile of the defendant, or place of the real estate in dispute, refers to the article, and determines the applicable law, without specifying the characteristic performance or the most significant relationship.[113]

Consumer contracts are governed by the law of the consumer's habitual residence, unless the business operator does not engage in any business activity in such place or the consumer chooses the law of the place where the commodity or the service is provided.

Employment contracts are governed by the law of the place where the employee works. If such working place cannot be ascertained, the law of the principal place of business of the employer shall apply.

Regarding unjust enrichment and *negotiorum gestio*, the applicable law failing choice of the parties is the law of their common habitual residence or, failing common habitual residence, the law of the place where the unjust enrichment or *negotiorum gestio* occurs.

[6] Torts

Torts are governed by the law of the place of the tortious act; where parties share a common place of habitual residence, the law of the place of their common habitual residence applies; where parties choose the governing law after tort occurs the chosen law applies.[114] The principle of double actionability is no longer required.[115]

Product liability is governed by the law of the place of the habitual residence of the victim; where the victim chooses the law of the place of the main business of the tortfeasor or the place of injury, or the tortfeasor has undertaken no business activity in the place of the habitual residence of the victim, the law of the place of the main business of the tortfeasor or the place of injury applies.[116]

Torts related to the protection of personality rights are governed by the law of the place of the habitual residence of the victim.[117]

The 1983 Marine Environment Protection Act applies to torts which occur abroad but cause damage to the territorial sea of China. Maritime torts are governed by the law of the place of the tort, the law of the forum, the law of common flagship of the ships under the Maritime Act.[118] Torts caused by civil aircraft on the grounds are governed

112. *Luzhiwei v. Hainan Hefa Real Estate, Haikou Intermediate People's Court* (final), (2011) 海中法民三终字第24号.
113. *Ni Weiting v. Hainan Yongsheng Real Estate Investment*, Haikou Intermediate People's Court (final), (2011) 海中法民三终字第7号.
114. Article 44 of the Act.
115. General Principles of Civil Law, Article 146.
116. Article 45 of the Act.
117. Article 46 of the Act.
118. Maritime Act, Articles 273 and 275.

by law of the place of the tort. Torts caused by civil aircrafts on the high seas are governed by the law of the forum.[119]

[7] Intellectual Property Rights

Ownership, contents and tort of intellectual property are governed by the law of the place where protection is sought,[120] though parties may choose the law of the forum after intellectual property tort occurs.[121] Parties may choose the law applicable to the transfer and license of intellectual property rights.[122] In the absence of such stipulation, the court will apply the conflict of laws rules for contracts.

[8] Incidental Questions

An incidental question arises where an issue with a foreign element can only be dealt with after tackling a subsidiary question which also has a foreign element. The issue of incidental questions for the purpose of conflict of laws is what law governs the subsidiary issue: the law governing the main issue, the law determined by the conflicts rule for the incidental issue, or some other law.[123]

The Act has no provision on incidental questions. Under the Interpretation, an incidental question is governed by the conflict of laws rule on the incidental question per se, independent of the conflict of laws rules on the main question.[124] Where a case has two or more civil relations, each civil relation is governed by independent conflict of law rules.[125] The latter seems to be redundant since it is normal that a case involving foreign relations has more than two matters governed under the conflict of law rules for each category. Choice of law rules are not designed on a case-by-case basis, but on an issue-by-issue basis.

The addition of incidental questions in the Interpretation is hardly necessary and may lead to rigidity. The incidental issue is a judicial process of a practical rather than a theoretical nature. Efforts to find a general solution have failed due to the diversity of situations and the inherent conflict between international harmony (incidental question subject to the governing law of the main question) and internal harmony (incidental question follows the conflict of laws rules of the forum for the category of the incidental question).[126] The realistic view that each situation has to be examined separately for finding the best solution in the case has become dominant.[127] It is not only in common law countries that the effort for a uniform solution has been abandoned, but also in some civil law countries.

119. Civil Aviation Act, Article 189.
120. Article 48 of the Act.
121. Article 50 of the Act.
122. Article 49 of the Act.
123. *Dicey, Morris and Collins*, *supra* n. 75, at [2-046].
124. Interpretation rule 12.
125. Interpretation rule 13.
126. *Dicey, Morris and Collins*, *supra* n. 75, at [2-048].
127. *Ibid.*, at [2-049].

[C] *Renvoi*

Under current Chinese law, *renvoi* is excluded in all matters. It is provided that the foreign law designated by the choice of law rules excludes the choice of law rules of the foreign law.[128] It has been criticised as rigid since it is generally recognised that in marriage and family law matters *renvoi* has a role to play.[129]

[D] Mandatory Rules of the Forum and of Third States

[1] Public Policy

Public policy may be used to reject the application of foreign law, or recognition or enforcement of foreign judgments and international arbitral awards, or requests for judicial assistance, if major interests of the forum, or basic principles of the law of the forum may be violated.

Public policy was firstly accepted in the 1982 Civil Procedure Act:[130] recognition or enforcement of a foreign judgment may be refused if public interest of the society is violated. The 1986 General Principles of Civil Law extended the public policy to exclude the application of foreign law: if the application of foreign law or international customs violates the social public interest of China, the foreign law or international customs should be excluded.[131] Nevertheless, it is doubtful that public policy can be used to exclude the application of international customs, since application of international customs is optional rather than mandatory.[132] If the mere violation of Chinese law or public interest leads to the exclusion of the foreign law, this may cause indiscreet resort to public policy. Thus it is recommended that a requirement of 'major interest' be added to the clause, so that only violation of major interest of public policy would exclude the application of foreign law. However, the Act still states that if the application of foreign law would violate the public interest of society of China (without any specific reference to 'major interests'), Chinese law would apply.[133]

Chinese courts have used public policy to refuse to recognise long-term separation of a Chinese spouse living in Argentina on the basis that there is no such mechanism under Chinese marriage law. This is considered incorrect.[134]

It is suggested that public policy may be applied with caution only where constitutional law is violated, national sovereignty and ethnic unity is violated, treaty obligations of China are violated, *jus cogens* norms are violated, or if foreign courts reject the application of Chinese law.[135]

128. Article 9 of the Act.
129. See Tu Guangjian, *supra* n. 50, at 15.
130. Article 204.
131. Article 150.
132. Xiao Yongping, *supra* n. 9, at 218.
133. Article 5.
134. Xiao Yongping, *supra* n. 9, at 219.
135. *Ibid.*, at 224-225.

[2] *Mandatory Rules*

Mandatory Chinese law applies directly regardless of the conflict of laws rules.[136] The Act uses the term 'mandatory rules', without providing any standard.[137] The Interpretation explains 'mandatory rules' by general description and specification with a view to balancing clarity and flexibility. Mandatory rules are defined as rules of law and regulations which are directly applicable to foreign-related civil relations in matters concerning the public interest of the Chinese society and cannot be excluded by party agreement, specifically concerning the protection of labour, food and public hygiene, environmental security, foreign exchange control and financial security, anti-trust and anti-dumping.[138] It is noted that mandatory rules under the Act and the Interpretation differ from mandatory rules under substantive contract law and should be applied with caution, akin to the public policy clause.

Chinese mandatory rules are applicable to cases which have substantive connection with China.[139] It is also submitted that the application of mandatory rules of Chinese law should take into consideration the consequences with regard to the interests of the forum, and the interests of the parties. Application of mandatory rules of Chinese law should be aimed at fostering transactions.[140]

It is not settled in the legislation whether mandatory rules of a third state may be applied by a Chinese court.[141] Given the vacuum of conflict of laws rules, mandatory rules of a third state can only be applied de facto by way of substantive law. In principle, mandatory rules of the country of the applicable law should be applied (even if they are public law rules),[142] unless they are contrary to the public policy of China.[143] Mandatory rules of a third state can be applied only through two mechanisms: (i) violation of mandatory rules of a third state may be invalidated for being in conflict with the public policy of China; (ii) mandatory rules of a third state may be held as impediment *ab initio* or *ex post facto* to the performance of a contract which justifies the revocation, rescission, or modification of the contract.

[E] Proof of Foreign Law

Where the parties choose the foreign law, they should provide the proof of such foreign law. If the foreign law cannot be ascertained or the foreign law is silent on the relevant issue, Chinese law should be applied.[144] The loopholes – solved by the Interpretation –[145] are:

136. Article 4 of the Act.
137. The Act.
138. Interpretation rule 10.
139. Xiao Yongping, *supra* n. 9, at 112.
140. *Ibid.*, at 114.
141. *Ibid.*, at 116.
142. *Ibid.*, at 115.
143. *Ibid.*
144. Article 10 of the Act.
145. Interpretation rules 17 and 18.

(i) The role of the court when the parties are obliged to provide the foreign law: The Interpretation provides that courts should hear both sides' understanding of the foreign law. Courts may hold that the foreign law has been ascertained if the parties have no challenge but shall review the foreign law if any party challenges the content of the foreign law.

(ii) The test to determine whether the foreign law cannot be ascertained: A court may hold that the foreign law cannot be ascertained where parties' submission, or channels in treaties binding on China, Chinese or foreign expert witness have been exhausted. If parties who are obliged to prove the foreign law (if parties choose the foreign law) fail to do so within the period specified by a court, a court may find that the foreign law cannot be ascertained.

The general approach is that the court takes judicial notice of foreign law unless foreign law is applicable because it is chosen by the parties as the governing law. The difficulty in finding foreign law by the court is taken into consideration and the obligation upon the parties to prove foreign law is enhanced where appropriate. It is a realistic attitude to give the court the discretion to review foreign law with the assistance of the parties, rather than the simplistic assertion that the court takes judicial notice of foreign law or the parties are obliged to prove foreign law.

The Interpretation is expected to provide a higher degree of certainty. Some past problematic cases are: (i) In a maritime transport contract case, a court of first instance found that the party claiming the application of Brazilian law failed to prove the Brazilian law and thus Chinese law was applied. The court of second instance found that the parties agreed to apply Chinese law without giving any evidence, but held that the party claiming exemption of liability under Brazilian law failed to prove the Brazilian law and thus Chinese law was applied to the exemption issue. The court of second instance is misleading in that it held that parties agreed to apply Chinese law in general but allows the application of Brazilian law to specific issues. A detail in the case is that the party provided the Brazilian law in un-notarised Portuguese and Chinese texts, and notarised English text without Chinese translation by a qualified translator. The submission of Brazilian law was thus found inadmissible;[146] (ii) In a case of a Hong Kong appellant against a mainland China respondent, the court consulted the website of the Hong Kong government and ascertained the applicable law;[147] (iii) In a case where both were foreign parties and designated the application of non-Chinese law but failed to submit the foreign law, the court held that foreign law cannot be ascertained and applied Chinese law under Civil Law Interpretation rule 193;[148] (iv) In a case of a Chinese appellant against a US respondent, the parties chose the US law as the governing law and the Chinese appellant submitted the US law while the US refused to

146. *Dafei Ship Company v. Shanghai Lizhi International Transport*, Shanghai High People's Court (final), (2011) 沪高民四(海)终字第205号.

147. *Chen Chengmiao v. Ye Qingchi*, Xiamen Intermediate People's Court (final), (2003) 厦经终字第44号.

148. *Kreditanstalt für Wiederaufbau v. Abu Dhabi* Container *Lines PJSC, Shanghai Maritime Court (first instance)*, (2002) 沪海法商初字第16号.

submit, the court considered itself obliged to ascertain the US law. US law was applied. The decision was in favour of the Chinese appellant.[149]

[F] Evasion of the Law

The Act has no provision on evasion of law, perhaps based on the thought that public policy is sufficient to deal with the evasion of law. However, public policy is considered not wide enough to cover evasion of law except when a major interest or morality of the forum is harmed. Thus, evasion of law is added in the Interpretation. If parties create a connecting factor with an intention to apply a foreign law and evade the mandatory rules of Chinese law and regulations, the foreign law will not be applied by courts.[150]

§1.04 PROCEDURAL ISSUES

[A] Service of Summons and Judicial Orders Abroad

Service is considered the exercise of judicial authority in civil law countries, which prohibit service by a foreign authority or foreign parties in its territory. In China service of judicial documents is considered as authority of courts.

The Civil Procedure Act applies where there is no bilateral treaty or international convention. It provides for service by a Chinese court on a person who has no domicile in China without classifying service on foreign nationals in China or abroad, or service on Chinese nationals abroad.[151] Service on a foreign national whose country is a party to treaties or conventions to which China is a party should be effected in the manner specified in those treaties or conventions.[152] If there is no applicable treaty or convention, service may be done through diplomatic channels where process is to be served on a foreign national or on a Chinese national residing abroad.[153] Service on a Chinese national residing abroad may be done by Chinese embassies or consulates based in that country,[154] subject to the consent of the foreign country. This is allowed under the Vienna Consular Convention.[155] Service on a foreign national in China by the embassy or consulate of that country in China is allowed.[156] Service of process by post abroad is allowed if the law of the home country of the person to be served permits service of process by post.[157] It is noteworthy that China opposes service by post in the

149. *US Sunshine International Ltd. v. China CSR Zhuzhou Electric Locomotive Co., Ltd.*, Hunan High People's Court (final), (2005) 湘高法民三终字第12号.
150. Interpretation rule 11.
151. Civil Procedure Act, Article 267.
152. *Ibid.*, Article 267(1).
153. *Ibid.*, Article 276(2).
154. *Ibid.*, Article 267(3).
155. Xu Hong, *International Judicial Assistance in Civil Matters* (2nd ed., Wuhan University Press, 2007), at 135.
156. Civil Procedure Act, Article 277.
157. *Ibid.*, Article 267(6).

territory of China.[158] Service by fax and email is allowed.[159] The last resort is public notice where service is completed after three months of notice.[160]

Under bilateral treaties, service is usually by exchange between central authorities. The Chinese central authority is the Supreme People's Court, which will forward requests for service from a foreign central authority to lower Chinese courts.[161] A foreign country can serve on its own nationals in the territory of China directly by its embassy or consular based in China as long as no compulsion is involved.[162]

China has been bound by the Hague Service Convention since 1992 with regard to other contracting states. Such convention allows transmission by central authorities, consular or diplomatic channels, direct communication between judicial officers, officials or other competent persons of the countries involved, and direct communication between an interested party and judicial officers, officials, or other competent persons of the requested state.[163] The Ministry of Justice is the central authority for transmission with foreign central authorities and foreign embassies and consulates under the Hague Service Convention. The Ministry of Justice transmits the requests from a foreign central authority to the Supreme People's Court which transmits to the competent lower courts, and the certificate of service back to the Ministry of Justice. The Supreme People's Court is responsible for transmission of requests for service on Chinese nationals abroad to Chinese embassies and consulates abroad.[164] The High People's Courts of Beijing Municipality, Shanghai Municipality, Guangdong, Zhejiang, and Jiangsu Provinces are authorised to send or forward requests to foreign central authorities under the Hague Service Convention, but not under bilateral treaties.[165] The Ministry of Justice is responsible for transmission to a foreign central authority a request from a Chinese court in other situations.

Where neither the Hague Service Convention nor any bilateral treaty applies, service by diplomatic channels is as follows.[166] A court of a country with diplomatic relations with China sends a request to service on Chinese nationals or third country nationals to the embassy in China, which transfers the request to the Consular Office of the Ministry of Foreign Affairs, which transfers it to a competent high court of the province, which transfers it to a competent intermediate court, which transfers it to the party. A court of a foreign country can serve on its own nationals in China subject to the sovereignty and security of China, and as far as there is no compulsion. A request to

158. China's reservation to the Hague Service Convention.
159. Civil Procedure Act, Article 267(7).
160. *Ibid.*, Article 267(8).
161. For example, China-France Treaty on Civil and Commercial Judicial Assistance (China-France Treaty), Article 5.
162. *Ibid.*, Article 7.
163. Hague Service Convention, Article 10.
164. Ministry of Justice, Supreme People's Court and Ministry of Foreign Affairs Notice on Implementing the Hague Service Convention SFT [1992] No. 93.
165. Supreme People's Court Notice on Assigning the High People's Courts of Beijing Municipality, Shanghai Municipality, Guangdong, Zhejiang, and Jiangsu Provinces to Directly Put Forward and Transfer Judicial Assistance Requests and Relevant Documents FB [2003] No. 297.
166. Supreme People's Court, Ministry of Foreign Affairs, and Ministry of Justice Notice on Selected Issues regarding the Service of Legal Documents through Diplomatic Channels between Chinese and Foreign Courts, WF [1986] No. 47.

serve abroad on a foreigner shall be examined by the competent high court before sending it to the Consular Office of the Ministry of Justice for forwarding to the foreign authority. A request to serve abroad on a Chinese national shall be forwarded to the Chinese embassy or consulate based in that country and will be subject to the law of that country.[167]

Service can be refused if compliance would infringe a law of the requested country or its sovereignty or security.[168] Requests can also be rejected on the basis of public policy under the Civil Procedure Act.[169] The Civil Procedure Act has wider grounds for refusing service which should be subject to the conditions contained in applicable bilateral treaties and conventions.[170]

A recently adopted Supreme People's Court interpretation confirms the practices on service and evidence-taking under international conventions and bilateral judicial assistance.[171] It enhances the systematic management of international service and evidence-taking.

[B] Obtaining Evidence Abroad[172]

Under the Civil Procedure Act, taking evidence abroad by Chinese authorities or taking evidence by foreigners in China can only be done as specified in international conventions, or on the principle of reciprocity,[173] or through diplomatic channels.[174] Foreign embassies and consulates based in China can take evidence from their nationals in China subject to Chinese law and without compulsion.[175]

Under bilateral treaties on judicial assistance, taking evidence abroad or taking evidence in China by foreign authorities can be done by central authorities or diplomatic channels.[176] China is a contracting state to the 1970 Hague Convention on the Taking of Evidence Abroad in Civil or Commercial Matters (Hague Convention on Taking Evidence). Bilateral treaties prevail over the Hague Convention on Taking Evidence regarding relevant countries. The central authority of China is the Ministry of Justice. As with service, several high courts are authorised to send or forward to foreign

167. See Xiao Yongping, *Principles of Private International Law* (2nd ed., Legal Press, 2007), at 405-407.
168. Article 11 of the China-France Treaty; Article 13 of the Hague Service Convention.
169. Civil Procedure Act, Article 276.
170. Xu Hong, *supra* n. 155, at 161-166.
171. Supreme People's Court Provisions on Service and Evidence-taking under International Conventions and Bilateral Judicial Assistance FS [2013] No. 11.
172. Chen Li, *Application of the Hague Convention on Taking Evidence in Trials of Foreign-Related Civil and Commercial Disputes in China*, Oriental Law 138 (2010); Li Shuangyuan (ed.), *Introduction to International Civil and Commercial Litigation* (Court Press, 2004), at 299-301.
173. Civil Procedure Act, Article 276.
174. *Ibid.*, Article 277.
175. *Ibid.*
176. Articles 3 and 7 of the China-France Treaty.

central authorities requests from other Chinese courts.[177] Common law discovery in China must be limited to documents clearly enumerated in the letters of request and of direct and close connection with the subject matter of the litigation.[178]

Taking evidence through diplomatic channels is similar to service through diplomatic channels.[179]

According to the Civil Procedure Act, a request for taking evidence in China will be rejected if it impairs the sovereignty, security or public policy of China.[180] This is the same with regard to countries which have entered into bilateral treaties on judicial assistance with China.[181] However, where the Hague Convention on Taking Evidence is applicable, rejections can only be made on the basis of sovereignty and security.[182]

[C] Restraint of Foreign Proceedings

There has been no case in which a Chinese court issued an injunction to prevent foreign proceedings or suspend its own proceedings because of an injunction issued by a foreign court. It has been suggested that Chinese courts should issue injunctions very exceptionally in order to protect Chinese parties and the jurisdiction of Chinese courts.[183] Chinese courts may issue injunctions where a foreign proceeding is commenced in violation of an exclusive choice of Chinese court or the public policy of China, where the foreign proceedings are unjust, where there is a need to defend the jurisdiction of Chinese courts and arbitral tribunals, or where a Chinese court has already rendered a valid judgment.[184]

[D] Proof of Foreign Public Documents

China is not a party to the 1961 Convention Abolishing the Requirement of Legalisation for Foreign Public Documents. The general rule for the admissibility of foreign judicial and extra judicial documents can be inferred from the Civil Procedure Act requirement that the letter of attorney of a foreigner, stateless person, foreign enterprise and organisation shall be notarised by the foreign public notary, and certified by the Chinese embassy or consulate based in the foreign country, or in accordance with the

---

177. Notice of the Supreme People's Court on Assigning the High People's Courts of Beijing Municipality, Shanghai Municipality, Guangdong, Zhejiang, and Jiangsu Provinces to Directly Put Forward and Transfer Judicial Assistance Requests and Relevant Documents FB [2003] No. 297.
178. 'China' Reservation to the Hague Convention on Taking Evidence.
179. SPC, Ministry of Foreign Affairs, and Ministry of Justice Notice on Selected Issues regarding the Service of Legal Documents through Diplomatic Channels between Chinese and Foreign Courts, WF [1986] No. 47.
180. Article 276.
181. Article 18 of the China-France Treaty.
182. Article 12 of the Hague Convention on Taking Evidence.
183. Ou Fuyong, *Injunctions in International Civil Litigations* (Peking University Press, 2007), at 249-250.
184. *Ibid.*, at 257.

certification procedures specified in applicable treaties.[185] Under bilateral treaties, certifying documents issued by a competent authority in accordance with the law of a foreign country are valid without certification procedures in China.[186]

[E] Statute of Limitations

Limitation periods are governed by the law applicable to the substantive matter.[187] It is accepted that statute of limitations affects the substantive rights of the parties and should be subject to the *lex causae* of the relative substantive issue.

[F] Remedies and Damages

There is no rule on whether remedies and damages are governed by the procedural law of the forum or the *lex causae*. It is generally accepted that remedies and damages are substantive rights of the parties and should be subject to the *lex causae* of the substantive issue.

[G] Foreign Currency Obligations

Chinese law is silent on whether foreign currency obligations can be recognised by the courts. There are cases where parties agree on the foreign currency obligations and interests, which are recognised by the court. It is thus held that the obligations calculated as agreed should be paid in the foreign currency.[188] In a case where parties agreed on the obligations in US dollars and interest, plaintiff claimed the dollar obligation, then changed to a RMB claim at the rate at the time the obligation was due, despite challenges from the other party. The court supported the RMB claim and ordered payment in the RMB, and interest for late payment according to bank loan interest of China.[189]

[H] Restraining Removal of Assets and Securing Evidence in Favour of a Foreign Arbitration/Judicial Process

In domestic proceedings, a people's court may order, at the request of a party or at its own discretion, protective measures with regard to the property (preservation of

185. Civil Procedure Act, Article 264.
186. For example, Article 7 of the China-Mongolia Bilateral Treaty on Civil and Criminal Judicial Assistance; Article 7 of the China-Italy Convention on Civil Judicial Assistance.
187. Article 7 of the Act.
188. *Bank of China Wenzhou Branch v. Wenzhou Dayang Import and Export Company*, Zhejiang Wenzhou Ouhai District Court (first instance), (2012) 温瓯商初字第298号; *Koyjco ltd v. Beijing Shiyuanda Electronics*, Beijing 1st Intermediate People's Court (first instance), (2012) 一中民初字第5442号.
189. *Haoteng Technology Company v. Shanghai Shangqi Circuit Board*, Shanghai 2nd Intermediate People's Court (final), (2012) 沪二中民四(商)终字第S408号.

property) or acts of a party (to do or not to do something) in order to facilitate enforcement of the judgment or protect the interest of a party.[190]

In urgent situations where a party would suffer irreparable damage if protective measures were not adopted, the party may apply for protective measures to the court of the place of the property, place of the domicile of the respondent, or other competent court, even before filing a lawsuit. Security is required for granting protective measures. If the applicant fails to start judicial proceedings or arbitration within thirty days after the adoption of the protective measures, the court will rescind them.[191] Preservation of property should be removed if the party against whom measures are taken provides security.[192] Preservation of evidence measures during litigation or before filing a lawsuit are subject to similar rules.[193]

These provisions were expressly made applicable to foreign-related proceedings under the 2007 revision – except for the fact that a court was not able to order the measures at its own discretion –[194] but the enabling provisions have been abolished under the 2012 revision. The intention of the legislature may be that the general provisions apply also to foreign-related proceedings and there is no need to insert specific provisions on foreign-related proceedings. Thus a court can take protective measures at its discretion in a foreign-related proceeding.

In maritime proceedings protective measures, preservation of property or evidence, are allowed both during the proceedings and before filing a lawsuit. Application for protective measures should be made to the maritime court of the place of the property or evidence,[195] regardless of any choice of court or arbitration clause between the parties.[196] The applicant should provide security.[197] Protective measures regarding property may be removed if the respondent provides security or provides justifications, or no litigation or arbitration is instituted within the time limit.[198] After protective measures regarding property or evidence have been ordered, parties should commence proceedings or arbitration.[199]

In foreign-related arbitral proceedings under a domestic arbitration commission, a party may apply for preservation of property pending arbitral proceedings to the arbitration commission, which will forward it to the intermediate court at the place of the respondent's domicile or where the property is located.[200] A party may also apply for preservation of evidence during an arbitral proceeding to the arbitration commission which will forward it to the court at the place where the arbitration commission is

190. Civil Procedure Act, Article 100.
191. *Ibid.*, Article 101.
192. *Ibid.*, Article 104.
193. *Ibid.*, Article 81.
194. Civil Procedure Act (2007 revision), Chapter 26.
195. Special Maritime Procedure Act, Articles 13 and 63.
196. *Ibid.*, Articles 14 and 64.
197. *Ibid.*, Articles 16 and 66.
198. *Ibid.*, Article 18.
199. *Ibid.*, Articles 19 and 72.
200. Civil Procedure Act, Article 272.

located.[201] The law is silent on whether preservation of property or evidence is allowed before the institution of arbitral proceedings.

The law is silent on whether a court will order preservation of property or evidence in favour of an ongoing or potential international arbitral proceeding. It is concluded that interim measures for the purpose of preserving property or evidence ordered by a foreign arbitral tribunal or a foreign court will not be recognised in China since the orders are interim rather than final.[202]

§1.05 RECOGNITION AND ENFORCEMENT OF FOREIGN DECISIONS

[A] Judicial Decisions: Requirements and Limitations

The recognition and enforcement of foreign judgments in China are subject to the Civil Procedure Act, bilateral treaties, international conventions, or the principle of reciprocity.[203]

Recognition or enforcement of a foreign judgment shall be rejected on any of the following grounds:

(1) The judgment is rendered by an incompetent court. The jurisdiction provisions of the Civil Procedure Act apply to determine whether a court which rendered the judgment is competent where no bilateral treaty or international convention applies. Jurisdiction provisions of bilateral treaties either list the circumstances where a court has jurisdiction,[204] or refer to the law of the requested country,[205] or provide that the country which rendered the judgment is competent as long as the matter does not fall within the exclusive jurisdiction of requested country.[206]
(2) The judgment is not final or enforceable. The standard for finality or enforceability is established in most bilateral treaties as the law of the country of origin.[207]
(3) The defendant was not duly serviced and a default judgment was made; or the defendant was not duly represented.[208] There is a case where recognition and enforcement of a French judgment was rejected since service on the Chinese national in China was done by post. Both China and France are contracting states to the Hague Service Convention but China has made a reservation against service by post. The China and France bilateral treaty on judicial

201. Arbitration Act, Article 68.
202. Zhang Shouzhi, Hu Ke and Xu Beibei, (February) China's Enforceability of Provisional Measures in Offshore Arbitration King & Wood Mallesons (China) China Bulletin (2011).
203. Civil Procedure Act, Article 281.
204. For example, China-Spain Treaty on Civil and Criminal Judicial Assistance (China-Spain Treaty), Article 21.
205. For example, China-France Treaty, Article 22.
206. For example, China-Russia Treaty on Civil and Criminal Judicial Assistance (China-Russia Treaty), Article 20.
207. For example, China-France Treaty, Article 22 and China-Russia Treaty, Article 20.
208. *Ibid.*

assistance also banned service by post. It was held the party against which enforcement was sought was not duly serviced and recognition and enforcement of judgments rejected.[209]

(4) The court where recognition and enforcement is sought has delivered a conclusive judgment on the same dispute between the same parties, or has recognised a foreign judgment on the same dispute between the same parties.[210]

(5) The applicable law determined in the judgment is not the law as required by the conflict of law rules of the requested state. Some treaties require that in respect of the status or capacities of natural persons, the applicable law is inconsistent with what is required by the choice of law of the forum unless the same substantive result is achieved.[211]

(6) The recognition and enforcement of a foreign judgment may be refused if recognition and enforcement would harm the national, social, and public interest of China.[212]

(7) Where there is no applicable treaty, recognition and enforcement of a foreign judgment can only be possible if it is required by reciprocity.[213]

It must be noted that some bilateral treaties (with Kuwait, UAE, and Tunisia) exclude interim injunctions form recognition and enforcement. Procedures for the recognition or enforcement of foreign judgments under bilateral treaties vary.[214] Some treaties require that parties alone can apply to a competent Chinese court for the recognition or enforcement of foreign judgments.[215] Some treaties provide that a central authority can apply to a Chinese court for the recognition or enforcement of foreign judgments in principle but parties can apply also if parties have domicile or residence in China.[216] Some treaties permit either a central authority or parties to apply to a Chinese court.[217] Some treaties allow only a central authority to apply.[218]

Regarding recognition of foreign divorce judgments, there are two Supreme People's Court interpretations which provide similar grounds for not recognising such judgments.[219] Foreign divorce judgments are often recognised and enforcement is not always necessary.

209. *Schneider Electric Industries SAS v. a Chinese company*, Zhejiang Wenzhou Intermediate People's Court (first instance), (2005) 温民三初字第155号.
210. For example, China-France Treaty, Article 22 and China-Russia Treaty, Article 20.
211. China-France Treaty, Article 22 and China-Spain Treaty, Article 22.
212. Civil Procedure Act, Article 282.
213. Civil Procedure Act, Article 281.
214. See Xiao Yongping, *supra* n. 167, at 427.
215. For example, China-France Treaty, Article 20.
216. For example, China-Russia Treaty, Article 17.
217. For example, China-Poland Treaty on Civil and Criminal Judicial Assistance, Article 18.
218. For example, China-Turkey Treaty on Civil, Commercial and Criminal Judicial Assistance, Article 22.
219. Provisions on the Procedures regarding the Application for Foreign Divorce Judgments by Chinese Nationals, FM [1991] No. 21, Article 12.

A court shall issue a ruling to recognise the legal force of a foreign judgment, as well as an order for enforcement, under the same procedures for enforcing a domestic judgment.[220]

[B] Arbitral Awards (Including ICSID Awards): Requirements and Limitations

The recognition and enforcement of foreign-related arbitral awards made by domestic arbitral tribunals may be rejected on the basis that (1) there is no valid submission to arbitration; (2) the respondent was not notified of the appointment of arbitrators or of the arbitral proceeding, or was not able to present his case for reasons beyond himself; (3) illegal composition of the arbitral tribunal or illegal procedures; (4) matters are unarbitrable or fall outside the arbitration agreement; (5) public policy would be violated.[221] Court examination over foreign-related domestic arbitral awards are relaxed in contrast with purely domestic awards. Under a Supreme People's Court notice, rejection of foreign-related domestic arbitral awards shall be reported to competent high courts for approval. Non-approval decision made by the high courts shall be approved by the Supreme People's Court.[222] The mechanism is designed to avoid intrusive examination of such awards and guarantee the finality of such awards.

The recognition and enforcement of international arbitral awards (i.e., rendered by foreign arbitral tribunals) may be rejected under the 1958 New York Convention to which China is a contracting state, applicable bilateral treaties, or the principle of reciprocity.[223] China is a party to the Convention on the Settlement of Investment Disputes between States and Nationals of Other States and has entered into a Comprehensive Investment Agreement with ASEAN.

§1.06 TREATIES FOR JUDICIAL COOPERATION

Apart from the already mentioned Hague Conventions, China has entered into numerous bilateral treaties on civil judicial assistance. Such international conventions on procedures or bilateral treaties on judicial assistance are directly applicable[224] and prevail over municipal Chinese law subject to the reservations of China.[225]

220. Civil Procedure Act, Article 282.
221. Arbitration Act, Article 71; Civil Procedure Act, Article 274.
222. Supreme People's Court Notice on Dealing with Foreign-Related Arbitration and Foreign Arbitration by the Courts FF [1995] No. 18.
223. Civil Procedure Act, Article 283.
224. Xiao Yongping, *supra* n. 9, at 364.
225. Civil Procedure Act, Article 260.

CHAPTER 2
Hong Kong

*Alan Gibb & Richard Morris**

§2.01 CODIFICATION OF PRIVATE INTERNATIONAL LAW AND RELEVANCE OF CASE LAW

[A] Codification and Case Law

In the major areas of private international – choice of jurisdiction and choice of law – Hong Kong follows the English common law rules and there is no codification of its laws. This stultifies development of the law in Hong Kong as the English jurisprudence in this area has considerably diminished with the increasing influence of European law. In *First Laser Ltd. v. Fujian Enterprises (Holdings) Ltd.*,[1] the Court of Appeal admonished the approach taken by the first instance judge where he applied by analogy the characteristic performance presumption of the European Rome I Regulation[2] in deciding the choice of law in contract; instead, the Court of Appeal applied the English common laws rules relying for assistance on English materials published before the advent of the European rules, such as the 1987 edition of Dicey & Morris on the Conflict of Laws!

The one exception to this is in the case of the rules on domicile. Under the Domicile Ordinance 2008,[3] the common law rules on domicile have been amended to make them less technical and to achieve a closer correlation between a person's legal domicile and the country he is most closely connected with. Thus, the very technical

* Alan Gibb, Barrister, Professional Consultant, The Chinese University of Hong Kong (CUHK). Richard Morris, Director of the Postgraduate Certificate in Laws, The Chinese University of Hong Kong (CUHK).

1. [2011] 2 HKLRD 45.
2. Regulation (EC) No. 593/2008 of the European Parliament and of the Council of 17 Jun. 2008 on the law applicable to contractual obligations.
3. Cap 596.

rules on domicile of origin and its revival on the abandonment of the domicile of choice have been abolished as has the wife's domicile of dependency! In their place, the legislation provides that a child takes the domicile of the country he is most closely connected with;[4] and when the child becomes an adult that domicile is retained until there is presence in another country with an intent to live there indefinitely.[5] A special rule was created to deal with the common problem of a person having a clear intention to live indefinitely in a country with more than one law district, such as the People's Republic of China (PRC),[6] but as yet no clear intention as to which law district s/he wishes to reside in. In this case their domicile is the law district within that country they are most closely connected with for the time being.[7]

The principle of *stare decisis* applies in Hong Kong.

[B] Multilateral Conventions Providing Uniform Substantive Law and/or International Jurisdictional Rules

Article 13 of the Basic Law stipulates that the Central Government of China is responsible for the foreign affairs relating to the Hong Kong Special Administrative Region (or HKSAR). Nevertheless, according to Article 151 of the Basic Law, Hong Kong can conclude some international agreements and join international organisations using the name of 'Hong Kong, China'. Furthermore, Article 153(1) of the Basic Law states that the HKSAR government has to be consulted before international agreements to which China is a party are extended to Hong Kong and Article 153(2) provides that with the authorisation of the Central Government of China, international agreements to which China is not a party may also continue to apply in the HKSAR.

International treaties have to be transposed into domestic legislation or accepted by a judicial decision in order for them to be binding in Hong Kong. As an example, Chapter 4A, order 69, rule 2(a) gives effect to the 1965 Hague Service Convention; the Will Ordinance gives effect to the 1961 Hague Forms of Will Convention; the Act of Recognition of Divorce and Judicial Separation gives effect to the 1971 Hague Divorce Convention; the Adoption Ordinance gives effect to the 1993 Hague Inter-Country International Children Convention; the Recognition of Trusts Ordinance gives effect to the 1985 Hague Trusts Convention; the Child Abduction and Custody Ordinance (Cap 512) gives effect to the Hague Child Abduction Convention; the Carriage of Air Ordinance (Cap 500) gives effect to several international conventions regarding international carriage by air. Similarly, several international maritime conventions are applicable to HKSAR even though China is not a party to them.

On the other hand, the UN Convention on Contracts for the International Sale of Goods (CISG), and the Convention on International Interest in Mobile Equipment (together with its Aircraft Protocol) are not applicable in Hong Kong.

4. Section 4.
5. Section 5.
6. The PRC comprises four law districts, the Mainland, Hong Kong, Macau, and Taiwan.
7. Section 10.

§2.02 JURISDICTION OF THE LOCAL COURTS IN FOREIGN-RELATED CASES

[A] Grounds for Jurisdiction

[1] General

The general grounds for jurisdiction of the Hong Kong courts depend on whether service can be lawfully made on the defendant. Order 11 of the Rules of the High Court[8] sets out a number of grounds upon which the Hong Kong Court may grant leave to bring proceedings against a foreign party, e.g., a contract made within Hong Kong, or by implication governed by Hong Kong Law, a tort committed within the jurisdiction even if the damage is sustained out of Hong Kong, or a tort committed out of the jurisdiction where the damage is sustained within the jurisdiction. The Order 11 grounds will be broadly similar to those of other Common Law countries within the Asia region. The Court has discretion to refuse leave on forum conveniens principles even where an Order 11 ground is established. Further, a party, even if served within the jurisdiction as of right, may also contest jurisdiction on forum non conveniens principles.

In March 2013, the High Court in *Re Pioneer Iron and Steel Group Company Limited*[9] – applying *Re Yung Kee Holdings Ltd*[10] – confirmed the three requirements that a petitioner seeking to wind up an unregistered company must establish in order for the Hong Kong courts to have jurisdiction: (i) there must be sufficient connection with Hong Kong (normally, the presence of assets); (ii) there should be a 'reasonable possibility that the winding up order would benefit those applying for it'; and (iii) the court must be able to exercise jurisdiction over one or more persons interested in the distribution of the assets (other than being a petitioner or creditor). In *Re China Medical Technologies Inc.*,[11] it was further clarified that: (i) those requirements are principles to be observed in exercising the jurisdiction and that (ii) in cases where the third requirement cannot be satisfied, discretion should be exercised considering whether the connection of the company's activities with Hong Kong is sufficiently strong and whether the benefits of the winding up are sufficiently substantial.

Hong Kong courts also have in rem jurisdiction. By virtue of section 12 of the High Court Ordinance (HCO), and with a number of exceptions, the provisions of the 1952 International Convention Relating to the Arrest of Seagoing Ships apply in Hong Kong.

[2] Submitted to Jurisdiction

Hong Kong courts also have jurisdiction when the defendant voluntary submits to their jurisdiction.

8. Chapter 4A Laws of Hong Kong.
9. [2013] HKEC 317.
10. [2012] 6 HKC 246.
11. HCCW 135/2012.

[3] Exclusive Jurisdiction

There are no specific provisions regarding exclusive jurisdiction, except by way of agreement of the parties.

[B] Exclusion of Jurisdiction

[1] Immunity

[a] Sovereign Immunity

There is no specific statute. Hong Kong, being now a part of Mainland China, adheres to Mainland China's absolute immunity approach.[12] It should be noted, however, that Mainland China does not claim immunity for its state owned enterprises, and these may be freely sued in the Hong Kong court or be the subject of arbitration proceedings in Hong Kong.

[b] Diplomatic and Consular Immunity

Both the 1961 Vienna Convention on Diplomatic Relations and the 1963 Vienna Convention on Consular Relations apply in Hong Kong.

[2] Non-justiciable Claims

Hong Kong courts do not have jurisdiction over issues regarding land located outside Hong Kong.

[3] Forum Agreements in Favour of Foreign Courts

In line with almost all private international law regimes Hong Kong respects the principle of party autonomy and leaves the parties free to determine the applicable law. The court will generally respect choice of forum unless the Hong Kong party would lose a juridical advantage or suffer a juridical disadvantage by being subjected to the overseas jurisdiction.

Proceedings cannot be brought outside the chosen jurisdiction under the exclusive jurisdiction clause unless there is an exceptional reason for doing so and it would be 'most unusual' for a Hong Kong court to stay proceedings brought in Hong Kong pursuant to a Hong Kong exclusive jurisdiction clause.[13]

---

12. *Democratic Republic of the Congo and others v. FG Hemisphere Associates LLC* (2011) 14 HKCFAR 395.
13. Per Lok DJ in *Hyundai Engineering & Construction v. UBAF (Hong Kong) Ltd.* [2012] HKLRD 620.

Similar principles would apply if the jurisdiction clause was in favour of a foreign country. Thus, in *Hyundai Engineering & Construction Co. Ltd. v. UBAF (Hong Kong) Limited and Bank of China Ltd,*[14] the court held that the presence of an exclusive jurisdiction clause is an important factor to be considered in determining whether to grant a stay of proceedings on the ground of forum non conveniens, particularly in case of international commercial disputes.

Indeed the Hong Kong courts have indicated it might be possible to have an exclusive jurisdiction clause in favour of more than one foreign jurisdiction.[15] Unlike many jurisdictions asymmetrical/unilateral jurisdiction clauses imposing exclusive jurisdiction on one party but not the other are permitted.

In the case of a non-exclusive jurisdiction clause where the plaintiff elects to litigate in the jurisdiction named in the clause, then the clause will be treated in the same way as an exclusive jurisdiction clause and forum non conveniens considerations will be irrelevant.[16].

In what circumstances will the Hong Kong court refuse to apply an exclusive jurisdiction clause? This is decided on a case by case basis but in recent years the courts have refused to apply such a clause where the party relying on the clause had broken it himself by initially instigating proceeding elsewhere (such conduct meant that he was estopped from relying on the clause)[17] and in order to avoid parallel proceedings.[18] The Hong Kong courts seem to be more willing to find a 'strong case' as why the exclusive jurisdiction clause should be departed from than their English counterparts where, for example, exclusive jurisdiction clauses have been upheld even if this created the danger of parallel proceedings.[19]

It should be noticed that according to the 2008 Reciprocal Arrangement between Mainland China and Hong Kong, the judgments rendered by a Hong Kong court based on non-exclusive jurisdiction clauses in favour of its courts will not be recognised and enforced in Mainland China; and vice versa.

[4] Arbitration Clause

Section 20 of Hong Kong's Arbitration Ordinance applies Article 8 of the UNCITRAL Model Law.[20] Where there is a valid arbitration clause, the Court will refer the parties to arbitration.[21]

14. [2013] HKEC 1530.
15. Per Reyes DJ in *Hwoo Huang Linda v. Fu Being San* [2012] HKEC 1668 commenting on an exclusive jurisdiction clause in favour of the USA!
16. *Noble Power Investments v. Nissei Stomach Tokyo* [2008] HKCU 1009.
17. *Pacific Aerosupplies v. Dakota Air Parts International* [2011] HKEC 916.
18. *S Net Freight (HK) Ltd v. Namsung Shipping Company Ltd* [2011] HKEC 1061.
19. *Morgan Stanley v. China Haisheng Juice Holdings* [2009] EWHC 2409 (Comm).
20. UNCITRAL Model Law on International Commercial Arbitration.
21. Chapter 609 Laws of Hong Kong.

[C] Non-exercise of Jurisdiction

[1] Forum Non Conveniens

Hong Kong adopts the English common law forum non conveniens principle as laid down in *Spiliada Maritime Corp. v. Cansulex Ltd.*[22] The only slight difference is that the Hong Kong courts adopt a three stage test rather than the *Spiliada's* two stages, see *The Adhiguna Meranti.*[23] The three stages are: (i) the defendant must prove that another jurisdiction, rather than Hong Kong, is the natural and appropriate forum (this burden of proof is reversed where the plaintiff does not have jurisdiction as of right but only by virtue of long-arm jurisdiction); (ii) if the defendant succeeds in proving stage 1, the plaintiff must then establish that if the claim went to the other jurisdiction this would deprive him/her of legitimate personal or juridical advantages; and (iii) if the plaintiff can prove stage 2, then the court must balance the advantages of the trial in the other jurisdiction against the disadvantages to be suffered by the plaintiff and decide whether 'substantial justice' will be done if the case is allowed to proceed in the other jurisdiction.

The test is very open textured, making it difficult to predict the outcome in many cases. At stage 1 level, the court takes into account factors such as location of witnesses and evidence, choice of law (is the issue of foreign law so complex it is best decided by the foreign court?), *lis albi pendens* (this is simply a factor the courts take into account), and the difficulty of enforcing the foreign judgment in Hong Kong. At stage 2 level, factors such as the fact that the plaintiff is time barred in the foreign jurisdiction, procedural fairness (will the plaintiff get a fair trial in the foreign court?) and the fact that the plaintiff will deprived of significant procedural advantages and remedies, are taken into account.[24]

Many cases in Hong Kong involve the court having to decide whether proceedings should be stayed in favour of the Mainland. On the whole, Hong Kong judges are quick to conclude that the Mainland is forum non conveniens taking the view that whilst they are competent to decide matters of Mainland law, Mainland judges lack the necessary English language skills to adjudicate in a case involving documents in English,[25] and recognizing also the fact that Mainland judgments are not normally enforceable in Hong Kong because they are not final and conclusive under Hong Kong's enforcement of judgment rules.

One particularly controversial matter is whether the Mainland is forum non conveniens because the plaintiff will be denied a fair trial there, especially in the context where the defendant is a state-owned enterprise. To date, no Hong Kong court

22. [1987] AC 460.
23. [1987] 2 HKC 126.
24. In *Shezhen Futaihing Precision Industry Co. Ltd. v. BYD Co. Ltd.* [2008] HKEC 1093 the fact that the plaintiff would be deprived of Hong Kong's superior discovery and interrogatories procedure, the remedies of constructive trust, tracing and mandatory injunction, and a much higher award of damages, if the case proceeded in the Mainland, convinced the judge that substantial justice required that proceedings should take place in Hong Kong.
25. *Botantic Ltd. v. China National Oil Corp.* [2008] HKCU 1312.

has concluded that this is the case because the evidence has not been sufficiently positive and cogent. Thus in *New Link Consultants v. Air China*[26] the court favoured the view of the defendant's legal expert on Mainland law who concluded:

> Whilst local protectionism does exist in some places in China, one cannot generalise to say that all courts in China suffer from the same problem. Judges in Beijing are well-trained and highly qualified, the legal 'environment' in Beijing is superior to the rest of China, Beijing courts are fully conscious of their external image and the Beijing Government has no need to interfere with justice ... Numerous examples [exist] in which courts in China (including those in Beijing) have held against Chinese parties in favour of foreign parties.

[2] Lis alibi pendens

The concept of proceedings being automatically stayed in favour of the first seised court is alien to Hong Kong law.

§2.03 APPLICABLE LAW

Procedural issues are governed by the *lex fori*, while questions of substance are governed by the law applicable according to the rules described below.

[A] Choice of Law

[1] Express Stipulation

Regarding choice of law in contract, the parties are free to agree on their choice of law. The only possible exception to this would be that if the chosen law has no real connection with the parties or the contract and the Hong Kong court considers it was inserted in bad faith in order to evade foreign law, then the court can refuse to give effect to the clause.[27] However, to date no Hong Kong court has found evidence of bad faith.

[2] Implied Choice

While in the absence of express choice, the Hong Kong courts have on occasion applied the implied choice of law test;[28] the preferred approach is to apply the proper law test of ascertaining the law district that the contract has the closest connection with.[29]

---

26. [2005] HKEC 815.
27. *Credit Agricole Indosuez v. Shanghai Erfangi* [2002] HKEC 301.
28. *Century Yachts Ltd. v. Xiamen Celestial Yacht Ltd.* [1994] 1 HKC 331.
29. In *First Laser v. Fujiian Enterprises Holdings Ltd.* [2012] HKEC 946 the Court of Final Appeal approved of the following summary of the law: 'But in practice the same result can be reached by the application of the second or third tests, and frequently the courts move straight from the first stage to the third stage. This is largely because the tests of inferred intention and close connection merged into each other, and because before the objective close connection test

This means the court must weigh up factors such as the country of the subject matter of the contract, country of legal terminology, country where the contract was made/negotiated, country of the parties domicile/residence, country of the language and currency of the contract, country of the related contract, country of intended performance (*lex solutionis*), and the country specified in a jurisdiction/arbitration clause. Case law establishes that the latter two carry the greatest weight and will usually trump other considerations.[30] It should also be noted that in the case of country of intended performance the emphasis is on the *place* where such performance was to be effected unlike most conflict of laws systems where the emphasis is on the place where the performing *party* is based. The fact that the contract would be illegal under the law of one country is an 'important but not a conclusive factor'[31] in favour of not applying its law.

On the grounds of comity, even if Hong Kong is the proper law, if it is the common intention of the parties to actually perform the contract in a country where it is illegal, the Hong Kong courts will not enforce it.[32]

[B] Other Cases

In the case of tort, Hong Kong retains the classic, and very parochial, common law rules on choice of law. This means that where the tort occurs in Hong Kong, then Hong Kong tort law will apply even if all the connecting factors, other than the place of the tort, connect the tort with another country.[33] If the tort occurs outside Hong Kong, then the double actionability rule is applied and in order to obtain a favourable judgment the plaintiff must establish that as well as being a civil wrong in the country where the tort occurred it is also a tort in Hong Kong. Thus in *Pei Zheng Middle School v. China Pui Ching Educational Foundation Ltd.*,[34] in order to succeed in a passing off claim the plaintiff had to prove not only that this was a tort in the Mainland but also that all requirements were fulfilled under Hong Kong's own law. The courts have the 'power to avoid injustice by introducing an element of flexibility into the rule'[35] and apply the law of the country which has 'the most significant relationship with the occurrence and with the parties'.[36] This is open to the objection that it makes the law very uncertain as there is no real guidance in the cases as to when the exception will be invoked. However, it has been used in Hong Kong where a road accident has occurred in the

became fully established the test of inferred intention was in truth an objective test designed not to elicit actual intention but to impute an intention which had not been formed.' (Dicey, para. 32-006).

30. *Ibid.; York Air Conditioning v. Lam Kwai Hung* [1995] 1 HKC 287.
31. *Hung Fung Enterprises Holdings v. Agricultural Bank of China* [2012] HKEC 870.
32. *Shenzen Development Bank v. New Century International (Holdings) Ltd.* [2002] HKEC 1087.
33. *GDH Ltd v. Creditor Co. Ltd.* [2008] HKEC 1780.
34. [2010] HKEC 658.
35. *Red Sea Insurance v. Bouygues* [1995] 1 AC 190.
36. *Ibid.*

Mainland involving two Hong Kong parties and no tort was involved in the Mainland because the concept of vicarious liability is not recognised there.[37]

Space does not permit detail on other areas of choice of law, however, Hong Kong follows the traditional English common law connecting factors such as the *lex situs* in the case of the transfer of property, the domicile of the testator at the time of death in the case of essential validity of a will (in relation to moveable property) and the domicile at the time the will was made in the case of its construction. The capacity of a party to enter into a contract is determined by the law of the party's domicile or by the law of the jurisdiction with which the party is most closely connected. The formal validity of a contract is governed by the law of the place the contract was entered into, though the contract could also be valid if the requirements of the proper law of the contract have been complied with.

In the case of marriage the dual domicile test applies in the case of essential validity and the place where the marriage was celebrated is the connecting factor in the case of formalities. A special Hong Kong point worth noting is that whereas concubinage was abolished in the Mainland in 1931 it was permitted in Hong Kong between persons of Chinese ethnic origin until 1971. Thus there are still cases being heard in the Hong Kong courts today, in relation to intestacy or succession under a will, where the plaintiff is seeking to establish that both parties were domiciled in Hong Kong before 1971 and went through the customary procedures required for a concubinage union, as under Hong Kong law concubines are recognised as having the same rights as wives in a monogamous marriage.[38]

[C] *Renvoi*

Presumably on the grounds of expense and/or lack of possible advantage to the litigant the issue of *renvoi* has never been argued in the Hong Kong courts. Indeed a data base search revealed that *renvoi* has only been referred to in a total of six cases either in a negative way, to confirm that it does not apply to in the field of contract,[39] or in relation to the fact that the expert witness on foreign law had not addressed this issue.[40]

[D] Mandatory Rules of the Forum and of Third States

In common with most jurisdictions, Hong Kong has legislation in place to prevent consumers and employees from losing their statutory rights by the use of a foreign choice of law clause. Thus both the Control of Exemptions Clauses Ordinance[41] (protecting consumers from unreasonable exemption clauses) and the Unconscionable Contracts Ordinance[42] (protecting consumers from unfair contract terms) provide that

37. *Kwok Yu Keung v. Yeung Pang Cheung and Others* [2006] HKC 107.
38. *Suen Toi Lee v. Yau Yee Ping*, Court of Final Appeal [2002] 1 HKLRD 196.
39. *Aoki Corporation v. Hong Kong Institute of Education* [2004] HKCFI 34 para. 122.
40. *Wong Zhong Lan Xiang & Others v. Wong & Another* [2003] HKCA 585 para. 85.
41. Cap 71, s. 17(2).
42. Cap 458, s. 7(2).

they have effect, notwithstanding a foreign choice of law clause, if either in the opinion of the court the intention of the term's inclusion is to wholly/mainly to evade the Ordinance or if the consumer is habitually resident in Hong Kong and the essential steps for making the contract were taken there.

In the case of employment law Hong Kong's four major statutory provisions preventing discrimination, Sex Discrimination Ordinance,[43] Family Status Ordinance,[44] Race Discrimination Ordinance,[45] and Disability Discrimination Ordinance[46] prohibit contracting out by the use of a choice of law clause if the actual or potential employment is at an 'establishment in Hong Kong'. (This is defined in a negative way as any employment 'unless the employee does his work ... mainly outside Hong Kong').[47]

The wording of Hong Kong's Employment Law Ordinance is less clear merely providing that '[a]ny term of a contract of employment which purports to extinguish or reduce any right, benefit or protection conferred upon the employee by this Ordinance shall be void.'[48] This provision has been subject to two conflicting first instance decisions.[49] However, the better view would seem to be that of *Reyes J* in the latter case: 'One cannot attempt to get around the protection afforded by the EO to employees working here through the expedient of choosing a foreign law.' This would mean that if, for example, an English employer sends an English employee on secondment to the employer's Hong Kong office then, whilst in Hong Kong, the employee is subject to Hong Kong's employment laws, such as the right of an employee to 'buy out' his notice period, a right not recognised in English employment law, despite the fact that the contract of employment is expressly governed by English law.

The fact that a particular law is mandatory in another state is not in itself a reason for the Hong Kong court to stay proceedings in favour of that state. Thus in *Yantai Wanhua Polyurethanes v. Pur Products*,[50] the court decided that Hong Kong was forum conveniens on the basis that if the case was stayed in favour of England the English court would not apply Hong Kong law, which was expressed in the contract as the choice of law, but mandatory European rules on commercial agents with the result that the defendant would be able to avoid the agreement he had made.

[E] Proof of Foreign Law

Hong Kong follows the English common law that there is presumption that foreign law is the same as domestic law, subject to a number of exceptions such as:

43. Cap 480.
44. Cap 527.
45. Cap 602.
46. Cap 487.
47. See, for example, the Sex Discrimination Ordinance s. 14(1).
48. Cap 57, s. 70.
49. *HSBC v. Wallace* [2008] 1 HGKLRD 613; *Cantor Fitzgerald Europe v. Boyer* [2012] HKEC 301.
50. [2013] HKLRD 590.

- It is not in the interests of justice to apply it.
- The foreign law is not based on the common law.
- It is inherently improbable that the foreign law is the same.
- The domestic law must be potentially universal.

Thus in *Dafni Igal v. CMA CGM SA*,[51] the Hong Kong court refused to assume Taiwanese tax laws were the same as Hong Kong's as this was highly improbable given '(i) the jurisprudential difference of the two jurisdictions and (ii) the highly specific nature of taxation law'. In addition it was stated 'tax statutes are not the type of laws that one could rationally assume to have any significant degree of universality'.

Once the issue of foreign law is raised and a party does not want to rely on the above presumption, foreign law must be proved as a fact with the assistance of expert evidence. Despite one dictum to the contrary,[52] the law of the Mainland is regarded as a matter of foreign law and must be established in the normal way. However, Hong Kong judges exhibit great confidence in deciding what Mainland law is. This is illustrated by *To DHCJ* in *Botanic Ltd. v. China National United Oil Corp.*,[53] where the judge stated (at paragraph [65]): 'In view of the ever increasing commercial relationship between Hong Kong and the PRC the Hong Kong courts had on numerous occasions to deal with issues of PRC law, including some complicated ones.' He added, among other points, that more literature on PRC law was now available and that more bilingual judges have been receiving legal education in PRC law. In light of the reasoning provided, the judge then went on to reject the view of the defendant's PRC legal experts, that the trial of the case would involve evidence in the nature of state secrets which could not be divulged in a Hong Kong court, and concluded (at paragraph [69]), after analysing Articles 2 and 8(3) of the State Secrets Law of the PRC, that 'their opinion does not even sound logical'.

To minimise the expense and inconvenience of proving foreign law as a matter of fact, the Evidence Ordinance[54] provides that where the High Courts of Hong Kong or England[55] (or on appeal from those Courts) have reached a decision on foreign law this is admissible as evidence in a later case as establishing the relevant foreign law unless the contrary is proved.

§2.04 PROCEDURAL ISSUES

[A] Service of Summons and Judicial Orders Abroad

Hong Kong is a party to the 1965 Hague Convention on the Service Abroad of Judicial and Extrajudicial Documents in Civil and Commercial Matters. Service of process

51. [2012] HKCFI 2082.
52. Per Liu JA in *Nan Tung Bank Ltd, Zhu Hai v. Wangfoog Transport Ltd.* [1999] 2 HKC 606.
53. *Botantic Ltd. v. China National Oil Corp.* [2008] HKCU 1312.
54. Cap 8, s. 59.
55. The reference to England is a reminder that pre-1997 handover English law remains valid in Hong Kong unless repealed or proved inconsistent with Basic Law.

abroad must, however, be consistent with the rules for domestic service and must not contravene the law of the country where service is to be effected.

[B] Obtaining Evidence Abroad

Hong Kong is also a party to the 1970 Hague Convention on the Taking of Evidence Abroad in Civil or Commercial Matters. Further, in relation to the taking of evidence, the court may either issue a letter of request to the judicial authorities of the country in which a witness resides to take the evidence of that witness, or, if the government of the country allows a person in that country to be examined before a person appointed by the court, the court may make an order appointing a special examiner to take the evidence of the witness in that country.[56]

[C] Restraint of Foreign Proceedings

The Hong Kong court may grant anti-suit injunctions to restrain the commencement of continuance of overseas proceedings (whether court proceedings or arbitration). In the grant of such injunctions, the Hong Kong court will follow the principles set out in the UK House of Lords decision *Airbus Industries GIE v. Patel*,[57] and such injunctions will only be granted where 'the foreign proceedings are vexatious or oppressive'[58] or where they are commenced in bad faith and are designed to subvert the Hong Kong proceedings. Thus in *Liaoyang Shunfeng Iron and Steel Co. Ltd. v. Yeung Tsz Wang*,[59] an anti-suit injunction was granted preventing the defendant litigating the same matter in the Mainland based on evidence that had been discredited in earlier Hong Kong proceedings.

[D] Proof of Foreign Public Documents[60]

Section 10 of the Oaths and Declarations Ordinance[61] provides that:

> An oath, affidavit, affirmation and notarial act administered, sworn, affirmed, or done before a diplomatic or consular officer of the People's Republic of China outside the People's Republic of China shall be as effectual as if duly administered, sworn, affirmed or done by or before any lawful authority in Hong Kong.

The effect is that a notarial act done before a diplomatic or consular officer of the People's Republic of China outside the People's Republic of China will be regarded as having the same effect as if administered before a notary public in Hong Kong and

56. Order 39/2 The Rules of the High Court, Chapter 4A Laws of Hong Kong.
57. [1999] 1 AC 119, applied in *Liaoyang Shunfeng Iron and Steel Co. Ltd. v. Yeung Tsz Wang* CACV234/2011.
58. *Airbus Industries GIE v. Patel*, p. 133 per Lord Goff.
59. [2012] HKEC 857.
60. This section was kindly supplied by Mr Alastair C. Macaulay, Vice-President of the Hong Kong Society of Notaries.
61. Chapter 10 Laws of Hong Kong.

hence may be admissible as evidence in the courts of Hong Kong under the relevant provisions of the Evidence Ordinance.[62]

Hong Kong is a party to the Hague Convention, but generally an apostille or legalisation is not required as a matter of law in the admission of duly notarised foreign public documents.

Documents filed in court or served on any person may be in English or Chinese.

[E] Statute of Limitations

Hong Kong has no statutory rules on this matter. There is dearth of case law on the issue the only instance where it has been raised in court occurred in *Peregrine Fixed Income Ltd. v. JP Morgan Chase Bank [2005] 3 HKLRD 922* the court refusing:

> to depart from the recognised common law position that, in terms of Hong Kong conflict of laws characterisation, statutes of limitation are regarded as matters of procedure and are governed by the law of the forum and to adopt the position – specifically achieved by statute in England and Australia – that defences of limitation are substantive defences and are governed by the proper law of the transaction.

This view is reflected in practice. As a matter of course, the Hong Kong courts apply their own limitation periods irrespective of the proper law of the dispute. This is particularly important as many cases in Hong Kong have the Mainland as the proper law which has far shorter limitation periods than Hong Kong.

To date there has been no consideration of the problem that if Hong Kong's limitation periods are classified as procedural and if under the foreign law, which is the proper law of the contract, its limitation periods are treated as substantive then, as potentially two different limitation periods apply, which one should the court adopt?

[F] Remedies and Damages

There is an assumption in Hong Kong that all non-monetary remedies such as injunctions are regarded as procedural and governed by the *lex fori*. As regards damages, the unsatisfactory distinction established in *Boys v. Chaplin*[63] between causation, remoteness and heads of damage (substantive and governed by the proper law), and quantification of damages (procedural and governed by the *lex fori)* applies. This distinction could potentially have serious consequences for a Hong Kong plaintiff in a tort action involving an accident on the Mainland, since pain and suffering is not recognised as a head of loss under Mainland law. As Hong Kong still applies the double actionability rule,[64] the fact that pain and suffering is not recoverable there would be a bar to a claim for this loss in Hong Kong. However, to evade this problem the Hong

62. Chapter 8 Laws of Hong Kong.
63. [1971] AC 356(HL).
64. See §2.03[B] above (in the case of a tort committed outside Hong Kong in order to recover for a head of loss it must be recognised as a head in both jurisdictions).

Kong courts, where both parties have a Hong Kong connection, have applied the exception to the double actionability rule and have concluded that, if the tort is more closely connected with Hong Kong, all of Hong Kong's law should apply including its rules on heads of loss.[65]

[G] Foreign Currency Obligations

Claims in Hong Kong may be brought and judgments awarded in foreign currencies.[66]

[H] Restraining Removal of Assets and Securing Evidence in Favour of a Foreign Arbitration/Judicial Process

The Hong Kong court may grant an injunction to restrain the removal of Hong Kong assets (Mareva Injunction) and/or to allow the plaintiff and/or its representatives to enter defendant's premises to search for, inspect and seize or make copies of evidence so that it may be preserved until trial (Anton Piller Order) even where there is no substantive jurisdiction. The injunction must relate to proceedings commenced or to be commenced overseas which proceedings are capable of giving rise to a judgment enforceable in Hong Kong.[67] The overseas proceedings could be arbitration proceedings as those are capable of giving rise to a judgment enforceable in Hong Kong.

Under section 76(1) of the Evidence Ordinance (Cap 8), the High Court can make an order for obtaining evidence to assist foreign proceedings. In *Kayne Creditors v. Roderick John Sutton and others*,[68] the judge noted that: (i) the evidence requested must be used for use at a trial; (ii) the wording of the request must specify precise documents rather than classes of documents; and (iii) fishing expeditions would not be tolerated by the court.

Section 45 of the Arbitration Ordinance empowers Hong Kong courts to grant certain interim measures in support of arbitral proceedings – seated in Hong Kong or outside – unless the court considers it more appropriate for the arbitral tribunal to grant them, if (i) the future award may be enforced in Hong Kong and (ii) the interim measure is one of the measures which may be granted in Hong Kong.

§2.05 RECOGNITION AND ENFORCEMENT OF FOREIGN DECISIONS

[A] Judicial Decisions: Requirements and Limitations

There are three separate regimes. The common law, the Foreign Judgments (Reciprocal Enforcement) Ordinance[69] (which replaces the common law rules for a limited number

65. *Kwok Yu Keung v. Yeung Pang Cheung and Others*. See n. 30 above.
66. Order 6/2/5 and 6/2/5 A Commentary in Hong Kong Civil Procedure 2013 Sweet & Maxwell.
67. Section 21M The High Court Ordinance, Chapter 4 Laws of Hong Kong; Order 11/1(oc) The Rules of the High Court, Chapter 4A, Laws of Hong Kong.
68. [2013] HKCU 2285.
69. Cap 319.

of countries) and in relation to the Mainland, the Mainland Judgments (Reciprocal Enforcement) Ordinance.[70] Enforcement only extends to enforcement of a money judgment and not to an order granting an injunction.[71]

[1] Common Law Regime

In the case of the *common law* regime, three conditions must be satisfied before a judgment will be enforced unless the defendant establishes a defence.

- Condition 1. The foreign court must have *competent* jurisdiction.

The Hong Kong courts decide this applying their *own rules* and not the jurisdictional rules of the foreign court. Hong Kong follows the leading English case of *Adams v. Cape Industries.*[72] In the case of individuals, there must be voluntary *physical* presence in the country at the date of the commencement of proceedings no matter how temporary this may be. Regarding companies the presence must be more substantial, the focus being on whether the company carries on business activities in the country. The company must have 'fixed place of business ... and for more than a minimal period of time has carried on its business ... from such premises' *per Slade LJ.*[73]

The issue of forum non conveniens is not relevant to enforcement. It is, therefore, not open to a Hong Kong court to refuse to recognise the judgment on the grounds the Hong Kong court and not the foreign court was the more appropriate court to hear the case.

Alternatively, there must be evidence of submission to the foreign court. For example, this would be the case if the contract has a clause giving the foreign court exclusive or non-exclusive jurisdiction or there is a voluntary appearance in the foreign court - such as participating in the proceedings by defending the case there, or starting an appeal.

- Condition 2. The judgment must be *final and conclusive*

The judgment must be a final one to comply with the principle of res judicata. However, the fact it could be appealed or being a default judgment the court has the power to set it aside does not stop it being final.[74] This requirement created particular difficulties in enforcing Mainland judgments, the Hong Kong courts refusing to enforce them on the basis there is a lack of finality in Mainland proceedings because the trial supervision system of the Mainland allows judgments to be opened by the original trial court on very broad grounds.[75] To solve this problem the Mainland Judgments (Reciprocal Enforcement) Ordinance was introduced in August 2008 (see below).

70. Cap 597.
71. *Westpac New Zealand v. Gao Hui* [2009] HKCU 769.
72. [1990] 1 Ch 433.
73. *Ibid.*
74. *Nintendo of America v. Bung Enterprises* [2002] 2HKC 629.
75. *Chiyu Banking Corporation v. Chan Tin Kwan* [1996] 2 HKLRD 395.

- Condition 3. The judgment must be for a fixed sum of money, and must not be *a tax or a penalty*

As it is not the function of Hong Kong courts to assist in enforcing another country's revenue or criminal law, if the foreign court order is in essence an order to pay tax or a sum payable as punishment for a crime it will not be enforced. What about punitive damages? Whilst English authorities takes the view that this can be recovered[76] and does not infringe the rule, in *Hung Fung Enterprises Holdings v. Agricultural Bank of China*[77] the Hong Kong Court of Appeal found an order by a Mainland court of double interest for late payment of damages to be a penalty and not enforceable.

Regarding defences it is no defence that foreign court got the law wrong or applied it incorrectly: 'the court is not re-trying the case. The question is not whether the decision of the foreign court is correct'.[78]

The usual range of common law defences apply in Hong Kong, namely the judgment was obtained by fraud, infringed natural justice, or it would contrary to public policy to enforce it. Hong Kong does not follow the much criticised ruling in *Abouloff v. Oppenheimer*[79] that a defendant is entitled to establish fraud even though this was rejected by the foreign court or never raised in the foreign proceedings, preferring the view that it would be abuse of process to relitigate the case in Hong Kong if satisfied that the foreign court has got a fair process in place for dealing with appeals based on fraud and these were either not used or the outcome was unsuccessful. See *Wang Hsiao Yu v. Wu Cho Cheng*[80] where the Hong Kong court refused to reopen the case when the issue of whether an IOU had been forged had gone through six rounds of appeal in Taiwan.

[2] Foreign Judgments (Reciprocal Enforcement) Ordinance[81]

This Ordinance applies to the judgments of fifteen countries (mainly British Commonwealth countries)[82] and provides for a slightly easier system of enforcement than under the common law regime. However, in order to succeed the judgment creditor must still satisfy the common law requirements as described above and the same defences apply. Also the statutory regime is tougher than the common law since, in case of an individual, *residence* rather than mere *presence* is required in the foreign country.[83]

76. SA *Consortium General Textiles v. Sun & Sand Agencies* [1978] 2 All ER 339.
77. [2012] HKEC 870.
78. Per Ching JA in *WFM Motors v. Malcolm Maydwell* [1996] 2HKLR 236.
79. (1882) 10 QBD 295.
80. [2000] HKEC 740.
81. Cap 319.
82. Australia, Austria, Belgium, Bermuda, Brunei, France, Germany, India, Italy, Israel, Malaysia, Netherlands, New Zealand, Singapore and Sri Lanka.
83. Section 6(2).

[3] *Mainland Judgments (Reciprocal Enforcement) Ordinance*[84]

This Ordinance allows Mainland judgments to be enforced in Hong Kong (the Mainland has equivalent legislation allowing Hong Kong judgments to be enforced in the Mainland). Its main feature is that it evades the common law rule that a Mainland judgment is not final and conclusive by enabling a judgment of the Supreme People's Court, Higher People's Court, Intermediate People's Court and 47 designated People's Courts[85] to be enforceable in Hong Kong 'as if it had been a judgment originally given in the Court of First Instance [in HK]'.[86] This is subject to defences such as fraud or that enforcement of the judgment is contrary to Hong Kong's public policy.[87]

However, the scope of the Ordinance (which is modelled on the Hague Choice of Court Agreements Convention 2005) is quite narrow as it only applies to *money judgments* in commercial contract disputes (non-commercial, family related and employment contracts are excluded),[88] and there must be an *exclusive jurisdiction clause* in favour of the Mainland.[89] This narrowness may explain why to date there has been no application of the Ordinance in Hong Kong.

While the Mainland has reciprocal enforcement arrangements with Macau,[90] there is no equivalent enforcement provision between Hong Kong and Macau, the common law regime therefore applying.

[B] Arbitral Awards (Including ICSID Awards): Requirements and Limitations

Mainland China is a contracting state to the 1958 New York Convention[91] (hereinafter the 'Convention') and upon its resumption of sovereignty over Hong Kong on 1 July 1997, it extended the territorial application of the Convention to Hong Kong. The provisions of the Convention are given statutory effect by the Arbitration Ordinance.[92] Thus awards from Convention countries are very easily enforced as judgments. Awards from Mainland China are enforceable in the same manner as those from Convention countries. The grounds for resisting enforcement in both cases are those set out in the Convention. In 2010, the Supreme People's Court issued a letter to the Higher People's Courts in Mainland China confirming the 'Mutual enforcement of arbitral awards between Mainland China and the Hong Kong SAR' (concluded in June 1999). According to the Agreement, the following awards rendered in Hong Kong are enforceable in Mainland China: (i) ad hoc arbitral awards made in Hong Kong;

84. Cap 597.
85. Section 6(2).
86. Section 14(1).
87. Section 18.
88. Section 2.
89. Section 3(2).
90. Arrangements between the Mainland and the Macao Special Administrative Region on the Mutual Recognition and Enforcement of Civil and Commercial Judgments (in force from 1 Apr. 2008).
91. The Convention on the Recognition and Enforcement of Foreign Arbitral Awards.
92. Chapter 609 Laws of Hong Kong.

(ii) arbitral awards made in Hong Kong by the ICC; and (iii) arbitral awards made in Hong Kong by other foreign arbitration institutions.

Awards from non-Convention countries can also be enforced as judgments and the grounds for resisting enforcement are those set out in the Convention save that the Hong Kong court may also refuse enforcement if it considers it just to do so. In its interpretation of the public policy ground for refusing enforcement of arbitration awards, Hong Kong is a very pro-enforcement jurisdiction.[93]

In *Pacific China Holdings Ltd. (in liquidation) v. Grand Pacific Holdings Ltd.*,[94] the court of Final Appeal confirmed in August 2013 that parties who unsuccessfully resist enforcement of an arbitral award in Hong Kong in the absence of special circumstances, will generally be ordered to pay costs on the indemnity basis.

On 16 December 2013, the Arrangement concerning Reciprocal Recognition and Enforcement of Arbitral Awards between the HKSAR and the Macao SAR (implemented by sections 98A-99D of the Hong Kong Arbitration Ordinance) come into force. A Macao award is to be enforced in Hong Kong either by action in the court or in the same manner as a Hong Kong or other non-Convention award (with leave of court). The grounds for refusal to enforce are in line with those contained in the Convention.

New sections 22A and B of the Arbitration Ordinance allow Hong Kong courts to support parties who want to enforce an emergency relief obtained outside Hong Kong.

Hong Kong is a party to the ICSID Convention[95] and has entered into a number of Bilateral Investment Treaties (BITs).[96]

§2.06 RECOGNITION OF OTHER FOREIGN PUBLIC DOCUMENTS[97]

An affidavit sworn outside Hong Kong before a notary public or a diplomatic or consular officer of the People's Republic of China may be used in the High Court of Hong Kong in all cases where affidavits are admissible.

Generally, if documents executed in Hong Kong are required to be executed in the presence of a solicitor or commissioner for oaths, the same documents, when executed outside Hong Kong should be executed in the presence of a notary public.

93. The leading case is *Hebei Import & Export Corp. v. Polytek Engineering Company Ltd.* [1999] 2 HKCFAR 111.
94. FAMV No. 18 of 201.
95. 1965 Convention on the Settlement of Investment Disputes between States and Nationals of Other States.
96. Mainland China has entered into many more BITs than Hong Kong and for a discussion of the coverage afforded to Hong Kong by those BITs see da Rosa and Choy 'One Country Two System and Country Risk Protection for Hong Kong Listed Companies' at http://law.lexisnexis.com/webcenters/hk.
97. This section was kindly supplied by Mr Alastair C. Macaulay, Vice-President of the Hong Kong Society of Notaries.

§2.07 TREATIES FOR JUDICIAL COOPERATION

Apart from the treaties referred to above, Hong Kong is a party to the following Hague Conventions:

- Civil Aspects of International Child Abduction
- Law applicable to Trusts and on their Recognition
- Protection of Children and Cooperation in Respect of Intercountry Adoption
- Recognition of Divorces and Legal Separations
- Conflicts of Laws Relating to the Form of Testamentary Dispositions.

CHAPTER 3

Indonesia

*Hendronoto Soesabdo, Reno Hirdarisvita & Ferry Artionang**

§3.01 CODIFICATION OF PRIVATE INTERNATIONAL LAW AND RELEVANCE OF CASE LAW

[A] Codification and Case Law

Indonesia still adopts the provisions inherited from the Dutch colonisation era in dealing with matters related to private international law, i.e., Articles 16, 17, and 18 of the *Algemene Bepalingen van Wetgeving voor Indonesia* (General Rules on Indonesian Laws/'AB'). Article 16 AB governs the law applicable to a citizen, and adopts the nationality principle. Article 17 AB governs the law applicable to movable and immovable goods, i.e., the law where the goods are located and Article 18 AB governs the law applicable to a tort, i.e., the law where the act is committed.

Those rules are still applicable as section II of the Transitional Provisions of the 1945 Constitution preserves the Dutch colonial regulations in Indonesia. Under this section, Dutch colonial regulations are still applicable where no new regulations have been enacted by the Indonesian legislature to replace them, and where they are not in conflict with the 1945 Constitution. As such, the old provisions on private international law under the AB, as aforementioned, are still in force.[1]

Efforts to codify private international law began as early as 1983; however, up to this day, there has been no noteworthy progress.

In developing private international rules, Indonesia relies on many sources, case law being one of them (though there is no application of the doctrine of *stare decisis*,

* Hendronoto Soesabdo, Partner, Commercial Dispute Resolution, Hadiputranto, Hadinoto & Partners. Reno Hirdarisvita & Ferry Artionang, Associates, Commercial Dispute Resolution, Hadiputranto, Hadinoto & Partners.

1. Sudargo Gautama, *Essays in Indonesian Law* (Second Edition, Jakarta, 1993), at 394.

some decisions of the Supreme Court have great authority – yet, they are not always published). There have been a number of cases where Indonesian judges applied the conflict of laws principles in foreign-related cases, albeit not significant in amount. Other sources include the aforementioned AB provisions, international conventions, and legal doctrines. Also the *Surat Edaran Mahkamah Agung*, SEMA (Supreme Court Circular Letters) or Supreme Court Decrees should be considered since they provide indications of the Supreme Court's perspective on certain legal issues (especially the application of former Dutch legislation). In practice, although those circular letters and decrees are highly respected, not always are applied by lower courts.

[B] Multilateral Conventions Providing Uniform Substantive Law and/or International Jurisdictional Rules

The Indonesian constitution is silent on the relationship between international and domestic

law. In practice, depending on the nature of the treaty, some of them have been implemented through domestic legislations/regulations, while others, not. Nevertheless, Law No. 24 of 2000 on International Agreements requires the publication in the official gazette of the instruments of ratification. International treaties in force in Indonesia prevail over domestic legislation.

Indonesia is a party to neither the UN Convention on Contracts for the International Sale of Goods (CISG), nor the Conventions for the International Carriage of Goods by Air and by Sea. However, Indonesia acceded to the 1993 Convention on Maritime Liens and Mortgages (through the Presidential Decree No. 44/2005 dated 8 July 2005)[2] and the Convention on International Interest in Mobile Equipment (together with its Aircraft Protocol) incorporated through Law No. 1 of 2009 on Aviation. In addition, Indonesia is a party to ten multilateral treaties administered by the World Intellectual Property Organization (WIPO).[3]

§3.02 JURISDICTION OF LOCAL COURTS IN FOREIGN-RELATED CASES

The current procedural laws in Indonesia are still influenced by the pre-1945 Dutch legal system: the *Het Herziene Indonesische Reglement* (HIR) – law governing procedures on the islands of Java and Madura; the *Rechtsreglement Buitengewestern* (RBg) – law governing procedures on the other islands; and the *Reglement op de Rechtsvordering* (Rv) – often applied by all judges when the HIR or the RBg do not regulate adequately a certain matter.

2. http://treaty.kemlu.go.id/index.php/treaty/index?Treaty%5Bwork_type_id%5D=2&Treaty%5Bsigned_year%5D=1999.
3. http://www.wipo.int/treaties/en/ShowResults.jsp?country_id=77C.

[A] Grounds for Jurisdiction

[1] General

Principally, Indonesian courts' authority adopt the territorial sovereignty doctrine, i.e., their authority covers only the areas of the Republic of Indonesia. Therefore, according to Article 118 HIR Indonesian courts' international civil jurisdiction is in principle limited to cases where the defendant's (or in cases where there are multiple defendants, one of the defendants) de facto or habitual residence is located within the jurisdiction of any of the Indonesian courts. Further, Article 100 Rv provides a basis for Indonesian courts to extend their jurisdiction to matters relating to foreign individuals. Under this rule, a party who is not domiciled in Indonesia can be sued before an Indonesian court in relation to agreements enforced in Indonesia or concluded with an Indonesian party (in cases where the parties do not specify their dispute settlement forum in the relevant agreements). In practice, Indonesian judges still refer to this provision in the absence of regulations concerning matters related to foreigners in the Indonesian civil procedural law.

Regarding jurisdiction In Rem, Article 222 of Law No. 17 of 2008 on Maritime Affairs regulates the seizure of ships located in an Indonesian port based on a court order in relation to a maritime claim (as defined in Article 223 of the Maritime Law). Although the law provides that further mechanism regarding arrest of ship will be developed by a Minister Regulation, until now no such regulation has been issued.

[2] Exclusive Jurisdiction

There is no rule that provides exclusive jurisdiction of Indonesian courts in civil disputes. However, for practical reasons, claimants should consider more on Indonesian courts (rather than foreign courts) in some cases (for example, cases over ownerships of assets located in Indonesia).

[B] Exclusion of Jurisdiction

[1] Immunity

[a] Sovereign Immunity

There is no specific Act or reported case concerning the sovereign immunity of foreign states.

[b] Diplomatic and Consular Immunity

Indonesia is a party to the 1961 Vienna Convention on Diplomatic Relations and the 1963 Vienna Convention on Consular Relations.

[c] Other Immunities

Indonesia is a party to the 1946 Convention on the Privileges and Immunities of the United Nations, the 1969 Convention on Special Missions and the 1947 Convention on the Privileges and Immunities of the Specialised Agencies.

[2] Non-justiciable Claims

There are claims that will be deemed as non-justiciable and would not be granted in Indonesia. For example, a claim in relation to a debt from gambling. Article 1788 of the Indonesian Civil Code (ICC) states that the law does not admit any legal claim with respect to a debt resulting from gambling. Note, however, that Indonesian courts are obliged to accept and examine any cases submitted to them. Indonesian courts may only issue their decision to dismiss or reject a case after examining the case.

[3] Forum Agreements in Favour of Foreign Courts

With regard to forum agreements in favour of foreign courts, parties are allowed to choose foreign courts to settle their disputes. This stems from the principle of freedom of contract as set out in Article 1338 of the Indonesian Civil Law which states that '[a] validly made agreement applies as law to the parties thereto'.

Note, however, that Indonesia is not a party to any international convention on recognition or enforcement of foreign court judgments. There are no procedures for an Indonesian court to recognise or enforce a foreign court's judgment.

[4] Arbitration Clause

A valid arbitration clause prohibits national courts from extending their jurisdiction to hear the case. Article 3 of the Arbitration Law expressly states that 'District Courts do not have jurisdiction to adjudicate a dispute between parties that are bound to an arbitration agreement.'

Further, Article 11 of the Arbitration Law (Law No. 30/1990) states that:

(1) A written arbitration agreement eliminates the rights of the parties to submit their dispute or differences of opinion arising from their agreement to the District Court.
(2) District Courts are obliged to reject and may not interfere in a settlement of dispute that has been determined to be settled through arbitration, except in certain cases as provided by this Law.

The absolutism of an arbitration clause is also confirmed in various decisions of the Supreme Court. Nevertheless in practice, parties are still trying to deviate from this principle and as Indonesian judges are not obliged to follow precedents, there are cases where Indonesian courts (especially at the first instance level) take jurisdiction over cases where the relevant parties had chosen the arbitration as the dispute settlement forum.

[C] Non-exercise of Jurisdiction

[1] Forum Non Conveniens

The doctrine of forum non conveniens is also applied by Indonesian courts. The determination of which court is the most appropriate forum should be based on the most real and substantial connecting factors related to the dispute. Whether a connecting factor is substantially related to a particular court depends on the type, nature, or form of the connecting factor itself. The following are the types or forms of connecting factors deemed to be significantly relevant with a dispute:[4]

- Convenience and expense of litigation.
- Availability of witnesses and documents.
- The place where the parties reside.
- The place where the parties carry on their business.
- Governing law.

The Indonesian Supreme Court in its decisions No. 1084 K/Pdt/1985, dated 17 July 1986, and No. 1537 K/Pdt/1989, dated 21 January 1991, determined that a foreign court is the most appropriate court or the court having substantial connecting factors with the case at hand, based on the following factors:

- The relevant governing law is foreign law.
- The choice of jurisdiction is a foreign court.
- The agreement was made in the foreign territory.

In both decisions, the Supreme Court also determined that as the court having substantial connecting factors with the case at hand, the foreign court and not an Indonesian court, is the court having jurisdiction to examine and adjudicate the case.

[2] **Lis alibi pendens**

In relation to the concept of *lis alibi pendens*, Indonesian courts do not have the authority and cannot order the cessation of foreign proceedings on the same matter/involving the same parties. Vice versa, Indonesian judges would normally take the view that foreign courts cannot restrain any Indonesian court from conducting proceedings on the same matter/involving the same parties since foreign judges cannot impose any order to Indonesian Judges. It seems that the root of this issue is that

4. M. Yahya Harahap, *Civil Procedural Law on Claim, Attachment, Evidence and Court Decision* (Sinar Grafika, Jakarta, 2005), at 246.

Indonesia is not a party to any international convention or agreement on the recognition and enforcement of foreign court judgment/order.

§3.03 APPLICABLE LAW

[A] Choice of Law

Indonesia recognises the parties' rights to choose the law applicable to their contracts provided that the relevant foreign law is not contrary to the Indonesian law. The basis is the freedom of contract principle embodied in Articles 1338[5] and 1320[6] of the ICC.

Under Indonesian law, parties to an agreement are free to contract to any terms and conditions, subject to such matters not being contrary to (i) any mandatory provision under Indonesian laws and regulations; and (ii) public policy.[7]

There are some limitations on the applicability of the principles of the freedom to choose the governing law of the contract:

(i) Indonesian law must be used in any employment contract of an Indonesian employee in Indonesia, or in government procurement contracts, or in franchise agreements.

(ii) Also, under Article 16 of AB,[8] where it concerns the legal status and the personal capacity of private individuals of Indonesian nationality, Indonesian law will be applicable whenever such individuals enter into a contract. This rule is generally applicable in the field of family law and more specifically in the case of, for example, marriage contracts and inheritances.

It should also be noted that in general, the principle of 'the most characteristic connection' is also applicable in Indonesian law. Under this principle, such choice of law must have connection with either the subject matter of the contract, or the parties to the contract or the location where the contract is to be performed.

In our view, the better interpretation of the Indonesian private international law (or conflict of law) on this point is as expressed above, namely that the parties' freedom to choose the governing law should be upheld unless there are grounds for voiding such a choice.

There were cases where courts in Indonesia would uphold the choice of law determined by the parties to the agreement. Below are some of those cases:

5. 'A validly made agreement shall apply as law to the parties thereto.'
6. 'In order to be valid, an agreement must satisfy the following four conditions: (i) there must be consent from the individuals who are bound thereby; (ii) the parties thereto must have the capacity to conclude the agreement; (iii) there must be a specific subject; and (iv) there must be a lawful cause.'
7. 'While point (i) arguably is certain as it refers to written law, point (ii) is less certain as it refers to unwritten law and the subjective view of good morals. There is no definition of what constitutes public policy in Indonesia. Therefore, determining whether or not a contract contradicts public policy is a matter subject to the courts' discretion and will be decided on a case-by-case basis.'
8. State Gazette 1847 No. 23, as amended in State Gazette 1915 No. 299 jo 652.

(i) In the case between *PT Friendship Prima Abadi v. PT Bandar Pasifik Lestari Cs* [1986], the court decided that since the parties had chosen English law as the governing law for the bill of lading and had chosen English courts as the choice of forum, the Indonesian court did not have jurisdiction over the case.
(ii) In the case between *Tat Lee Bank Limited v. Giantono Djali Cs* [1988], the court decided that since the parties had chosen Singapore law and Singapore courts, the Indonesian court did not have jurisdiction over the case.
(iii) In the case between *PT Khaded Salameh v. United Arab Shipping Cs* [1998] where the parties had chosen English law or Kuwait law, the Indonesian court decided that the case must be decided using the choice of law under the contract in the respective jurisdiction.
(iv) In the case between *PT Indokaya Nissan Motor v. Marubeni* [1983] the District Court of Central Jakarta examined the dispute by applying Japanese law in a dispute over property. In its decision, the District Court respected the parties' agreement on the choice of law. When the court examined the Japanese law, it appeared that the Japanese law required the case to be decided in accordance with the governing law where the property is located, which is in Indonesia (*renvoi* principle).

However, from time to time we have seen cases where courts have applied Indonesian law to examine disputes, notwithstanding the choice of law provisions in the relevant contract. It should be noted that Indonesian courts would consider the parties arguments in examining their cases. Thus, whether or not the parties were arguing on the use of foreign law is an important factor.

[B] Other Cases

In theory, if the parties to a contract have made no choice of law, it will be the function of judges to determine which system of law will apply. Indonesian Law does not contain an express rule for determining the governing law of a contract. Various points of connection may be taken into account in determining the applicable system of law, such as the nationality of the parties involved, the place where the relevant contract/agreement was signed, or the place where the object in dispute is located. In this regard, 'the most characteristic connection' theory will be applied by the court. By this theory, the court will also consider the intention of the parties as a connecting factor which determines the law to be applied in the contracts.

In practice, unless the parties argue otherwise, Indonesian courts will likely apply the Indonesian law.

[C] *Renvoi*

There is no specific written law that regulates *renvoi*, but it is not excluded in Indonesia. It has long been accepted in administrative practices in Indonesia. For instance, it was discovered in the year 1922 that an official circular letter was distributed at the request of the government by the attorney general (*Procureur Generaal* at the time) to the civil registration officers. The circular letter set out the positions that the burgerlijke stand officers would have to take in addressing marriages involving foreign nationals. One of the core issues was whether or not a foreign adult would still need the consent of his/her parents to marry. In this regard, Article 42 of the ICC stipulates that an individual, even though he or she is already an adult but has not reached the age of 30, would need a consent from his/her parents to marry. Indonesia adopts the principle of nationality to determine personal status. A foreign national's personal status is determined by his/her own national law according to Article 16 of AB by analogy. Thus, determining whether it is required for a foreign national below 30 years of age that wishes to marry in Indonesia to obtain a parental consent must be done based on the national law of that individual. However, the scenario would be different when the private international law system of the foreign national's state adopts the principle of domicile in determining personal status. British nationals who wish to marry and be domiciled in Indonesia are subject to the provisions in the ICC.[9]

A scholar, Sudargo Gautama, subscribes to the view that *renvoi* is accepted in Indonesia primarily for practical reasons, as the national/internal law of Indonesia is the one that would be employed by the judges.[10] Sudargo Gautama also opined that *renvoi* does not apply to any contract where the parties to that contract are given the freedom to choose any internal law of a country to govern the contract.[11]

[D] Mandatory Rules of the Forum and of Third States

Under Indonesian laws, the parties' freedom to choose the governing law to a contract is not unfettered. This freedom is subject to the application of certain mandatory rules found under, for instance: the competition law; the capital market law; the labour law; and the consumer protection law. An example of mandatory rule of a public law nature is Presidential Decree No. 59 of 1972 as well as Decree of the Minister of Finance No. 261 of 1973 on the borrowing of offshore loans. The borrowing of an offshore loan by a state-owned enterprise or a regional enterprise must generally be approved by the Minister of Finance. The borrowing state-owned/regional enterprise is also obliged to periodically report the repayment of the loan. Thus, the Presidential Decree and the Minister of Finance Decree as mandatory rules of a public law nature affect the enforceability of the loan agreement.

Article 31 of Law No. 24 of 2009 on Flag, Language and Symbol of State and National Anthem (Law No. 24) mandates that all contracts and MOUs involving an Indonesian national or entity must be written in Indonesian. In 2009, the Ministry of Law and Human Rights issued two letters confirming that agreements written in English would remain valid and enforceable. Nevertheless, in a recent decision currently under appeal, the West Jakarta District Court considered that all agreements

9. Sudargo Gautama, *Pengantar Hukum Perdata Internasional Indonesia* (Binacipta Bandung, 1987, 5th Ed.), at 102.
10. *Ibid.*, at 117.
11. *Ibid.*, at 118.

involving an Indonesian private or public entity entered into after 9 July 2009 which are not in Bahasa Indonesia will be in violation of Law No. 24 and therefore void.[12]

[E] Proof of Foreign Law

Under Indonesian law, the party who argues on an issue has the burden to prove its argument. Thus, Indonesian courts will rely on evidence submitted by the parties in determining whether or not the elements that may cause the application of a foreign law exist. The existence of any foreign element in a case may lead the panel of judges to employ a foreign law in examining the case. Further, if the use of foreign law is not proved, it is likely that the relevant court will apply Indonesian law to examine disputes (*lex fori*).

According to the Memorandum of Understanding with Australia[13] and Belarus[14] regarding Legal Cooperation, Indonesia can exchange legal materials, concerning the laws, legal systems, and legal institutions of each country, including legislation and related material with each of those countries. In addition, Indonesia also has a Memorandum of Understanding with China,[15] which allows Indonesia and China to exchange their legal experts for giving lectures or studies and participate in seminars, workshops, or other legal trainings held by either of the two countries.

[F] Evasion of the Law

There is no specific regulation that prohibits evasion of the law. There are two schools of thought with regard to evasion of the law. The first one considers that where an evasion of the law is proven, foreign elements are instantly disregarded and the national law would be employed. According to the second one, where a certain right is validly obtained on the basis of the recognised and honoured foreign law, that right would not be instantly disregarded by the local court.[16] Indonesian courts would usually take the conservative approach in dealing with any evasion of the law, where it would be deemed as a violation of public order, thus deemed as an unlawful act. Any rights which may have been obtained under the foreign law would likely be set aside by the judges upon finding that there has been an evasion of the law by the parties.

Evasion of the law is tightly related to the topic of public policy. Both are intended to have the national law applied and to set aside foreign laws. In other words, evasion of the law and public policy are meant to guard the national law against foreign laws. The main difference between the two is that with public policy, a national law is generally deemed to be applicable, whereas with evasion of the law the national law would only apply in certain circumstances.[17]

12. Decision No. 451/Pdt.G/2012/ PN.Jkt.Bar., 10 Jul. 2013.
13. http://treaty.kemlu.go.id/uploads-pub/4271_AUS-2000-0130.pdf.
14. http://treaty.kemlu.go.id/uploads-pub/4270_BLR-2013-0017.pdf.
15. http://treaty.kemlu.go.id/uploads-pub/4234_CHN-1992-0029.pdf.
16. Sudargo Gautama (1987), *supra* n. 9, at 149.
17. *Ibid.*, at 148.

§3.04 PROCEDURAL ISSUES

[A] Service of Summons and Judicial Orders Abroad

Based on the Technical and Administrative Guidelines for Judicial System in the field of General and Specific Civil Cases issued by the Supreme Court of the Republic of Indonesia,[18] in a case where the defendant is domiciled abroad, the claim is filed at the district court where the plaintiff is domiciled. The chairman of that district court must then forward the claim through the Ministry of Foreign Affairs[19] Further administrative steps, e.g., consularisation process, are dealt with in accordance with the internal policy of each consular office. These administrative issues are not regulated in the abovementioned guidelines.

Nevertheless, Indonesia has entered into a bilateral Agreement on Judicial Cooperation with the Kingdom of Thailand for serving judicial documents and obtaining evidence in civil and commercial matters.[20] Indonesia is not a party to the 1965 Hague Convention on the Service Abroad of Judicial and Extrajudicial Documents in Civil or Commercial Matters.

[B] Obtaining Evidence Abroad

There are no regulations under Indonesian law that pertain to the obtaining of evidence abroad. Thus, this matter is left to the discretion and also effort of the parties to the dispute in presenting piece(s) of evidence obtained from another state before Indonesian courts.

Nevertheless, Indonesia has entered into a bilateral Agreement on Judicial Cooperation with the Kingdom of Thailand, above mentioned, providing for the obtainment of evidence in civil and commercial matters. Indonesia is not a party to the 1979 Hague Convention on the Taking of Evidence Abroad in Civil or Commercial Matters.

[C] Restraint of Foreign Proceedings

Indonesian courts do not have the authority and cannot order the cessation of foreign proceedings on the same matter/involving the same parties. Vice versa, Indonesian judges would normally take the view that foreign courts cannot restrain any Indonesian court from conducting proceedings on the same matter/involving the same parties due to the reason that Indonesian judges are independent and that foreign judges cannot issue any order to Indonesian Judges.

18. Pedoman Teknis Administrasi dan Teknis Peradilan Perdata Umum dan Perdata Khusus, Buku II (Ed. 2009), Mahkamah Agung Republik Indonesia.
19. *Ibid.*, at 51-52.
20. http://treaty.kemlu.go.id/uploads-pub/4226_THA-1978-0009.pdf.

[D] Proof of Foreign Public Documents

Indonesia is neither a party to the 1961 Hague Convention Abolishing the Requirement for Legalisation for Foreign Public Documents nor to any treaty that addresses this matter.

Pursuant to the Appendix of Foreign Minister Affairs Regulation No. 09/A/KP/XII/2006/01, every foreign public document to be used in Indonesia needs to be legalised by the authorised ministry of the country where the document originated and then by the representative of the Republic of Indonesia in that country. In practice, a foreign document will be notarised by the notary public where the document originates from and is then legalised by the Indonesian consulate in that country. For some special cases where a notary public is not available in the particular country, then legalisation alone would suffice. It is noteworthy that the purpose of legalisation is only to legitimise the signature in the document, not the content of the document.

Documents in a foreign language must be translated into Indonesian by a sworn, registered translator before being submitted to the court.

[E] Statute of Limitations

The general statute of limitations under Indonesian Civil Code is thirty years. There is also exemption to this statutes of limitations under the Indonesian Civil Code, i.e., Consumer Protection Law stipulates that the statute of limitations is four years after the date of purchase of the goods or the within the agreed period (guarantee period).

Statute of limitations is generally regarded as procedural issues and must thus be resolved according to the *lex fori*, i.e., Indonesian law. However, a dispute which involves a statute of limitation on the obtaining of a certain right is substantive in nature and therefore shall be resolved pursuant to the applicable law, which would first be determined by the judges.[21]

[F] Remedies and Damages

Due to the fact that the issues on remedies that are available to a plaintiff in proceedings before an Indonesian court concern the authority of that court to grant the relief being sought and thus are procedural in nature, the *lex fori* would be applicable to the dispute, i.e., Indonesian law. However, questions on quantum of damages which concern the substantive rights of plaintiffs by law should be resolved by relying on the applicable law.

21. Bayu Seto, *Dasar-Dasar Hukum Perdata Internasional* (Buku Kesatu, Edisi Ketiga; Penerbit PT. Citra Aditya Bakti, Bandung 2001), at 77.

[G] Foreign Currency Obligations

A claim may be made in a foreign currency, provided that the claim concerns the default of an agreement where the parties have agreed that repayment or payment will be done in a foreign currency. This of course excludes costs/fees for the legal proceedings and other administrative costs that would be borne by the losing party in the case.

[H] Restraining Removal of Assets and Securing Evidence in Favour of a Foreign Arbitration/Judicial Process

A request for restraining removal of assets and/or securing evidence an attachment cannot be granted in support of substantive proceedings that are taking place in foreign courts or arbitral tribunals.

§3.05 RECOGNITION AND ENFORCEMENT OF FOREIGN DECISIONS

[A] Judicial Decisions: Requirements and Limitations

As a general rule, foreign court judgments are not enforceable in Indonesia. Indonesia is not a party to any international (either multilateral or bilateral) treaty on recognition and enforcement of foreign judicial decisions. One possible strategy in dealing with this situation is for the creditors to commence proceedings afresh before the relevant Indonesian District Court. Under this strategy, foreign judgments can be presented as evidence before Indonesian courts and the judge will evaluate, on a case-by-case basis, whether and to what extent the foreign judgment will be accepted.

[B] Arbitral Awards (Including ICSID Awards): Requirements and Limitations

Before being enforced in Indonesia, a foreign arbitral award must be recognised through the issuance of an exequatur, which gives the award the standing of res judicata. After obtaining exequatur, a writ of execution may be applied for. The District Court of Central Jakarta will only deny exequatur to a foreign arbitral award if:

(a) The award is rendered in a state which is not bound by a bilateral or multilateral convention or treaty on the recognition and enforcement of foreign arbitral awards by which Indonesia is bound.
(b) The legal relationship on which the award was based cannot be considered as commercial under Indonesian law.
(c) The recognition or enforcement of the award would be contrary to public policy.

Indonesia is a party to the 1958 New York Convention. Pursuant to Presidential Decree No. 34 of 1981 referring to Article I(3) of the New York Convention, Indonesia will only apply the Convention on the basis of reciprocity (foreign arbitral awards can only be enforced if the country granting the award is also a Contracting Party to the New York Convention) and only to differences arising out of legal relationships, either contractual or otherwise, which are considered as commercial under Indonesian law (commonly called as the 'commercial reservation').

Together with the Arbitration Law, also relevant is Supreme Court Regulation No. 1 of 1990 on Enforcement of Foreign Arbitral Awards (it provides greater detail on the procedure and requirements). Any application must attach a certificate from the Indonesian diplomatic representative in the country were the award was rendered, confirming that such country and Indonesia are bound by a bilateral or multilateral treaty.[22] If the Government of Indonesia is a party to the award, only the Supreme Court has jurisdiction to grant exequatur.[23] Only rejection of the *exequatur* can be appealed to the Supreme Court.

Indonesia is a party to the Convention on the Settlement of Investment Disputes between States and Nationals of Other States ('ICSID Convention'), and has ratified the 2009 ASEAN Comprehensive Investment Agreement, according to which has to provide for the enforcement in its territory of the awards rendered under its investment dispute settlement mechanism.

§3.06 RECOGNITION OF OTHER FOREIGN PUBLIC DOCUMENTS

Foreign public documents will be regarded as evidence and the Judges have their discretion to weight such evidence.

§3.07 TREATIES FOR JUDICIAL COOPERATION

Indonesia has entered into one bilateral treaty for judicial cooperation in the field of civil law: Thailand (the first bilateral agreement entered into as a result of the ASEAN Declaration on Concord on Judicial Co-Operation). Additionally, Indonesia entered into some bilateral agreements for legal cooperation (China, Belarus, and Australia). Indonesia is not a party to any of the Hague Conventions on Private International Law issues.

22. Article 67(2)(c) of the Arbitration Law.
23. Article 66(e) of the Arbitration Law.

CHAPTER 4
Japan

*Naoki Iguchi & Naoko Kamimura**

§4.01 CODIFICATION OF PRIVATE INTERNATIONAL LAW AND RELEVANCE OF CASE LAW

[A] Codification and Case Law

The main body of codified private international law in Japan is the 'Act on General Rules for Application of Laws'[1] (AGRAL). In addition, there are several Acts codifying international agreements on private international law: the 'Act on the Law Applicable to the Form of Wills',[2] 'Act on the Law Applicable to the Obligation of Support',[3] Articles 88-94 of the 'Act on Bill of Exchange and Promissory Notes',[4] and Articles 76-81 of the 'Act on Checks'.[5]

The Code of Civil Procedure (CCP),[6] the Civil Provisional Remedies Act,[7] and the Civil Execution Act[8] have several provisions regarding international civil proceedings. Furthermore, there are special acts for international private procedures: the 'Act on the Civil Jurisdiction of Japan with respect to a Foreign State, etc.',[9] and the 'Act on Recognition of and Assistance for Foreign Insolvency Proceedings'.[10]

---

* Naoki Iguchi, Partner, Nagashima Ohno & Tsunematsu. Naoko Kamimura, Special Counsel, Nagashima Ohno & Tsunematsu.

1. Act No. 78 of 2006, *Ho no Tekiyo ni kansuru Tsusoku-Ho.*
2. Act No. 100 of 1964, *Igon no Houshiki no Jyunkyo-Ho ni kansuru Houritsu.*
3. Act No. 84 of 1986, *Fuyo-gimu no Jyunkyo-Ho ni kansuru Houritsu.*
4. Act No. 20 of 1995, *Tegata-Ho.*
5. Act No. 57 of 1932, *Kogitte-Ho.*
6. Act No. 109 of 1996, *Minji-Sosho Ho.*
7. Act No. 91 of 1989, *Minji-Hozen Ho.*
8. Act No. 4 of 1979, *Minji-Shikko Ho.*
9. Act No. 24 of 2009, *Gaikoku-tou ni taisuru Wagakuni no Minji-Saiban-ken ni kansuru Houritsu.*
10. Act No. 29 of 2000, *Gaikoku Tousan Shori Tetsuzuki no Shounin Enjyo ni kansuru Houritsu.*

Although Japan does not apply the *stare decisis* principle, decisions of the Supreme Court are taken into consideration for interpreting the codified law.

[B] Multilateral Conventions Providing Uniform Substantive Law and/or International Jurisdictional Rules

According to Article 98 of the Constitution, a treaty duly concluded by Japan and general international law have to be faithfully observed. In order to have domestic effect, treaties need to be promulgated in the official gazette.

Japan is a party to the UN Convention on Contracts for the International Sale of Goods (CISG), the 1910 Convention for the Unification of Certain Rules of Law with respect to Collisions between Vessels, the 1910 International Convention for the Unification of Certain Rules of Law Relating to Assistance and Salvage at Sea, and the 1929/1999 Conventions for the Unification of Certain Rules relating to International Carriage by Air.[11] In addition, Japan is a party to eighteen multilateral agreements and protocols administered by the World Intellectual Property Organization (WIPO).[12]

§4.02 JURISDICTION OF LOCAL COURTS IN FOREIGN-RELATED CASES

[A] Grounds for Jurisdiction

[1] General

In 2011, Japan introduced for the first time in the CCP special provisions on international jurisdiction in civil and commercial matters. Most of the new provisions codified the two leading decisions of the Supreme Court on the international competence of Japanese courts.[13]

According to Article 3(2) of the CCP, the general rule for establishing the international jurisdiction of Japanese courts is:

- in case of actions against a natural person, the existence in Japan of domicile, habitual residence or prior domicile before the filing of the action; and
- in case of actions against legal persons, associations or foundations, the location in Japan of its principal office or the domicile of its representative or any other principal person in charge of its business.

---

11. By a Note dated 24 Oct. 2003 signed by the Minister for Foreign Affairs, Japan informed ICAO 'that, in accordance with Article 57(a) of the Convention for the Unification of Certain Rules for International Carriage by Air, done at Montreal on 28 May 1999, the Government of Japan declares that this Convention shall not apply to international carriage by air performed and operated directly by the Government of Japan for non-commercial purposes in respect to its functions and duties as a sovereign State'.
12. http://www.wipo.int/treaties/en/ShowResults.jsp?country_id=87C.
13. *Goto et al. v. Malaysian Airline System*, 134 Minshu 115, Supreme Court, 16 Oct. 1981; and *Family Co. Ltd. v. Miyahara*, 186 Minshu 1, Supreme Court, 11 Sep. 1997.

Apart from the general rule, Article 3(3) of the CCP regulates the international jurisdiction of the Japanese courts in relation to specific actions:

- Enforcement of a contractual obligation, damages for the breach of a contractual obligation and actions arising from *negotiorum gestio* or unjust enrichment in connection with a contractual obligation: where, according to the contract or to the law chosen in the contract, the place of performance of the obligation is located in Japan.
- Payment of a bill of exchange, promissory note or check: where the place of payment is in Japan.
- In relation to property rights: where the object of the claim is located in Japan or, if the action seeks payment, where the defendant has sizeable assets in Japan. It includes intangible assets (e.g., Intellectual property rights are deemed to be located where they are registered or have been created.).
- Against a person (natural or legal) when it relates to the activities carried out in his office (including non-profit activities) located in Japan.
- Against a person engaged in business (including non-profit activities) in Japan in relation to such business carried out in Japan. It includes a foreign company that continuously carries out transactions in Japan even though it has no offices in Japan (e.g., through agencies/subsidiaries or through internet).
- Any claim secured by a ship (including those related to maritime liens), where the ship is located in Japan.
- Several actions related to company law when the association or foundation is a legal person incorporated in Japan or, if it is not a legal person, when its principal office is located in Japan.
- An action relating to a tort occurred in Japan. If the harmful act and the damage take place in different countries, it suffices that either of them takes place in Japan (except when the harmful act took place abroad and the damage is unforeseeably sustained in Japan).
- Damages related to an accident at sea: where the first place at which the damaged ship arrives is located in Japan.
- Salvage: when it was performed in Japan or when the first place at which the salvaged ship arrives is located in Japan.
- In relation to immovable property located in Japan.
- Succession: when the deceased was domiciled or had the habitual residence in Japan at the commencement of the succession or had ever been domiciled in Japan prior to the commencement of the succession.

Similarly, Article 3(4) of the CCP provides for special rules on international jurisdiction for consumer contracts and for employment relations:

- Consumer contracts: if the domicile of the consumer at the time of filing the action or when the contract was concluded is located in Japan.
- Employment relations: if the place of work under the employment contract (or, if no specified, the office which hired the employee) is located in Japan.

According to Article 3(12) of the CCP, the jurisdiction of the Japanese courts must be determined at the time when the action is filed.

Furthermore, Article 3(6) of the CCP states that when two or more claims are made jointly against one defendant and the Japanese courts have jurisdiction only over one of the claims, the action may be filed in Japan only if all the claims have a close connection. In case of more than one defendant or plaintiff, the foregoing applies only if the rights or obligations are common to all of them or based on the same legal or factual grounds.

Finally, Article 146 CCP states that counterclaims may be filed if the Japanese court (i) has jurisdiction over such claim or (ii) the claim has a close connection with the plaintiff's claim or with the defence thereto (except when a foreign court has exclusive jurisdiction over the substance of the counterclaim).

[2] Submitted to Jurisdiction

Article 3(7) of the CCP allows for choice of court agreements even in favour of foreign courts. For being enforceable, such agreements must be in writing clearly indicating the designated court, must relate to a specific legal relationship and the foreign court must be able to exercise jurisdiction. Article 3(7) of the CCP further limits the cases where such choice of court is allowed in case of consumer or employment contracts.

According to Article 3(8) of the CCP, Japanese courts have jurisdiction if the defendant, without objecting to the jurisdiction, makes arguments on the merits.

[3] Exclusive Jurisdiction

Article 3(5) of the CCP provides for special rules on exclusive jurisdiction:

- Several actions[14] contained in the Companies Act, the 'Act on General Incorporated Associations and General Incorporated Foundations' and analogous actions relating to associations or foundations incorporated in Japan.
- An action related to a registration in Japan.
- An action with respect to the existence and effect of an intellectual property right created by registration, if the registration takes place in Japan.

According to Article 312 of the CCP, only when the exclusive jurisdiction of the Japanese courts has been violated there is a 'right' to appeal. In other cases, leave for appeal may be sought but the final appellate court has wide discretion to grant or not the petition.

14. For example, actions concerning the organisation of a company, actions for pursuing the liability or dismissal of officers ... .

[B] Exclusion of Jurisdiction

[1] Immunity

[a] Sovereign Immunity

In *X et al. v. Islamic Republic of Pakistan,*[15] the Supreme Court switched its position from the absolute immunity to the limited immunity. The court's position was codified as 'Act on the Civil Jurisdiction of Japan with Respect to a Foreign State, etc.' (Act No. 24 of 2009), which does not take precedence over treaties or customary international law.[16]

The Act regulates also (i) the express or implied consent to jurisdiction, (ii) the specific cases (labour contracts, proceedings concerning the existence or effect of arbitration agreement...) in which a foreign state shall not be immune from jurisdiction, (iii) immunity from enforcement, and (iv) some specific procedural issues.

[b] Diplomatic and Consular Immunity

Japan is a party to the 1961 Vienna Convention on Diplomatic Relations and the 1963 Vienna Convention on Consular Relations.

[c] Other Immunities

Japan is a party to the 1946 Convention on the Privileges and Immunities of the United Nations and the 1947 Convention on the Privileges and Immunities of the Specialised Agencies.

[2] Forum Agreements in Favour of Foreign Courts

As mentioned before, Article 3(7) of the CCP allows the parties to choose a foreign court except when the Japanese courts have exclusive jurisdiction.

[3] Arbitration Clause

Although not specifically referred to in the CCP, according to court practice and Article 14 of the Arbitration Act, a valid arbitration agreement excludes court's jurisdiction over any dispute covered by such arbitration agreement. Article 14(2) of the Arbitration Act specifically provides that the arbitral tribunal may commence or continue arbitral proceedings and make an arbitral award even while the court's decision on its jurisdiction is pending.

15. 60 Minshu 2542, Supreme Court, 21 Jul. 2006.
16. Article 3 of the Act.

[C] Non-exercise of Jurisdiction

[1] Forum Non Conveniens

In *Family Co. Ltd. v. Miyahara*,[17] the Supreme Court stated that in case of 'extraordinary factors (*tokudan-no-jijo*)' in a particular dispute, Japanese courts would not exercise jurisdiction. This rule has been codified in Article 3(9) of the CCP, according to which Japanese courts may dismiss (without prejudice) a claim (or part of it) if taking into account some factors such as the nature of the case, the location of evidence... the court considers that it would impair fairness between the parties or hinder the efficient conduct of the hearing.

[2] Lis alibi pendens

During the preparatory works for the new provisions of the CCP, there were discussions on whether or not to codify the 'foreign *lis alibi pendens*'. However, since the circumstances in the cases mentioned before vary widely and it was considered difficult to codify the rulings and positions taken by the Japanese courts, the idea was abandoned.

While Article 142 of the CCP prohibits a party to a pending case in Japan to file another concurrent action in Japan, there are no express provisions regarding foreign proceedings.

In *Miyakoshi Kiko Co. Ltd. v. Gould Inc.*,[18] a Japanese company sought a declaratory judgment in Japan after being sued by an American company in a US federal court. The Japanese court held that:

(i) 'court' in Article 142 of the CCP means a court in Japan and therefore Article 142 of the CCP does not apply to overlapping lawsuits in Japan and a foreign jurisdiction;
(ii) there is no globally accepted principle on handling internationally overlapping lawsuits;
(iii) for the avoidance of conflicts of judgments, for equitable treatment of parties, and for the efficiency of the judicial system, the *lis alibi pendens* doctrine is applicable if it is almost certain that:
  - a final and binding judgment will be rendered by a foreign court; and
  - such a judgment will probably be recognised by Japanese courts.

The court further found that because the US lawsuit procedures were not yet in a phase of examination of substantial issues, it was too early to say that it was almost certain that a final and binding judgment would be rendered and would be recognised by Japanese courts. The court also stated that it was too early to determine whether or

17. *Supra* n. 13.
18. 1348 Hanji 91, Interim judgment of Tokyo District Court, 30 May 1989; 703 Hanta 240.

not the potential judgment would meet the requirement of Article 118(3) of the CCP (no contradiction with public policy in Japan).

On the contrary, in *Mazaki Bussan Co. Ltd. v. Nanka Seimen Company*,[19] the jurisdiction of a Japanese court over the dispute was denied. In Japan, the plaintiff sought a declaratory judgment confirming that he was not obliged to indemnify the defendant for any damages or losses caused by the California lawsuits. The court held that although the Japanese court potentially had jurisdiction over the defendant's product liability related claim, such jurisdiction should be denied due to 'extraordinary factors (*tokudan-no-jijo*)':

(i) since plaintiff's obligation was dependent on the Californian lawsuits, the Japanese lawsuit might ultimately be in vain unless the defendant lost the California lawsuits;
(ii) there had been great progress in the California lawsuits; and that
(iii) almost all of the evidence was located in California.

§4.03 APPLICABLE LAW

[A] Choice of Law

Article 7 of the AGRAL states that the contract shall be governed by the law chosen by the parties at the time the contract was made. Under the AGRAL, the parties can also agree on the governing law applicable to torts, unjust enrichment, agency by necessity (*negotiorum gestio*),[20] and with some limitations, to the matrimonial property regime.[21]

Since Article 7 is silent on how the choice should be made, it is considered that no formality is required and that the choice of governing law can also be made by the implied will of the parties.

Article 9 allows parties to change the governing law of the contract without imposing any temporal limitation. However, if the change of the governing law would prejudice the rights of a third party, the change cannot be asserted against such third party. Article 9 does not require any explicit formality and thus the change of the governing law can be made by the implied will of the parties. In practice, Article 9 may be used to recognise the implied will of the parties to change the governing law to Japanese law when one party asserts its claims under Japanese law and the other makes counterarguments or rebuttals under Japanese law without claiming that Japanese law is not applicable.

19. 1390 Hanji 98, Tokyo District Court, 29 Jan. 1991; 764 Hanta 256.
20. Article 16 (unjust enrichment and *negotiorum gestio)* and 21(tort).
21. Article 26, para. 2 of the AGRAL.

[B] Other Cases

[1] Contract without Choice of Law - General

If there is no choice of governing law, the contract shall be governed by the law of the place with which the contract was most closely connected at the time it was made (Article 8, paragraph 1 of the AGRAL).

Article 8, paragraphs 2 and 3 contain a rebuttable presumption based upon the characteristic performance. Namely, if only one of the parties is to provide characteristic performance under the contract, the law of the habitual residence of the party providing said performance is presumed to be the law of the place with which the contract is most closely connected. However, if the party providing characteristic performance has an establishment related to the contract, the law of the place where the establishment is located (or the principal establishment if several establishments in different jurisdictions are related to the contract) is presumed to be the law of the place with which the contract is most closely connected. Notwithstanding the foregoing, if the object of the contract is an immovable, the law of the place where the immovable is situated is presumed to be the law of the place with which the contract is most closely connected.

Nevertheless, the AGRAL does not define or include examples of what is considered as characteristic performance.

[2] Consumer and Labour Contracts

The AGRAL somewhat restricts the party autonomy in order to protect weaker parties in certain types of contract, i.e., consumer contracts and labour contracts.

[a] *Consumer Contracts*

Even if parties can choose the governing law of a consumer contract, the specific mandatory rules of the law of the consumer's habitual residence shall also apply to matters subject to such mandatory rules with regard to the formation and effect of the consumer contract, provided that the consumer expresses (within or outside judicial proceedings) his/her will to the business operator to the effect that such mandatory rules should apply (Article 11, paragraph 1).

However, the AGRAL does not protect all consumers. 'Active consumers' (those who go to the jurisdiction of the business operator's establishment and conclude consumer contracts or receive performance exclusively in that jurisdiction, without there being a 'solicitation' by the business operator), are not protected under the mandatory provision of the law of their habitual residence. What constitutes a 'solicitation' is not defined in the AGRAL.

In addition, the consumer is not protected (even if he/she is not an 'active consumer') when: (i) the business operator was unaware of the location of the consumer's habitual residence, or (ii) the business operator has misidentified the counterparty as not being a consumer, and had reasonable grounds for such unawareness or for such misidentification (Article 11, paragraph 6, items 3 and 4).

If the parties have not chosen a law to govern the formation and effect of their consumer contract, the formation and effect of the consumer contract shall be governed by the law of the consumer's habitual residence (Article 11, paragraph 2).

[b] *Labour Contracts*

Almost the same protective rules apply for labour contracts. The difference is that the law most closely connected with the labour contract should be referred to the law of place where the labour is to be carried out (Article 12, paragraphs 1 and 3). The law of the place where the labour is to be carried out according to the labour contract (if the place where the labour is to be carried out cannot be identified, the law of the place of the establishment at which the employee has concluded the labour contract) is presumed to be the law of the place with which the labour contract is most closely connected (Article 12, paragraph 2). Therefore, the employee must express its will to the employer to apply the mandatory provisions of the law most closely connected with the labour contract (usually the law of the place where the labour is to be carried out) to enjoy the protections under the AGRAL.

In the absence of a choice of law by the parties, the law of the place where the work is to be carried out is presumed to be the law of the place with which the contract is most closely connected (Article 12, paragraph 3).

[3] Rights in Rrem, etc.

Rights in rem and other rights requiring registration with regard to movables or immovables shall be governed by the law of the place where the subject property is located. Notwithstanding the foregoing, the acquisition and loss of the rights shall be governed by the law of the place where the subject property is located at the time when the events causing the acquisition or loss are completed. (Article 13)

[4] Torts

If no law is chosen by the parties after the occurrence of the tort, the formation and effect of a claim arising from a tort shall be governed by the law of the place where the result of the wrongful act occurred (unless such place was unforeseeable) (Article 17).

However, there are particular provisions for specific torts: (i) in case of *product liability*, the law of the place where the product was delivered to the victim applies (unless such place was unforeseeable, in which case the law of the place of the principal establishment or habitual residence of the producer applies) (Article 18); (ii) in case of *defamation*, the law of the habitual residence of the person defamed applies (Article 19).

Notwithstanding the previous rules, Article 20 of the AGRAL requires the Japanese courts to apply the law of the place with which the tort is manifestly more closely connected. Limitations apply to torts due to public policy: if a tort is governed by a foreign law, the facts must also constitute a tort under Japanese law, and even if the actions causing tort are unlawful both under that foreign law and Japanese law, the recovery of damages is limited to the extent available under Japanese law (Article 22).

[5] Negotiorum Gestio and Unjust Enrichment

Claims arising from *negotiorum gestio* or unjust enrichment shall be governed by the law of the place where the facts constituting the cause of it occurred, unless another place is obviously more closely connected (Article 14).

[6] National Law

Matters of personal status, family law and succession[22] apply the principle of national law. The AGRAL does not include any provision on the law applicable to legal persons or associations, though it is generally accepted that the law of the place of incorporation applies.

[7] Formalities for Contracts

A contract shall be valid if it complies with either the law applicable to the formation of the contract or the law of the place where the said contract was made (Article 10, paragraphs 1 and 2). Even if the governing law is changed, the initially applicable law prior to the change shall be the law applicable to the formation of the contract. With regard to a declaration of intention to a person who is in a different jurisdiction, the law of the place where the declaration was made is deemed to be the place where the contract was made (Article 10, paragraph 3).

Article 10 also sets forth the formalities for a contract concluded between persons in different jurisdictions. In such case, notwithstanding the foregoing, the contract shall be formally valid if it conforms with the law of the place from which the notice of offer or that of acceptance has been sent (Article 10, paragraph 4).

Notwithstanding the foregoing, the formalities for contracts that create or dispose of rights in rem or other rights requiring registration to movables or immovables shall be governed only by the law of the place where the subject property of the right is situated.

22. Japan follows the principle of unity.

[C] *Renvoi*

When a case should be governed by a person's national law and such law requires that Japanese law should apply, the Japanese law shall apply (Article 41). However, such rule does not apply in case of Article 25 (effect of marriage) - which is applied *mutatis mutandis* to the marital property regime and divorce under Article 26 and 27, respectively - and Article 32 (legal relationship between parents and children). Both Article 25 and 32 provide what is called the 'cascade system'.

[D] Mandatory Rules of the Forum and of Third States

According to Article 42 of the AGRAL, if the application of the provisions of the foreign law is against public policy, those provisions shall not apply.

The AGRAL does not have any express provision regarding the applicability of mandatory rules. Many scholars divide 'mandatory rules' into 'overriding' mandatory rules, which should be applied irrespective of the governing law, and 'relative' mandatory rules, which should be applied only when the governing law is the same law that sets forth the mandatory rules in question. Based on this argument, the 'mandatory rules' discussed in consumer contracts and labour contracts above (under Articles 11 and 12) should mean 'relative' mandatory rules. 'Overriding' mandatory rules of the forum (i.e., Japan) and third states may be applied by the Japanese courts irrespective of the governing law of the contract, as necessary.

[E] Proof of Foreign Law

There is an argument on whether a foreign law should be treated as 'law' or 'fact' since neither the AGRAL nor the CCP include any provision on the proof of foreign laws. It is generally understood that a foreign law should be treated as a 'law' and thus the courts should be responsible for finding and applying ex officio a foreign law.

[F] Evasion of the Law

There are no specific regulations in Japan (including the AGRAL) that prohibit or prevent the evasion of the law.

§4.04 PROCEDURAL ISSUES

[A] Service of Summons and Judicial Orders Abroad

According to Article 98(1) of the CCP, judicial documents must be served by the authority of the court. Although Japan became a signatory to the 1965 Hague Service Convention, it expressly declared its objection to the use of the methods of service referred to in sub-paragraphs (b) and (c) of Article 10.

Japan also entered into bilateral treaties with the United States (Japan-US Consular Treaty) and the United Kingdom (Japan-UK Consular Treaty) for the service of judicial documents. However, those bilateral treaties do not provide any special requirements or exemptions.

In *Hiroko Saeki Incorporated v. Ozaki*,[23] the court held that the service or notice required by Article 118.ii of CCP for recognition in Japan of a foreign judgment[24] is a 'foreign court's official summons or order served in accordance with the necessary procedures for judicial co-operation' by a person who has an ordinary capacity. In addition, the court emphasised that a translation should be attached to the service or notice, regardless of the actual language capability of the recipient. In *Hiroko Saeki Incorporated*, since the judicial documents were not translated into Japanese, the court found that no appropriate service took place and concluded that the Hawaiian judgment should not be recognised and enforced in Japan.

However, eight years later, the Supreme Court, in *Sadhwani v. Sadhwani*,[25] considered that in case an existing international treaty with the country where the judgment is rendered stipulates that judicial documents for commencement of litigation must be served in accordance with the treaty, any service of documents which is not made in accordance with the treaty shall not qualify as due 'service' required by Article 118.ii CCP. In *Sadhwani*, the Supreme Court concluded that private service was invalid since it was not permitted either under the Hague Service Convention or the Japan-UK Consular Treaty.

Article 20 of the 'Act on the Civil Jurisdiction of Japan with Respect to a Foreign State, etc.', prescribes the special mechanism for serving a complaint, a writ of summons or any other similar document upon a foreign state.

[B] Obtaining Evidence Abroad

According to Article 184 of the CCP, the examination of evidence to be conducted in a foreign country shall be commissioned to the competent government agency of that country or the Japanese ambassador/consul stationed in that country; and, even where it contravenes any laws of that country, shall be effective if it does not contravene the Japanese CCP. In recent practice, this provision is rarely used since the foreign witness/expert usually appears voluntarily before the Japanese courts.

Furthermore, Article 186 of the CCP allows a Japanese court to commission a government agency or public office, a foreign government agency or public office, or school, chamber of commerce, exchange or any other organisation to conduct a necessary examination. This provision may be used to establish details of foreign laws. In practice, Article 186 of the CCP is also rarely used.

23. 857 Kinhan 39, Tokyo District Court, 26 Mar. 1990.
24. Article 118(ii) of the CCP requires that: 'The losing party has received service (excluding service by publication or any other service similar thereto) of a summons or order necessary for the commencement of the suit.'
25. 188 Minshu 313, Supreme Court, 28 Apr. 1998.

Any documentary evidence should be submitted to the court with a Japanese translation.[26]

[C] Restraint of Foreign Proceedings

Japanese courts have not yet imposed an order to stay, a provisional prohibition on the filing of a lawsuit, or any other similar measure, in relation to foreign proceedings.

[D] Proof of Foreign Public Documents

Japan is a party to the 1961 Convention Abolishing the Requirement of Legalisation for Foreign Public Documents ('the Hague Apostille Convention').

A foreign public document that appears to be prepared by an authorised public officer in the course of his/her duties may be assumed to be an authentically created document. If there is any doubt about the authenticity of the creation of an official document, the court, by its own authority, may make an inquiry to the relevant government agency or public office concerned.

[E] Statute of Limitations

There is no statutory 'limitation' in the CCP for parties to file their claims. Although there is no authoritative precedent rendered by the Supreme Court of Japan, it is understood that the limitations applicable to the dispute are those in the *lex causae*, instead of the *lex fori*.

[F] Remedies and Damages

Damages, including interest issues, are governed by the *lex causae*, not the *lex fori*. However, in *Oregon State Union v. Mansei Kogyo Co. Ltd.*,[27] the Supreme Court expressly stated (in relation to the enforcement in Japan of a US judgment) that the purpose of damages under Japanese laws is to compensate the injured for the loss suffered and held that the portion of 'punitive' damages exceeding the compensatory damages was invalid because it violated public policy in Japan. Although the Supreme Court's position is firm and clear, there are some controversies on the theoretical case where parties have expressly agreed on a governing law the jurisdiction of which clearly allows punitive damages.

Similarly, foreign parties should be mindful that a Japanese court could intervene (based on the public policy theory)[28] as to the amount of liquidated damages if it finds the amount to be exorbitant.

26. Article 74 of the Court Act (Act No. 59 of 1947, *Saibansho-Ho*).
27. 51 Minshu 2573, Supreme Court, 11 Jul. 1997.
28. Article 90 of the Civil Code.

[G] Foreign Currency Obligations

Courts are not prohibited from issuing a judgment or any order in a foreign currency. In fact, there are some precedents.

In an enforcement action, if a payment amount is calculated and designated in a foreign currency, the obligor may make a payment in either Japanese Yen or such designated foreign currency. The Supreme Court, in *Bank of the Ryukyus v. Toenec Corporation*,[29] stated that the exchange rate for currency conversion is the rate on the date of closing of the hearing.

[H] Restraining Removal of Assets and Securing Evidence in Favour of a Foreign Arbitration/Judicial Process

The Civil Provisional Remedies Act[30] allows Japanese courts to adopt provisional attachments (*kari-sashiosae*) and provisional injunctions (*kari-shobun*) in favour of foreign proceedings if:

- the subject matter of the provisional attachment or dispute is located in Japan;[31] and
- it is showed (i) prima facie evidence (*somei*) of rights to be provisionally protected; and (ii) necessity for provisional protection.[32]

Article 15 of the Japanese Arbitration Act (JAA) allows a party to request a provisional measure before or during arbitral proceedings as long as the subject matter of such provisional measure is located in Japan and is the subject of the arbitration.

§4.05 RECOGNITION AND ENFORCEMENT OF FOREIGN DECISIONS

[A] Judicial Decisions: Requirements and Limitations

Article 118 of the CCP states that a final and binding foreign judgment shall be recognised in Japan only if all of the following requirements are met:

(i) The foreign court had jurisdiction over the dispute according to the provisions on international civil jurisdiction contained in Japanese law and treaties.

The Supreme Court in *Sadhwani* explicitly referred to this concept and described this foreign court's hypothetical jurisdiction issue as 'indirect jurisdiction (*kansetsu-kankatsu*)'.[33] *Sadhwani* is an interesting case because the judgment was the outcome of 'third party proceedings', which are not

29. 29 *Minshu* 1029, Supreme Court, 15 Jul. 1975.
30. Act No. 91 of 1989, *Minji-Hozen-Ho*.
31. Article 11 of the Provisional Remedies Act.
32. Article 13 of the Provisional Remedies Act.
33. *Supra* n. 25.

common among civil law jurisdictions. However, the Supreme Court took a substantive approach to find that the third-party claim had justifiable reasons to be consolidated with the original proceedings and that the Hong Kong court did have jurisdiction over such claims even from a Japanese law perspective. The Supreme Court upheld the High Court's decision and enforced the Hong Kong judgment.

On the other hand, in *X et al. v. Y et al.*,[34] the Tokyo District Court found no jurisdiction of a US federal court and rejected an enforcement request. The court denied the US jurisdiction since it did not find any 'objective causation' between the alleged tortious conduct that took place outside the US and the damage suffered in the US.

(ii) The losing party has received service (excluding a service by publication or any other service similar thereto) of a summons or order necessary for the commencement of the suit, or has appeared without receiving such service. The Supreme Court ruled in *Sadhwani*[35] that in case an existing international treaty with the country where the judgment is rendered stipulates that judicial documents for commencement of litigation must be served in accordance with the treaty, any service of documents which is not made in accordance with the treaty shall not qualify as due 'service' required by Article 118(ii) of the CCP.

(iii) The content of the judgment is not contrary to public policy in Japan. Although Japanese courts usually do not rely on this ambiguous concept, they have declined recognition and enforcement in the following cases:
   (a) 'punitive damages': e.g., the Supreme Court in *Oregon State Union*;[36] and
   (b) conflicting judgments: in *Marubeni America Corporation v. Kansai Tekko Co. Ltd.*,[37] a district court held that any foreign judgment conflicting with a judgment rendered by Japanese courts shall not be recognised and enforced, regardless of the timing of the filing of the complaint, issuing of the judgment and the judgment becoming final and binding since it would lead to a violation of the 'public policy'.

(iv) Reciprocity. So far, Japan has recognised judgments of California;[38] Singapore;[39] the United Kingdom;[40] New York;[41] Nevada;[42] West Germany

34. 2101 Hanji 67, Tokyo District Court, 15 Apr. 2010.
35. *Supra* n. 25.
36. *Supra* n. 27.
37. 261 Hanta 127, Osaka District Court, 22 Dec. 1977.
38. *X v. Y, 1351 Hanta 241,* Tokyo District Court, 28 Mar. 2011.
39. *X v. Y, 1229 Hanta 334,* Tokyo District Court, 19 Jan. 2006.
40. *Barclays Bank plc et al. v. Japan Planning Association Co. Ltd., 837 Hanta 300,* Tokyo District Court, 31 Jan. 1998.
41. *Concept Generation International Inc. v. Japan Design Network Co. Ltd., 864 Hanta 267,* Tokyo District Court, 14 Jan. 1998.
42. *Las Vegas Hilton Corporation v. Aomatsu, 794 Hanta 246,* Tokyo District Court, 16 Dec. 1992.

(Federal Republic of Germany);[43] Washington DC;[44] Hawaii;[45] and Switzerland.[46] Japanese courts have not yet recognised a judgment rendered by the People's Republic of China (PRC).

Although according to the CCP, the court has to determine whether or not those requirements are fulfilled, in practice the court bases its decision on the evidence provided by the party who seeks recognition. If additional evidence is needed, the court may require further evidence.

A foreign judgment recognised under Article 118 of the CCP, will be enforced in Japan according to the Civil Execution Law (CEL). In particular, the CEL provides for the specific means of enforcement available in Japan.

[B] Arbitral Awards (Including ICSID Awards): Requirements and Limitations

Japan is a party to the 1958 Convention on the Recognition and Enforcement of Foreign Arbitral Awards (the New York Convention),[47] the 1927 Geneva Convention on the Execution of Foreign Arbitral Awards (the Geneva Convention), and to the 1966 Convention on the Settlement of Investment Disputes between States and Nationals of Other States ('ICSID Convention').

Japan followed the UNCITRAL Model Law on International Commercial Arbitration[48] and the New York Convention when it enacted the JAA in 2003. Accordingly, Articles 45 and 46 (Recognition and Enforcement) of the JAA are in line with the globally accepted standards for recognition and enforcement of arbitral awards.

A foreign arbitral award may be enforced by making an application to the court for an exequatur (Article 46.1 of the JAA). Japanese courts must issue an exequatur unless grounds for refusing recognition or enforcement exist (with respect to certain grounds, the burden of proof lies with the defendant to the enforcement proceedings) and even if such grounds exist, the court has discretion not to dismiss the application for the enforcement. Japanese courts have discretion over dismissing the enforcement proceedings of an arbitral award being set aside by the courts at the place of the arbitration.

The competent court will be the district court having jurisdiction over the domicile of the obligor (if located in Japan) or the location of the object of the claim or seizable assets.

Although the JAA requires 'a document certifying that the content of said copy is identical to the arbitral award', it does not request 'a Japanese translation of the arbitral

43. *X Company v. Y Company, 1236 Hanji 13*, Nagoya District Court, 6 Feb. 1987.
44. *X Company v. Y, 37 Minshu 611*, Supreme Court, 7 Jun. 1983.
45. *PF Carrier Incorporated v. Gates, 625 Hanji 66*, Tokyo District Court, 24 Oct. 1970.
46. *X Company v. Maruman Co. Ltd., 215 Hanta 173*, Tokyo District Court, 13 Nov. 1967.
47. In accordance with Article I(3) and Article X(1) of the New York Convention, Japan declared that it would apply the New York Convention only to recognition and enforcement of awards in the territory of another contracting State.
48. Japan has not yet incorporated UNCITRAL's amendments adopted in 2006.

award' to be certified by the authority. Once the exequatur is obtained, the award will be enforced in accordance with the Civil Execution Act.

Furthermore, the JAA adopted an expedited procedure without mandatory oral argument (*kettei-tetsuzuki*) and the form of the court's determination is not a 'judgment' (*hanketsu*) but a 'decision' (*kettei*). On the other hand, one negative effect of this new legislation is that not all the 'decisions' are available in the public domain, although almost all judgments are publicly available.

So far, Japanese courts have not declined recognition and enforcement of a substantial number of foreign awards. Many arbitral awards issued in the PRC have been recognised and enforced by Japanese courts.[49]

§4.06 RECOGNITION OF OTHER FOREIGN PUBLIC DOCUMENTS

Japan is a party to the Convention Abolishing the Requirement of Legalisation for Foreign Public Documents and thus public documents issued by a foreign country party to the same convention shall be recognised without legalisation if they have an apostille.

§4.07 TREATIES FOR JUDICIAL COOPERATION

Japan is a party to the 1954 Hague Convention on Civil Procedure and the 1965 Hague Convention on the Service Abroad of Judicial and Extrajudicial Documents in Civil or Commercial Matters. In order to implement these treaties, a special act was promulgated.[50] Japan is also a party to the 1961 Convention Abolishing the Requirement of Legalisation for Foreign Public Documents.

Japan entered into agreements providing for judicial cooperation with the US, United Kingdom, and several other countries, such as Thailand, Brazil, and Australia.

In case no treaty for judicial cooperation may be applied in a particular case, the provisions contained in the Act relating to the Reciprocal Judicial Aid to be given at the Request of Foreign Court[51] will apply.

49. As a recent example: *X v. MIT Co Ltd, 2122 Hanji 122*, Osaka District Court, 25 Mar. 2011.
50. Act No. 115 of 1970, *Minji-sosho-tetsuzuki ni kansuru joyaku to no jisshi ni tomonau minji -sosho-tetsuzuki no tokurei tou ni kansuru houritsu*.
51. Act No. 63 of 1905, *Gaikoku-saibansho no shokutaku ni yoru kyojyo ho*.

CHAPTER 5
Republic of Korea

*Young Seok Lee, Sae Youn Kim & Sy Nae Kim**

§5.01 CODIFICATION OF PRIVATE INTERNATIONAL LAW AND RELEVANCE OF CASE LAW

[A] Codification and Case Law

Private international law in the Republic of Korea (Korea) was originally codified in the Conflict of Laws Act of 1962. In 2001, the Conflict of Laws Act was repealed and the Private International Act (PIA) was enacted and promulgated in its place.

The PIA was enacted to accommodate the needs of modern international society and to reflect the contemporary trends and recent developments in private international law. The following are some examples of the changes adopted in the PIA: addition of a general provision on international jurisdiction; introduction of the concept of 'habitual residence' in determining the applicable law; and supplementation of many choice of law provisions regarding legal capacity, legal entity or organisation, attorney-in-fact, means of transportation, goods in transit, security for contractual rights, intellectual property, etc.

There have been internal discussions within the Ministry of Justice (MOJ) regarding possible amendments of the present PIA. However, the specific scope of, or the specific provisions that would be subject to amendment have not been decided yet. On 30 June 2014, MOJ launched a Private International Act Revision Committee to further discuss the issues and prepare a draft amendment proposal to be submitted to the National Assembly. According to the news, the Committee is aiming for submission of a draft amendment proposal during the latter half of 2015, which will reflect recent

* Young Seok Lee, Partner and Chair of the International Dispute Resolution Practice, Yulchon. Sae Youn Kim, Partner and Vice-Chair of the International Dispute Resolution Practice, Yulchon; & Sy Nae Kim, Associate at Yulchon.

international trends in the conflict of laws, taking into consideration the on-going discussions at the Hague Conference on Private International Law and domestic Supreme Court precedents that have accumulated since the PIA's enactment in 2001.

Korea is a civil law country heavily influenced by the German and French legal systems as adopted and construed by Japanese law.[1] Therefore, codified law is the primary source of law. The principle of *stare decisis* is not recognised under Korean law. However, Korean courts do play a major role in construing and supplementing the codified law. This is especially true of the decisions by the Korean Supreme Court, which have de facto binding effect on all lower courts and even on itself. The Supreme Court can only change its former rulings by an en banc decision. Hence, lower courts and the Supreme Court respect judicial precedents.

When the PIA was enacted in 2001, some of the principles set forth in decisions by the Supreme Court in cases involving international elements were introduced into the act. One such example is Article 2 of the PIA, which is a reflection of the rulings of the Supreme Court that established basic principles in determining which country's court had jurisdiction over the matter at hand. Two leading cases regarding the determination of international jurisdiction are Supreme Court Decision 91*da*41897 rendered on 28 July 1992 and Supreme Court Decision 93*da*39607 rendered on 21 November 1995.

However, Article 2 of the PIA only lays down the main principles applicable to determine international jurisdiction, and does not include specific guidelines for the application of such principles. Therefore, it is still up to the courts to provide such guidelines for the determination of international jurisdiction.

[B] Multilateral Conventions Providing Uniform Substantive Law and/or International Jurisdictional Rules

According to Article 6(1) of the Constitution, a treaty duly concluded has the same effect as the domestic laws of the Republic of Korea. In order to have domestic effect, treaties need to be promulgated in the official gazette.

The Republic of Korea is a party to the UN Convention on Contracts for the International Sale of Goods (CISG) and the 1999 Convention for the Unification of Certain Rules relating to International Carriage by Air. In addition, the Republic of Korea is a party to eighteen multilateral agreements and protocols administered by the World Intellectual Property Organization (WIPO).[2]

1. The modern Korean legal system originated from the legal system of Imperial Japan, which was applied in Korea during the Japanese rule. During that time, the French and German legal systems were introduced in Korea through Japanese scholars and legal practitioners. After World War II, Korea became independent from Japan, but the French and German influences integrated by the Japanese remained in the modern Korean legal system.
2. http://www.wipo.int/treaties/en/ShowResults.jsp?country_id = 95C&start_year = ANY&end_year = ANY&treaty_all = ALL&search_what = C.

§5.02 JURISDICTION OF LOCAL COURTS IN FOREIGN-RELATED CASES

[A] Grounds for Jurisdiction

[1] General

Article 2 of the PIA states:

> (1) The court shall have international jurisdiction over disputes, in which a party or the subject matter of the dispute is substantially connected to the Republic of Korea. When determining whether there is substantial connection, the court shall follow reasonable standards that are compatible with the ideology of the allocation of international jurisdiction.
> (2) The court shall determine whether it has international jurisdiction with reference to the domestic law provisions regarding jurisdiction and shall take full account of the unique nature of international jurisdiction in light of the intentions set out in paragraph (1).

According to the above provisions, the basic criterion used in determining the competent court for foreign-related cases is whether there is 'substantial connection' between either a party to the dispute or the subject matter and the forum. Whether there is substantial connection should be determined by the court after taking into consideration the following factors: personal interests of the parties such as fairness between the parties, convenience of the forum and predictability, and public interests of the court and state such as adequacy, speed, and efficiency of the legal proceedings and effectiveness of the judgment.[3]

Another important criterion that the court also needs to consider is whether the relevant court would have jurisdiction if one followed the Korean domestic rules on territorial jurisdiction. According to the said territorial jurisdiction rules in the Korean Civil Procedural Code, general jurisdiction is recognised at the defendant's address (Article 2). Cases of special jurisdictions, which usually relate to the subject matter of the claim, are then enumerated in Articles 7 through 24 of the Civil Procedural Code. Some examples are: the workplace or office of the defendant when a lawsuit is brought against a person who works continuously at the workplace or the office (Article 7); *locus delicti* for tort claims (Article 18); the place where immovable property is situated (Article 20), etc. As clearly set forth in Article 2(2) of the PIA, these domestic rules should not overrule the unique nature of international jurisdiction. Thus, the court ultimately has to take into account the various factors mentioned in the paragraph above.

The Korean courts usually exercise considerable leniency when determining the competent court and they have rarely denied their jurisdiction over the subject matter at hand.[4]

3. See Supreme Court case 2002*da*59788 rendered on 27 Jan. 2005.
4. See Supreme Court case 2009*da*22549 rendered on 24 May 2012 and Supreme Court case 2010*da*18355 rendered on 15 Jul. 2010.

[2] Exclusive Jurisdiction

There is no specific regulation on express or implicit submission to the court, other than regulations on domestic jurisdiction with respect to bankruptcy cases,[5] patent cases,[6] etc. The PIA provides for exclusive jurisdiction over special types of disputes, i.e., disputes relating to certain consumer contracts[7] and employment contracts. More specifically, Article 27(5) of the PIA provides that the courts of the country of the consumer's habitual residence shall have exclusive jurisdiction over disputes arising out of the consumer contract when the consumer is a defendant. Similarly, Article 28(4) of the PIA provides that the courts of the country of the employee's habitual residence shall have exclusive jurisdiction over disputes arising out of the employment contract, when the employee is a defendant.

Parties may also agree to exclusive jurisdiction by way of contract. However, if the agreed forum is a foreign court, the Korean courts may not accept the validity of such an agreement, unless certain requisites are met. The details of such requisites are found in section 5.02[B][3] below.

[B] Exclusion of Jurisdiction

[1] Immunity

[a] Sovereign Immunity

Foreign states enjoy immunity in accordance with the customary international law. The Korean courts' approach towards such immunity is restrictive. In the case 97*da*39216, en banc, rendered on 17 December 1998, the Supreme Court ruled that sovereign acts of a state are subject to immunity, but not the private acts.

[b] Diplomatic and Consular Immunity

Diplomatic immunity is recognised under the Vienna Convention on Diplomatic Relations of 18 April 1961, which Korea ratified on 26 October 1970, and consular

5. Article 3 of the Debtor Rehabilitation and Bankruptcy Act regulates exclusive domestic jurisdiction of rehabilitation cases and bankruptcy cases.
6. Patent Act Article 186(1) stipulates that the Patent Court of Korea shall have original jurisdiction over any action against a trial decision or dismissal of a request for trial or retrial. A trial proceeding is an administrative proceeding where the Intellectual Property Tribunal hears and renders decisions regarding patent applications and other IP related claims.
7. The consumer contracts that are subject to special treatment under Article 27 of the PIA must have been signed by the consumer without professional or business purposes and must fall under one of following cases: (i) the other party to the contract has conducted professional or business activities such as invitation by advertisement in the country of applicable law, or if the advertisement or other business activities have been conducted from another country into that country, the consumer has taken necessary actions to execute the contract in that country; (ii) the other party to the contract has received an order from the consumer in that country; or (iii) the other party to the contract induced the consumer into going to a foreign country to place an order.

immunity under the Vienna Convention on Consular Relations of 24 April 1963, which Korea ratified on 16 December 1976.

[c] Other Immunities

Members or employees of the United States Armed Forces, including those employees who are nationals of, or ordinarily resident in the Republic of Korea, shall not be subject to any proceedings for the enforcement of any judgment rendered against them in the Republic of Korea in a matter arising from the performance of their official duties (Agreement under Article IV of the Mutual Defense Treaty between the Republic of Korea and the United States of America, regarding Facilities and Areas and the Status of United States Armed Forces in the Republic of Korea, Article 23(f)).

The United Nations (including organisations under its auspices), representatives of the United Nations and its officials enjoy immunity pursuant to Article 105 of the Charter of the United Nations and the United Nations Convention on Jurisdictional Immunities of States and their Property.

[2] Non-justiciable Claims

Korean Law does not specify claims that are non-justiciable. However, if the Korean court finds that a certain claim does not meet the criteria for its jurisdiction under Article 2 of the PIA it is considered non-justiciable. Such non-justiciable claims would usually arise when the claim at hand lacks the necessary connection with Korea.

Although there is no specific legislation in this regard, the Korean courts do acknowledge that if the issue at hand deals with the constitution, validity and/or cancellation of a right that is registered in a foreign country, such as a registered patent, the court of the registered country would have the exclusive jurisdiction over the matter, and renders such claim non-justiciable. However, if the issue is the breach of an obligation to register or transfer the title to another person, it is a mere contractual claim and the Korean court may find that it has jurisdiction over such claim if necessary connections are found.[8]

[3] Forum Agreements in Favour of Foreign Courts

Forum agreements in favour of foreign courts are valid, but under strict requirements. In its ruling rendered on 9 September 1997 in the case 96*da*20093, the Supreme Court held that:

> In order for a forum agreement that excludes the jurisdiction of the Korean courts in favour of foreign courts to be valid, the considered dispute should not be a dispute over which the Korean courts have exclusive jurisdiction, the designated foreign court should have competence over the dispute at hand, and there should be a reasonable connection between the dispute and the forum under the law of

8. See, Supreme Court case 2009*da*19093 rendered on 28 Apr. 2011.

> that forum. On the other hand, if the forum agreement is noticeably unreasonable and unfair, such forum agreement is invalid on grounds of public policy.

Some scholars have criticised the Supreme Court for requiring reasonable connection in order for the forum agreement to be valid, since it is quite usual for parties with different nationalities involved in international trade to designate a third party state as a neutral forum to settle their potential disputes. Therefore, if the Supreme Court requires that the designated forum have a reasonable connection to the matter at hand, it runs counter to the will of the parties to settle their disputes in a neutral forum. Nevertheless, the Korean courts have maintained the position taken by the Supreme Court in case 96*da*20093 and there have been only few cases where a Korean court has actually denied its competence because of a forum agreement in favour of foreign courts.

According to Articles 27 and 28 of the PIA, forum agreements in consumer contracts and employment contracts must be in writing. In addition, the agreement is valid only if it was made after a dispute has arisen or if the agreement is in effect adding on additional fora to the competent forum under the PIA.

[4] Arbitration Clause

A valid arbitration clause should prevent national courts from hearing the case. When the court recognises that a valid arbitration clause is applicable to the dispute at hand, it must dismiss the case pursuant to Article 9(1) of the Korean Arbitration Act, which states:

> A court before which an action is brought in a matter that is the subject of an arbitration agreement shall, if the respondent raises a plea that an arbitration agreement exists, dismiss the action, unless it finds that the agreement is null and void, inoperative or incapable of being performed.

It should be noted however, that under Korean law, in principle, only an exclusive arbitration clause, i.e., one which allows disputes to be resolved only through arbitration and not litigation, is valid. This issue has been controversial. Korean courts generally consider elective or optional arbitration clauses, i.e., ones which allow a dispute to be resolved through arbitration or litigation, as invalid and allow the objecting party to resort to court action as long as the objection was made in a timely manner. The Korean Supreme Court has held that an elective or optional arbitration clause may be considered valid if a party elects, and proceeds with, arbitration and the other party takes part to the arbitration without raising any objection.[9]

9. In the Supreme Court case 2005*da*12452 rendered on 27 May 2005, the losing party in an arbitration case filed a motion before a Korean court to set aside the arbitral award on the grounds that the arbitration clause was an invalid elective arbitration agreement. The Supreme Court held that since that party did not raise any objection as to the jurisdiction of the arbitral tribunal at the

[C] Non-exercise of Jurisdiction

[1] Forum Non Conveniens

When the current PIA was drafted, there were some discussions on whether to include a provision in the PIA codifying the doctrine of forum non conveniens. After some debate however, the provision whereby national courts may dismiss or stay proceedings if it is clear that a foreign forum is more convenient was deleted from the draft. Therefore, the statute remains silent as to whether forum non conveniens can be applied in Korea.

In practice, Korean courts usually consider the issue of forum non conveniens in their reasoning, i.e., in obiter dictum.[10] However, no case has been reported where a Korean court has relied on that the doctrine to dismiss a case or to stay proceedings pending in Korea. Actually, Korean courts are usually reluctant to deny judicial assistance on the grounds that the dispute should be settled elsewhere, especially if the matter has reasonable connection to the forum e.g., the nationality of both parties is Korean.

[2] Lis alibi pendens

The current PIA does not contain any provisions dealing with the treatment of a local judicial proceeding in the event where there is an on-going foreign proceeding or proceedings on the same matter between the same parties. Besides, to our knowledge, the Supreme Court has not rendered any ruling dealing directly with this issue. However, there are lower court cases where a Korean court actually dismissed the lawsuit on the grounds that the same matter was already pending in another country.

A leading case, where a Korean court dismissed a lawsuit on the grounds of foreign *lis alibi pendens* is the Seoul District Court case 2000*gahap*90940 rendered on 13 December 2002. In this case, the court reasoned that:

> If a lawsuit is pending in the courts of a foreign country and it can be predicted that the judgment that will be rendered in the foreign lawsuit will be recognised in Korea pursuant to Article 217 of the Civil Procedural Code, it should be regarded as *lis alibi pendens* under Article 259 of the Civil Procedural Code. Therefore, if the same case is filed in the Korean courts, it is a duplicate lawsuit that is illegitimate and shall be dismissed.

---

outset of the arbitration proceeding, such challenge is time-barred under Article 17(2) of the Korean Arbitration Act and the elective arbitration clause amounts to a valid arbitration agreement.

10. An example of a boilerplate phrase often found in the reasoning would be: 'In light of all the circumstances drawn from the records, it cannot be acknowledged that Korea is a noticeably inconvenient forum to exercise judicial competence over the instant matter'. See Supreme Court case 2002*da*59788 rendered on 27 Jan. 2005.

Other courts seem to have adopted the reasoning by the Seoul District Court in the case above and similar rulings have been rendered since.[11]

According to the judgments of these lower courts, in order to dismiss a case on grounds of foreign *lis alibi pendens*, the following requirements should be met: (i) the case pending overseas and the case brought before the local court should be the same (e.g., same parties, same subject matter, etc.); (ii) the latter case should have been filed with the local court while the former case is pending in a foreign court; and (iii) one should be able to predict that the judgment to be rendered in the former case pending before the foreign court would eventually be recognised in Korea.

The predictability of the judgment to be rendered in the former case pending before the foreign court eventually being recognised in Korea depends on whether the judgment meets the requirements for recognition under the Korean Civil Procedural Code.

Article 217 of the Civil Procedural Code lays out the requirements for a foreign judgment to be recognised in Korea. The requirements are as follows:

(i) The judgment must be final with no further appeal available.
(ii) The foreign court that rendered the judgment must have jurisdiction under the principles of international jurisdiction according to Korean law or international treaties.
(iii) The defendant who is the losing party must have been properly served with a complaint (petition) or a similar litigation document and a summons or notification of the hearing date (with the exclusion of notification by public notice or similar means) with sufficient time to prepare a defence, or if the defendant has not been served, has voluntarily submitted to the jurisdiction of the foreign court.
(iv) The recognition of the foreign judgment must not be contrary to Korean public policy or Korean social values.
(v) The foreign jurisdiction must provide reciprocity with respect to the enforcement of judgments rendered in Korea.

If the judgment expected to be rendered in the former lawsuit pending in a foreign court cannot meet one or more of the above requirements, the Korean court may go ahead and hear the case filed before it, regardless of the foreign proceeding. However, the Korean court may be reluctant to arrive at a different conclusion than that of the foreign court, unless special circumstances compel the court to do so (e.g., the judgment to be rendered in the foregoing lawsuit is contrary to the public policy of Korea).[12]

11. For example Seoul Central District Court judgment 2005*gahap*43314 rendered on 14 Oct. 2005. See Kwang Hyun Suk, *International Civil Procedure Law* (Pakyoungsa, 2012), 208. See also Busan District Court judgment 2000*gahap*7960 rendered on 2 Feb. 2007.
12. In the Supreme Court case 2009*da*22549 rendered on 24 May 2012 (*supra* n. 4), the issue at stake was whether to dismiss the claims brought by the plaintiffs on the basis that there was a foreign judgment regarding that same lawsuit issued in a foreign country. The Busan High Court, which heard the appeal on the matter, dismissed the claims on the basis that the foreign judgment was likely to be recognised in Korea under Article 217 of the Civil Procedural Code and therefore the

§5.03 APPLICABLE LAW

[A] Choice of Law

[1] Express Stipulation

The PIA has a comprehensive set of rules regarding choice of law in various types of legal relationships and these rules are divided into chapters titled persons, legal actions, real rights, contractual rights, family, succession, bills, notes and *cheques*, as well as maritime affairs. In the case of *negotiorum gestio*, unjust enrichment or tort, parties are allowed to agree on the application of Korean law after the occurrence of the event, provided that rights of third parties shall not be prejudiced by such agreement (PIA, Article 33).

Party autonomy in the choice of applicable law is both recognised and supported especially for the chapter on contractual rights. According to Article 25(1) of the PIA, parties to a contract may choose the law applicable to their contract by express stipulation or implied choice. Choosing the applicable law for only certain parts of a contract or choosing different applicable laws for respective parts of a contract is allowed under Article 25(2) of the PIA. Changing the choice of law or agreeing on the choice of law after the execution of the relevant contract is also allowed, provided that the rights of third parties are not affected by the change or by the new choice of law between the parties. Parties may choose the applicable law before or after a dispute has arisen and even after a lawsuit has been filed.[13]

Korean Courts also recognise and support party autonomy. In a case where the parties had referred to the 'law of the United States' without specifying which state law was to be applied, the Korean Supreme Court ruled that such choice of law should not be considered invalid straightaway because of its obscurity. The Supreme Court further ruled that the court should investigate whether the intention of the parties was to choose the law of a certain state, as it could reasonably be inferred from the context, including the text of the contract, circumstances before and after the contract was entered into, standard practices, etc. Even if the parties' choice of a state law cannot be reasonably established after such an investigation, if there is any uniform federal law regarding a certain subject matter that can be applied in all of its Member States, the parties' choice of law regarding that subject matter will be considered as a valid agreement to apply that uniform federal law.[14]

---

claims filed by the plaintiffs were not legitimate in light of the res judicata effect of the foregoing foreign judgment. The High Court judgment was repealed and remanded by the Supreme Court, which reasoned that the recognition of the foreign judgment was contrary to the public policy of Korea. After the case was remanded, the Busan High Court rendered a judgment in favour of the plaintiffs. The post-appeal case has been appealed again and is currently pending in the Supreme Court.

13. For example, in Seoul High Court Case 2012*na*59871 rendered on 19 Jul. 2013, the parties have agreed on the applicable law during the appeal proceedings.
14. Supreme Court Case 2009*da*77754 rendered on 25 Oct. 2013.

According to Article 8(2) of the PIA, substantial connection between the contract and the choice of law is not necessary.

The law that would be applicable if the agreement were valid, i.e., the law chosen by the parties, determines the validity of the parties' agreement regarding the choice of law. If it is clearly unreasonable to determine the validity of the agreement according to the law that was chosen by the parties in the agreement, a party may rely on the law of the country where he has his habitual residence to establish that he did not consent to the choice of law (PIA Article 25(5) and 29).

[2] Implied Choice

Implied choice is recognised only if it can be reasonably inferred from the contents of the contract and other circumstances.

[B] Other Cases

The PIA generally adopts the 'closest relationship' principle and even introduces a general exception clause (Article 8), which requires the application of the law of the country which has the closest connection if the governing law designated by the PIA – except choice of law – only has a slight connection.

According to Article 26 of the PIA, if the parties have not chosen the governing law, the contract is governed by the law of the country with which it is the most closely connected. In relation to certain contracts,[15] the most closely connected law is presumed to be the law of the country where the party responsible for performing the contract (i.e., the performer) has his habitual residence –according to Article 4, if it is impossible to ascertain the habitual residence, the law of the residence shall govern – or, if that party is a corporate entity or an organisation, the law of the country where its principal office is located. However, if the contract is entered into in the course of that party's professional or business activities, the law of the country where the party's business office is located shall be presumed to be most closely connected. If the subject matter of the contract is a right in immovable property, the law of the country where the immovable property is situated shall be presumed to be most closely connected.

Notwithstanding Article 26 of the PIA as described above, special rules apply to determine the law applicable to certain consumer and employment contracts in the absence of choice by the parties. According to PIA Article 27(2), consumer contracts in such cases are governed by the law of the country in which the consumer has his habitual residence. Employment contracts in such cases are governed by the law of the country in which the employee habitually carries out his work. However, if the employee does not habitually carry out his work in any one country, the contract shall

15. See Article 26(2): (i) where the contract concerns the assignment of rights: the performance of the assignor; (ii) where the contract concerns the lease of goods or of a right: the performance of the lessor, and (iii) where the contract concerns the provision of service: the performance of the service provider.

be governed by the law of the country of the company's place of business where the employee was engaged.

The PIA was greatly influenced by the Convention on the Law Applicable to Contractual Obligations 1980 ('Rome Convention'),[16] which was the instrument that created a common choice of law system in contracts within the European Union at the time. Therefore, the provisions in the PIA regarding the choice of law for contractual obligations greatly resemble those of the Rome Convention, but for a few differences. A detailed comparison of the Rome Convention and the relevant provisions of the PIA are set out in the table below.

[1] A Comparison of the Rome Convention and Relevant Provisions of the Korean Private International Law

	Rome Convention	*Private International Law*
Scope of application	Contractual obligations involving choice of law with some explicit exceptions	A comprehensive set of rules regarding choice of law in various legal relations, including contractual obligations
Freedom to choose applicable law	Expressed or demonstrated with reasonable certainty. Partial agreement and variations after contract possible to the extent that it does not adversely affect the rights of third parties	Expressed or demonstrated with reasonable certainty. Partial agreement possible. A variation to the choice of law must not affect the validity of the contract and the rights of third parties
Applicable law in the absence of choice	The law of the most closely connected country Presumption provision for performance and special provision for immovable property	The law of the most closely connected country Habitual residence of the performer for certain contracts and the place of immovable property for rights related to immovable property are presumed to have most close connection

16. The Rome Convention has been replaced by the Rome I Regulation (593/2008) and a revision committee has been formed in order to update the PIA in accordance with the recent trends in international private law.

	Rome Convention	*Private International Law*
Certain consumer contracts	Choice of law made by the parties cannot have the result of depriving the consumer of the protection afforded to him by the mandatory rules of law of the country of his habitual residence	Choice of law made by the parties cannot have the result of depriving the consumer of the protection afforded to him by the mandatory rules of law of the country of his habitual residence
Employment contracts	Choice of law made by the parties cannot have the result of depriving the employee of the protection afforded to him by the mandatory rules of law of the country of his habitual residence	Choice of law made by the parties cannot have the result of depriving the employee of the protection afforded to him by the mandatory rules of law of the country of his habitual residence
Mandatory rules	Mandatory rules of another country with close connection are inevitable	Mandatory rules of the most closely connected country are inevitable even if the parties choice of law is that of another country
Material Validity	To be determined by the law which would govern if the contract or term were valid	To be determined by the law which would govern if the contract or term were valid
Formal Validity	To be determined by the law which governs the contract under the Rome Convention or the law of the country where it is concluded	To be determined by the law which would govern if the contract or term were valid
Scope of applicable law	Interpretation, performance, consequences of breach, extinguishing obligations, the consequences of nullity	N/A
Incapacity	The law applicable	The law of the person's nationality
Voluntary assignment	The law applicable to the contract between the assignor and the assignee	The law applicable to the contract between the assignor and the assignee
Subrogation	Determined by the law which governs the third person's duty to satisfy the creditor	Determined by the law which governs the third person's duty to satisfy the creditor
Burden of proof	According to the law governing the contract	N/A
Exclusion of *renvoi*	Rules of private international law excluded	N/A

	Rome Convention	*Private International Law*
Public policy of the forum	Application of a rule may be refused if such application is manifestly incompatible with the public policy of the forum	The provisions of the applicable law which are evidently contrary to public policy of Korea shall not be applied

*[2] Management of Affairs (**negotiorum gestio**), Unjust Enrichment, and Tort Claims*

The law applicable to the management of affairs (*negotiorum gestio* or *gestion d'affaires*) is the law of the place where the management took place. However, if the management was performed based on a legal relationship between the relevant parties, the governing law of that legal relationship shall apply. If the claim arises out of payment of another person's debt, the governing law shall be the law applicable to the debt (PIA Article 30).

The law applicable to unjust enrichment is the law of the place where the enrichment occurred. However, if the unjust enrichment results from a legal relationship existing between the relevant parties, the governing law of such legal relationship shall apply (PIA Article 31).

The law applicable to tort is the law of the place where the tortious act took place. However, if the habitual residence of both the tortfeasor and the victim are in the same country at the time of the tortious act, the law of that country shall apply. Notwithstanding the foregoing, if a pre-existing legal relationship between the parties was infringed by the tortious act, the law governing that legal relationship shall apply. If the governing law determined by the above rules is a foreign law, and the nature of the damages under that law is clearly not a suitable restitution for the victim (e.g., punitive damages) or if the damages under that law exceeds the amount necessary for reasonable compensation, the foreign law shall not be applicable to that extent (PIA Article 32).

[3] Persons

The legal capacity of a natural person is governed by the law of that person's nationality. Once legal capacity is acquired, it cannot be taken away or limited by a change of nationality (PIA Article 13).

There are certain limitations to the allegation of incapacity, especially in transactions where one party was not aware of the other's incapacity (PIA Article 15).

Legal entities and organisations are governed by the law of the country of their place of incorporation. However, if a legal entity or organisation incorporated in a foreign country has its principal office in Korea or conducts its main businesses in Korea, Korean law shall be the applicable law.

[4] Legal Actions

The formal requirements of a legal action are governed by the law applicable to that legal action. Notwithstanding the foregoing, if the legal action meets the formal requirements of the law of the country where the action takes place, said action shall be considered valid (PIA Article 17).

The law governing the relationship between the principal and the agent in a voluntary or consensual agency is the law applicable to the legal relationship between the principal and the agent. Whether the legal actions of the agent have effect on the principal is determined by the law of the country where the agent's office is located. However, if the agent does not have an office or if the third person could not have been aware that the agent had an office, the law of the country where the agent's legal actions took place shall apply. If the agent is an employee of the principal but does not have an office, the main office of the principal is deemed to be the office of the agent. Notwithstanding the above, the principal may choose the law governing the legal relationship between the principal and the agent so long as such choice is made in writing, either in a document evidencing the agent's authority or a notice to the opposing party (PIA, Article 18).

[5] Real Rights **(jura in re** ***or rights in rem*****)**

The law governing real rights with respect to movable/immovable property and other real rights that require registration is the law of the country where that property is located (PIA, Article 19).

Real rights with respect to airplanes are governed by the law of the country where the airplane is registered and real rights with respect to trains are governed by the law of the country in which the train permit was issued (PIA, Article 20).

Real rights with respect to goods in transit are governed by the law of the country where the goods are to be delivered (PIA, Article 22), and security rights for bonds, stocks and other negotiable instruments are governed by the law governing the rights that are being secured (PIA, Article 23).

Intellectual property rights are protected by the law of the country where such rights were infringed (PIA, Article 24).

[6] Family

According to PIA Article 36, the substantive requirements of marriage are governed by the respective national law of each spouse while the formal requirements are governed by the law of the country where the marriage takes place or the national law of one of the spouse. However, Korean law shall apply if the marriage takes place in Korea and one of the spouses is Korean.

According to Article 37 of the PIA, the law governing the legal effects of marriage is determined in the following order:

(i) The law of the country of which the spouses are both nationals.
(ii) The law of the country where the spouses have mutual habitual residence.
(iii) The law of the country to which the spouses are the most closely connected.

Article 37 of the PIA applies *mutatis mutandis* to marital property. However, the spouses may agree to apply a different law to marital property, provided their choice leads to one of the following: (i) the law of the country of which one of the spouse is a national; (ii) the habitual residence of one of the spouse; (iii) the law of the place where immovable property is located in case of immovable marital property. Their agreement must be made in writing, dated and signed by both spouses (printed name and seal imprint or handwritten signature).

Application of foreign law to legal actions arising out of the marriage and to marital assets within Korea cannot adversely affect the rights of a *bone fide* third party. If the foreign law cannot apply as a result, the law of Korea would govern the issue of marital property in relation to that third party. Notwithstanding the foregoing, if the marital property agreement containing a choice of foreign law clause is registered in Korea, the foreign governing law may still be applied against the third party (PIA Article 38).

Article 38 of the PIA is applied *mutatis mutandis* to divorce cases. However, if one of the spouses is Korean with habitual residence in Korea, Korean law shall be the governing law (PIA Article 39).

Articles 40-48 of the PIA also set out the rules regarding the law governing parental relationships within or without marriage, as well as the laws governing adoption, support, and guardianship.

[7] Succession

In principle, the governing law in matters of succession is the national law of the deceased at the time of death. Such law will govern the entire estate of the deceased. Other laws may become applicable if the deceased explicitly designated the following laws as applicable law in a formal will: (i) the law of the country where the deceased had his habitual residence at the time his/her will was written; (ii) in case of immovable property, the law of the country where the immovable property is located (PIA Article 49).

Wills are governed by the law of country of which the testator is a national (PIA Article 50).

[8] Bills, Notes, and Cheques

The legal capacity of the obligor on a negotiable instrument (bills of exchange, promissory notes, and *cheques*) is governed by the country of which the obligor is a national. However, if the law of the country of which the obligor is a national provides that the law of another country shall apply, that other law shall apply. Even if the obligor does not have legal capacity according to the foregoing applicable laws, the obligor is deemed to have capacity to bear the obligation if he signed the relevant note in another country and has legal capacity to do so in that country (PIA Article 51).

The formal requirements relating to bills of exchange, promissory notes, and *cheques* are governed by the law of the country where the relevant negotiable instrument was signed (PIA Article 53). The formal requirements of *cheques* can also be governed by the law of the country where payment is to be made.

The obligations of the guarantor in a bill of exchange and of the issuer in a promissory note are governed by the law of the country where payment is to be made, and obligations arising from *cheques* are governed by the law of the country where it was signed (PIA Article 54).

[9] Maritime Affairs

The law of the country where the ship is registered generally governs: (i) the real rights in a ship; (ii) the priority of security rights on the ship; (iii) the scope of ship-owner's obligations for the actions of the captain and his crew; (iv) the limitation of liabilities; (v) general average; and (vi) the scope of the captain's power of representation (PIA Article 60).

[10] Contractual Assignment of Claims and Assumption of Obligations

The legal relationship between the assignor and the assignee is governed by the law which governs the contract between them, while the law governing the claim to be assigned determines its assignability and the effect of the assignment against the debtor and third parties. The same rules apply in case of assumption of obligations (PIA 34).

[C] *Renvoi*

According to the PIA, the doctrine of *renvoi* is applied as a principle. However, there are some exceptions to the application of *renvoi*, which are laid out in Article 9(2) of the PIA. The exceptions are as follows:

(i) when the parties have chosen the governing law by agreement;
(ii) when the applicable law of a contract is designated by the PIA;
(iii) when the law applicable to support is designated pursuant to Article 46 of the PIA;
(iv) when the law applicable to the method of a will is designated pursuant to Article 50(3) of the PIA;
(v) when the law of the country of registry of a ship is designated pursuant to Article 60 of the PIA; and
(vi) when the application of *renvoi* goes against the purpose of designation pursuant to the PIA.

[D] Mandatory Rules of the Forum and of Third States

According to Article 7 of the PIA, mandatory provisions of the forum (in this case the mandatory rules of Korea), which must be applied regardless of the applicable law (similar to the 'overriding mandatory rules' in Rome I and Rome II Regulations) in light of the purpose of the legislation, will apply even if the law of a foreign country has been designated as the applicable law pursuant to the PIA.

Furthermore, according to Article 10 of the PIA, the application of provisions of a foreign law is excluded if such application is evidently contrary to the good morals and other public order of the Republic of Korea.

On the other hand, there is no separate provision for the application of the mandatory rules of third states. This area is left to the precedents and scholarly opinions. That being said, Article 6 of the PIA, by stating that the foreign laws that are designated by the PIA will not be excluded just because they are of administrative nature, is understood to be declaring the principle for application of the mandatory rules of third states, albeit in a passive way.[17]

There are some specific references to the mandatory provisions of third countries. For example, for certain consumer and employment contracts, protection afforded to the consumer or the employee by the mandatory rules of the country in which the consumer or employee has his habitual residence is applied regardless of choice of law. Also if all of the elements are related to one single country and the parties nevertheless choose the law of another country, the mandatory provisions of that single relevant country cannot be excluded (Article 25(4) of the PIA).

[E] Proof of Foreign Law

According to Article 5 of the PIA, the contents of a foreign law designated by the PIA shall be investigated and applied by the court on its own initiative, but the court may request cooperation from the parties for such purposes. This provision has been introduced in the PIA after the Supreme Court first recognised the principle in case 89*daka*20252 rendered on 10 April 1990. The Supreme Court ruled that the contents of a foreign law are a matter of law and not a matter of fact. Therefore, it is subject to an investigation that is initiated by the court. The court may investigate the foreign law by any means it deems reasonable. There is no requirement that the court's investigation take the form of an expert report or an expert witness statement and the court is not obliged to request an investigation or send out an inquiry to domestic and foreign public institutions/schools.

In short, the court must investigate the contents of the foreign law as the applicable law in any international case where such law is applicable. The court should apply and construe the contents and meanings of the foreign law as they are actually applied and construed in that foreign country. However, if the materials evidencing the standards of interpretation under the foreign law (e.g., court precedents of the foreign

17. Kwang Hyun Suk, *Private International Law* (Pakyoungsa, 2013), 149.

country) were not submitted in the proceedings, making it impossible to verify their content, the court may confirm the meaning and the contents of the foreign law pursuant to the general standards for law interpretation under Korean law.[18]

If, despite the court's best effort to investigate, the court cannot confirm the contents of the foreign law, then the court can apply the customary law of that foreign country. If the contents of the customary law of that foreign country cannot be confirmed either, then, and only then, shall the court apply 'sound reasoning'.[19]

[F] Evasion of the Law

There is no specific regulation in Korea that deals with evasion of the law directly. Evasion of the law is not recognised in Korea as a general doctrine either.

However, certain provisions in the PIA (Article 7, 25(4), 27(1), and 28(1)) and certain rulings of the Korean courts, in particular those denying the validity of exclusive jurisdiction agreements on grounds of public policy and social order, seem to demonstrate the necessity to regulate evasion of the law.

§5.04 PROCEDURAL ISSUES

[A] Service of Summons and Judicial Orders Abroad

Korea is a signatory to the Hague Convention on the Service Abroad of Judicial and Extrajudicial Documents in Civil or Commercial Matters ('1965 Hague Convention'). Korea is also a signatory to bilateral treaties regarding judicial assistance in civil and commercial matters with Uzbekistan, Mongolia, China and Australia.[20] There is also a statute, i.e., the Act on International Judicial Mutual Assistance in Civil Matters ('Judicial Assistance Act'), which applies in cases where the relevant country is neither a member of the 1965 Hague Convention nor a party to any bilateral treaties with Korea. The Judicial Assistance Act can also be applied on a supplementary basis to the relevant actions of other 1965 Hague Convention Signatories. In some circumstances, the Civil Procedural Code is also applied, usually on a supplementary basis.

Pursuant to Article 2 of the 1965 Hague Convention, Korea designated the National Court Administration as the Central Authority under the 1965 Hague Convention. In addition to the National Court Administration, the staff of the court that has jurisdiction over the place of service has been designated for the purpose of completion of the certificate provided for in Article 6 of the 1965 Hague Convention.

According to the 1965 Hague Convention, service of judicial documents between Contracting States may be conducted through various channels besides the Central Authority. In Korea, however, service by diplomatic or consular agents (with the

18. For example Supreme Court case 2008*da*88375 rendered on 25 Mar. 2010.
19. Supreme Court case 2000*da70064* rendered on 10 Jan. 2003.
20. It should be noted that in the case of bilateral treaties judicial assistance with regard to service of documents is limited to judicial documents. Therefore service of extrajudicial documents is not subject to bilateral treaties.

exception of service to a national of the country from which the documents originate, Article 8), and service by postal channels directly to persons abroad, direct service between judicial officers, officials or other competent persons of the State of origin and the State of destination, and service by any person interested in a judicial proceeding directly to competent persons of the State of destination are not allowed (Reservations of Articles 8 and 10 of the 1965 Hague Convention).[21]

In practice, when a document originating from a Korean court needs to be serviced to a party in a foreign country, the presiding judge of the case requests service of the documents through the National Court Administration, which in turn entrusts the service of the documents with the relevant authority of the foreign country through the Ministry of Foreign Affairs and Trade in Korea.[22] The foreign authority that has been entrusted with the document then effects service to the party by means available pursuant to the laws and regulations of that country. Theoretically, the service process effected between Contracting States pursuant to the 1965 Hague Convention should be reasonably speedy. In reality however, it may take months for the documents to be serviced to the relevant party.

[B] Obtaining Evidence Abroad

Korea is a signatory to the Hague Convention on the Taking of Evidence Abroad in Civil or Commercial Matters ('1970 Hague Convention'). Bilateral treaties regarding judicial assistance in civil and commercial matters with Uzbekistan, Mongolia, China, and Australia also deal with the taking of evidence for civil and commercial matters within these respective countries. The Judicial Assistance Act is applied when taking evidence in foreign countries that are not signatories to any of the above treaties.

When Korea acceded to the 1970 Hague Convention in 2009, it made reservations regarding the language of the Letters of Request pursuant to paragraph 2 of Article 4 and Article 33 of the Convention, so that it will only accept Letters of Request in Korean or English. Korea pointed out in its reservation that the execution of Letters of Request that are not accompanied by a translation into Korean would take longer than that of Letters of Request with a Korean translation. Korea will accept Letters of Request in

---

21. Korea has also made reservations pursuant to Article 15 of the 1965 Hague Convention, thereby allowing a Korean judge to render judgment even if no certificate of service or delivery has been received, insofar as all of the following conditions have been fulfilled:
    a) The document was transmitted by one of the methods provided for in the 1965 Hague Convention
    b) A period of time not less than six months, considered adequate by the judge in the particular case, has elapsed since the date of the transmission of the document,
    c) No certificate of any kind has been received, even though every reasonable effort has been made to obtain it through the competent authorities of the State addressed.
22. Australia is an exception to this process. According to the Treaty on Judicial Assistance in Civil and Commercial Matters between the Republic of Korea and Australia, the National Court Administration sends documents directly to the Central Authority of Australia, which is the Attorney General's Department.

Korean only from Contracting States that do not accept Letters of Request in Korean or English.

Korea has also made reservations for the application of Articles 16 (taking of evidence by a diplomatic officer or a consular agent of another Contracting State) and 17 (taking of evidence by a person duly appointed as commissioner for the purpose in the territory of a Contracting State in aid of proceedings commenced in the courts of another Contracting State).

Korea has designated the National Court Administration as the Central Authority under the 1970 Hague Convention which will undertake to receive Letters of Request coming from a judicial authority of another Contracting State and to transmit them to the authority competent to execute them.

When a witness is located outside Korea, he/she cannot be summoned by the Korean court. Therefore, unless the witness comes forward voluntarily, evidence can be obtained from the witness by written inquiries or witness statements. The witness is not required to take an oath when providing evidence by written inquiry or a witness statement. According to Article 341(1) of the Korean Civil Procedural Code, the court may request examination by an expert that must be a public institution of a foreign country. The court may order the party who is outside Korea to submit certain documents, but the court may not order a third party outside Korea to submit certain documents.

[C] Restraint of Foreign Proceedings

Anti-suit injunctions and anti-arbitration injunctions are not recognised in Korea.

[D] Proof of Foreign Public Documents

According to Article 356 of the Korean Civil Procedural Code, a document is presumed to be an authentic public document if that document can be recognised as a document prepared by a public official in the course of performing his duty, based on the way the document was drafted and the purpose of the said document. Foreign public documents are treated in the same way, provided that it was acknowledged that the foreign public document was created by the foreign public institution in the course of its duty. If in doubt, the Korean civil court can inquire about the authenticity of the foreign document to the foreign public institution, but the foreign public institution is not obliged to reply. Therefore, in order for the parties to prove that the foreign document was created by the foreign public institution in the course of its duty, legalisation is often used.

On 14 July 2007, the Convention of 5 October 1961 Abolishing the Requirement of Legalisation for Foreign Public Documents ('Apostille Convention') entered into force in Korea. Therefore, Korea does not require the public documents executed in another Member State to be legalised in order to acknowledge it as a public document. However, legalisation is still required for public documents executed in foreign countries that are not signatories to the Apostille Convention. In this case, legalisation must be made by a Korean consulate located in that foreign country.

All foreign documents submitted to court must be translated into Korean.

[E] Statute of Limitations

Limitation periods are determined according to the law applicable to the dispute.

In a case before the Busan High Court, the court ruled that the law applicable to the dispute arising out of a contract between a German company and a Russian company was Russian law. Applying the statutes of limitations under Russian law, and not the statutes of limitations under Korean law, the court ruled that the limitation period had run out.[23]

[F] Remedies and Damages

Remedies and damages are determined according to the law applicable to the dispute, but the scope of remedies and damages that can be awarded to the injured party can be limited in certain cases.

There is no provision in the PIA that applies to remedies and damages in general. Therefore, the law applicable to the dispute will be determined by the underlying legal action that forms the basis of the claim for remedies and damages.

When the request for remedies and damages result from a contractual claim, the applicable law is the law of the country which is the most closely connected to the contract, unless the parties have agreed otherwise. As seen in section 5.03[B], there are some limitations in the law that the parties to certain consumer or employment contracts may choose.

When the request for remedies and damages results from a tort claim, the applicable law is the law of the place where the tortious act occurred (Article 32(1) of the PIA). If the habitual residences of the tortfeasor and the injured party are located in the same country at the time the tort occurred, the law of that country shall be the applicable law, regardless of the place where the tort occurred (Article 32(2) of the PIA). Furthermore, if the tortious act impacted upon a pre-existing legal relationship between the tortfeasor and the injured party, the law applicable to that legal relationship shall apply irrespective of the place where the tort occurred and the habitual residences of the party (Article 32(3) of the PIA). There is a certain limit to applying foreign law in determining the scope of damages, as was shown in section 5.03[B][2] above. Korean courts do not recognise punitive damages or treble damages provided for by Article 4 of the 1914 Clayton Act or Article 1964 of the RICO-Act.[24]

---

23. Busan High Court 99*na*5033 rendered on 2 Feb. 2001.
24. Similarly, a foreign judgment awarding punitive damages or treble damages to the injured party shall not be recognised in Korea on grounds that it is contrary to public policy. This does not mean that the judgment will be denied recognition in full, but just the portion that exceeds the usual amount of damages. See Seoul Eastern District Court case 93*gahap*19069 rendered on 10 Feb. 1995. This principle has been further affirmed by the recent amendment to the Korean Civil

[G] Foreign Currency Obligations

Claims in foreign currency are recognised in Korea. According to Article 377(1) of the Korean Civil Code, if a contract provides for payment to be made in a foreign currency, the obligor may make payment with any kind of monies in that foreign currency.

As a practical matter, however, the claimant who files a claim in a foreign currency, must specify the amount of the claim converted into Korean won and the currency rate that is applied. This is for the convenience of the courts, since the amount of the stamp fees and other legal costs incurred for processing a claim in the Korean courts, which are paid in Korean won, is determined according to the claimed amount.

[H] Restraining Removal of Assets and Securing Evidence in Favour of a Foreign Arbitration/Judicial Process

It is possible to restrain the removal of assets in favour of a foreign arbitration/judicial process by applying for a provisional seizure of the assets or a provisional injunction preventing the owner, or the person in possession of the assets, from transferring or in any way disposing of the assets.

In order to be granted such measure, the applicant must show good cause, i.e., the likelihood of success on merits and the urgent need for such measure. Although the degree of evidence required in such cases is not as high as that required in the case on the merits, the applicant must still be able to provide the court with sufficient grounds to persuade it that he has relatively high chances of winning, and also that there is a risk that without the requested measure, the assets may disappear.

When the court issues an order for provisional seizure or provisional injunction, it is common practice for the court to order the applicant to post a certain amount of security in cash or in surety bonds. If the applicant is a foreign entity without any substantial connection to Korea, the court may request the security to be paid partly or entirely in cash.

Anton Piller orders are not provided for in Korea.

§5.05 RECOGNITION AND ENFORCEMENT OF FOREIGN DECISIONS

[A] Judicial Decisions: Requirements and Limitations

Judicial decisions may be recognised in Korea pursuant to Article 217 of the Korean Civil Procedural Code when the following requirements are met: (i) the foreign judgment must be final; (ii) the foreign judgment must have been rendered by a

Procedural Code. Article 217-2 was added and its first paragraph states that 'the court shall not recognise, in whole or in part, a finalised judgment awarding damages if the said judgment significantly goes against the Korean law or basic order of international treaties to which Korea is a party'.

competent court; (iii) the defendant must have been provided with an opportunity to defend himself; (iv) the recognition must not be contrary to Korean public policy; (v) and the country where the judgment was rendered must provide reciprocity with respect to enforcement of Korean judgments.

In the case of foreign insolvency proceedings, the Korean Debtor Rehabilitation and Bankruptcy Act, which adopted the UNCITRAL Model Law on Cross-Border Insolvency, provides a separate set of rules regarding recognition. According to Article 631 of the Korean Debtor Rehabilitation and Bankruptcy Act, the representative of a foreign insolvency proceeding may file an application for recognition of the foreign proceeding with the Korean court by submitting relevant documents, including: (i) a statement describing the general process and legal basis of the foreign proceeding; (ii) a document proving the commencement of the foreign proceeding; (iii) a document proving the qualification and authority of the representative of the foreign insolvency proceeding; and (iv) a statement describing the main points of application for the foreign insolvency proceeding including descriptions regarding creditors, debtors and interested parties to the proceeding.

[B] Arbitral Awards (Including ICSID Awards): Requirements and Limitations

Korea is a party to the 1958 New York Convention on the Recognition and Enforcement of Foreign Arbitral Awards (hereinafter 'New York Convention'), to the 1966 Convention on the Settlement of Investment Disputes between States and Nationals of Other States (hereinafter 'ICSID Convention') and to the ASEAN-Korea Investment Agreement.

Therefore, foreign arbitral awards, including ICSID awards that are subject to these Conventions, may be recognised and enforced in Korea in accordance with these Conventions.

§5.06 RECOGNITION OF OTHER FOREIGN PUBLIC DOCUMENTS

Foreign public documents may be recognised in Korea as public documents pursuant to Article 356 of the Korean Civil Procedural Code, as mentioned above.

However, foreign deeds and extrajudicial public documents cannot be directly enforced in Korea and a lawsuit must be initiated in the Korea court, but the existence of the foreign deed or extrajudicial public document would be prevailing evidence in the lawsuit. Public documents executed in a foreign country are recognised in Korea through: (i) the *apostille* process, if the document was executed in a country that is a signatory to the Apostille Convention; or (ii) legalisation by a Korean Consulate in the relevant country, if the document was executed in a country that is not a signatory to the Apostille Convention.

§5.07 TREATIES FOR JUDICIAL COOPERATION

Korea is a party to the following list of bilateral treaties:

- Treaty on Judicial Assistance in Civil and Commercial Matters between the Republic of Korea and the Republic of Uzbekistan.
- Treaty on Judicial Assistance in Civil and Commercial Matters between the Republic of Korea and Mongolia.
- Treaty between the Republic of Korea and the People's Republic of China on Judicial Assistance in Civil and Commercial Matters.
- Treaty on Judicial Assistance in Civil and Commercial Matters between the Republic of Korea and Australia.

Apart from the already mentioned Hague Conventions, Korea is also a party to the Convention on Civil Aspects of International Child Abduction, which provides for certain judicial cooperation to secure the prompt return of children and to achieve other objects of the Convention.

CHAPTER 6
Macau

*Jorge Menezes**

§6.01 CODIFICATION OF PRIVATE INTERNATIONAL LAW AND RELEVANCE OF CASE LAW

[A] Codification and Case Law

The legal system of Macau is very similar to the Portuguese law that was in effect in 1999, when the Government of the People's Republic of China took over the exercise of sovereignty over the Territory. It is, therefore, part of the Roman-Germanic, or civil law, system. The main source of law in Macau is therefore written law, essentially codified.

Macau is an autonomous region of China and has, therefore, a complex, territorially based legal system, which establishes rules of conflict, whether international or interlocal. Hence the legal designation of 'external jurisdiction' to situations that are commonly designated as 'international jurisdiction' (e.g., Hong Kong thus constitutes an external legal system belonging to the same country).

Despite the existence of international and interlocal sources, Macau Private International Law has a mainly domestic origin. Private International Law rules regarding the law applicable to transnational situations (conflict of laws) are codified in Articles 13–62 of the Macau Civil Code (MCC). It is, by comparison with the common substantive law of Macau, a special substantive law applicable to plurilocal situations.

* Partner at Legal Macau. He has practiced law for 20 years in Portugal and Macau. He has worked as a legal advisor for the Macau Government (Legislative Affairs Office), both before and after the handover. Jorge is also qualified as a Private Notary in Macau and lectured law subjects at universities in Lisbon, Guinea-Bissau and Oxford. He would like to thank João Redinha for his contribution and advice on relevant sections of this chapter.

Private International Law rules are also contained in the Law of Recognition (Articles 1199–1205 of the Macau Civil Procedure Code, MCPC), which regulates the recognition of foreign judgments; and in the Law of International and External Jurisdiction of the Courts of Macau (Articles 15–20 and 29 of the MCPC).

As Macau has a civil law system, judicial decisions do not constitute binding precedents. The decisions of the courts of appeal have, however, great persuasive value. In this regard it is relevant to note that there is only one Court of Appeal, with nine judges, and one Court of Final Appeal, with just three judges, which generates relatively uniform decisions.

There is no legislation project underway to amend the rules of Private International Law in force in Macau, and the legal community has not signalled the need for such amendment.

[B] Multilateral Conventions Providing Uniform Substantive Law and/or International Jurisdictional Rules

Article 13 of the 'Basic Law' states that the Central Government of China is responsible for the foreign affairs relating to the Macau Special Administrative Region. Nevertheless, according to Article 136 of the Basic Law, Macau can conclude some international agreements. Furthermore, Article 138 of the Basic Law states that Macau has to be consulted before international agreements to which China is a party are extended to Macau and provides that with the authorisation of the Central Government of China, international agreements to which China is not a party may also continue to apply in Macau.[1]

The following conventions apply in Macau:[2] the 1910 and 1952 International conventions for the unification of certain rules of law relating to Collision between vessels; the 1924 International Convention for the Unification of Certain Rules of Law relating to Bills of Lading; the 1929 and 1999 Conventions for the Unification of Certain Rules relating to International Carriage by Air; the 1930 Convention Providing a Uniform Law for Bills of Exchange and Promissory Notes; the 1930 Convention for the Settlement of Certain Conflicts of Laws in Connection with Bills of Exchange and Promissory Notes (and Protocol); the 1931 Convention Providing a Uniform Law for Cheques (Annexes and Protocol); the 1931 Convention for the Settlement of Certain Conflicts of Laws in Connection with Cheques (and Protocol); the 1948 Convention on the International Recognition of Rights in Aircraft; the 1952 International convention for the unification of certain rules relating to Arrest of sea-going ships; and the 1957 International convention relating to the Limitation of the liability of owners of sea-going ships. In addition, several treaties administered by the World Intellectual Property Organization (WIPO) are applicable in Macau.[3]

1. http://www.dsrjdi.ccrj.gov.mo/en/tratadospt.asp.
2. For a more detailed list, see http://yearbook.gcs.gov.mo/files/yearbook/2014/myb2014eAP11.pdf.
3. https://www.economia.gov.mo/en/web/public/pg_ip_it.

§6.02 JURISDICTION OF LOCAL COURTS IN FOREIGN-RELATED CASES

[A] Grounds for Jurisdiction

[1] General

The rules regarding the Macau courts' external jurisdiction are defined in Articles 15-17 of the MCPC. All these rules have to be interpreted as part of the Macau legal system and, therefore, according to its own rules.

Article 15 of the MCPC establishes general jurisdiction based on three criteria or principles:

- The criterion of *causality*: which applies when the fact or any of the facts that form the basis for the action have taken place in Macau.
- The criterion of *reciprocity*: which applies when the respondent is a non-resident and the applicant is a resident, provided that the applicant could be sued in an identical action brought by the respondent in the courts of the respondent's place of residence. It is a rule that has been abandoned in many jurisdictions, including the Portuguese, as it is understood to be based on a criterion of retaliation, with a foundation more political than legal, but it remains in force in Macau.
- The criterion of *necessity*: which intervenes when the substantive right cannot be effected except by means of the action proposed in a Macau court and provided that there is a serious element of personal or material connection between the action proposed and Macau. The rule is intended to prevent the right being unprotected. The inability to effect the right in a different jurisdiction may be either legal or factual. With regard to the aforementioned elements of connection, the elements most frequently invoked are those of nationality and of the location of goods.

Article 16 of the MCPC establishes special attribution rules for international or external jurisdiction for certain actions, without prejudice to the general criteria for the attribution of jurisdiction of Article 15. *Inter alia*:

- contractual obligations: when the obligation has to be fulfilled in Macau or if the respondent is domiciled in Macau;
- concerning non-real rights over real estate located in Macau; and
- concerning the forum of domicile or residence, in divorce actions.

Article 17 of the MCPC defines subsidiary criteria, applicable without prejudice to the general criteria set out in Article 15 and where none of the actions provided for in Article 16 are involved. These criteria are -with regard to individuals- the domicile or residence of the respondent in Macau or the domicile or residence of the applicant in Macau, if the defendant is not normally resident or the residence is uncertain or absent; and -with regard to legal entities- the location in Macau of its headquarters or management, or even its branch, agency, subsidiary, or representative.

[2] Exclusive Jurisdiction

There are criteria attributing exclusive jurisdiction to the courts of Macau set out in Article 20 of the MCPC. This concerns only actions relating to real rights over real estate located in Macau and actions to declare legal entities headquartered in Macau bankrupt or insolvent. In these cases, the Macau legal system does not allow the parties to agree to attribute jurisdiction to a foreign court, and does not recognise judgments by foreign courts that considered themselves competent in this regard (Articles 29(3)(d) and 1200(1)(c) of the MCPC).

[B] Exclusion of Jurisdiction

[1] Immunity

[a] *Sovereign Immunity*

In Macau there is no absolute conception of jurisdictional immunity of States. The Macau legal system considers that, as a rule, a foreign State enjoys jurisdictional immunity in respect of acts performed in the exercise of public authority (*iure imperii*). The classification of the act as an act of public authority is according to the rules of Public International Law, which can lead to a different result than that of the Macau domestic law. A State may, moreover, waive this immunity. In particular, the State that entered into an arbitration agreement cannot claim immunity before the arbitral tribunal or before the state court exercising control functions over it.

[b] *Diplomatic and Consular Immunity*

Both the 1961 Vienna Convention on Diplomatic Relations and the 1963 Vienna Convention on Consular Relations apply in Macau.

[c] *Other Immunities*

Both the 1946 Convention on the Privileges and Immunities of the United Nations and the 1947 Convention on the Privileges and Immunities of the Specialised Agencies apply in Macau

[2] Forum Agreements in Favour of Foreign Courts

Article 29 of the MCPC allows, subject to certain requirements being met, forum or jurisdiction agreements curtailing or conferring jurisdiction. The agreement has a curtailing nature when it removes the jurisdiction to hear the action from the Macau courts and attributes it to one or several foreign courts. It is attributive when it confers jurisdiction to the courts of Macau. According to Article 29(2), the agreement can confer to an exterior court exclusive jurisdiction or alternative jurisdiction with the Macau courts, assuming, in case of doubt, that it is alternative.

The requirements, applied cumulatively, for the validity of the forum agreement are set down in Article 29(3)(a)-(e) of the MCPC:

- The forum agreement applies to 'disposable rights' (rights that can be disposed of or waived by the will of the parties) and is not contrary to the Macau courts' exclusive jurisdiction rules, established in Article 20 of the MCPC.
- The attribution of the forum is accepted by the law of the designated court.
- The attribution is justified by a serious interest of one or both of the parties, in the former case not involving a significant inconvenience to the other party. This rule serves to safeguard the position of the weaker party.
- The agreement is in writing, expressly mentioning the attributed jurisdiction.

[3] Arbitration Clause

According to Article 8 of Decree-Law no. 55/98/M, of 23 November, a court of Macau before which an action is brought in a matter which is the subject of a valid and operative arbitration agreement shall, if a party so requests before submitting his first statement on the substance, refer the parties to arbitration. Arbitral proceedings may nevertheless be commenced or continued, and an award may be made, while the issue is pending before the court.

[C] Non-exercise of Jurisdiction

[1] Forum Non Conveniens

The forum non conveniens doctrine, justified by the flexible criteria for determining international jurisdiction that prevail in common law systems, is not used in the Macau legal system. In the Macau legal system, as in most civil law systems, the legal criteria for determining jurisdiction result from exact rules, and the rules concerning agreements are limited by the need to correspond to a serious interest of a party or of both parties, provided that in the former case it does not involve any significant inconvenience to the other party (Article 29(3)(c) of the MCPC, aforementioned).

[2] **Lis alibi pendens**

In Macau, local judicial proceedings cannot be stopped because there are ongoing foreign proceedings on the same matter and parties. Article 416(3) of the MCPC establishes that the fact that a case is pending in a jurisdiction external to Macau is irrelevant, unless another solution was established by international treaty or by agreement on judicial cooperation. But there is no such treaty or agreement applicable in Macau.

§6.03 APPLICABLE LAW

Macau's conflict of laws rules are statutory, derived from the Civil Code approved in 1999, just before the handover. Macau's conflict of laws system closely follows that of Portugal, which has been in place since 1966 (save for international agreements that Portugal is party to), but developed and adapted to Macau's specific circumstances.

Macau is not an independent political entity or sovereign state, but an autonomous region of the People's Republic of China (PRC). Therefore, and although having a fully autonomous legal system, it is in a particular way part of a pluralistic or composite legal system. This peculiarity justifies the use of the concept of *residence* instead of *nationality*, as the latter does not exist as such in Macau. The notion of citizenship is expressed under the surrogate legal concept of residency, which delimits the sphere of those whom the law in principle addresses. This distinctiveness is noticeable not only regarding connecting factors, but also in the first provision of the conflict of laws chapter of the Civil Code (Article 13), which addresses the legal status of 'non-residents' (as opposed to 'foreigners'). This provision establishes the general principle that non-residents enjoy the same civil rights as Macau residents, except where a legal provision states differently. For these purposes, Chinese nationality is immaterial, as the operative concept is that of Macau residency.

For similar reasons, the conflict of laws rules use the phrase 'external law' instead of 'foreign law' in reference to the laws of other legal systems within the PRC, since they are laws of the same sovereign state (Articles 15, 20, 21, and 22 of the MCC). In this chapter, however, the phrase 'foreign law' should normally be taken as any law other than the *lex fori*, and therefore as including reference to PRC and Hong Kong law, which cannot, strictly speaking, be considered foreign laws.

The attribution of competence to foreign law only covers rules that, by virtue of their content and the role they play in the foreign legal system, correspond to the rules of the legal institution or concept referred to in Macau's conflict of laws rules (Article 14 of the MCC). This refers to the classification or characterisation (named 'qualification' by the MCC) stage of the conflict process.

[A] Choice of Law

In some limited domains specified by the conflict of laws rules, the parties are at liberty to choose the applicable law, either by express stipulation or implied choice. Once this choice has been made, choice of law rules and *renvoi* do not apply (Article 17(2) of the MCC).

Choice of law is allowed in voluntary transactions or contracts, although limited in the terms referred to below, as well as in the interpretation of wills or agreements as to the succession (Articles 40 and 61(a) of the MCC). Moreover, international organisations are free to have their personal law designated in the conventions creating them or in their Articles (Article 32 of the MCC). Finally, as noted below, Article 51(3) of the MCC allows for a limited freedom regarding the choice of law governing the matrimonial regimes under Macau law.

[B] Other Cases

Where the parties do not choose the applicable law, subsidiary connecting factors apply.

[1] Personal Law

The status, capacity, family relations, and succession of natural persons, as well as the beginning and extinction of legal personality, rights of personality, and guardianship are governed by the personal law of the individual (Articles 24, 25, 26, and 29 of the MCC). However, Article 26(2) of the MCC establishes that a non-resident does not benefit from any legal protection in Macau that is not acknowledged by the local law. In accordance with Article 28 of the MCC, changing one's personal law does not affect majority or emancipation acquired in accordance with one's prior personal law.

Similarly, the capacity, formation, operation, and authority of the organs of a legal person, as well as the acquisition and relinquishing of the position of partner or shareholder, its rights and obligations, liability and its transformation, dissolution and extinction, are governed by the personal law of the legal person (Article 31 of the MCC).

The personal law of natural persons is that of their habitual residence (and not that of nationality as, for the reasons stated, Macau law would never be directly applicable in personal matters), which is the place where the persons have the actual and stable centre of their personal life. For an individual to be deemed a habitual resident in Macau, no administrative formality is required, but those entitled to Macau resident identity cards are presumed habitual residents. If an individual has more than one habitual residence, one being in Macau, the personal law is the law of Macau; where an individual has no habitual residence, the personal law is the law of the place with which the individual's personal life is most closely connected. Regarding transactions undertaken abroad, the governing law is that of the country of the nationality of those concerned, provided that it considers itself applicable. The relevance of nationality is, however, disregarded, and this rule no longer applies if the person in question is a national of a country with a composite legal system and has habitual residence in that country, in which case the connecting element of habitual residence has primacy, provided that the law of the person's habitual residence considers itself the governing law (Article 30 of the MCC).

The personal law of a legal person is the law of the place where its principal and effective headquarters is located. If it transfers its principal and effective headquarters to a place with a different legal system, its legal personality is not extinguished, if both legal systems so determine. Similarly, the merging of entities with different personal laws is subject to both personal laws (Article 31 of the MCC).

Articles 27 and 33 of the MCC set forth some specific rules deviating from the principle that capacity issues of both natural and legal persons are governed by the personal law. These articles hold, except for a specified category of cases, as valid a transaction that would have been considered as invalid by the personal law on the basis of incapacity, if the law of the place where the transactions was executed considers it valid.

*[2] Transactions (**negócio jurídico**)*

Articles 34-39 of the MCC designate the applicable law concerning a transaction (*negócio jurídico*), that is, a declaration intended to have legal effect. The completion, interpretation, and gap-filling of a declaration and the lack or defects of consent are governed by the law applicable to the substance of the transaction (to be designated by the respective choice of law rules). The issue of whether silence or non-verbal conduct shall be deemed to be legally binding (implied-in-fact agreement) is governed by the law of the common habitual residence of the persons who make and who accept the offer, in the absence of which the situation is governed by the law of the place where the conduct took place (regarding conduct) or where the offer was received (regarding silence) (Article 34 of the MCC).

According to Article 35 of the MCC, the form of the declaration is also governed by the law applicable to the substance of the transaction. The observance of the law of the place where the declaration was made, or of the law referred to by the latter's choice of law rules is, however, sufficient (unless the law of the substance of the transaction requires a specific form even for transactions entered into abroad).

The law applicable to legal representation governs the legal relationship from which representative authority is derived (Article 36 of the MCC), and the representation of legal persons by its governing bodies is governed by the legal person's personal law (Article 37 of the MCC). Voluntary or contractual representation is governed by the law of the place where the representative's authority is effected, except if the representative uses its powers in a country or territory different from the one specified by the principal, and the third (contracting) party is aware of this, in which case the law of the principal's normal residence prevails. If the representative acts in a professional capacity, and the third (contracting) party is aware of this, the law of the representative's professional domicile applies. If the representation pertains to the transfer or administration of real estate, the law of the location of the real estate applies (Article 38 of the MCC).

[3] Obligations

This section covers obligations derived from contracts, *negotiorum gestio*, unjust enrichment, and tort (including delict, risk, and strict liability). Obligations arising from a *negócio jurídico*, that is, voluntary obligations such as contracts, are governed by the law designated or envisaged by the parties, that is, by an express or implicit choice of law. This freedom of choice is limited, as the parties can only designate a law whose application fulfils a serious interest of the contractors or that contains one of the connecting elements within the pertaining Macau conflict of laws rules (Article 40 of the MCC). In the absence of a choice of law by the parties, the law of the place with the closest connection to the transaction shall apply (Article 41 of the MCC).

Negotiorum gestio, or uncommissioned agency, is governed by the law of the place where the main activity of the uncommissioned agent takes place, and unjust enrichment, on the other hand, is governed by the law under which the transfer of the asset to the enriched person took place (Articles 42 and 43 of the MCC). Tort (including delict, risk, and strict liability) is governed by the law of the place where the principal conduct causing the damage occurred or, in the case of omission, where the liable person should have acted. In the case where the tortfeasor is considered liable by the law where the injury occurred but not by the law of the place of action, the former law applies if the tortfeasor should have foreseen the occurrence of damages, in accordance with the law where injury occurred, as a consequence of the action or omission (however, the law does not specify according to which law the said foreseeability should be determined). Furthermore, when the tortfeasor and the injured party normally have the same habitual residence, but happen to be occasionally abroad, the law of their common habitual residence is applicable. As a consequence of the doctrine of mandatory rules, however, it the situation shall be governed by the provisions of the law designated in accordance with the above two sentences where they stipulate that these provisions shall be applied to everyone, without distinction (Article 44 of the MCC).

[4] Property and Copyright

Possession, ownership, and other real rights regarding immovable or movable property are governed by the *lex situs* (Article 45 of the MCC). *Lex situs* also governs the capacity to acquire or transfer real rights in immovable property as long as the *lex situs* so determines; where it does not, the personal law applies (Article 46 of the MCC). In particular, according to paragraphs 2 and 3 of Article 45 of the MCC, the acquisition or transfer of goods in transit is governed by the law of the place of destination, and the acquisition and transfer of means of transportation subject to registration is governed by the law of the place where the means of transportation is registered.

Copyright and related rights, as well as industrial property rights, either of domestic or international origin, are governed by the law of the place where their protection is claimed.

[5] Family Relationships and Cohabitation

The capacity to marry and to enter into marriage contracts, as well as matters of validity or lack of consent, are governed by the personal law of each betrothed (Article 48 of the MCC). The law applicable to the form of marriage is that of the place where the marriage is undertaken. Two foreigners can, however, marry before their respective consular agent in accordance with the formal requirements of the law of the nationality of either party, which is a manifestation of the principle of *favor negotii* (Article 49 of the MCC). There is no Macau consulate abroad, and there is no legal provision regulating marriage of Macau residents abroad under the formalities of Macau law, and therefore Article 49 does not constitute a reciprocity requirement.

The relationship between spouses is governed by the law of their common habitual residence or, in the absence of a common habitual residence, by the law of the place with which the family is most closely connected (Article 50 of the MCC), which is also the case for divorce (Article 53 of the MCC), postnuptial contracts, and modifications to the matrimonial property regime (Article 52 of the MCC). The matrimonial property regime and prenuptial contracts are regulated by the law of the common habitual residence at the time of the marriage, in the absence of which the situation shall be governed by the law of the first conjugal residence. The law allows the parties to agree on one of the matrimonial regimes in place under Macau law, even where Macau law would not otherwise be the applicable law, provided that one of the spouses is a habitual resident in Macau (Article 51 of the MCC).

The requirements and legal effects of cohabitation are governed by the law of the common residence of the cohabitees and, in its absence, by the law of the place with which the situation is most closely connected (Article 57 of the MCC).

The establishment of filiation is governed by the personal law of the parent at the time when the relationship is established (Article 54 of the MCC). The same rule applies to adoption. However, where husband and wife, or cohabitants are the adopters or the adoptee is the child of the adopter's spouse or cohabitator, the establishment of adoption shall be governed by the law of the spouses or cohabitators' common habitual residence and, in its absence, by the law of the place most closely connected with the family life of the adopters (Articles 54 and 56 of the MCC). If the personal law of the child to be recognised or adopted requires the consent of the child, this requirement shall be respected, which results in the cumulative application of two laws: the law designated in Article 54 or 56 of the MCC and the personal law of the child (Article 57 of the MCC).

The parent-child relationship, including that of adoption, is governed by the law of the common habitual residence of the parents and, in its absence, by the personal law of the child. If the filiation is established regarding only one parent, the relationship is governed by the personal law of the parent or, if one of them is deceased, by the personal law of the survivor. The relationship between the adoptee and the biological family is also regulated by the personal law of the adopter or adopters in the terms referred to in the preceding sentence (Articles 55 and 56 of the MCC).

[6] Succession

Succession on death and the powers of the administrator of the estate and the executor of the will are governed by the personal law of the deceased at the time of death (Article 59 of the MCC). The capacity to make, modify, or revoke any disposition upon death, as well as the special formal requirements for dispositions by virtue of the disposing party's age are subject to the personal law of the party at the time the declaration. If a person acquires a new personal law after having made a disposition, the capacity necessary to revoke it in accordance with the previous law is retained (Article 60 of the MCC).

The interpretation of provisions and dispositions is governed by the law designated by express stipulation or implied choice of the deceased, in the absence of which the applicable law is the personal law of the deceased at the time the declaration was made. The personal law also governs lack or defect of will, as well as the admissibility of joint wills (not admissible under Macau's substantive law) and succession agreements (Article 61 of the MCC).

Regarding the formal validity of dispositions upon death, Macau law states an alternative choice of law rule fostering *favor negotii*: dispositions, their revocation, and modification are formally valid if they fulfil the requirements of the law of the place where the act was carried out (local law), the law referred to by the choice of law rules of the local law, or the personal law of the deceased at the time the declaration was made or at the time of death (Article 62 of the MCC).

[C] *Renvoi*

The *general principle* is that reference in the conflict of laws rules to any foreign law determines the application of the substantive provisions of that system of law if there is no Macau rule stipulating otherwise (Article 15 of the MCC).

In order to attain international uniformity, *renvoi* is allowed in two situations. First, where the conflict of laws rules of the foreign law selected refer (directly or through the conflict of laws rules from yet another country) to the law of another jurisdiction that considers itself the competent law, the latter's substantive provisions apply (Article 16(1) of the MCC). Second, where the conflict of laws rules of the foreign law selected refer back (directly or through the conflict of laws rules from yet another country) to Macau substantive provisions, the case shall be governed by Macau law (Article 16(2) of the MCC).

However, in order to uphold the principle of the *favor negotii*, *renvoi* is excluded whenever it leads to the invalidity or unenforceability of a transaction, or to the lack of legitimacy or standing that would otherwise not be the case (Article 17(1) of the MCC). In these cases, the goal of upholding the validity of contracts has priority over that of international uniformity. Moreover, where free choice of law is allowed (Articles 32, 40 and 61 of the MCC), *renvoi* rules do not apply if the foreign law has been nominated by the parties, a consequence of the specific nature of free choice as a connecting factor (Article 17(2) of the MCC). In all these cases, Article 16 of the MCC applies and the dispute is governed by the substantive provisions of the legal system designated by the Macau conflict of laws rules.

There are also rules where the principle of the *favor negotii* acts as a specific and autonomous source of *renvoi*, referring to another legal system (even if it does consider itself the competent law) where the formal validity of a transaction or declaration intended to have legal effect is upheld (Articles 35(1) and 65(1) of the MCC).

Where the conflict of laws rules refer to a pluralistic or composite legal system and the specific or sub-legal system applicable is not designated, the competent legal system is determined in accordance with the criteria followed in that jurisdiction (Article 18(1) of the MCC). Where such criteria prove to be ineffective, the court applies the law of the sub-legal system with the greatest connection to the cause of action (Article 18(2) of the MCC).

[D] Mandatory Rules of the Forum and of Third States

Pursuant to Article 21 of the MCC ('rules of immediate application'), substantive rules of Macau, which by virtue of their specific scope and purpose are mandatorily applied, prevail over the provisions of the foreign law designated by the choice of law rules. There is no specific provision regarding mandatory rules of third States.

[E] Proof of Foreign Law

The Macau legal system treats foreign law as law, not as fact, and its application is not subject to a burden of proof, but instead to cooperation efforts between the parties and the judge. Although the parties are supposed to play an active role, the judge investigates the content and application of foreign law independently, whether or not the application of foreign law has been pleaded and evidence submitted by the parties. This applies even to situations where the opposing party has acknowledged, or not opposed, its existence and content. The law does not require any specific type of evidence, and therefore the parties or the judge may use any appropriate kind of evidence (e.g., expert testimony or documentary evidence, including practising lawyers and academics' legal opinions). The judge is also required to consider the applicability of conflict of laws rules, even if neither party invokes the private international nature of the dispute or pleads the applicability of foreign law.

If it does not prove possible to ascertain the content of the otherwise applicable foreign law, the court refers to subsidiary connecting factors established in conflict of laws rules (e.g., Article 30(5) of the MCC). If the relevant rule does not have a subsidiary connecting factor or if it is also not possible to establish the content of the foreign law referred to by the subsidiary connecting factor, recourse shall instead be made to Macau ordinary law (Articles 22 and 341 of the MCC).

Foreign law shall be interpreted and its gaps shall be filled from the viewpoint of the legal system to which it belongs and in accordance with the standards and practices of interpretation therein followed (Article 22 of the MCC).

[F] Evasion of the Law

The doctrine of the evasion of law is enshrined in Article 19 of the MCC, which states that in the application of conflict of laws rules, the situations of fact or of law conceived with the fraudulent intent of avoiding the application of otherwise applicable law are deemed irrelevant. It requires fraudulent intent in successfully evading otherwise applicable mandatory rules, and applies to the evasion of both domestic and foreign law rules. Where the laws are evaded, the sanction consists simply in applying the rules that the fraudulent action sought to avoid.

§6.04 PROCEDURAL ISSUES

Lex fori applies to procedural issues.

[A] Service of Summons and Judicial Orders Abroad

[1] Service Abroad

Regarding service of Macau proceedings abroad, international conventions and bilateral agreements are followed. Where international conventions and bilateral agreements do not apply, service of summons abroad is effected by mail, or when service by mail is not possible, by letter rogatory, as described hereinafter (Article 193 of the MCPC). Service of judicial orders abroad follows the same doctrine (Articles 200(2), 202, and 203 of the MCPC).

The Hague Service Convention applies in Macau, and there is a bilateral agreement in force since 15 September 2001 between Macau and mainland China on the Service Abroad of Judicial Documents and on the Taking of Evidence in Civil or Commercial Matters. There is no other bilateral agreement in this field.

According to a declaration made by the People's Republic of China (PRC), the documents to be served in Macau under Article 5(1) of the Hague Convention must be written, or be accompanied by a translation, in either Chinese or Portuguese. No objection was made to the methods of direct service mentioned in Article 10 of the Service Convention. The average time required for performance of requests for service in Macau is around one month and can go up to five months.

With effect from the reunification of Macau and China on 20 December 1999, the Service Convention has ceased to apply to service between Macau and mainland China or Hong Kong, as the Convention only applies between State parties, and Macau (like Hong Kong) is now a special region of the PRC. Even regarding service effected in Mainland China *before* the 1999 transfer of sovereignty, the Court of Second Instance stated that 'there are still doubts on whether [the Convention] is applicable to acts between Macau and China' as Macau was a Chinese territory under Portuguese Administration.[4] This is no longer the case since the transfer of sovereignty, as the abovementioned 15 September 2001 bilateral agreement with mainland China indicates. However, in a 7 March 2013 judgment issued by the Macau Court of Second Instance[5] on an appeal regarding the validity of service of Macau legal proceedings in Hong Kong by mail, the Court stated that the Convention is applicable to service between Macau and Hong Kong. The issue was apparently not raised by the parties, the Court did not provide reasons or discuss the matter, the comment was not central to the case, and the judgment does not set a precedent. Therefore, it is still the case that the Service Convention does not apply to service effected in mainland China or in Hong Kong.

4. Case no. TSI-A-73-2006-VP, 3 Mar. 2007.
5. Case no. TSI-A-808-2012.

The 15 September 2001 bilateral agreement determines that if one party requests service in the other party's jurisdiction, it will be effected through the courts in accordance with the rules of the served party's jurisdiction, except if the requesting party requests the observance of certain formalities that do not conflict with the other party's laws. Service is undertaken in Chinese (including the documents to be served), within two months. Service can only be refused if it violates the fundamental principles or the public order of the other party. Exclusive jurisdiction and lack of merit of the claim are not valid reasons to refuse service. Service in Mainland China by mail pursuant to Article 193 of the MCPC not effected under the Macau-China bilateral agreement should still be considered valid in Macau proceedings, as the agreement's goal is that of facilitating service and not of imposing a requirement.

The Civil Procedure Code establishes that, in the absence of international conventions or bilateral agreements, service abroad (including in Hong Kong) is made by registered letter with acknowledgment of receipt. The notice is signed by the addressee of the service or by the postal official, according to the local regulation of the postal services. If service by mail is not possible or was frustrated, service is by letter rogatory. If the addressee is absent in an unknown location, service will then be effected through publication (Article 193 of the MCPC).

In summary, the Service Convention governs service in all countries that are parties to the Convention, service in China is governed by the 15 September 2001 bilateral agreement, and service in Hong Kong and all countries that are not parties to the Service Convention is effected by registered mail, as described in the previous paragraph.

[2] Service of Foreign Proceedings in Macau

Service of foreign proceedings in Macau follows international conventions (the 1965 Hague Service Convention) or bilateral agreements (the 15 September 2001 agreement with Mainland China), as mentioned in the previous section. Otherwise, and since this topic is not specifically regulated in Macau's domestic law, the foreign court can effect service as it sees fit, in accordance with its own law, by letter rogatory or by direct means, such as mail or Macau legal counsel (legal counsels are also authorised to serve summons in domestic proceedings).

If the foreign court chooses to request service by letter rogatory, the Public Prosecutor is responsible for advancing its terms, but the court is responsible for the fulfilment. The Public Prosecutor may oppose the fulfilment of the letter rogatory on grounds of public interest: the judge will then decide whether it shall be fulfilled or not, against which the Public Prosecutor can lodge an appeal (Article 134 of the MCPC). The judge observes the formalities requested in the letter rogatory by the foreign court as long as they do not conflict with the laws of Macau (Article 135 of the MCPC).

Unless otherwise provided in international convention or agreement, the court shall refuse to execute the letter rogatory if:

- it does not have the jurisdiction to effect the act requested, if the request is for an act that Macau law forbids absolutely;

- the act is contrary to public policy;
- the act involves execution of a decision by a court or arbitrator from outside Macau that is not reviewed and confirmed, where the law so requires; and
- there are any doubts about the authenticity of the letter rogatory (Article 136 of the MCPC).

The domestic law does not require that letters rogatory for service of summons be translated into Chinese or Portuguese (the general requirement found in Article 89 of the MCPC that acts should be undertaken in one of the two official languages applies only to domestic proceedings); hence the courts have discretion on whether to order service in a foreign language or not (this is not the case regarding service effected in Macau under the Service Convention, which shall be written, or be accompanied by a translation, in either Chinese or Portuguese, according to a declaration made by the PRC to Article 5(1) of the Hague Convention).

[B] Obtaining Evidence Abroad

Unless otherwise provided by an international convention or bilateral agreement, evidence abroad is obtained through letter rogatory, as is the case with any other request for procedural acts requiring the intervention of courts or other authorities outside Macau (Articles 126(1), 130(1), 481, 505(2), and 524 of the MCPC). The letter is sent directly to the foreign court or authority (except where it is otherwise provided by an international convention or bilateral agreement) and the Macau judge specifies the time limit for the foreign authority to comply with the request, although it should normally not be more than three months (Articles 130(1) (2) and 131 of the MCPC). Expert witnesses are deposed in Macau, and not through rogatory letter (Article 495(1) of the MCPC).

The 1970 Hague Convention on the Taking of Evidence Abroad in Civil or Commercial Matters was extended to Macau with effect from 14 December 1999. In accordance with Article 23 of the Convention, the PRC has declared, by letter of notification of 16 December 1999, that Macau will not execute Letters of Request issued for the purpose of obtaining pre-trial discovery of documents.

[C] Restraint of Foreign Proceedings

Macau law does not allow for anti-suit injunctions or court orders halting or restraining foreign proceedings, either arbitral or judicial. Also, as mentioned above, parallel litigation abroad is irrelevant for domestic proceedings (Article 416(3) of the MCPC).

[D] Proof of Foreign Public Documents

The Hague Convention of 5 October 1961 Abolishing the Requirement of Legalisation for Foreign Public Documents (Convention) was extended to Macau with effect from 21 December 1969.

[E] Statute of Limitations

Statutes of limitation are more appropriately known in Macau's legal system as prescription, as this is not classified as a procedural issue, but a substantive one, since the expiration of the applicable period extinguishes the substantive right. Coherently with the substantive nature of the concept, and pursuant to Article 39 of the MCC, the law governing the limitation period is the law that governs the substantive right: the law applicable to the dispute, and not the *lex fori*.

[F] Remedies and Damages

Remedies and damages are generally of a substantive nature and, therefore, to be determined by the law applicable to the dispute. According to the conflict of laws rules, all these issues are governed by the law applicable to the dispute (Articles 40, 41, 43, and 44 of the MCC).

There are interim or precautionary measures, similar to preliminary injunctions, that are of procedural nature, regulated by the Civil Procedure Code, and determined by the *lex fori* (except where they are also covered by the MCC as substantive matters). These include the following preliminary remedies: (a) provisional restitution of possession and use, (b) suspension of corporate resolutions, (c) provisional maintenance or alimony, (d) provisional compensation in death or physical harm suits, (e) seizure orders, (f) stop-work orders, and (g) listing and seizure of assets.

Pursuant to Article 1(2) of the MCPC, it is a fundamental principle of civil procedure that, even if not specifically provided by law, for every substantive right there is a procedural remedy 'appropriate to recognise it in court, to prevent or remedy its violation, and to enforce it coercively, including the steps necessary to safeguard the effectiveness of the action'. This rule applies to foreign law as well: if the foreign law provides the parties with certain substantive rights, the domestic court should ensure that there is a procedural remedy that effectively enforces those rights. If there is no specific remedy in the domestic procedural law to enforce those rights, the judge shall fill the gap in the law by applying or adapting some of the existent remedies of the domestic procedural law.

[G] Foreign Currency Obligations

Foreign currency obligations can be agreed upon by the parties, but as such they do not give rise to symmetrical rights and duties: pursuant to Article 551(1) of the MCC, while the creditor can only demand to be paid in the foreign currency (and not to be paid in the domestic currency), the debtor is endowed with the alternative of paying in the foreign currency or in the domestic currency (Patacas). For this reason, these are known as fictional foreign currency obligations. Where the debtor chooses to pay the foreign obligation in the domestic currency, the exchange rate applicable is the one in force at the time and in the place of effective fulfilment (unless the creditor is in default or temporary breach regarding his performance, in which case the debtor may choose between the date of effective fulfilment or of the creditor's default).

However, the parties may establish in the contract that the debtor waives its legal right to choose to pay in the domestic or in the foreign currency. The latter is known as a proper foreign currency obligation, where both parties are contractually bound to pay and be paid in the foreign currency agreed upon in the contract. Differently from the two cases referred above, the parties can also agree to be paid in an amount corresponding to a certain amount in a foreign currency. This is not a foreign currency obligation, and both parties are contractually bound to pay and be paid in the domestic currency (at the exchange rate in force at the date of fulfilment).

Notwithstanding the above, these are all matters of substantive, not procedural law, and therefore are to be determined by the law applicable to the dispute, and not by the *lex fori*.

[H] Restraining Removal of Assets and Securing Evidence in Favour of a Foreign Arbitration/Judicial Process

There are no specific provisions regarding restraining removal of assets in favour of a foreign process.

§6.05 RECOGNITION AND ENFORCEMENT OF FOREIGN DECISIONS

[A] Judicial Decisions: Requirements and Limitations

Macau has a system of individualised recognition of decisions passed outside of Macau and there is a special procedure, provided for in Articles 1199-1205 of the MCPC, that is common to the reviews of decisions about private-rights handed down by both state and arbitral courts outside Macau. The private-rights nature of the decision is defined by the Macau Law of Recognition. There are questionable situations on whether certain decision are about private-rights, such as the US courts' decisions granting punitive damages (although it is generally understood to have a predominantly private nature).

Essentially, recognition covers the reception of the effects and the granting of enforceability in Macau to external decisions. The reception of the effects covers, on the one hand, the direct effects of the judgment, which are those covered by the res judicata, as determined by the law of the State of origin of the decision. It also covers, on the other hand, the definition of the legal situation object of the proceeding and its indirect effects as determined by the law designated by the conflict of laws rules.

Article 1199(2) of the MCPC states, however, that no review is required when the decision is invoked in an action pending in the courts of Macau only as a simple means of proof presented to the court (and not for the purpose of receiving or recognising the effects of, and attributing, enforceability).

The recognition of the decision is dependent on the finding of the Court of its own motion of certain requirements, which all have to be present, as provided for in Article 1220(1) (a-f) of the MCPC:

- There is no doubt about the authenticity of the document containing the decision, or about the meaning of the decision.
- The decision is final (res judicata) according to the law of the place where it was rendered.
- The decision was from a court whose jurisdiction did not derive from or was not caused by an evasion of law situation and does not involve issues over which the courts of Macau have exclusive jurisdiction.
- Lis pendens or res judicata based on a case pending before a Macau court cannot be invoked, unless the first action was brought in a court outside Macau. This rule seeks to avoid contradictory cases in the Macau legal system. This solution harmonises with the rule of the aforementioned direct irrelevance of *foreign lis pendens* established in Article 416(3) the MCPC, which allows the recognition of foreign judgments. As the respondent cannot invoke lis pendens in the externally pending proceedings, this can be done in the recognition proceedings in Macau as a ground of opposing the confirmation of the judgment.
- The respondent was duly served, under the law of the originating State, and the principles of *audi alteram partem* and equality of the parties were observed.
- Confirmation of the decision does not produce a result manifestly incompatible with public policy. This rule should also be used to evaluate the effect of external judgments that, for reasons of principle, are unknown in Macau law.

These requirements may, under Article 1202(1) of the MCPC, be invoked by the respondent as grounds for opposing the recognition of the decision. But this precept also provides other grounds for challenging that can be invoked by the respondent.

A first group of grounds is defined by reference to Article 653(a), (c), and (g), which establishes the grounds of the extraordinary remedy of review of a judgment (a sort of appeal available in special circumstances to review res judicata judgments). Particularly relevant in this regard is paragraph (g), under which the fact that the foreign judgment is contrary to another that constitutes an antecedent res judicata is a ground for challenge. This rule is in conflict with the aforementioned Article 1200(1)(d), meaning that prevalence has to be given to one of the two. A more correct understanding of this is that a judgment may not be recognised when it contradicts Macau res judicata, even if the proceedings were in the first place instituted in a court outside Macau.

Another ground for opposition is where the external decision has been made against a Macau resident, if the result of the action would have been more favourable to the Macau resident if substantive Macau law had been applied to the case. It is also required that, under the Macau rules of conflict, the matter in dispute should have been resolved by Macau substantive law.

The action for recognition of decisions passed outside Macau must be filed with the Court of Second Instance (Court of Appeal), with the Court of Final Appeal hearing the appeal (Article 36(13) of the Law 9/2009, of 25 May, and Article 1205(1) of the MCPC).

[B] Arbitral Awards (Including ICSID Awards): Requirements and Limitations

Decree-Law no. 55/98/M, which was based on the UNCITRAL Model Law, governs international commercial arbitration. According to its Article 35, '[a]n arbitral award, irrespective of the State or Territory in which it was made, shall be recognized as binding and, upon application in writing to the competent court, shall be enforced' after the duly authenticated original award (or a certified copy thereof), and the original arbitration agreement (or a certified copy thereof) have been provided - with a certified translation into one of the official languages of Macau. Grounds for refusal (Article 36) are based on the 1958 New York Convention on the Recognition and Enforcement of Foreign Arbitral Awards.

Macau applies the 1958 New York Convention only to disputes arising out of commercial relations. In addition to the agreement with Mainland China for the recognition and enforcement of arbitral awards (in force since 2008), in December 2013 entered into force an agreement with Hong Kong on reciprocal recognition and enforcement of arbitral awards. In both arrangements the confirmation and recognition of the arbitral award is not automatic; it must be requested by a party and may be rejected by the court according to the requirements contained in the agreements. The Convention on the Settlement of Investment Disputes between States and Nationals of Other States ('ICSID Convention') applies to Macau.

§6.06 TREATIES FOR JUDICIAL COOPERATION

Macau has entered into an Agreement on Juridical and Legal with the Republic of Portugal. In addition, the following Hague Conventions are in force for Macau:

- Convention of 1 March 1954 on Civil Procedure.
- Convention of 24 October 1956 on the Law Applicable to Maintenance Obligations in Respect of Children.
- Convention of 15 April 1958 on the Recognition and Enforcement of Decisions Relating to Maintenance Obligations in Respect of Children.
- Convention of 5 October 1961 concerning the Powers of Authorities and the Law Applicable in Respect of the Protection of Minors.
- Convention of 5 October 1961 Abolishing the Requirement of Legalisation for Foreign Public Documents.
- Convention of 15 November 1965 on the Service Abroad of Judicial and Extrajudicial Documents in Civil or Commercial Matters.
- Convention of 18 March 1970 on the Taking of Evidence Abroad in Civil or Commercial Matters.
- Convention of 25 October 1980 on the Civil Aspects of International Child Abduction.
- Convention of 29 May 1993 on Protection of Children and Co-operation in Respect of Intercountry Adoption.

CHAPTER 7

Malaysia

Effendy Othman[*]

§7.01 CODIFICATION OF PRIVATE INTERNATIONAL LAW AND RELEVANCE OF CASE LAW

[A] Codification and Case Law

Common law is one of the recognised sources of Malaysian law. Section 3 of the Malaysian Civil Law Act 1956 (CLA), which applies to West Malaysia (i.e., excluding the states of Sabah and Sarawak) provides that the Common law of England and the Rules of Equity, as administered in England on 7 April 1956, are to be applied in Malaysian Courts, subject to local conditions. In the state of Sarawak the date of reception is 12 December 1949 whilst for the State of Sabah it is 1 December 1951. These two states, i.e., Sarawak and Sabah also import statutes of general application of the United Kingdom. Islamic law, which is only applicable to Muslims and is applied by the Syariah Courts, is restricted to Islamic personal law relating to marriage, divorce, guardianship, maintenance, adoption, legitimacy, family law, gifts or succession, testate, and intestate.

Malaysia does not have any general legislation or code for Private International Law. Conflict of laws rules are disseminated amongst several legislations: the Reciprocal Enforcement of Judgment Act 1958 (REJA), the Malaysian Arbitration Act 2005 ('Arbitration Act 2005')...

The principle of *stare decisis* applies in Malaysian law. In the area of Public and Private International law, there is a significant reliance on Common law especially court decisions of other Common law jurisdictions, notably England and Australia.

* Partner, Zaid Ibrahim & Co. (a member of ZICOlaw).

[B] Multilateral Conventions Providing Uniform Substantive Law and/or International Jurisdictional Rules

International treaties have to be transposed into domestic legislation in order for them to be binding in Malaysia.

Malaysia is not a party to the UN Convention on Contracts for the International Sale of Goods (CISG). Nevertheless Malaysia is a party to the 1910 International Convention for the Unification of Certain Rules of Law Relating to Collision between Vessels, the 1910 International Convention for the Unification of Certain Rules of Law Relating to Assistance and Salvage at Sea, the 1924 International Convention for the Unification of Certain Rules of Law Relating to Bills of Lading (Hague Rules), the 1929/1999 Conventions for the Unification of Certain Rules relating to International Carriage by Air, and the Convention on International Interest in Mobile Equipment (together with its Aircraft Protocol). In addition, Malaysia is a party to eight multilateral treaties administered by the World Intellectual Property Organization (WIPO).[1]

§7.02 JURISDICTION OF LOCAL COURTS IN FOREIGN-RELATED CASES

[A] Grounds for Jurisdiction

[1] General

The jurisdiction of the Malaysian courts is governed by statute, namely the Court of Judicature Act 1964 (CJA), whereby first and foremost, the local jurisdiction of the Malaysian courts is territorially demarcated between the states situated in West Malaysia and the states of Sabah and Sarawak;

In so far as civil matters are concerned, the jurisdiction of the Malaysian courts over a defendant (local or foreign) is attached to the defendant's or place of business. His mere presence within the jurisdiction will not necessarily confer the Malaysian courts with jurisdiction over him. Section 23 of the CJA provides that the High Court shall have jurisdiction to try all civil proceedings where:

(i) the cause of action arose within the local jurisdiction of the Court; or
(ii) the defendant or one of several defendants reside or has his place of business within the local jurisdiction; or
(iii) the facts on which the proceedings are based exist or alleged to have occurred within the local jurisdiction; or
(iv) any land the ownership of which is disputed is situated within the local jurisdiction.

In other words, there must be some form of nexus between the parties and the forum for the Malaysian courts to exercise their local (territorial) jurisdiction. In the

1. http://www.wipo.int/treaties/en/ShowResults.jsp?country_id=124C.

context of their general jurisdictional powers over a defendant, it would depend on the type of actions before them, namely whether the action is:

(a) in personam, i.e., an action directed against a person to compel him to do or not to do something or to order him to pay damages; or
(b) in rem, i.e., an action brought in relation to a specific *res* or thing, e.g., a sea vessel.

[a] In Personam Jurisdiction

The jurisdiction of the Malaysian courts over the defendant can be invoked by reason of:

(i) the defendant's presence within the jurisdiction (irrespective of whether his presence is temporary or long term); or
(ii) the defendant's submission to the jurisdiction of the Malaysian court which can take different forms such as:
  - acceptance of service of Court process;
  - entry of unconditional appearance to an action filed in the Malaysian courts;
  - pleading the merits of the case;
  - contractual submission via the incorporation of the relevant contractual clauses, e.g., choosing Malaysian Courts as the forum;
  - submission by instituting a Malaysian court action; and
  - an extended jurisdiction of the Malaysian courts through service of process out of jurisdiction in accordance with Order 11 of the Malaysian Rules of Court 2012 ('RC 2012').[2]

Service of process out of jurisdiction is aimed at a defendant who is either a foreigner or a Malaysian who is resident or domiciled out of jurisdiction but is nevertheless called upon to answer claims against him in Malaysia. To effect service out of jurisdiction, the Plaintiff must obtain the leave of the Malaysian court and must satisfy a Malaysian court that:

- that service out of jurisdiction is appropriate in that the Plaintiff has a good cause of action;
- that he has a good arguable case that he comes within one of the categories set out in Rule 1 of Order 11, e.g., that it concerns an action for breach of a contract where the breach was committed within the jurisdiction notwithstanding that the contract may have been made outside the jurisdiction;[3]
- that he is able to identify the country the defendant is or may probably be found; and

2. The Rules of Court 2012 are rules of procedure which govern court proceedings of civil cases in the Subordinate Courts (i.e., Sessions and Magistrates' Courts) and the High Court in Malaysia.
3. Order 11 Rule 1(1) (G) RC 2012.

- that the Malaysian court is the most convenient forum for the action to proceed.[4]

[b] In Rem Jurisdiction

Order 70 rule 1(2) of RC 2012 provides that 'action in rem' means an *Admiralty action* in rem.

Following the English position, a Malaysian court's jurisdiction in respect of Admiralty actions in rem does not depend on the connection of the dispute with the forum nor is it affected by the nationality or flag or registration of the ship, the residence or domicile of her owners, or the place where the claim arose;[5] and it has to be noted that pursuant to Order 70 rule 3(3) RC 2012, service out of jurisdiction of a writ or notice of writ does not apply to Admiralty action in rem.

According to the International Interest in Mobile Equipment (Aircraft) Act of 2006, Malaysian courts also have jurisdiction in rem in relation to aircrafts located in Malaysia.

In Malaysia, the High Court has the power to try Admiralty cases by virtue of section 24(b) of the Courts of Judicature Act 1964.

[2] Exclusive Jurisdiction

There are no specific actions over which only the Malaysian courts have jurisdiction, unless the parties agreed to confer exclusive jurisdiction to Malaysian courts.

[B] Exclusion of Jurisdiction

[1] Immunity

Certain individuals and bodies have immunity from the jurisdiction of the Malaysian courts. However the extent of the immunity may vary depending on their identities and the nature of the claims which are brought against them;

[a] Sovereign Immunity

[i] Rulers of the States of Malaysia

In the past, Rulers in Malaysia had absolute immunity from being sued in any courts in Malaysia. However, following an amendment to the Malaysian Federal Constitution in 1993, a Special Court was set up to hear claims brought against any Ruler in his

---

4. The Malaysian courts have accepted the principles set out in the English case of *Spiliada Maritime Corp. v. Cansulex Ltd., The Spiliada* [1986] 3 WLR 972 in determining this point.
5. Malaysian Rules of Court 2012 (Annotation) at p. 1262. Contrast this position with s. 23 of the CJA.

personal capacity, whereby Article 181(2) of the Federal Constitution provides that 'no proceedings whatsoever shall be brought in any court against the Ruler of a state in his personal capacity except in the Special Court established under Part XV'.

[ii] Foreign States

Generally, a defendant has immunity from being sued in court when it is a foreign sovereign or state. This foreign state or sovereign is required to be certified by the Malaysian Minister of Foreign Affairs as has been shown in the case of *Village Holdings Sdn Bhd v. Her Majesty The Queen in right of Canada.*[6]

However, this immunity is not absolute as Malaysia adopts a restrictive immunity approach in that the immunity ceases if the acts of the sovereign state are commercial in nature as can be seen in case of *Bank Bumiputera Malaysia Bhd v. International Tin Council & Anor* which cited with approval the opinion of Lord Denning MR in the *Trendtex* case:[7]

> a foreign sovereign has no immunity when it enters into a commercial transaction with a trader here and a dispute arises which is properly within the territorial jurisdiction of our courts...international comity requires that it (the foreign sovereign) should abide by the rules of the market...

[b] Diplomatic and Consular Immunity

The Diplomatic Privileges (Vienna Convention) Act 1966 [revised-2004] (DPA) provides diplomatic immunity to persons according to their rank in a diplomatic mission or consular post in Malaysia by exempting diplomats from local jurisdiction so that they can perform their duties with freedom, independence, and security.

Article 31 of the Schedule to the DPA provides that diplomatic agent (defined under Article 1 as the head of the mission or a member of the diplomatic staff of the mission), shall enjoy immunity from the criminal, civil and administrative jurisdiction, except in the case of:

(i) a real action relating to private immovable property situated in the territory of the receiving State, unless he holds it on behalf of the sending State for the purposes of the mission;
(ii) an action relating to succession in which the diplomatic agent is involved as executor, administrator, heir or legatee as a private person and not on behalf of the sending State; and
(iii) an action relating to any professional or commercial activity exercised by the diplomatic agent in the receiving State outside his official functions.

6. [1998] 2 MLJ 656.
7. *Trendtex Trading Corp. v. Central Bank of Nigeria* [1977] 1 QB 529.

Be that as it may, Article 32(1) of the Schedule provides that the immunity from jurisdiction of diplomatic agents and of persons enjoying immunity under Article 37 may be waived by the sending State.

Article 32(3) of the Schedule states that the initiation of proceedings by a diplomatic agent or by a person enjoying immunity from jurisdiction under Article 37 shall preclude him from invoking immunity from jurisdiction in respect of any counterclaim directly connected with the principal claim,.

Lastly, Article 32(4) provides that a waiver of immunity from jurisdiction in respect of civil or administrative proceedings shall not be held to imply waiver of immunity in respect of the execution of the judgment, for which a separate waiver shall be necessary.

[c] Other Immunities

Malaysia is a party to the 1961 Convention on the Privileges and Immunities of the United Nations and the 1947 Convention on the Privileges and Immunities of the Specialised Agencies.

[2] Non-justiciable Claims

Malaysian courts do not have jurisdiction over foreign land.

[3] Forum Agreements in Favour of Foreign Courts

Under Malaysian law, in line with parties' freedom to contract, it is possible to confer exclusive or non-exclusive jurisdiction to a court of a particular forum by contractually providing for the same.

However, it is not an absolute exclusion of the court's jurisdiction because the Malaysian courts retain the discretion to decide whether the selected forum or another forum elsewhere is more appropriate to adjudicate the dispute. In such instance, the party who disputes the exclusive jurisdiction clause must show strong case/reasons why the clause should not be enforced.[8] This position has been followed by the recent case of *Nutri Mills Products Sdn Bhd v. CMA CGM Malaysia Sdn Bhd.*[9]

A party who commences an action in a Malaysian court instead of in the agreed foreign court commits a breach of contract and he has the burden of satisfying the Malaysian court that Malaysia is the appropriate forum to adjudicate the dispute. This was fortified by the Malaysian Federal Court in *Globus Shipping and Trading Co. (Pte) Ltd. v. Taiping Textiles Bhd*[10] which held as follows:

8. *Inter Maritime Management Sdn Bhd v. Kai Tai Timber Co Ltd., Hong Kong* [1995] 1 MLJ 322 (which followed the English case of *The Eleftheria* [1969] 1 Lloyd's Rep 237).
9. [2013] 8 MLJ 877.
10. [1976] 2 MLJ 154.

> it would seem abundantly clear from the authorities that where a cause of action in respect of any dispute in relation to a contract arises and is therefore properly within its jurisdiction, the court has a discretion whether or not to adjudicate upon the claim in the action even where the parties have agreed to refer such dispute to a foreign court, and that the question of jurisdiction is quite separate from the question of the proper law of the contract to be applied...;[11]

In exercising its discretion whether to hear the action or to stay the same in favour of the agreement to litigate the dispute in a foreign court, the Malaysian court will consider the following factors as enunciated in the English case of '*The Eleftheria*':[12]

(i) in what country the evidence on the issues of fact was available, and the relative cost and convenience of trials;
(ii) whether foreign law applied and, if so, to what extent it differs from English law in any material respect;
(iii) with which country either party is connected, and how closely;
(iv) whether the defendant genuinely desires trial in a foreign country, or only seeks procedural advantages there; and
(v) whether the plaintiff will be 'prejudiced' by having to sue in a foreign country, either by losing security for his claim, being unable to enforce any judgment obtain there, being faced with a time-bar not applicable locally, or being unlikely to get a fair trial.

[4] Arbitration Clause

The Arbitration Act 2005[13] limits the Malaysian courts' jurisdiction to adjudicate on a matter which parties' have agreed to arbitrate irrespective of whether the seat of arbitration is in Malaysia or overseas in that the Malaysian court is bound to accede to an application to stay local proceedings in breach of such agreement unless it finds that the agreement is null and void, inoperative or incapable of being performed. These are the only exceptions on which the court may refuse to stay an action before it in favour of arbitration.

[C] Non-exercise of Jurisdiction

[1] Forum Non Conveniens

Malaysian courts recognise and will, in appropriate cases, apply the Common law doctrine of Forum Non Conveniens to stay local proceedings in favour of another forum.

A stay of the local proceedings will only be granted on the ground of Forum Non Conveniens if the Malaysian court is satisfied that there is some other available forum, having competent jurisdiction, which is the appropriate forum for the trial of the

11. [1976] 2 MLJ 154 p. 156.
12. *Supra* n. 8.
13. Section 10(1) of the Arbitration Act 2005.

action, i.e., in which the case may be tried more suitably for the interests of all the parties and the ends of justice.[14]

Where a contracting party has filed an action in Malaysia, disregarding the agreement to submit to another forum, the burden is on him to show why the action should proceed in Malaysia. For example, he would not obtain a fair hearing in the foreign court.[15] This is because the agreement creates a strong prima facie case that the agreed jurisdiction is the appropriate forum.

[2] Lis alibi pendens

Malaysian courts recognise and will, in appropriate cases, apply the Common law doctrine of *Lis Alibi Pendens*. However, there are very few decisions on this point. In *J.H. Rayner (Mincing Lane) Ltd & Ors v. Manilal & Sons (M) Sdn Bhd & Anor*,[16] the High Court considered it was an abuse of process and stayed proceedings in Malaysia against the first defendant because the plaintiffs had started similar proceedings in London. This is in line with the principles of res judicata.

§7.03 APPLICABLE LAW

[A] Choice of Law

[1] Express Stipulation

Malaysian law recognises parties' freedom to contract including to choose the law to govern their contractual relationship. The exception to this is where the choice would be contrary to public policy or if there is lack of nexus with the subject matter of the agreement. Any choice of law clause contained in a contract must comply with the provisions contained in the Contracts Act 1950.[17]

[2] Implied Choice

When there is an absence of an express choice, the court may infer a choice from the contract and surrounding circumstances at the time of the making of the contract including parties' choice of jurisdiction.[18]

14. The Malaysian High Court case of *Southern Acids (M) Berhad v. Standard Chartered Bank Malaysia Berhad* (Suit No: D-22NCC-658-2010) applying the principles laid down in the English case of *Spiliada Maritime Corporation v. Cansulex Ltd* [1987] 1 AC 460.
15. Cf. *Purcell v. Khayat* (1987) Times, 23 November.
16. [1987] 1 MLJ 312.
17. *Ngui Mui Khin & Anor v. Gillespie Bros & Co. Ltd.* [1980] 2 MLJ 9.
18. *The Government of India v. Cairn Energy India Pty Ltd.*, [2011] 6 MLJ 441.

[B] Other Cases

If the parties have not chosen the governing law of the contract, then the Malaysian court would look at the 'localizing elements' or 'connecting factors', i.e., the law of the country or jurisdiction with the closest and has the most real connection with the transaction and the parties.

[C] *Renvoi*

Under Malaysian law, the doctrine of *Renvoi* only applies to the following circumstances and when a Malaysian court accepts the reference back to it. In such instance, the domestic or internal laws of Malaysia would apply:

(i) a Malaysian dies domiciled in a country by whose law succession is governed by the *lex patriae*, i.e., law of citizenship;
(ii) cases involving legitimatisation of subsequent marriage and formal validity of a marriage.

[D] Mandatory Rules of the Forum and of Third States

There are no judicial decisions by the Malaysian courts specifically on the treatment of mandatory rules. However, the concept of mandatory rules is reflected in legislations as exemplified by section 24 of the Malaysian Contracts Act 1950 which provides as follows:

> The consideration or object of an agreement is lawful, unless—
>
> (a) it is forbidden by a law;
> (b) it is of such a nature that, if permitted, it would defeat any law;
> (c) it is fraudulent;
> (d) it involves or implies injury to the person or property of another; or
> (e) the court regards it as immoral or opposed to public policy.

In each of the above cases, the consideration or object of the agreement is said to be unlawful and every agreement of which the object or consideration is unlawful is void under Malaysian law;

It is more likely than not that the Malaysian courts would give cognisance to the mandatory rules of Malaysia notwithstanding that the parties have opted for the law of another forum to regulate their contractual relationship; and

It is also an established legal position that a Malaysian court will not enforce the revenue, penal and expropriation laws of another country nor would it recognise any foreign law which is repugnant to Malaysian public policy.

[E] Proof of Foreign Law

Under Malaysian law, foreign law is a matter of fact which has to be pleaded and proven. The burden of proof of foreign law lies on the party who is relying upon it.

However, unlike the position under Common law where in the absence of evidence to the contrary, the foreign law is presumed to be same as that of the *lex fori*, under Malaysian law, if a party fails to lead evidence on the foreign law which he is relying on, his claim will fail.[19]

Section 38 of the Malaysian Evidence Act 1950 (EA) states that:

> When the court has to form an opinion as to a law of any country, any statement of that law contained in a book purporting to be printed or published under the authority of the Government of that country, and to contain any such law, and any report of a ruling of the courts of that country contained in a book purporting to be a report of such rulings, is relevant.

Furthermore, section 45(1) of the EA refers to the value of experts in the foreign law when the court has to form an opinion upon a point of such foreign law.

Additionally, Malaysian courts shall take judicial notice of all public Acts passed or to be passed by the Parliament of the United Kingdom.

[F] Evasion of the Law

There is no specific provision to regulate the evasion of the law, but Malaysian public policy requirements will prevail in certain circumstances where there is an attempt to avoid any particular domestic law requirement. Public policy decisions may also be relevant where certain actions may be incompatible with the social, moral or political climate of Malaysia.[20]

§7.04 PROCEDURAL ISSUES

[A] Service of Summons and Judicial Orders Abroad

Malaysia is not a signatory to the 1965 Hague Convention on the Service Abroad of Judicial and Extrajudicial Documents in Civil or Commercial Matters.

Under Malaysian law, service of a Writ of Summons or a Notice of Writ out of jurisdiction is permissible with the leave of court and by complying with the requirements set out in Order 11 RC 2012.[21]

The grant of leave is discretionary and the court will consider the jurisdiction most appropriate for the trial of the action. However, Malaysian law does not prescribe any specific mode or process for the service of Malaysian judicial orders abroad.

[B] Obtaining Evidence Abroad

Malaysia is not a party to the 1970 Hague Convention on the taking of Evidence Abroad in Civil or Commercial Matters.

---

19. *Chan Kwong Fong v. Fong v. Chan Wah* [1977] 1 MLJ 232.
20. RH Hickling & Wu Min Aun, *Conflict of Laws in Malaysia* (1995), at p. 50.
21. Order 11 RC 2012.

Under Order 39 RC 2012, a Malaysian court may, if it appears necessary for the purposes of justice, order for the taking of depositions of any person whether within Malaysia or abroad. For example, where the witness is residing abroad and is too ill to travel to attend court in Malaysia. The Malaysian court may also invoke its inherent powers to order for the taking of depositions in the interest of justice.[22]

The party in the Malaysian court proceedings who intends to obtain evidence by depositions must make a formal application to the court[23] and if the court allows this application, the court will issue a request to the judicial authorities of the foreign country where the witness is residing to facilitate the examination of the said witness.[24] This process is subject to the agreement of the foreign judicial authorities who may refuse such a request.

[C] Restraint of Foreign Proceedings

Provided the Malaysian court has personal jurisdiction over the party who has commenced separate court actions against the same defendant in Malaysia and elsewhere, the Malaysian court may by way of an anti-suit injunction, restrain the said party from proceeding as a plaintiff in the foreign court.[25] However given the fact that such injunction orders would indirectly affect the foreign proceedings, the Malaysian courts would generally exercise greater scrutiny and caution before granting such injunction orders.

Based on the English Privy Council decision in *Societe Nationale Industrielle Aerospatiale v. Lee Kui Jak & Anor*,[26] it would appear that the principles governing the Malaysian court's discretion to grant an anti-suit injunction to restrain foreign proceedings are more stringent than those in respect of staying of proceedings in a Malaysian court action. The principles are as follows:

(i) the jurisdiction to stay was to be exercised when the '*end of justice*' requires it;
(ii) when the court decides to grant an injunction restraining foreign proceedings, its order is against the party so proceeding or intending to do so and not against the foreign court;
(iii) such an injunction would only be issued against a party who is amenable to the jurisdiction of the court, if it was an effective remedy against the said party;
(iv) as the order is one which indirectly affects the foreign court, the jurisdiction has to be exercised with caution.

22. The Malaysian Courts inherent powers provided under Order 92 rule 4 RC 2012.
23. Order 39 rule 2 RC 2012.
24. Order 39 rule 3 RC 2012.
25. See RH Hickling & Wu Min Aun, *supra* n. 20, at 87.
26. [1987] 2 MLJ 397 PC.

In *Berjaya Industrial Bhd v. Public Bank (L) Ltd.*,[27] the court granted an injunction in respect of the foreign proceedings on the basis that:

> there cannot be two sets of judicial proceedings in different jurisdictions on the same subject matter between the parties as this would give rise to multiplicity of proceedings and possible conflicting judgments.[28]

An application to obtain an injunction on grounds of *lis alibi pendens* will not be allowed where the nature of the action is different. For example, where one action is in the form of an Admiralty action in rem whereas the other action is an action in personam.

[D] Proof of Foreign Public Documents

All cause papers filed before the courts must be in the Malay language except if such document is to be used as an exhibit in the court proceedings. Additionally, under Order 41 Rule 13, RC 2012, an affidavit of a deponent affirmed outside Malaysia may be filed into the Malaysian court in the English language and need not be accompanied by the Malay language translation unless the court orders so.

Malaysia is not a signatory to the Hague Apostille Convention, which provides for international certification of public documents of its signatory states. Under Malaysian law, the proof of foreign public documents is governed and regulated by the Malaysian Evidence Act 1950.

Section 74 of the EA defines public documents to include:

(i) documents forming the acts or records of the acts of:
  - the sovereign authority;
  - official bodies and tribunals; and
  - public officers, legislative, judicial and executive, whether Federal or State or of any part of the Commonwealth or of a foreign country; and

(ii) public records kept in Malaysia of private documents.

There are several ways to prove foreign public documents under section 78 of the EA:

(i) proclamations, orders or regulations issued by the Crown in the United Kingdom or by the Privy Council of by any Minister or department of Crown can be proved by copies or extracts contained in either London *Gazette*, or in the *Gazette*, in any State *Gazette* or purporting to be printed by Her Britannic Majesty's Printer;[29]

(ii) the acts of the Executive or the proceedings of the legislature of a foreign country can be proved by journals published by their authority or commonly received in that country as such by a copy certified under the seal of the

27. [1996] 5 MLJ 389.
28. *Ibid.* at p. 404.
29. Section 78(1)(c) EA.

country or sovereign or by a recognition thereof in some Act, Ordinance or Enactment of Malaysia or any State;[30]

(iii) public documents of any other class in a foreign country can be proved by the original or by a copy certified by the lawful keeper thereof, with a certificate under seal of a notary public or of a consular officer of Malaysia that the copy is duly certified by the officer having the lawful custody of the original and upon proof of the character of the document according to the law of the foreign country.[31]

Sections 79 and following contain several rules regarding the presumption as to the genuineness of several documents.

[E] Statute of Limitations

In line with section 3 of the CLA,[32] and applying the English Common law as it stood prior to the enactment of the English Foreign Limitation Periods Act, 1984, the laws of limitation are treated as a matter of procedure under Malaysian law and will be governed by the *lex fori*.[33]

[F] Remedies and Damages

Under Malaysian law, following the English Common law, a plaintiff in a Malaysian court action can only obtain remedies which are available under Malaysian law, i.e., the *lex fori*. A Malaysian court will not grant remedies which are available under foreign law (*lex causae*) which are unknown to it.[34]

In terms of damages, the issue of remoteness of damage would be considered as a substantive issue under Malaysian law and therefore governed by the *lex causae*. On the other hand, the measure or quantum of damages is considered a procedural point and would be governed by the *lex fori*.[35]

[G] Foreign Currency Obligations

A Malaysian court has the jurisdiction to enter judgment in a foreign currency.[36] The judgment should be for payment of the amount in the foreign currency or the Malaysian currency equivalent converted at the time of payment.[37]

30. Section 78(1)(d) EA.
31. Section 78(1)(f) EA.
32. Pursuant to s. 3 of the Civil Law Act 1956 which applies to West Malaysia (i.e., excluding the states of Sabah and Sarawak), the Common law of England and the Rules of Equity, as administered in England on 7 Apr. 1956, are to be applied in Malaysian courts, subject to local conditions.
33. RH Hickling, Wu Min Aun, *supra* n. 20, at pp. 35-37.
34. *Ibid.* at p. 41.
35. *Ibid.* at pp. 41-42.
36. *New Kok Ann Realty Sdn Bhd v. Development & Commercial Bank Ltd., New Hebrides (In liquidation)* [1987] 2 MLJ 57.
37. *Miliangos v. George Frank (Textile) Ltd.* [1976] AC 443.

[H] Restraining Removal of Assets and Securing Evidence in Favour of a Foreign Arbitration/Judicial Process

A Malaysian court has the power pursuant to section 25(2) of the Courts of Judicature Act 1964 as well as Order 29 of RC 2012, to grant an interlocutory injunction to restrain the removal or dissipation of assets located within or outside of its jurisdiction pending the disposal of the court actions before it. This is to ensure that the plaintiff will have a meaningful source of recovery, if it obtains a judgment in its favour against the defendant;

This form of injunction is commonly referred to as the Mareva Injunction after the English case of *Mareva Compania Naviera SA v. International Bulk Carriers SA*[38] through which such order was first granted. A Mareva Injunction in respect of assets of the defendant which are situated abroad is known as a '*Worldwide Mareva*'.

Malaysian courts would generally be slow to grant a Mareva Injunction especially a *Worldwide Mareva* unless the plaintiff can demonstrate that it has a strong prima facie case against the defendant[39] and that there is danger of dissipation of such assets by the defendant.[40] Similarly, Malaysian courts can also grant Anton Piller Orders to avoid the disposal or destruction of incriminating evidence, but only where it is essential in the interest of justice. The plaintiff must satisfy the court that it has an extremely strong prima facie case, that the actual or potential damage is very serious, and that there is clear evidence that the defendant has in its possession incriminating documents/things and there is a real possibility that the defendant may destroy such material before proceedings are started.

However, Malaysian courts are unlikely to grant an interlocutory Mareva Injunction or an Anton Piller Order in aid of foreign court proceedings because interlocutory injunction is not in itself a cause of action but merely a recourse to facilitate and preserve a pre-existing cause of action against the defendant.[41]

The position is different where it concerns a foreign arbitration. This is because under section 11 of the Arbitration Act 2005, a Malaysian court has the jurisdiction and powers to make an order for the preservation of any property (the subject matter of the dispute) or for the purpose of ensuring that any award made in the arbitral proceedings is not rendered ineffectual by the dissipations of assets by the counter-party. This right to obtain such an order extends to an international arbitration where the seat of arbitration is not in Malaysia.[42]

38. [1980] 1 All ER 213.
39. *Bank Bumiputra Malaysia Bhd v. Lorrain Osman* [1985] 2 MLJ 36.
40. *Supra* n. 38.
41. *The Siskina* [1979] AC 210.
42. Section 11(3) of the Arbitration Act 2005.

§7.05 RECOGNITION AND ENFORCEMENT OF FOREIGN DECISIONS

[A] Judicial Decisions: Requirements and Limitations

Subject to the qualifications set out below, a final and conclusive monetary judgment of any of the superior courts of reciprocating countries[43] listed in the First Schedule of REJA (other than a judgment of such court given on appeal from a lower court and not being a sum payable in respect of taxes) could be registered and enforced in Malaysia in accordance with the requirements set under REJA and the RC 2012. The judgment creditor must apply for registration within six years after the date of the foreign decision.

Registration will be denied when the foreign judgment has been wholly satisfied or it could not be enforced in the country where it was rendered. If the sum payable is expressed in a currency other than Malaysian currency,[44] the judgment shall be registered as if it were a judgment for such sum in Malaysian currency applying the exchange rate existing at the date of the judgment of the original court.[45] In addition to the sum of money payable under the original judgment, including any interest, the judgment shall include costs incurred for the registration, including the costs of obtaining a certified copy of the judgment from the original court.

Once registered, the foreign monetary judgment can be enforced in Malaysia as if it were a domestic judgment.[46] On an application duly made by any party against whom a registered judgment may be enforced, the registration will not be set aside if the registering court is satisfied that:[47]

(i) the foreign judgment was not obtained by fraud;
(ii) the enforcement of the foreign judgment would not be contrary to natural justice or the public policy of Malaysia;
(iii) the enforcement of the foreign judgment is not an enforcement of penal or revenue laws of the foreign country;
(iv) the foreign judgment was not obtained in proceedings in which the defendant did not (notwithstanding that process may have been duly served on him in accordance with English laws) receive notice of those proceedings in sufficient time to enable it to defend the proceedings and did not appear;
(v) there has not been an earlier judgment of a competent court;
(vi) the judgment is for a fixed sum and not for multiple damages;
(vii) the enforcement of proceedings is instituted within six years after the date of the judgment;

---

43. The United Kingdom; Hong Kong; Singapore; New Zealand; the Republic of Sri Lanka; India (excluding State of Jammu and Kashmir, State of Manipur, Tribal areas of State of Assam, and Scheduled areas of the States of Madras and Andhra) and Brunei Darussalam.
44. *Inter Diam Pte Ltd v. PJ Diamond Centre Sdn Bhd* [2002] 4 AMR 4613.
45. *Ibid.*, at p. 142.
46. Section 4(2) REJA.
47. Section 5 REJA.

(viii) there is no appeal pending before the foreign court, and the judgment debtor is not entitled and intending to appeal, against the foreign judgment;
(ix) the foreign judgment was made by a court of competent jurisdiction; and
(x) the foreign judgment has not been wholly satisfied and is enforceable by execution in the English courts.

In any other case involving monetary claim where a foreign judgment has been obtained but does not fall within REJA, a fresh suit has to be instituted in the courts of Malaysia based either on the foreign judgment or on the original cause of action;

[B] Arbitral Awards (Including ICSID Awards): Requirements and Limitations

Under section 38 of the Arbitration Act 2005, a foreign arbitral award from a state party to the 1958 Convention on the Recognition and Enforcement of Foreign Arbitral Awards (or better known as the 'New York Convention') can, on an application to the High Court in Malaysia, be recognised and enforced as if it were a domestic judgment. There are only limited grounds upon which recognition and enforcement of such arbitral award will be refused. These grounds are set out in section 39(1)(a) and (b) of the Arbitration Act 2005 which are based on the New York Convention.

Malaysia is also a party to the Convention on the Settlement of Investment Disputes Between States and Nationals of Other States ('ICSID Convention') applied through the Convention on the Settlement of Investment Disputes Act 1966, which Article 3 stipulates that an award made by an arbitrator under the Convention shall be binding and may be enforced in the same manner as if it is a decree judgment or order of the court. Malaysia is also a party to the 2009 ASEAN Comprehensive Investment Agreement.

§7.06 RECOGNITION OF OTHER FOREIGN PUBLIC DOCUMENTS

Foreign public documents can be recognised under Malaysian law by going through the process of legalisation which essentially requires authentication from the relevant office of the foreign country responsible for the issuance of such document and subsequently endorsed by a certificate under seal of a notary public or of a consular officer of Malaysia.[48]

§7.07 TREATIES FOR JUDICIAL COOPERATION

Malaysia is not a signatory to any treaties for judicial cooperation although it is a member of the Hague Conference for Private International Law and the Malaysian Attorney General's office is studying the Conventions with a view of ascertaining whether Malaysia can become a party to any of them.

48. See s. 7.04[D].

CHAPTER 8
Mongolia

Munkhselenge Purevdorjiin[*]

§8.01 CODIFICATION OF PRIVATE INTERNATIONAL LAW AND RELEVANCE OF CASE LAW

[A] Codification and Case Law

Since early 1990s, after the enactment of the new constitution, Mongolia has undertaken the complete reformation of the legislative system and structure from a socialist regime to a civil law system. Nevertheless, there is no independent and separate codification of private international law in Mongolia. Different conflict of laws rules are contained in the Civil Code (Part VI), the Civil Procedure Law, the Family Law...

Precedent is not considered to be a source of law. Furthermore, judges do not expound legal analysis in their decisions. Therefore, there is not much interpretation as to the direction of the law or to the merits of a case or to what judges find convincing evidence.

[B] Multilateral Conventions Providing Uniform Substantive Law and/or International Jurisdictional Rules

According to Article 539(2) of the Civil Code, the provisions of international treaties shall prevail unless they contradict the Constitution of Mongolia. Similar provision is contained in Article 2(2) of the Civil Procedure Law.

Mongolia is party to the UN Convention on Contracts for the International Sale of Goods (CISG), the 1929/1999 Conventions for the Unification of Certain Rules relating

* Lecturer at School of Foreign Service, National University of Mongolia; received LL.B. degree from Hitotsubashi University, Tokyo, Japan and LL.M. degree from Wake Forest University, School of Law, USA; Ph.D. candidate at School of Law, NUM; Lawyer.

to International Carriage by Air, the Agreement on International Goods Transport by Rail (SGMS), the Convention on the Contract for the International Carriage of Goods by Road and the Convention on International Interest in Mobile Equipment (together with its Aircraft Protocol). In addition, Mongolia is a party to sixteen multilateral agreements and protocols administered by the World Intellectual Property Organization (WIPO).[1]

§8.02 JURISDICTION OF LOCAL COURTS IN FOREIGN-RELATED CASES

[A] Grounds for Jurisdiction

According to Article 2(2) of the Civil Procedure Law, rules contained in an international treaty ratified by Mongolia will prevail (unless they are contrary to the Mongolian constitution).

[1] General

International Civil jurisdiction of Mongolian courts is founded on Article 189 of the Civil Procedure Law:

- Defendant has habitual residence and does business in the territory of Mongolia.
- One of the plaintiffs has habitual residence in the territory of Mongolia.
- Claims concerning an obligation to be performed in the territory of Mongolia.
- Torts committed in the territory of Mongolia.
- Dispute relating to the branch or representative office located in the territory of Mongolia.
- Claims of foreign citizens, stateless persons permanently residing in the territory of Mongolia or Mongolian citizens concerning payment of alimony and determination of fatherhood.
- Claims relating to wills and inheritance of a deceased who before his death had habitual residence in the territory of Mongolia or property is located in the territory of Mongolia.

Article 192 of the Civil Procedure Law states that cases involving family law (divorce, parentage, adoption...) have jurisdiction in Mongolian courts, when:

- Both parties are Mongolian nationals or at least one of them had Mongolian nationality when getting married.
- Foreign or stateless defendant is a Mongolian resident.
- One of the plaintiffs (in actions to determine the relationship between children and parents) has Mongolian nationality or permanent residence in Mongolia.
- Either adopter or child who is being adopted has Mongolian nationality or has permanent residence in Mongolia.

1. http://www.wipo.int/treaties/en/ShowResults.jsp?country_id=117C.

[2] *Exclusive Jurisdiction*

In accordance with Article 190 of the Civil Procedure Law, the following international disputes are referred to the special jurisdiction of Mongolian courts:

- disputes related to ownership, possession, and use of immovable properties which are located in the territory of Mongolia;
- disputes related to reorganisation and bankruptcy of legal persons which are incorporated in Mongolia, and the decision raised by the legal persons, their branches, and their representative offices;
- disputes regarding the validity of registration by Mongolian courts and other authorised organisations;
- disputes related to the registration and applications for registration of patent, trademark, and other intellectual properties by Mongolian Intellectual Organization;
- court decisions enforced in Mongolia and personal requests for enforcing court decisions in Mongolia.

[B] Exclusion of Jurisdiction

[1] *Immunity*

[a] *Sovereign Immunity*

There is no express provision within the Civil Procedure Law or reported case concerning the sovereign immunity of foreign states. Nevertheless, Article 4 of the Civil Procedure Law requires equality of the parties before the court and several statutes (Mining Law, Tax Law...) allow foreign companies to file a claim in Mongolia against the government. Similarly, Mongolia has entered into agreements providing for arbitration in case of breach of the contractual obligations.[2] However, Mongolia has contended before the courts of New York its immunity from jurisdiction.[3] Mongolia has not signed yet the 2004 UN Convention on Jurisdictional Immunities of States and Their Property.

[b] *Diplomatic and Consular Immunity*

Mongolia is party to the 1961 Vienna Convention on Diplomatic Relations and the 1963 Vienna Convention on Consular Relations. Article 193 of the Civil Procedure Law expressly refers to the exclusion of civil jurisdiction in relation to diplomatic immunities.

2. For example, Oyu Tolgoi Investment Agreement (http://www.ot.mn/en/node/316).
3. 551 U.S. 193 (2007).

[c] Other Immunities

Mongolia is a party to the 1961 Convention on the Privileges and Immunities of the United Nations and the 1947 Convention on the Privileges and Immunities of the Specialised Agencies.

[2] Non-justiciable Claims

There is no specific provision regarding non-justiciable claims.

[3] Forum Agreements in Favour of Foreign Courts

According to the Civil Procedure Law, parties are free to choose any foreign jurisdiction to resolve their contractual disputes, except for the matters referred especially to Mongolian jurisdiction as noted above. It is common business practice for Mongolian parties to voluntarily submit to foreign jurisdictions in relation to commercial contracts.

[4] Arbitration Clause

In principle, according to Article 13(2) of the Civil Procedure Law, an agreement to arbitrate will take precedence. However, the general article regulating the stay of court proceedings (Article 80 of the Civil Procedure Law) does not include a stay of proceedings brought in breach of an agreement to arbitrate. Nonetheless, since Mongolia is a signatory to the 1958 New York Convention on the Recognition and Enforcement of Foreign Arbitral Awards, a Mongolian court would be obliged under Article II of such convention, upon application by one of the parties, to refer the parties to arbitration unless it finds that the arbitration agreement is null and void, inoperative or incapable of being performed.

[C] Non-exercise of Jurisdiction

[1] Forum Non Conveniens

The doctrine of forum non conveniens is not applied by Mongolian courts.

[2] **Lis alibi pendens**

Under Article 65 of the Civil Procedure Law of Mongolia, a judge may dismiss the action in the following cases:

- a court decision or decree (or an arbitral award) that has come into force or a decree on dismissal of an action/case relates to facts alleged in the new legal action and regarding fault of parties;
- the court is considering another case about the matter in dispute;
- a case related to the claim is being investigated through criminal procedures (though Article 65 does not expressly mention it, foreign criminal proceedings could also be considered);
- the court has no appropriate jurisdiction (e.g., because the parties agreed to submit their dispute to a foreign court or arbitration).

§8.03 APPLICABLE LAW

[A] Choice of Law

[1] Express Stipulation

According to Article 549(1) and (2) of the Civil Code, the rights and obligations of the parties to a contract, the content of the contract, the fulfilment of obligations, the termination or revocation, the implementation of duties under the contract, or the failure shall be regulated by the law of the country designated by the parties to the contract. Such choice of law can be changed by the mutual consent of the parties even after signing the contract (in which case, the initial contractual provision would be void).

[2] Implied Choice

If the parties did not choose the applicable law, then Article 549(4) of the Civil Code provides for the following presumptions or guidelines to ascertain the preferences of the parties to a contract:

- sale contract: the law of the seller;
- leasing contract: the law of the lesser;
- deposit contract: the law of the depository;
- commission contract: the law of the commission agent;
- agency contract: the law of the agent;
- transportation contract: the law of the transportation agent;
- insurance contract: the law of the insured;
- loan contract: the law of the lender;
- gift contract: the law of the donor;
- warranty: the law of the guarantor;
- pledge contract: the law of the pledger.

[B] Other Cases

According to Article 549(8) of the Civil Code, in case of contracts where there is no express choice of law and the above-mentioned guidelines are not applicable, the rights and obligations shall be determined by the law of the country where the party performing the principal obligations has its place of residence or carries out its core business activities.

The only exceptions are contained in Article 549(5)-(7) of the Civil Code:

- contracts for joint production, specialised training, cooperation, construction, assembling and other works shall be governed by the law of the country where those activities are being carried out or where the results of those contracts occur, unless otherwise agreed by the parties;
- joint venture agreements involving foreign legal entities and citizens shall be governed by the law of the country where the joint venture has its place of business;
- a contract concluded as a result of stock exchange transaction or an auction sale shall be governed by the law of the country where the transaction took place or where the auction sales were conducted.

According to Article 10(5) of the Civil Procedure Law, a court may apply universally accepted international norms in case proceedings related to international civil law provided that they do not conflict with the Constitution of Mongolia.

[1] Property Rights

Regarding property rights, Article 547 of the Civil Code states that they shall be determined by the law of the country where the property is located or registered; relations pertaining to the creation and termination of the property ownership rights are governed by the law of the country where such rights were first created, unless the Mongolian law provides otherwise. In case of goods transported under international contracts, the law of the country from where the shipment was dispatched applies, unless the parties agreed otherwise. In case of intangible, non-economic rights, the law of the country where these rights are being used applies.

[2] Form of Legal Transactions

According to Article 548 of the Civil Code, the form of a legal transaction is governed by the law chosen by the parties living in different countries, or the law of the state in which the transaction is concluded or the law applicable to the content of the transaction. If the standards of Mongolian law are met, it is not possible to revoke a transaction made abroad even if it doesn't comply with the foreign standards. In case of real estate located in Mongolia, the form of transaction is determined by Mongolian law. The authorisation form and term shall be determined by the law of the country where the authorisation was issued, but will always be valid if it meets the requirements of Mongolian law.

[3] Legal Capacity

According to Article 543 of the Civil Code, the legal capacity of foreign nationals shall be determined by the law of their nationality, of their country of residence (in case of stateless persons), or of the country that provided asylum. Nevertheless, in relation to contracts or torts that take place in Mongolia, the legal capacity of foreign and stateless persons shall be determined by Mongolian law. The deprivation or restriction of legal capacity of any person present in Mongolia shall be determined by Mongolian law.

In case of foreign entities, Article 544 of the Civil Code provides that their legal capacity shall be determined by the law of the state of which they are nationals (registration, centre of administration...). Nevertheless, a foreign legal entity entering into agreements cannot apply restrictions not specified by Mongolian law.

[4] Succession

Inheritance relations shall be regulated by the laws of the country of permanent residence of the heir. The questions of legal capacity of the testator, form of the will, drafting and amendment are governed by the laws of the country of the permanent residence of the testator at the time of drafting or amending the will. In so far as the will was drafted and amended according to the requirements of the laws of the country where it was made or the laws of Mongolia, it cannot be considered void on the basis of problems with its form. Inheritance and bequeathing, change of successors of immovable property located on the territory of Mongolia are determined by the laws of Mongolia.

[5] Family

According to Article 6 of the Family law of Mongolia, if Mongolian citizens marry in a foreign country or a Mongolian citizen marries to a foreign citizen or stateless person in a foreign country, (i) the marriage is valid unless the foreign law contradicts Mongolian Family law (e.g., only civil law marriage is legitimate in Mongolia) and (ii) the material and immaterial property rights are regulated by the law of the foreign country unless they choose otherwise. If a divorce of Mongolian citizens from foreign citizens or stateless persons in a foreign country does not contradict an international agreement and/or Mongolian Family law, then it is valid in Mongolia. Additionally, Articles 14, 23, 58, and 67 of the Family Law regulate conflict of laws issues in relation to parentage, adoption, and custody.

[C] *Renvoi*

According to Article 540(2) of the Civil Code, 'if the foreign laws stipulate the prevalence of Mongolian law, the Mongolian legislation shall be applied'. There are no other statutory provisions regarding the application of the principle of *renvoi*.

[D] Mandatory Rules of the Forum and of Third States

According to Article 540(1) of the Civil Code, foreign laws, legislative acts and internationally accepted practice not in contradiction with Mongolian law or the international treaties to which Mongolia is signatory may apply to civil litigations, disputes and for regulating other civil legal relations.

[E] Proof of Foreign Law

According to Article 541 of the Civil Code, when applying a foreign law, also its official interpretation and practice shall be considered. In order to ascertain the contents, interpretation and practice of foreign laws, the court may request the Ministry of Justice, other competent authorities in Mongolia or abroad to provide legal assistance and interpretations as well as to invite experts. Parties to the proceedings can provide the court with documents that explain foreign laws, or invite foreign specialist as experts. Mongolian law shall be applied in case it is impossible to ascertain the content of foreign law.

Interestingly, Article 540(3) of the Civil Code provides also for the contrary situation: in case Mongolian law does not specify clearly the civil relation or defines it under different legal context or it is impossible to solve the case through interpretation of Mongolian law, foreign laws and acts can be considered.

[F] Evasion of the Law

There is no specific regulation on evasion of the law.

§8.04 PROCEDURAL ISSUES

Mongolian law applies to procedural issues unless there is an applicable international treaty.

[A] Service of Summons and Judicial Orders Abroad

Article 77 of the Civil Procedure Law regulates the service of summons to defendants in Mongolia (by certified mail or by a court officer personally to their place of residence or work; to the relevant senior officers or employees; by mass media) and it is considered applicable even where the defendant is outside the territory of Mongolia (unless an international treaty applies).

Mongolia is not a party to the 1965 Hague Convention on the Service Abroad of Judicial and Extrajudicial Documents in Civil or Commercial Matters. Nevertheless, Mongolia is a party to the 1954 Hague Convention on Civil Procedure, which provides for communication of judicial and extrajudicial documents, as well as for mutual support in legal matters. Also, some of the bilateral treaties entered into by Mongolia provide for the service of judicial documents abroad.

[B] Obtaining Evidence Abroad

Article 39 of the Civil Procedure Law states that the competent authority may apply to the appropriate foreign authorities for obtaining foreign evidence required by the court. In case there is no specific international agreement for those requests of mutual legal assistance, diplomatic channels will be used. In the meantime, proceedings are stayed.

Mongolia is not a party to the 1970 Hague Convention on the Taking of Evidence Abroad in Civil and Commercial Matters. Therefore, obtaining evidence abroad is mainly based on specific bilateral agreements in force, mutual legal assistance based on the 1954 Hague Convention or by diplomatic channels.

[C] Restraint of Foreign Proceedings

Mongolian courts do not recognise the concept of anti-suit injunctions.

[D] Proof of Foreign Public Documents

Although Mongolia is a party to the Hague Convention Abolishing the Legalisation of Foreign Public Documents, several Contracting Parties raised an objection and therefore, the Convention is not in force between Mongolia and Austria, Belgium, Finland, Germany, and Greece. Documents issued in those countries require legalisation.

According to Article 7(4) of the Civil Procedure Law, evidence written in a foreign language shall be translated by an officially licensed translator into Mongolian language and certified by notary public.

[E] Statute of Limitations

According to Article 542(1) of the Civil Code, liability period shall be determined in accordance with Mongolian law or the international treaties to which Mongolia is a signatory.

[F] Remedies and Damages

The rights and obligations of the parties for the damage caused shall be governed by the laws of the country where the damage occurred or the compensation claim was originally raised and where documents are held. Nevertheless, if the party held liable for damage abroad is a citizen or legal entity of Mongolia, the laws of Mongolia shall apply (Article 551 of the Civil Code).

[G] Foreign Currency Obligations

The Mongolian courts do not enter judgments in foreign currency. All claims have to be paid in Mongolian currency, the tugrik. According to Article 63 of the Civil Procedure Law, the exchange rate to be applied is the official one announced by the Central Bank of Mongolia.

[H] Restraining Removal of Assets and Securing Evidence in Favour of a Foreign Arbitration/Judicial Process

According to Article 69 of the Civil Procedure Law, *after instigation of proceedings*, if deemed necessary, a judge may decree the following measures for affirmation at the request of the plaintiff; (1) seizure of defendant's assets in the amount of the claim; (2) prohibition of any concrete operations of defendant in the amount of the claim; (3) seizure of current accounts of defendant in the amount of the claim; or (4) transfer of money in the amount of the claim to court. Nevertheless, the State Agency for Executing Judgments rarely deals with extraterritorial attachments. Article 50 of the Civil Procedure Law also regulates the possibility to secure evidence.

Although the Civil Procedure Law is silent about attachment of assets on the merits of foreign proceedings, some of the bilateral international agreements signed by Mongolia provide for the seizing of assets. Furthermore, restraining removal of assets and securing evidence could be requested by a foreign court based on the 1954 Hague Convention on Civil Procedure or by diplomatic channels.

Article 33 of the Arbitration Law allows the arbitral tribunal or a party with the approval of the arbitral tribunal to request from the Court of Appeal assistance in taking evidence. However, Article 3 of the Arbitration Law limits the application of such possibility to arbitrations taking place in Mongolia.

§8.05 RECOGNITION AND ENFORCEMENT OF FOREIGN DECISIONS

[A] Judicial Decisions: Requirements and Limitations

Mongolian courts enforce foreign court judgments according to Mongolian laws, bilateral and multilateral treaties:

- If there is a bilateral treaty regarding enforcement of foreign decisions: the bilateral treaty, the 'Law on Enforcement of Court Judgments', Supreme Court's Decree No. 9 issued on 28 February 2008 ('Implementation of Mongolian International Treaties and Universally Accepted International Norms and Principles in Judicial Practice') and the Civil Procedure Law will apply. The previous statute of limitations for enforcement of foreign decisions (three years) has been abolished.
- If there is no bilateral treaty providing for enforcement of foreign decisions, the court will not enforce the foreign court decision (with the exception of foreign court decisions related to legal costs when the 1954 Convention on Civil Procedure applies).

In order to be enforced in Mongolia, a foreign court decision must be confirmed and accepted by the court that made the decision. Further, the foreign court decision must be officially translated into Mongolian and delivered in accordance with the proper regulation under the bilateral treaty.

If any of the following situations occur during the enforcement of the foreign court judgment in Mongolia, the foreign court decision will not be enforced in Mongolia:

- if damage to the independence and national security of Mongolia may occur;
- if it contradicts commonly accepted norms;
- if there is a valid court decision made by Mongolian courts on the case in question;
- if the court decision is related to litigation that belongs to the special jurisdiction of Mongolian courts;
- if the court decision is not yet validated; or
- if the statute of limitations for enforcing a foreign court judgment has lapsed.

[B] Arbitral Awards (Including ICSID Awards): Requirements and Limitations

According to Article 3 of the Arbitration Law, foreign arbitral awards shall be recognised in Mongolia and enforcement proceedings shall be regulated in conformity with the New York Convention of 1958 on the Recognition and Enforcement of Foreign Arbitral Awards, which applies in Mongolia on the basis of reciprocity and only to those disputes of commercial character.

The party applying for its enforcement shall supply the authenticated original award or a certified copy thereof, and the original arbitration agreement or a certified copy thereof (together with a certified translation). Civil Procedure Law applies to enforcement of foreign arbitration decisions before Mongolian courts.

Mongolia is a party to the 1965 Washington Convention on the Settlement of Investment Disputes between States and Nationals of Other States, which established the International Centre for the Settlement of Investment Disputes (ICSID).

§8.06 RECOGNITION OF OTHER FOREIGN PUBLIC DOCUMENTS

Apart from what has been mentioned in section 8.04[D], Mongolian law is silent on requirements for recognition of other foreign public documents.

§8.07 TREATIES FOR JUDICIAL COOPERATION

Since the collapse of the socialist regime in early 1990s, Mongolia started to enter into bilateral and multilateral agreements for judicial cooperation. Up to date, Mongolia has entered into an agreement on judicial cooperation with the following countries (some of them including recognition and enforcement of court judgments): Hungary, Bulgaria, Romania, Czech Republic, Slovakia, Republic of Korea, Democratic People's Republic of Korea, Cuba, China, France, Kazakhstan, Poland, Russia, Ukraine, Vietnam, Turkey, India, and Canada.

In addition, Mongolia is also a party to the following Hague Conventions: the 1954 Convention on Civil Procedure, the 1961 Convention on Abolishing the Requirement of Legalisation for Foreign Public Documents and the 1993 Convention on Protection of Children and Co-operation in Respect of Intercountry Adoption.

The Supreme Court of Mongolia has also established close cooperation with the Supreme Courts of the United States of America, the Russian Federation, the People's Republic of China, and the Republic of Korea.[4]

4. http://www.supremecourt.mn/english/International_Cooperation.htm.

CHAPTER 9

Philippines

Elizabeth H. Aguiling-Pangalangan[*]

§9.01 CODIFICATION OF PRIVATE INTERNATIONAL LAW AND RELEVANCE OF CASE LAW

[A] Codification and Case Law

Having been colonised by Spain for 333 years, the Philippine Civil Code which entered into force on 30 August 1950, was derived from Spanish law. The principal provisions on conflict of laws found in the Spanish Civil Code were adopted in the Philippine Civil Code. It is in here and the Family Code, which amended provisions in the Civil Code pertaining to persons and family relations, where many of the conflict of laws rules are contained.

Special statutes have also been enacted in the Philippines to govern cases involving foreign elements, among which are the following: The Corporation Code (B.P. Blg. 68) in 1980; the General Banking Act No. 337 (1948); the Act Instituting the Foreign Currency system in the Philippines, Rep. Act No. 426 (1972); the Philippine Foreign Law Guarantee Corporation under Presidential Decree No. 550 (1974); the Insurance Code (P.D. No. 1460 (1978); the Philippine Overseas Shipping Act (Rep. Act No. 1407 (1955); the Investment Incentives Act (Rep. Act No. 5186); and the Export Incentives Act (Rep. Act No. 6135), and Republic Act No. 7722 (1994) liberalising the entry of foreign banks in the Philippines.

* Professor at the University of the Philippines College of Law where she has taught Family Law, Contracts, Conflict of Laws and Child's Rights for more than 20 years. She obtained her Bachelor of Arts (AB), major in Political Science and her Bachelor of Laws (LLB) degrees from the University of the Philippines and her Master of Laws (LLM) form Harvard Law School, Cambridge, MA, USA. She attended the Private International Law sessions of the Hague Academy of International Law in 1998. She thanks law students, Cielo Marjorie Gono and Mark Bejemino for their assistance.

The other legal system that has directly influenced our laws is that of American law. The Philippines was granted independence from America only on 4 July 1946[1] and thus Philippine public law, including Constitutional law as well as rules of procedure and evidence, is largely based on American law. The 1987 Constitution is patterned after the US Constitution[2] and contains principles on nationality and comity.

Of late, the Philippines has witnessed an influx of cases which necessitate the knowledge and application of conflict of laws principles. Judicial decisions undoubtedly form the main bulk of source of conflict rules in the light of the Civil Code of the Philippines, which provides that all 'judicial decisions applying or interpreting the laws or the Constitution shall form a part of the legal system of the Philippines'.[3] Nevertheless, only decisions of the Supreme Court constitute binding case law.

[B] Multilateral Conventions Providing Uniform Substantive Law and/or International Jurisdictional Rules

Under its Constitution, the Philippines follows the 'incorporation' theory in the national law treatment of international law obligations. Under its 'Incorporation Clause', the Philippines 'adopts the generally accepted principles of international law as part of the law of the land'.[4] Moreover, the Constitution provides that a treaty, once ratified by at least two-thirds of the Philippine Senate, shall be 'valid and effective'.[5]

The Philippine Supreme Court has construed treaty ratification as partaking of a legislative character thus making a treaty directly enforceable before Philippine courts.[6] As consequence, however, the same court has accordingly applied the 'later-in-time' rule, thus allowing domestic rules to supersede and override an earlier treaty obligation.[7] On the other hand, the Philippines is a party to the Vienna Convention on the Law of Treaties, which provides that '[a] party may not invoke the provisions of its internal law as justification for its failure to perform a treaty'.[8]

The Philippines is a party to neither the UN Convention on Contracts for the International Sale of Goods (CISG), nor the Conventions for the International Carriage of Goods by Sea. Nevertheless, the Philippines is a party to the 1929 Convention for the

1. In March 1947, the Philippines and the United States signed a military assistance pact and the Philippines gave the United States a 99-year lease on designated military, naval, and air bases. Questions over Philippine sovereignty led the Philippine Senate to reject the bases treaty September 1991 and in 1992, the US forces departed.
2. R. Pangalangan, *Political Emergencies in the Philippines: Changing Labels and the Unchanging Need for Legitimacy*, in V. Ramraj and A. Thiruvengadam (eds), *Emergency Powers in Asia: Exploring the Limits of Legality* (Cambridge University Press, 2009), at 412.
3. Civil Code of the Philippines, Article 8.
4. *1987 Constitution*, Article II, s. 2.
5. *Ibid.*, Article VII, s. 21.
6. *Guerrero's Transport v. Blaylock*, G.R. No. 41518 (1976).
7. *Abbas v. Commission on Elections*, G.R. No. 89651 (1989).
8. Vienna Convention on the Law of Treaties, Article 27.

International Carriage of Goods by Air[9] and to nine multilateral treaties and protocols administered by the World Intellectual Property Organization (WIPO).[10]

§9.02 JURISDICTION OF LOCAL COURTS IN FOREIGN-RELATED CASES

[A] Grounds for Jurisdiction

[1] General

Philippine courts will assume international civil jurisdiction over cases involving a foreign element if they have jurisdiction over the subject matter, the property, or the parties involved.

Subject matter jurisdiction is the general power conferred by law to courts to take cognisance of cases of a general class or nature. It cannot be bestowed by consent of the parties and is instead 'conferred by the Constitution and the law and by the material allegations in the complaint, irrespective of whether claims or reliefs sought therein'.[11]

Jurisdiction over the person is acquired (i) over the plaintiff, the moment he invokes the aid of the court by filing a suit; (ii) over the defendant, when he voluntarily enters his appearance or is properly served with the legal process. In *Facilities Management Corporation v. De la Rosa*,[12] the Supreme Court ruled that:

> Indeed, if a foreign corporation, not engaged in business in the Philippines, is not barred from seeking redress from courts in the Philippines, *a fortiori*, that same corporation cannot claim exemption form being sued in Philippine courts for acts against a person or persons in the Philippines.

According to the Rules of Civil Procedure:[13]

> If any of the defendants does not reside and is not found in the Philippines, and the action affects the personal status of the plaintiff, or any property of said defendant located in the Philippines, the action may be commenced and tried in the court of the place where the plaintiff resides, or where the property or any portion thereof is situated or found.

Under special laws, certain courts or special boards are granted jurisdiction over specific disputes. For example, the Civil Aeronautics Board (aviation disputes involving air carriers, general sales agents, cargo sales agents and air freight forwarders),[14]

9. The Philippines has deposited the following reservation: 'Article 2, paragraph 1, of the Convention shall not apply to international air transport effected by the Republic of the Philippines.'
10. http://www.wipo.int/treaties/en/ShowResults.jsp?country_id = 168C.
11. *Raytheon v. Rouzie*, Jr., G.R. No. 162894, 26 Feb. 2008.
12. G.R. No. L-38649, 26 Mar. 1979; also in *Wang Laboratories v. Mendoza*, G.R.No. 72147, 1 Dec. 1987.
13. Rule 4, s. 3.
14. RA No. 776.

the National Labor Relations Commission (disputes arising from employer-employee relations)[15]...

Jurisdiction over the property results either from the seizure of the property under a legal process or from the institution of legal proceedings wherein the court's power over the property is recognised and made effective. Where the action is in rem, the situs could 'bind the world' and not just the interest of specific persons. The basis for the exercise of jurisdiction is the presence of the property within the territorial jurisdiction of the forum.

Another form of jurisdiction based on the state's physical power over property found within its territory is quasi in rem jurisdiction, but affects only interests of particular persons in that thing. In proceedings in rem and quasi in rem, all that due process requires is that the defendant be given adequate notice and opportunity to be heard. Both requirements are met in service of summons by publication.[16]

[2] Submitted to Jurisdiction

As mentioned in the previous section, the court can gain jurisdiction over the defendant also by his voluntary appearance or submission, which – according to the Rules of Civil Procedure – is considered equivalent to service of summons.[17] In *Tijam v. Sibonghanoy*,[18] the Supreme Court considered that after voluntary submission to the jurisdiction of the courts it had become 'too late for the loser to question the jurisdiction or power of the court'.

[3] Exclusive Jurisdiction

There is no express provision of law specifying exercise of exclusive jurisdiction by Philippine courts.

[B] Exclusion of Jurisdiction

[1] Immunity

[a] Sovereign Immunity

As mentioned before, the general principles of international law are considered as part of the law of the land. Accordingly, the Supreme Court has confirmed that the doctrine of state immunity applies restrictively: no immunity applies 'when the proceedings arise out of commercial transactions of the foreign sovereign, its commercial activities or economic affairs'.[19]

15. Presidential Decree No. 21.
16. Rules of Court, Rule 14, s. 15.
17. *Ibid.*, s. 23.
18. G.R. No. L-21450, 15 Apr. 1968.
19. *United States of America v. Ruiz*, G.R. No. L-35645, 22 May 1985.

The Supreme Court, in the case of *United States of America v. Guinto*,[20] categorically stated that this immunity likewise applies to 'state officials for acts allegedly performed in their official capacity'. However, the immunity for sovereign acts is impliedly waived when the state officials engage in acts *juris gestionis*.[21]

[b] Diplomatic and Consular Immunity

The Philippines is a party to the 1961 Vienna Convention on Diplomatic Relations and the 1963 Vienna Convention on Consular Relations.

[c] Other Immunities

The Philippines is a party to the 1961 Convention on the Privileges and Immunities of the United Nations, the 1969 Convention on Special Missions and the 1947 Convention on the Privileges and Immunities of the Specialised Agencies. Furthermore, several court decisions have confirmed the immunity enjoyed by regional international organisations and specialised agencies.[22]

[2] Forum Agreements in Favour of Foreign Courts

Under the principle of freedom of contract (Article 1306 of the Civil Code), parties may include a choice of forum clause in their contract agreement. While recognising the choice of forum clause, the Philippine Supreme Court has consistently asserted its jurisdiction to hear these cases.

The choice of court agreement should be exclusive, in writing and entered into before the filing of the suit.[23]

In *King Mau v. Sycip*,[24] the Court ruled that when the law confers concurrent jurisdiction in different courts, a choice of court in favour of one of those venues would be valid. In *Hong Kong and Shanghai Banking Corporation v. Sherman*,[25] Eastern Book Supply Service (Company), a company incorporated in Singapore was granted by HSBC an overdraft facility in the amount of SGD 200,000.00. As a security for the repayment by the company of the sum advanced by the petitioner Bank, both private respondents Jack Robert Sherman and Deodato Reloj who were then directors of the Company, acted as guarantor. Upon failure of the Company and the guarantors to pay their obligation, HSBC filed a case in the Regional Trial Court of Quezon City, which jurisdiction was contested by private respondents because of a stipulation in their

20. *M.H. Wylie v. Rarang*, G.R. No. 74135, 28 May 1992.
21. *Ibid.*
22. For example, in *Southeast Asian Fisheries Development Center-Aquaculture Department et al., v. National Labor Relations Commission* (GR. No. 86773, 14 Feb. 1992); *World Health Organization v. Aquino* (48 SCRA 242, 1972).
23. *Pilipino Telephone Corporation v. Tecson*, GR. No. 156966, 7 May 2004.
24. G.R. No. L-5897, 23 Apr. 1954.
25. G.R. No. 72494, 11 Aug. 1989.

Guarantee, which gave the courts of the Republic of Singapore 'jurisdiction over all disputes arising under this guarantee'. Asserting jurisdiction, the Philippine Supreme Court ruled that:[26]

> the parties did not thereby stipulate that only the courts of Singapore, to the exclusion of all the rest, has jurisdiction. Neither did the clause in question operate to divest Philippine courts of jurisdiction. In international law, jurisdiction is often defined as the right of a State to exercise authority over persons and things within its boundaries subject to certain exceptions... A State is competent to take hold of any judicial matter it sees fit by making its courts and agencies assume jurisdiction over all kinds of cases brought before them.

In the recent case of *Raytheon v. Rouzie, Jr*,[27] the Philippine Supreme Court once again reiterated jurisdiction of Philippine courts, this time by correctly distinguishing between a choice of forum clause and a choice of law provision.Here,Brand Marine Services, Inc. (BMSI), a corporation existing under the laws of the State of Connecticut, USA, and Stockton W. Rouzie, Jr, an American citizen, entered into a contract whereby BMSI hired Rouzie to negotiate the sale of services in several government projects in the Philippines for an agreed remuneration. Rouzie, Jr, obtained a service contract with the Republic of the Philippines on behalf of BMSI for the dredging of rivers affected by the Mt. Pinatubo eruption and mudflows. A legal problem ensued between the parties and Rouzie commenced a suit for illegal dismissal and non-payment of commissions. He filed a labour case as well an action for damages. The case centred on whether or not the choice of law clause in the contract affected the exercise of judicial jurisdiction by the Philippine courts. The court held that, although 'the subject contract included a stipulation that the same shall be governed by the laws of the State of Connecticut (this) does not suggest that the Philippine courts, or any other foreign tribunal for that matter, are precluded from hearing the civil action'.

[3] Arbitration Clause

Arbitration, as an alternative mode of dispute resolution, has long been recognised in the Philippines as embodied in Book IV of the Civil Code, which has been in force since 1950. The Philippine Arbitration Law (Republic Act No. 876), enacted on 19 June 1953, continues to be the governing law on Domestic Arbitration. Under Resolution No. 71 of the Philippine Senate[28] reciprocal recognition and enforcement of international arbitration agreements between parties of different nationalities within a contracting state are viable.

Moreover, in 2004 the Congress of the Philippines passed Republic Act 9285, known as the Alternative Dispute Resolution Act, which governs international commercial arbitration. This law expressly adopts the United Nations Commission on International Trade Law (UNCITRAL) 'Model Law'.

---

26. *Ibid.*
27. *Supra* n. 11.
28. Passed on 10 May 1965.

The pro-arbitration policies of the Philippines are encapsulated in Rule 2: Statement of Policies of the Special Alternative Dispute Resolution (ADR) Rules. These were passed 'to encourage and promote the use of ADR, particularly arbitration and mediation, as an important means to achieve speedy and efficient resolution of disputes, impartial justice, curb a litigious culture and to de-clog court dockets'. By these Rules, courts are further constrained to 'intervene only in the cases allowed by law or these Special ADR Rules' in exercise of the power of judicial review.

According to Rule 2.2, where the parties have agreed to submit their dispute to arbitration, courts have the duty to refer the parties to arbitration pursuant to Republic Act No. 9285. The arbitration agreement is deemed as the law between the parties and consistent with the general rule on contracts, parties are expected to abide by it in good faith.[29] In addition, courts cannot refuse to refer parties to arbitration even on the following grounds:

(a) The referral tends to oust a court of its jurisdiction.
(b) The court is in a better position to resolve the dispute subject of arbitration.
(c) The referral would result in multiplicity of suits.
(d) The arbitration proceeding has not commenced.
(e) The place of arbitration is in a foreign country.
(f) One or more of the issues are legal and one or more of the arbitrators are not lawyers.
(g) One or more of the arbitrators are not Philippine nationals.
(h) One or more of the arbitrators are alleged not to possess the required qualification under the arbitration agreement or law.

In *Puromines, Inc. v. Court of Appeals*,[30] the court stressed that arbitration is 'valid and constitutional' and that 'the rule now is that unless the agreement is such as absolutely to close the doors of the courts against the parties, which agreement would be void, the courts will look with favour upon such amicable arrangements and will only interfere with great reluctance to anticipate or nullify the action of the arbitrator'.

In a recent case,[31] petitioner Korea Technologies Co., Ltd. (KOGIES), a Korean corporation, executed a contract to set up a Liquified Petroleum Gas (LPG) Cylinder Manufacturing Plant in Cavite for Pacific General Steel Manufacturing Corp. (PGSMC), a domestic corporation. After a problem arose regarding payment, KOGIES instituted an application for arbitration before the Korean Commercial Arbitration Board (KCAB) in Seoul, Korea, pursuant to the arbitration clause contained in the Contract. PGSMC filed an opposition to the temporary restraining order (TRO) arguing that KOGIES was not entitled to the TRO since the arbitration clause which ousted the local courts of jurisdiction was null and void for violating public policy. On appeal, the Supreme Court, referring to Article 2044 of the Civil Code (which 'sanctions the validity of

29. Article 1159 of the Civil Code states that '[o]bligations arising from contracts have the force of law between the contracting parties and should be complied with in good faith'.
30. G.R. No. 91228, 22 Mar. 1993.
31. *Korea Technologies Co. v. Hon. Lerma*, G.R. No. 143581, 7 Jan. 2008.

mutually agreed arbitral clause or the finality and binding effect of an arbitral award'), held that the arbitration clause stipulating that the arbitration must be done in Seoul and that the arbitral award is final and binding, does not offend public policy.

[C] Non-exercise of Jurisdiction

[1] Forum Non Conveniens

Even if the court may assume international jurisdiction over the case, it may decline to try it on the ground that the controversy may be more suitably tried elsewhere. A court may choose not to exercise jurisdiction based on forum non conveniens in order to prevent the plaintiff from forum shopping. Instead of making a definite choice of forum from their action, litigants file actions in all available courts and execute the judgment which is most favourable to them. It may also consist in a party against whom an adverse judgment has been rendered in one forum, seeking a more favourable opinion in another forum other than by appeal or special civil action of certiorari.[32] Moreover, non-resident litigants' choice of forum wherein to sue may be 'for malicious reasons, such as to secure procedural advantages, to annoy and harass the defendant, to avoid overcrowded dockets, or to select a more friendly venue'.[33] The proscription against forum shopping is aimed at avoiding conflicting decisions by different courts, a situation antithetical to the concept of an orderly and fair administration of justice.

The Supreme Court in the case of *First Philippine International Bank v. Court of Appeals*[34] underscored that:

> [t]o combat these less than honorable excuses, the principle of forum non conveniens was developed whereby a court, in conflicts of law cases, may refuse impositions on its jurisdiction where it is not the most 'convenient' or available forum and the parties are not precluded from seeking remedies elsewhere.

In the *Bank of América v. Court of Appeals*,[35] citing an earlier court ruling in *Communication Materials and Design, Inc. v. Court of Appeals*,[36] the Court held that:

> Whether a suit should be entertained or dismissed on the basis of said doctrine depends largely upon the facts of the particular case and is addressed to the sound discretion of the trial court... [w]hile it is within the discretion of the trial court to abstain from assuming jurisdiction on this ground, it should do so only after vital

32. *Velasquez et al. v. Hernandez*, GR 1507732, 31 Aug. 2004, citing *Bangko Silangan Development Bank v. Court of Appeals*, G.R. No. 110480, 29 Jun. 2001; *Philippine Economic Zone Authority v. Vianzon*, G.R. No. 131020, 20 Jul. 2000; *Progressive Development Corporation, Inc. v. Court of Appeals*, G.R. No. 123555, 22 Jan. 1999.
33. G.R. No. 120135, 31 Mar. 2003.
34. G.R. No. 115849, 24 Jan. 1996.
35. G.R. No. 120135, 31 Mar. 2003.
36. GR No. 154618, 14 Apr. 2004. The Court ruled that 'a Philippine Court may assume jurisdiction over the case if it chooses to do so; provided, that the following requisites are met: (1) that the Philippine Court is one to which the parties may conveniently resort to; (2) that the Philippine Court is in a position to make an intelligent decision as to the law and the facts; and, (3) that the Philippine Court has or is likely to have power to enforce its decision'.

facts are established, to determine whether special circumstances require the court's desistance; and that the propriety of dismissing a case based on this principle of forum non conveniens requires a factual determination, hence it is more properly considered a matter of defense.

[2] Lis alibi pendens

Lis alibi pendens is a Latin term that literally means 'action elsewhere pending'. *Lis alibi pendens* arises from international comity and provides that where proceedings involving the same cause of action are pending in a court elsewhere, any court other than the court first seized must refuse to exercise jurisdiction during the pendency of parallel litigation.[37]

The Philippine Rules of Court[38] thus require a plaintiff filing a case in court to certify under oath in the complaint that:

(a) he has not theretofore commenced any action or filed any claim involving the same issues in any court, tribunal, or quasi-judicial agency and, to the best of his knowledge, no such other action or claim is pending therein;
(b) if there is such other pending action or claim, a complete statement of the present status thereof; and
(c) if he should thereafter learn that the same or similar action or claim has been filed or is pending, he shall report that fact within five days therefrom to the court wherein his aforesaid complaint or initiatory pleading has been filed.

Failure of a plaintiff to comply with these requirements shall be cause for the dismissal of the case without prejudice. The Rules further state that 'if the acts of the party or his counsel clearly constitute wilful and deliberate forum shopping, the same shall be ground for summary dismissal with prejudice and shall constitute direct contempt, as well as a cause for administrative sanctions'.[39]

Thus given the broad language of the Rules, filing of a case involving the same subject matter, parties and issues in a court or tribunal within or outside the Philippines gives the latter Philippine courts reason to decline jurisdiction over the case in favour of the other court which first seized jurisdiction. The purpose of this is to prevent parallel proceedings from taking place at the same time that could give rise to irreconcilable judgments.

In the case of *Societe Generale de Surveillance (SGS) v. Republic of the Philippines*,[40] the ICSID Tribunal held that SGS was bound by the terms of the 'exclusive jurisdiction clause' found in Article 12 of the three-year agreement (CISS Agreement) between the Swiss corporation and the. Philippines. In the CISS Agreement, SGS agreed

37. <definitions.uslegal.com/l/lis-alibi-pendens/> Accessed on 8 Aug. 2014.
38. Rules of Civil Procedure, Rule 7, s. 5.
39. *Ibid.*
40. ICSID Case No. ARB/02/6, 29 Jan. 2004.

to provide specialised services to assist the Philippines in improving its customs clearance and control. Article 12 thereof required all contractual disputes to be submitted to Philippine courts to be decided in accordance with Philippine law. The Tribunal held that the arbitrations proceedings should be stayed while the Philippine court was still deciding on the matter of how much amount was due but still unpaid under the CISS Agreement.

§9.03 APPLICABLE LAW

Subject-procedure characterisation determines the extent to which a court of justice may apply forum law. Substantive law refers to 'that part of the law which creates, defines, and regulates rights' in contrast to procedural law which 'prescribes the method of enforcing rights or obtaining redress for their invasion'.[41]

If the issue is one that pertains to substantive law the court may apply *lex fori* or foreign law, but if it is procedural or remedial in character, the court must apply *lex fori*. The application of the law of litigation aims at relieving a court or tribunal the burden, impracticality and inconvenience caused by demands to conduct a trial in accordance with a foreign law. Thus, the *lex fori* governs procedural matters such as service of summons, filing and service if pleadings, judgments and other papers as well as periods of appeal.

[A] Choice of Law

[1] Express Stipulation

Contract being the law between the parties, parties to a contract may include any 'stipulation, clauses, terms and conditions as they may deem convenient'.[42] The Civil Code provides that when the 'terms of the contract are clear and leave no doubt upon the intent of the contracting parties, the literal meaning of its stipulation shall control'.[43] The stipulations and clauses in a contract as well as the object of the contract should however not be contrary to law, morals, good customs, public order, or public policy.[44]

Thus in the case of *Pakistan International Airlines Corporation v. Ople*,[45] the Supreme Court referred to the provisions of the employment agreement entered into by two Filipino citizens with the foreign airline doing business in the Philippines. The court held that although the contract specifically identified the law of Pakistan as the

41. Black's Law Dictionary Free (2nd Ed.) and The Law Dictionary: http://thelawdictionary.org/substantive-law/#ixzz2cbmehSlV.
42. Article 1306.
43. Article 1370.
44. Civil Code, Articles 1306, 1347, and 1352.
45. G.R. No. 61594, 28 Sep. 1990.

applicable law to govern disputes arising from the contract, such was in violation of the Philippines' public policy. The court stated that said clause:

> cannot be invoked to prevent the application of Philippine labor laws and regulations to the subject matter of this case, i.e., the employer-employee relationship between PIA and private respondents. We have already pointed out that the relationship is much affected with public interest and that the otherwise applicable Philippine laws and regulations cannot be rendered illusory by the parties agreeing upon some other law to govern their relationship.

A choice of a law clause that violates public policy may be set aside. This is one of the limitations to choice of law given that the court is faced with 'counter balancing the principle of autonomy of contracting parties [and] the equally general rule that...provisions relating to matters affected with public policy are deemed not written in to the contract'.[46]

[2] *Implied Choice*

A contract is defined in Article 1305 of the Civil Code as 'a meeting of minds between two persons whereby one binds himself, with respect to the other, to give something or to render some service'. Parties who enter into a contract may have intended a particular law to apply without having categorically stated it. Their intention shall be gauged principally by 'their contemporaneous and subsequent acts'.[47] In case of doubt as to the parties' real intention, their implied intent may be presumed using the principle of validity. This is contained in the Civil Code, which states that: 'Art. 1373. If some stipulation of any contract should admit of several meanings, it shall be understood as bearing that import which is most adequate to render it effectual'.

The Philippine Civil Code further provides that when it is certain that there was meeting of the minds of the parties to the contract but their true intent is not expressed in the contract, one of the parties may ask for a reformation of the contract for it to reflect their true intention.[48]

These rules apply to contracts involving a foreign element except if prohibited by the *lex loci contractus* of a state other than the Philippines. The law of the place where the contract was made may be determined by looking at the last act necessary to create a binding agreement between the parties. In the absence of an express choice of law, it may be presumed that the parties contemplated the application of the law of the place where the contract was entered into.

---

46. *Manila Resources Development Corporation v. NLRC*, G.R. No. 75242, 2 Sep. 1992.
47. Article 1371.
48. Article 1359. When, there having been a meeting of the minds of the parties to a contract, their true intention is not expressed in the instrument purporting to embody the agreement, by reason of mistake, fraud, inequitable conduct or accident, one of the parties may ask for the reformation of the instrument to the end that such true intention may be expressed.

[B] Other Cases

Where the parties have not made a choice, the following rules apply:

> Article 15, Civil Code: Laws relating to family rights and duties, or to the status, condition and legal capacity of persons are binding upon citizens of the Philippines, even though living abroad.
>
> Article 16, Civil Code: Real property as well as personal property is subject to the law of the country where it is stipulated. However, intestate and testamentary successions, both with respect to the order of succession and to the amount of successional rights and to the intrinsic validity of testamentary provisions, shall be regulated by the national law of the person whose succession is under consideration, whatever may be the nature of the property and regardless of the country wherein said property may be found. Article 17, Civil Code: The forms and solemnities of contracts, wills, and other public instruments shall be governed by the laws of the country in which they are executed. When the acts referred to are executed before the diplomatic or consular officials of the Republic of the Philippines in a foreign country, the solemnities established by Philippine laws shall be observed in their execution. Prohibitive laws concerning persons, their acts or property, and those which have, for their object, public order, public policy and good customs shall not be rendered ineffective by laws or judgments promulgated, or by determinations or conventions agreed upon in a foreign country.
>
> Article 26, Family Code: All marriages solemnized outside the Philippines, in accordance with the laws in force in the country where they were solemnized, and valid there as such, shall also be valid in this country, except those prohibited under Articles 35 (1), (4), (5) and (6), 36, 37 and 38. Where a marriage between a Filipino citizen and a foreigner is validly celebrated and a divorce is thereafter validly obtained abroad by the alien spouse capacitating him or her to remarry, the Filipino spouse shall have capacity to remarry under Philippine law.

[C] *Renvoi*

Philippine courts have the option of either rejecting or accepting the *renvoi*. In many more cases, it has accepted the *renvoi* by referring to the foreign state's 'whole law' composed of its internal law as well as choice of law rules.

In *Aznar v. Garcia*,[49] an American citizen residing in the Philippines executed a will leaving the bulk of his estate to one daughter and merely bequeathing an amount of money to another, who opposed the partition of properties since the distribution did not follow Philippine laws giving children equal shares of their parent's estate. The court ruled that since the testator, 'was a citizen of the United States and of the State of

49. 61 O.G. No. 46 p. 7303 (1963).

California at the time of his death, the successional rights and intrinsic validity of the provisions in his will are to be governed by the law of California'. The problem however was that under the California Probate Code, a testator may dispose of his property by will in the form and manner he desires but the conflict of laws rules of California provided otherwise. Article 946 of the Civil Code of California, stated that: 'If there is no law to the contrary, in the place where personal property is situated, it is deemed to follow the person of its owner, and is governed by the law of his domicile.'

Since the deceased was domiciled in the Philippines, the Supreme Court accepted the *renvoi*. However, there is no law - substantive or procedural - that will prevent the court from rejecting the *renvoi* should it decide that this would give rise to a just result.

Renvoi is inapplicable in a false conflict, where both countries involved have identical substantive laws or where one of the countries has no real interest in ensuring that its law is applied.[50]

[D] Mandatory Rules of the Forum and of Third States

Under the principles of comity and reciprocity, the court or administrative agency should look into the application of foreign law and apply it. There are instances, however, when the law of forum must be applied in spite of the presence of a foreign element. The exceptions fall under three main categories, namely: (1) when the local law expressly so provides; (2) when there is failure to plead and prove the foreign law or judgment; and (3) when the case falls under any of the exceptions to the rule of comity.

According to Article 17, paragraph 3 of the Philippine Civil Code:

> Prohibitive laws concerning persons, their acts or property, and those which have for their objective public order, public policy and good customs shall not be rendered ineffective by laws or judgments promulgated, or by determinations or conventions agreed upon in a foreign country.

As such, a foreign law contrary to an important public policy of the forum cannot be applied. Dismissal of a case on grounds of public policy is not a dismissal on the merits and the plaintiff can go elsewhere to file another suit. Closely related to this is the prohibition in applying a foreign law that is contrary to good morals. It is difficult to define the standard of *contra bonos mores* but one could argue that this would necessarily include laws that are universally considered as contrary to good morals. In the final analysis, however, the determination of what is *contra bonos mores* is better left to the forum court. Resort to this exception should not be abused given its inherent subjectivity. The danger in disregarding a clear choice of law on the ground of *contra bonos mores* is that it could be a mere ruse to decide it no differently from a domestic case in order to apply internal law.

Moreover, when the issue involved in the case is the enforcement of a foreign claim that is fiscal or administrative, the State is not obliged to enforce the revenue law of another. This reasoning has led courts to deny enforcement of tax claims brought by

50. J. Coquia and E. Aguiling-Pangalangan, *Conflict of laws: cases, materials and comments* (2000).

foreign countries on local residents. Similarly, when the foreign law is penal in charater, it cannot be applied. The penal law exception has its roots in a statement of US Supreme Court Chief Justice Marshall that 'the Courts of no country execute the penal laws of another'. In *Lorenzo v. Posadas*,[51] the Philippine Supreme Court considered that:

> a statute is penal when it imposes punishment for an offense committed against the state which, under the Constitution, the Executive has the power to pardon. In common use, however, this sense has been enlarged to include within the term 'penal statutes' all statutes which command or prohibit certain acts, and establish penalties for their violation, and even those which, without expressly prohibiting certain acts, impose a penalty upon their commission.

[E] Proof of Foreign Law

Courts can take judicial cognisance only of domestic laws. Foreign law must be proved like any other fact. Section 24, Rule 132 of the Rules of Court requires proof of foreign law, either by (1) official publications or (2) copies attested by the officer having legal custody of the documents. If the copies of official records are not kept in the Philippines, these must be (a) accompanied by a certificate issued by the proper diplomatic or consular officer in the Philippine foreign service stationed in the foreign country in which the record is kept and (b) authenticated by the seal of his office. Nevertheless, in *Willamette Iron and Steel Works v. Muzzal*,[52] the Supreme Court considered the testimony under oath of an attorney-at-law of San Francisco, California, who quoted verbatim the relevant provision of California Civil Code and testified that that was the law in force at the time the obligations were contracted, as sufficient evidence to establish the existence of said law. The Court ruled that 'Section 41, Rule 123 (Section 25, Rule 132 of the Revised Rules of Court) does not exclude the presentation of other competent evidence to prove the existence of a foreign law.'

Regarding the lack of proof, in the case of *Zalamea v. Court of Appeals*,[53] the Supreme Court held that:

> The U.S. law or regulation allegedly authorizing overbooking has never been proved. Foreign laws do not prove themselves nor can the courts take judicial notice of them. Like any other fact, they must be alleged and proved... Respondent TWA relied solely on the statement of Ms. Gwendolyn Lather its customer service agent, in her deposition dated January 27, 1986 that the Code of Federal Regulations of the Civil Aeronautics Board allows overbooking. Aside from said statement, no official publication of said code was presented as evidence. Thus, respondent court's finding that overbooking is specifically allowed by the US Code of Federal Regulations has no basis in fact.

The Court held further that even if the Code of Federal Regulations did exist and was proven, it would not govern this legal situation following the principle of *lex loci*

51. 64 Phil 353 (1937).
52. GR No L-42538, 21 May 1935.
53. 228 SCRA 27 (1993).

contractus. Hence, Philippine law is the governing law when the tickets were sold and issued in the Philippines.

In *Miciano v. Brimo*,[54] a Turkish national left a will expressly choosing Philippine law on succession to govern the partition of his properties. His brother opposed the partition on the ground that it was in violation of the Philippine Civil Code; but he failed to prove that the said testamentary dispositions were not in accordance with Turkish laws and to present any evidence showing what the relevant Turkish laws were. The Court held that '[i]n the absence of evidence on such laws, they are presumed to be the same as those of the Philippines'. Further,there was 'no evidence in the record that the national law of the testator Joseph G. Brimo was violated in the testamentary dispositions in question which, not being contrary to our laws in force, must be complied with and executed'.

Considering that the testator's last will and testament was the definitive occasion in which he could decide how his properties should be distributed, the Supreme Court should have instead used a modern approach to choice of law, such as the most significant relationship theory. With this the court could have established that the Philippines had the most significant connection with the case, which would have led it to arrive at the same conclusion (e.g., application of Philippine law) without flouting the testator's express intentions.

Garcia v. Recio[55] is an interesting case that illustrates another option available to the court when there is failure to prove foreign law. In 1987, Rederick Recio, a Filipino, married an Australian citizen in the Philippines. After two years, they obtained a decree of divorce from an Australian family court. In 1992, Recio became an Australian citizen and in 1994 married Garcia, a Filipina, in the Philippines citing in their application for a marriage license, that he was 'single' and 'Filipino'. By 1995, Recio and Garcia lived separately and their conjugal assets were divided in accordance with their Statutory Declarations secured in Australia. Garcia filed a petition for nullity of marriage in the Philippines on the ground of bigamy, claiming that she was unaware of Recio's subsisting marriage at the time he married her. While the suit was pending, Recio secured a divorce decree from a family court in Sydney on the ground that the marriage had irretrievably broken down. The trial court declared the marriage dissolved because of the divorce decree was valid and recognised in the Philippines.

The Supreme Court underscored that although Philippine law does not provide for absolute divorce, it recognises a divorce secured by the alien spouse in a mixed marriage involving a Filipino and a foreigner. Under Article 26 of the Family Code, Filipino spouse may contract a subsequent marriage in case the divorce is 'validly obtained abroad by the alien spouse capacitating him or her to remarry'. Thus, the court held that 'before a foreign divorce decree can be recognised by our courts, the party pleading it must prove the divorce as a fact and demonstrate its conformity to the foreign law allowing it. Presentation solely of the divorce decree is insufficient'. The court pointed out that the trial court:

54. 50 Phil. 867 (1924).
55. 366 SCRA 437 (2001).

> erred in finding that the divorce decree ipso facto clothed respondent with the legal capacity to remarry without requiring him to adduce sufficient evidence to show the Australian personal law governing his status; or at the very least, to prove his legal capacity to contract the second marriage.

But neither could the Supreme Court declare her marriage to respondent null and void on the ground of bigamy since it may turn out that under Australian law, one of the effects of the divorce decree is termination of the marriage bond which would have capacitated him to marry. The court remanded the case to the trial court to receive evidence to show Recio's legal capacity to marry petitioner.

§9.04 PROCEDURAL ISSUES

[A] Service of Summons and Judicial Orders Abroad

The Philippines is not a party to the 1965 Hague Convention on the Service Abroad of Judicial and Extrajudicial Documents in Civil or Commercial Matters.

Personal service is the general rule.

In case of a foreign company doing business in the Philippines, service of summons is effected by personal service on its resident agent designated in accordance with the law, or the government official designated by the law (i.e., the Securities and Exchange Commission, who shall transmit a copy by mail to the foreign corporation), or upon any of the foreign company's officers or agents in the Philippines.[56]

In case of natural persons, Rule 14, section 15 of the Rules of Court states that when the defendant is not a resident of the Philippines and is not found within the territory, and the action affects the personal status of the plaintiff or relates to property within the Philippines in which the defendant has or claims an interest, service may, by leave of court, be effected out of the Philippines by personal service: a copy of the papers is delivered personally to the party or his counsel, or by leaving it in his office with a person having charge thereof. If no person is found in his office, or his office is not known, then a copy may be left at the party's or counsel's residence, with a person of sufficient age and discretion then residing therein. The Rules of Court further provides that service of summons may likewise be made 'by publication in a newspaper of general circulation in such places and for such time as the court may order, in which case a copy of the summons and order of the court shall be sent by registered mail to the last known address of the defendant, or in any other manner the court may deem sufficient'. Nevertheless, in *Sahagun v. Court of Appeals*,[57] it was ruled that summon by publication is not proper in actions strictly in personam (which would require personal service of summons), so the plaintiff should transform the action into an in rem *or* quasi in rem by attaching property the Philippines of the defendant (under Rule 57, section 1.f of the Rules of Court). In *State Investment House Inc. v. Citibank,*

56. Rules of Court, Rule 14, s. 12. Section 128 of the Corporation Code requires designation of a resident agent before the issuance of a license to transact business in the Philippines.
57. GR. No. 78328, 3 Jun. 1991.

NA,[58] the Supreme Court explained that such possibility does not apply in case of foreign companies since Rule 57, section 1.f of the Rules of Court does only refer to natural persons.

Following the Supreme Court's ruling in *Northwest*,[59] it is the procedural law of the country from where the judgment originated that determines whether or not extraterritorial service of summons is allowed. In the mentioned case, a passenger sales agency agreement entered onto by Northwest and CF Sharp through its Japan branch. Sharp was authorised by Northwest to sell its airline tickets but failed to remit proceeds of the sale leading to a suit in Tokyo for collection of the unremitted amount. The Tokyo District Court of Japan issued a writ of summons against Sharp at its Yokohama office. After two failed attempts at serving summons, the court decided to have summons served at Sharp's head office in Manila. Though Sharp accepted the writs it failed to appear at the hearing leading to the judgment against it for more than JPY 83 million. Northwest was unable to execute the decision in Japan so it went to the Philippines to enforce the Japanese judgment. After Sharp questioned the validity of the foreign judgment, the Supreme Court held that:

> It is settled that matters of remedy and procedure such as those relating to the service of summons upon the defendant are governed by the lex fori or the internal law of the forum. In this case, it is the procedural law of Japan where the judgment was rendered that determines the validity of the extraterritorial service of process on Sharp.

The Supreme Court further discussed its two options in the face of Sharp's failure to prove Japanese procedural law that invalidates extraterritorial service of summons. It applied the Philippine presumption of validity and regularity in the service of summons and decision rendered by the foreign court. It further held that: 'In the light of the absence of proof regarding Japanese law, the presumption of identity or similarity or the so called processual presumption may be invoked.'

The court then referred to its Rules of Court on service of summons to foreign corporations doing business in the Philippines and held that service to Sharp followed the Rules of Court in relation with the Corporation Code.

[B] Obtaining Evidence Abroad

The Philippines is not a party to the 1979 Hague Convention on the taking of Evidence Abroad in Civil or Commercial Matters.

The Rules of Court, under the modes of discovery, allow the taking of deposition in foreign countries as provided under Rule 23. Depositions may be taken: (a) on notice before a secretary of embassy or legation, consul general, consul, vice-consul, or consular agent of the Republic of the Philippines; (b) before such person or officer as may be appointed by commission or under letters rogatory; or (c) before persons

58. G.R. No. 70026-27, 17 Oct. 1991.
59. *Northwest Orient Airline, Inc. v. Court of Appeals and C.F. Sharp and Company, Inc.*, G.R. No. 11222573, 9 Feb. 1995.

authorised to administer oaths as stipulated in writing by the parties.[60] When parties so stipulate in writing these depositions may be used like other depositions.[61]

Furthermore, section 12 of Rule 23 allows for the issuance of a commission or letters rogatory only when necessary or convenient, on application and notice, and on such terms and with such direction as are just and appropriate. Officers may be designated in notices or commissions either by name or descriptive title and letters rogatory may be addressed to the appropriate judicial authority in the foreign country.

In the *Pfeger R. Dulay v. Rodrigo S. Dulay*,[62] the Supreme Court explained that:

> [L]eave of court is not required when the deposition is to be taken before a secretary of embassy or legation, consul general, consul, vice-consul or consular agent of the Republic of the Philippines and the defendant's answer has already been served.

However, if the deposition is to be taken in a foreign country where the Philippines has no secretary of embassy or legation, consul general, consul, vice-consul, or consular agent, it may be taken only before such person or officer as may be appointed.[63] Letters rogatory, on the other hand, may be defined as:

> (a)n instrument sent in the name and by the authority of a judge or court to another, requesting the latter to cause to be examined, upon interrogatories filed in a cause pending before the former, a witness who is within the jurisdiction of the judge or court to whom such letters are addressed.[64]

Section 12, Rule 24 states that a commission is addressed to 'officers . . . designated . . . either by name or descriptive title,' while letters rogatory are addressed to some 'appropriate judicial authority in the foreign state.' Noteworthy in this connection is the indication in the Rules that letters rogatory may be applied for and issued only after a commission has been 'returned unexecuted'.[65]

With regard to international commercial arbitration, Article 27 of the UNCITRAL Model Law (applicable by virtue of R.A. 9285) enables the arbitral tribunal 'to request from a competent court of this State assistance in taking evidence. The court may execute the request within its competence and according to its rules on taking evidence'.

[C] Restraint of Foreign Proceedings

Anti-suit injunctions in restraint of foreign proceedings are a relatively unfamiliar concept in Philippine jurisprudence. Nevertheless, under the Rules of Court, preliminary injunction may be issued requiring a party or a court, agency or a person to refrain

60. Section 11. Persons before whom depositions may be taken in foreign countries.
61. Section 14. Stipulations regarding taking of depositions.
62. G.R. No. 158857, 11 Nov. 2005.
63. J. Feria, *Civil Procedure* (1969 ed.), at 415, citing *Cyclopedic Law Dictionary*, at 200.
64. *Ibid.*, at 653.
65. *Dasmarinas Garments, Inc. v. Hon Ruben Reyes and American President Lines, Ltd.*, G.R. No. 108229, 24 Aug. 1993.

from a particular act or acts or performance of a particular act or acts as provided under Rule 58. Thus, an injunction may be applied to restraint a person from continuing or initiating a proceeding in a foreign forum.

A preliminary injunction may be granted by the court where the action or proceeding is pending when it is established:

(a) That the applicant is entitled to the relief demanded, and the whole or part of such relief consists in restraining the commission or continuance of the act or acts complained of, or in requiring the performance of an act or acts, either for a limited period or perpetually.
(b) That the commission, continuance or non-performance of the act or acts complained of during the litigation would probably work injustice to the applicant.
(c) That a party, court, agency or a person is doing, threatening, or is attempting to do, or is procuring or suffering to be done, some act or acts probably in violation of the rights of the applicant respecting the subject of the action or proceeding, and tending to render the judgment ineffectual.

The Supreme Court further explained that:

> To be entitled to the injunctive writ, petitioners must show that (1) there exists a clear and unmistakable right to be protected; (2) this right is directly threatened by an act sought to be enjoined; (3) the invasion of the right is material and substantial; and (4) there is an urgent and paramount necessity for the writ to prevent serious and irreparable damage.[66]

[D] Proof of Foreign Public Documents

The Philippines is not a signatory to the 1961 Hague Convention Abolishing the Requirement for Legalisation for Foreign Public Documents.

Under Philippine Law, foreign public documents may be evidenced by an official publication thereof or by a copy attested by the officer having the legal custody of the record, or by his deputy, and accompanied, if the record is not kept in the Philippines, with a certificate that such officer has the custody.[67] In *Asiavest Limited v. Court of Appeals*[68] the Supreme Court, citing the Rules of Court held:

> Under Sections 24 and 25, Rule 132 of the New Rules of Evidence, the record of public documents of a sovereign authority, tribunal, official body, or public officer may be proved by (1) an official publication thereof or (2) a copy attested by the officer having the legal custody thereof, which must be accompanied, if the record is not kept in the Philippines, with a certificate that such officer has the custody. The certificate may be issued by the secretary of the embassy or legation, consul general, consul, vice consul, or consular agent, or any officer in the foreign service

66. *Australian professional realty, Inc., jesus garcia, and lydia marciano v. municipality of padre garcia batangas province*, G. R. No. 183367, 14 Mar. 2012.
67. Section 24, Rule 132, Rules of Court.
68. *Asiavest Limited v. Court of Appeals*, G.R. No. 128803, 25 Sep. 1998.

of the Philippines stationed in the foreign country in which the record is kept, and authenticated by the seal of his office. The attestation must state, in substance, that the copy is a correct copy of the original, or a specific part thereof, as the case may be, and must be under the official seal of the attesting officer.

This certification requirement is not a mere technicality but is intended to justify the giving of full faith and credit to the genuineness of a document in a foreign country.[69] In *Heirs of Arcilla v. Teodoro*,[70] the Supreme Court clarified that this rule does not apply to documents acknowledged before a notary public abroad, it held:

> From the foregoing provision [referring to Section 24, Rule 132, Rules of Court], it can be gathered that it does not include documents acknowledged before [a] notary public abroad. For foreign public documents to be admissible for any purpose here in our courts, the same must be certified by any officer of the Philippine legation stationed in the country where the documents could be found or had been executed. However, after judicious studies of the rule, Sec. 24, Rule 132 of the 1997 Rules of Court basically pertains to written official acts, or records of the official of the sovereign authority, official bodies and tribunals, and public officers, whether of the Philippines, or of a foreign country. This is so, as Sec. 24, Rule 132 explicitly refers only to paragraph (a) of Sec. 19. If the rule comprehends to cover notarial documents, the rule could have included the same.

Thus, the Supreme Court reiterated that although the certificate of forum shopping that was submitted did not bear the certification provided under section 24, Rule 132 of the Rules of Court, '[what] is important is the fact that the respondent-applicant certified before a commissioned officer clothed with powers to administer oath that [s]he has not and will not commit forum shopping'.

Notwithstanding this pronouncement, the Supreme Court recognised certain exceptions. *Asiavest Limited*[71] pointed out that '[a]lthough it is desirable that foreign law be proved in accordance with the above rule' the Supreme Court has held in several naturalisation cases that:

> evidence of the law of a foreign country on reciprocity regarding the acquisition of citizenship, although not meeting the prescribed rule of practice, may be allowed and used as basis for favorable action, if, in the light of all the circumstances, the Court is 'satisfied of the authenticity of the written proof offered'. Thus, in a number of decisions, mere authentication of the Chinese Naturalization Law by the Chinese Consulate General of Manila was held to be competent proof of that law.

All documents submitted to the court must be in English or Filipino, or accompanied with a translation by an official, sworn translator or by a diplomatic or consular agent.

69. *Wildvalley Shipping Co. Ltd, v. Court of Appeals*, G.R. No. 119602, 6 Oct. 2000.
70. *Heirs of the Deceased Spouses Arcilla v. Teodoro*, G.R. No. 162886, 11 Aug. 2008.
71. *Supra* n. 68.

[E] Statute of Limitations

In *Cadalin v. Philippine Overseas Employment Association (POEA)*,[72] Cadalin and company instituted a class suit with the POEA for money claims arising from non-payment of the unexpired employment contracts with a foreign corporation based in Texas. One of the issues therein raised was whether or not the complainants' claim for benefits had already expired in light of the Amiri Decree of 1976 that required the filing of a claim arising out of a contract within one year from the date of expiry of such contract. The Supreme Court held that the Philippine prescriptive period of ten years[73] applied not only because prescription and borrowing statues could be characterised as matters of procedure, but also due to policy of protection for labour embedded in the Constitution.[74]

[F] Remedies and Damages

As confirmed by the Supreme Court in the already-mentioned *Northwest* case, matters of remedy are governed by the *lex fori* or the internal law of the forum.

[G] Foreign Currency Obligations

The former regime (contained in Republic Act 529) was repealed by Republic Act 8183 in 1996. The new law provides that 'parties may agree that the obligation or transaction shall be settled in any other currency at the time of payment'.[75] This removed the prohibition on stipulation on payment of currency other than Philippine currency. Parties may now freely transact in the currency agreed upon by them. As to the applicable exchange rate, the Supreme Court held in *C.F. Sharp & Co. v. Northwest Airlines*[76] that it is based on the prevailing rate at the time of payment:

> Just like R.A. 529, however, the new law does not provide for the applicable rate of exchange for the conversion of foreign currency-incurred obligations in their peso equivalent. It follows, therefore, that the jurisprudence established in R.A. No. 529 regarding the rate of conversion remains applicable. Thus, in *Asia World Recruitment, Inc. v. National Labor Relations Commission* (313 SCRA 1, 17 [1999]), the Court, applying R.A. No. 8183, sustained the ruling of the NLRC that obligations in foreign currency may be discharged in Philippine currency based on the prevailing rate at the time of payment. The wisdom on which the jurisprudence interpreting R.A. No. 529 is based equally holds true with R.A. No. 8183. Verily, it is just and fair to preserve the real value of the foreign exchange-incurred obligation to the date of its payment.

72. G.R. No. L-104776, 5 Dec. 1994.
73. Civil Code of the Philippines, Article 1144.
74. 1987 Constitution, Article 13, s. 3.
75. Section 1, Republic Act No. 8183.
76. *C.F. Sharp & Co. v. Northwest Airlines, Inc.*, G.R. No. 133498, 18 Apr. 2002.

[H] Restraining Removal of Assets and Securing Evidence in Favour of a Foreign Arbitration/Judicial Process

As mentioned before, preliminary injunction requiring a person to refrain from doing a particular act may be granted at any stage prior to judgment or final order. This is particularly available against a party who resides out of the Philippines. Nevertheless, such injunctions have to be granted by the court where the action is pending, so there is no specific provision in support of foreign proceedings.

§9.05 RECOGNITION AND ENFORCEMENT OF FOREIGN DECISIONS

[A] Judicial Decisions: Requirements and Limitations

Before enforcing a foreign civil or commercial judgment or final order, it must be recognised by the Philippine courts. No recognition will be granted if the foreign judgment or order is contrary to public order, public policy, or good customs.[77] Furthermore, the court must be convinced that the defendant had an opportunity for full and fair trial,[78] the judgment must have disposed of the controversy on its merits[79] and the original court must have been impartial and competent.[80] The Supreme Court held in *Asiavest Merchant Bankers (M) Berhard v. Court of Appeals* that to assail a foreign judgment the party must present evidence of want of jurisdiction, want of notice to the party, collusion, fraud, or clear mistake of law or fact. Otherwise, the foreign judgment enjoys the presumption of validity as long as it was duly certified and authenticated.[81] Comity could also be considered as an additional factor to be taken into account.

According to Rule 39, section 48, of the Rules of Civil Procedure:

> The effect of a judgment or final order of a tribunal of a foreign country, having jurisdiction to pronounce the judgment is as follows:
>
> (a) In case of a judgment upon a specific thing, the judgment is conclusive upon the title to the thing; and
> (b) In case of a judgment against a person, the judgment is presumptive evidence of a right as between the parties and their successors in interest by a subsequent title.

In either case, the judgment or final order may be repelled by evidence of a want of jurisdiction, want of notice to the party, collusion, fraud, or clear mistake of law or fact.

In *Hang Lung Bank Ltd. v. Saulog*,[82] the Supreme Court clarified that 'an action for recognition is also one for enforcement'. The respondent 'may present evidence of

77. *Bank of America v. America Realty Corporation et al.*, GR. 133876, 29 Dec. 1999.
78. *Philippine Aluminium Wheels v. Fasgi Enterprises*, GR. No. 137378, 12 Oct. 2000.
79. *Oil and Natural Gas Commission v. Court of Appeals*, GR. 114323, 28 Sep. 1999.
80. *Ramirez v. Gmur*, G.R.. No. L-11992, 5 Aug. 1918.
81. GR. No. 110263, 20 Jul. 20001.
82. G.R. No. 73765, 26 Aug. 1991.

lack of jurisdiction, notice, collusion, fraud or clear mistake of fact and law, if applicable'. In fact, a foreign judgment is presumed to be valid and the foreign court to have acted correctly, so the respondent has the burden of proof to the contrary.[83]

In *Corpuz v. Sto. Tomas and the Solicitor General*[84] petitioner was a former Filipino citizen who acquired Canadian citizenship through naturalisation in November 2000. In January 2005, he married a Filipina. Soon after he returned to Canada and filed a petition for divorce, which was granted in 2005. Two years later, planning to marry his new Filipina fiancée in the Philippines, he registered the Canadian divorce decree on his previous marriage certificate. Despite the registration of the divorce decree, the National Statistics Office informed him that his former marriage still subsisted under Philippine law and that to be enforceable, the foreign divorce decree must first be judicially recognised by a competent Philippine court. He thus filed a petition for judicial recognition of foreign divorce and/or declaration of marriage as dissolved with the family Court in the Philippines. The trial court denied Gerbert's petition saying that Gerbert was not the proper party to institute the action for judicial recognition of the foreign divorce decree as he is a naturalised Canadian citizen and that only the Filipino spouse can avail of the remedy, under the second paragraph of Article 26 of the Family Code, in order for him or her to be able to remarry under Philippine law.

The Supreme Court held that the foreign divorce decree is presumptive evidence of a right that clothes the party with legal interest to petition for its recognition in this jurisdiction. Furthermore, although:

> the second paragraph of Article 26 of the Family Code bestows no rights in favor of aliens ... the unavailability of the second paragraph of Article 26 of the Family Code to aliens does not necessarily strip Gerbert of legal interest to petition the RTC for the recognition of his foreign divorce decree. The foreign divorce decree itself, after its authenticity and conformity with the alien's national law have been duly proven according to our rules of evidence, serves as a presumptive evidence of right in favor of Gerbert.

The court remanded the case to the trial court to determine whether the divorce decree was consistent with the Canadian divorce law given that 'a remand, at the same time, will allow other interested parties to oppose the foreign judgment and overcome a petitioner's presumptive evidence of a right by proving want of jurisdiction, want of notice to a party, collusion, fraud, or clear mistake of law or fact'. It stressed that the divorce obtained by an alien abroad may be recognised in the Philippines, as long as the divorce is valid according to the alien spouse's national law. The Supreme Court expounded on this point, as follows:

> The starting point in any recognition of a foreign divorce judgment is the acknowledgment that our courts do not take judicial notice of foreign judgments and laws... This means that the foreign judgment and its authenticity must be proven as facts under our rules on evidence, together with the alien's applicable national law to show the effect of the judgment on the alien himself or herself. The

83. See *Northwest* (*supra* n. 59), *Asiavest Merchant* (*supra* n. 81).
84. G.R. No. 186571, 11 Aug. 2010.

recognition may be made in an action instituted specifically for the purpose or in another action where a party invokes the foreign decree as an integral aspect of his claim or defense.

[B] Arbitral Awards (Including ICSID Awards): Requirements and Limitations

The Philippines is a party to the New York Convention on the Recognition and Enforcement of Foreign Arbitral Awards 1958 (New York Convention).

In *LM Power Engineering Corporation v. Capitol Industrial Construction Groups, Inc.*,[85] the Supreme Court clarified that although the parties mutually stipulate an arbitration clause to be final and binding, it is not immediately enforceable. It requires recognition by a competent court for enforcement. Under section 42 of R.A. 9285 the recognition and enforcement of such arbitral awards shall be filed with the Regional Trial Court (RTC).[86] When the RTC confirms these awards, the foreign arbitral awards shall be immediately enforced in the same manner as final and executory decisions of courts of the Philippines.[87]

The court can only refuse recognition and enforcement based on the grounds of the New York Convention. In the case of *Chung Fu Industries, Inc. v. Court of Appeals*,[88] involving a special civil action of certiorari, it was held that the Supreme Court will not engage in a review of the facts found nor even of the law as interpreted or applied by the arbitrator, unless there be on the part of the arbitrator a grave abuse of discretion or that he has acted without or in excess of jurisdiction.

Appeal exists in case of non-recognition or non-enforcement.

§9.06 TREATIES FOR JUDICIAL COOPERATION

The Philippines has entered into some bilateral judicial cooperation treaties. Under these treaties, the Philippines is able to obtain the assistance of foreign authorities in obtaining information, evidence or testimony necessary for civil proceedings. Apart from the United States, the Philippines also has existing bilateral treaties for mutual legal assistance with China, Korea, Hong Kong, Australia, United Kingdom, Swiss Confederation, and Spain.

The Philippines is not a party to the Hague Conventions dealing with International legal cooperation, except for the 1993 Hague Convention on Protection of Children and Co-operation in Respect of Intercountry Adoption.

---

85. G.R. No. 152471, 26 Mar. 2003.
86. SEC. 47. *Venue and Jurisdiction* – Proceedings for recognition and enforcement of an arbitration agreement or for vacations, setting aside, correction or modification of an arbitral award, and any application with a court for arbitration assistance and supervision shall be deemed as special proceedings and shall be filed with the Regional Trial Court (i) where arbitration proceedings are conducted; (ii) where the asset to be attached or levied upon, or the act to be enjoined is located; (iii) where any of the parties to the dispute resides or has his place of business; or (iv) in the National Judicial Capital Region, at the option of the applicant.
87. Republic Act 9285 (2004), s. 44.
88. G.R. No. 169332, 25 Feb. 1992.

CHAPTER 10

Singapore

*Harish Kumar & Jonathan Toh**

§10.01 CODIFICATION OF PRIVATE INTERNATIONAL LAW AND RELEVANCE OF CASE LAW

[A] Codification and Case Law

Singapore is a city-state governed by a single set of national laws and regulations. It is a common law jurisdiction. As the Singapore courts continually develop their jurisprudence in the area of private international law, English and Commonwealth cases are considered persuasive (but not binding) in instances where there is no local case law on the subject. Private international law rules are not codified and there are no plans to do so.

[B] Multilateral Conventions Providing Uniform Substantive Law and/or International Jurisdictional Rules

International treaties have to be transposed into domestic legislation in order for them to be binding in Singapore.

Singapore is a party to the UN Convention on Contracts for the International Sale of Goods (CISG),[1] the 1910 Convention for the Unification of Certain Rules of Law with respect to Collisions between Vessels, the 1910 International Convention for the Unification of Certain Rules of Law Relating to Assistance and Salvage at Sea, the 1924 International Convention for the Unification of Certain Rules of Law relating to Bills of

* Harish Kumar, Partner, Rajah & Tann Singapore LLP. Jonathan Toh, Senior Associate, Rajah & Tann Singapore LLP.

1. Singapore declared that it would not be bound by para. 1(b) of Article 1.

Lading (Hague Rules) together with its Protocol (Visby Rules), the 1929/1999 Conventions for the Unification of Certain Rules relating to International Carriage by Air[2] and the Convention on International Interest in Mobile Equipment (together with its Aircraft Protocol). In addition, Singapore is a party to thirteen multilateral agreements and protocols administered by the World Intellectual Property Organization (WIPO).[3]

§10.02 JURISDICTION OF LOCAL COURTS IN FOREIGN-RELATED CASES

[A] Grounds for Jurisdiction

[1] General

Civil jurisdiction of the Singapore court is founded on statute. Judicial power is derived from Article 93 of the Constitution of the Republic of Singapore.[4] The Supreme Court and the State Courts are set up under the Supreme Court of Judicature Act (Cap. 322, 2007 Rev Ed) (SCJA) and the State Courts Act (Cap. 321, 2007 Rev Ed) (SCA), respectively. According to the doctrine of *stare decisis*, courts of the same or lower status are bound by the legal precedent set by preceding judgments. In 1994, all appeals to the Privy Council were abolished.

[a] In Personam Jurisdiction

In personam jurisdiction[5] is properly founded against a defendant upon due service of originating process, either inside or outside Singapore, in a manner authorised by Singapore law founding such jurisdiction. In order to invoke the jurisdiction of the Supreme Court, a plaintiff seeking to sue a foreign defendant must satisfy section 16(1) of the SCJA. The jurisdiction of the State Courts is similarly invoked, save that its subject matter jurisdiction is limited expressly by statute.[6]

Defendant in Singapore

The Singapore courts have jurisdiction over a defendant who is served personally with originating process when he is present in Singapore.[7] Therefore, a person passing through Singapore may be served with process. If the person refuses to accept service, service may be effected by informing the person of the nature of the document and

2. Singapore declared that the Convention shall not apply to: (a) international carriage by air performed and operated directly by the Republic of Singapore for non-commercial purposes in respect to its functions and duties as a sovereign State; and (b) the carriage of persons, cargo and baggage for its military authorities on aircraft registered in or leased by the Republic of Singapore, the whole capacity of which has been reserved by or on behalf of such authorities.
3. http://www.wipo.int/treaties/en/ShowResults.jsp?country_id = 154C.
4. The Constitution of the Republic of Singapore, 1992 Reprint.
5. That is, the ability of the court to make a decision that is personally binding on a party.
6. Section 19(2) and (3), SCA.
7. Section 16(1)(a)(i), SCJA; Order 10 r 1(1), Rules of Court (Cap. 322, R5, 2006 Rev Ed) ('Rules of Court').

leaving it as near as possible to the defendant so that he is in a position to easily retrieve it.[8] Service may also be affected by any method agreed between the parties.[9]

Defendant outside Singapore

Where the defendant cannot be served within Singapore, the plaintiff may seek leave from the court for service of the originating process outside Singapore. A defendant cannot be served out of Singapore without leave of court even if the agreement between the parties provide for it.[10]

[b] In Rem Jurisdiction

The High Court can order the arrest of a ship within its territorial waters through its in rem jurisdiction.[11] Similarly, in case of a claim in the nature of towage or pilotage in respect of an aircraft, the admiralty jurisdiction of the High Court may be invoked by an action in rem against that aircraft if at the time when the action is brought it is beneficially owned by the person who would be liable on the claim in an action in personam. A recent case of the Court of Appeal,[12] provides the various steps and standards of proof applicable for ordering the arrest of a ship:

> Step 1: prove, on the balance of probabilities, that the jurisdictional facts under the s. 3(1) HCAJA heads of claim exist; and show an arguable case that its claim is of the type or nature required by that provision.
> Step 2: prove, on the balance of probabilities, that the claim arises in connection with a ship.
> Step 3: identify, without having to show in argument, the person who would be liable in an action *in personam*.
> Step 4: prove on the balance of probabilities, that the relevant person was, when the cause of action arose, the owner or charterer or in control or possession of the ship.
> Step 5: prove on the balance of probabilities, that the relevant person was, at the time when the action was brought, the beneficial owner of the offending ship or the sister ship.

[c] Jurisdiction of the Singapore International Commercial Court

The Singapore International Commercial Court (SICC) was officially launched on 5 January 2015.
The SICC has jurisdiction to try an action or a claim that is:[13]

(a) international and commercial in nature;
(b) one that the High Court may hear and try in its original civil jurisdiction;

8. Order 62 rule 3(1)(a), Rules of Court.
9. Order 62 rule 3(2), Rules of Court.
10. Order 10 rule 3, Rules of Court.
11. High Court (Admiralty Jurisdiction) Act, HCAJA.
12. *The Bunga Melati 5* [2012] 4 SLR 546.
13. Section 18D, SCJA.

(c) one that parties have submitted to the SICC's jurisdiction under a written jurisdiction agreement; and[14]
(d) one where parties do not seek any relief in the form of, or connected with a prerogative order.[15]

A claim is international in nature if:[16]

(a) the parties to the claim have, by a written jurisdiction agreement, agreed to submit the claim for resolution by the SICC and, at the time the agreement was concluded, the parties have their places of business in different States;
(b) none of the parties to the claim have their places of business in Singapore;
(c) one of the following places is situated outside any State in which any of the parties have their places of business:
    i. any place where a substantial part of the obligations of the commercial relationship between the parties is to be performed;
    ii. the place with which the subject-matter of the dispute is most closely connected; or
(d) the parties to the claim have expressly agreed that the subject matter of the claim relates to more than one State.

A claim is commercial in nature if the subject matter of the claim arises from a relationship of a commercial nature. The Rules of Court set out a non-exhaustive list of relationships similar to Article 1(1) of the Model Law[17] (any trade transaction for the supply or exchange of goods or services; distribution agreement; commercial representation or agency; factoring; leasing; construction of works; consulting; engineering; licensing; investment; financing; banking; insurance; exploitation agreement or concession; joint venture and other forms of industrial or business co-operation; carriage of goods or passengers by air, sea, rail or road).[18]
While SICC jurisdiction is generally founded upon the parties' agreement to submit to the jurisdiction of the SICC,[19] there are two exceptions: First, the SICC has jurisdiction to hear and determine a case transferred to it from the High Court where appropriate;[20] and second, the SICC may hear an originating summons for leave to commit a person for contempt in respect of any judgment or order made by the Court.[21]

The SICC has certain unique characteristics that are not available in the High Court or State Courts. It has a panel of international judges that hail from both civil and

14. Order 110 rule 7(1)(b), Rules of Court.
15. Order 110 rule 7(1)(c), Rules of Court.
16. Order 110 rule 1(2)(a), Rules of Court.
17. See First Schedule, International Arbitration Act (Cap. 143A, 2002 Rev Ed) (IAA).
18. Order 110 rule 1(2)(b), Rules of Court.
19. Order 110 rule 7(1), Rules of Court.
20. Order 110 rule 12(4), Rules of Court.
21. Order 110 rule 7(2), Rules of Court.

common law jurisdictions;[22] Parties may apply for the case to be confidential;[23] Parties may apply for foreign law to be determined by way of submissions and not proved as fact;[24] Domestic rules on evidence may not apply;[25] the rules on production of documents and interrogatories are similar to the *IBA Rules on the Taking of Evidence in International Arbitration*;[26] and there is scope for foreign counsel to represent parties in 'offshore' cases, i.e., cases which have no substantial connection with Singapore.[27]

[2] Submitted to Jurisdiction

Jurisdiction will also be found over a defendant who has submitted voluntarily to the jurisdiction of the Singapore court.

[a] Agreement

Agreement is commonly the basis for submission to jurisdiction. Where parties have agreed that the Singapore courts have jurisdiction; the agreement provides for a means for service of originating process within Singapore; and service is accordingly effected, then the court has jurisdiction over such defendant.[28] The party invoking the jurisdiction generally has to prove to the standard of a good arguable case that the jurisdiction agreement exists. The construction of a jurisdiction agreement is governed by the law of the contract.

Non-exclusive jurisdiction clauses could allow proceedings to be brought in jurisdictions other than the one named in the clause. Nevertheless, depending on the contractual context and true intention of the parties, the court could conclude that a clause labelled as non-exclusive should be given the effect of an exclusive jurisdiction clause[29] (see below, at section 10.02[B][3]).

[b] Participation

A defendant voluntary submits to the Singapore court's jurisdiction, if he takes a step in the proceedings which amounts to a recognition of the court's jurisdiction. Filing a substantive defence would clearly be such a step. However, a step taken early in the proceedings while the defendant was not reasonably aware of the grounds of jurisdictional challenge may not amount to submission.[30] The entry of an appearance merely to protest the existence of jurisdiction is a submission only to the jurisdiction of the

22. Presently, these are the United States of America, Australia, Austria, France, the United Kingdom, Hong Kong and Japan.
23. Order 110 rule 30, Rules of Court.
24. Order 110 rule 25, Rules of Court.
25. Order 110 rule 23, Rules of Court.
26. Order 110 rules 14–22, Rules of Court.
27. Order 110 rule 1(2), Rules of Court.
28. Order 10 rule 3(1), Rules of Court.
29. *Orchard Capital I Ltd. v. Ravindra Kumar Jhunjhunwala* [2012] SGCA 16.
30. *International SOS Pte Ltd. v. Overton Mark Harold George* [2001] 2 SLR(R) 777 at [7].

court to determine its own jurisdiction, and not a submission to jurisdiction for the determination of the merits of the claim.[31]

While jurisdiction may be procedurally founded, the defendant may nevertheless apply to stay the proceedings on the ground that the Singapore court is not the natural forum to try the case (see section 10.02[C][1] below). However, this is an application to persuade the court that jurisdiction *should not be* exercised, and therefore is likely to constitute submission to jurisdiction of the court to determine the merits of the case.

[c] Deemed Submission

The defendant will be deemed to have submitted to the jurisdiction of the court if he enters an appearance without an application to challenge jurisdiction[32] or if the application fails.[33]

[3] Exclusive Jurisdiction

The Singapore court may have exclusive jurisdiction only where parties have agreed to such effect. In such cases, it is important to determine what exactly parties have agreed. This is a question of construction governed by the proper law of the jurisdiction agreement, which is usually the proper law of the contract of which it forms a part. In the most straightforward case, an exclusive jurisdiction agreement would provide that parties submit to the jurisdiction of Singapore and agree not to commence proceedings in any jurisdiction other than Singapore.

[B] Exclusion of Jurisdiction

[1] Immunity

[a] Sovereign Immunity

The doctrine of sovereign immunity applies in Singapore and is restated in the State Immunity Act (Cap. 313 Rev Ed) (SIA). Common law principles are relevant where the Act is silent.

The Singapore court has no jurisdiction in respect of a sovereign state except as provided for in the SIA.[34] The executive has the final say on whether a country counts as a 'state'.[35] This includes the sovereign or head of state in his public capacity; its government or any such department.[36] Entities distinct from the executive organs of the foreign state capable of suing or being sued do not enjoy such immunity unless the

31. Order 12 rule 7(5), Rules of Court.
32. Order 12 rule 7(6), Rules of Court.
33. Order 12 rule 7(5), Rules of Court.
34. Section 3, SIA.
35. Section 18(a), SIA.
36. Section 16(1), SIA.

proceedings relate to its acts in the exercise of sovereign authority in such circumstances where a state would be so immune.[37]

The Singapore Court of Appeal has agreed with the observations of English courts that the sovereign immunity doctrine is not absolute and should not be extended unnecessarily.[38] Sovereign immunity does not apply in a number of situations (sections 4-10 SIA): Where the state has submitted to the jurisdiction of the Singapore court; where the proceedings relate to a commercial transaction entered into by the state or a contractual obligation (whether arising from a commercial transaction or not) of the state that is to be performed wholly or partly in Singapore; contracts of employment between the state and an individual made in Singapore or to be performed wholly or partly in Singapore; death or personal injury or damage or loss to tangible property occurring in Singapore; ownership or possessory interests in immovable property in Singapore or obligations arising out of such interests; patents, trademarks, or designs protected in Singapore or the use of trade or business names in Singapore; and membership of an incorporated or unincorporated body which has members other than states and which is constituted under Singapore law or is controlled from or has its principal place of business in Singapore. Further exceptions are made in respect of arbitration agreements, admiralty proceedings, and customs duties (sections 11-13 SIA). In case an agreement entered into by the state is allegedly void *ab initio*, any waiver of immunity contained in the dispute resolution clause survives under the doctrine of separability.[39]

[b] Other Immunities

Immunity from the in personam jurisdiction of the Singapore court can also arise as a result of immunities conferred under the Diplomatic and Consular Relations Act,[40] and the International Organisations (Immunities and Privileges) Act.[41]

[2] Non-justiciable Claims

Some claims are regarded as non-justiciable in the Singapore courts, such as claims based on the enforcement of foreign penal, revenue[42] or other public laws, or claims which involve transactions between foreign states which the civil court is not in a position to resolve in a dispute between private parties.

---

37. Section 16(2), SIA.
38. *Republic of the Philippines v. Maler Foundation* [2008] 2 SLR(R) 857 at [37] and [46] (CA).
39. *Maldives Airports Co. Ltd. and Another v. GMR Male International Airport Pte Ltd.* [2013] SGCA 16.
40. Cap 82A 2006 Rev Ed – an Act giving certain provisions of (i) the 1961 Vienna Convention on Diplomatic Relations adopted and (ii) the 1963 Vienna Convention on Consular Relations force of law in Singapore.
41. Cap 145 1985 Rev Ed.
42. For example, *Relfo Ltd. (in liquidation) v. Bhimji Velji Jadva Varsani* [2008] 4 SLR(R) 657 (non-enforcement of foreign revenue claim). Recently, the plaintiff in *Her Majesty's Revenue & Customs v. Hashu Dhalomal Shahdadpuri* [2011] 2 SLR 967 was struck out for attempting to enforce a foreign revenue rule. The case was overturned on appeal in [2011] 3 SLR 1186 on the

In addition, Singapore courts do not have subject matter jurisdiction over disputes involving the determination of title or right of possession to foreign immovable property. This is derived from the English rule in *The British South Africa Company v. The Companhia de Mocambique* [1893] AC 602, commonly known as the *Mocambique* rule and reflects the practical fact that only at the *situs* of the land can there be an effective determination of title.[43] The *Mocambique* rule is subject to three exceptions:

(a) *In personam actions*: The Singapore court has jurisdiction to determine issues of personal obligations between the parties founded on contract or equity between the parties, commonly known as the rule in *Penn v. Baltimore* (1750) 1 Ves Sen 444.
(b) *Trusts and Estates*: The court also has jurisdiction where it is called upon to administer a trust or estate which includes local and foreign property.[44]
(c) *Admiralty Jurisdiction*: The *Mocambique* rule has not been applied in an action in rem to enforce a maritime lien for tortious damage to foreign immovable property.[45]

[3] Forum Agreements in Favour of Foreign Courts

The Singapore courts will generally give effect to an agreement between the parties that proceedings are to be brought in a foreign court (commonly known as an exclusive choice of court clause). The choice of court clause is usually governed by the same law that governs the entire contract. Unilateral choice of court clauses are valid.

Where a plaintiff has commenced an action in the Singapore court in breach of an exclusive choice of court clause, the court will ordinarily stay the proceedings to give effect to the agreement of the parties, unless the party commencing the action in breach of contract can show exceptional circumstances amounting to *strong cause* why the agreement should not be adhered to.[46] In determining strong cause, the court will have regard to the following matters:[47]

(a) In what country the evidence on the issues of fact is situated or more readily available, and the effect of that on the relative convenience and expense of trial as between the Singapore and foreign courts.

ground that it was not plain and obvious that the foreign revenue rule was infringed – the Court of Appeal found that it was at least arguable that it was a private law claim. The foreign revenue rule was upheld.

43. *Murakami Takako (executrix of the estate of Takashi Murakami Suroso, deceased) v. Wiryadi Louise Maria and others* [2009] 1 SLR(R) 508 at [6] (CA).
44. See *Re Duke of Wellington* [1948] Ch. 118, [1947] 2 All ER 854; *Nelson v. Bridport* (1846) 8 Beav 547, 50 ER 215; *Re Piercy* [1895] 1 Ch. 83; *Re Hoyles* [1911] 1 Ch. 179; *Re Ross* [1930] 1 Ch. 377.
45. *The Tolten* [1946] P 135, [1946] 2 All ER 372 (CA).
46. *The Vishva Apurva* [1992] 1 SLR(R) 912 at [13] (CA).
47. *The Hyundai Fortune* [2004] 4 SLR(R) 548 at [16] (CA).

(b) Whether the law of the foreign court applies, and whether it differs from Singapore law in any material respect.
(c) With what country either party is connected and, if so, how closely.
(d) Whether the defendant genuinely desires trial in the foreign country, or is only seeking procedural advantages.
(e) Whether the plaintiff would be prejudiced by having to sue in the foreign court because it would:
   (i) be deprived of security for its claim;
   (ii) be unable to enforce any judgment obtained;
   (iii) be faced with a time-bar not applicable in Singapore;
   (iv) for political, racial, religious or other reasons is unlikely to get a fair trial.

Although the factors are similar to those considered for determining the natural forum where there is no choice of court agreement, the two tests are different. The burden on the plaintiff is not merely to show that one forum is clearly more appropriate than another, but whether there are sufficient grounds to allow the plaintiff to renege on the agreement (whether it would cause '*unreasonableness and injustice*'[48] to enforce the agreement). There is a strong bias in favour of enforcing the agreement.

An exclusive choice of court clause may not be given effect to if it will lead to the contravention of an international mandatory rule of the forum or fundamental public policy of the forum. The Singapore court has refused to do so where it would lead to the foreign court applying a limitation to the plaintiff's claim that is lower than that provided for under its mandatory statute giving effect to an international convention.[49] In such a case, the law of the forum applies as mandatory law to override any foreign governing law.

Another example is the protection of the mandatory provisions of the Unfair Contract Terms Act (Cap 396, 1994 Rev Ed) (UCTA). An exclusive choice of court clause may contravene the statute if it imposes unreasonably restrictive or onerous conditions for the enforcement of the terms of the contract.[50] The UCTA provisions have mandatory effect if it was found that the choice of court clause was imposed primarily for the purpose of evading the operation of the statute, or if one of the contracting parties had acted as a consumer and the essential steps necessary for the making of the contract had been taken in Singapore.[51] This statutory protection applies only to choice of court agreements, and does not apply to arbitration agreements.[52]

48. *The Vishva Apurva*, *supra* n. 31, at [19].
49. *The Epar* [1984-1985] SLR 409.
50. Section 13(1), UCTA.
51. Section 27(2), UCTA.
52. Section 13(2), UCTA.

[4] Arbitration Clause

If a plaintiff has instituted proceedings in the Singapore court in breach of an arbitration clause for an international arbitration,[53] it is mandatory for the court to grant a stay of court proceedings. A stay must be granted upon the court finding that (i) the parties in the action are parties to the arbitration agreement;[54] (ii) the agreement covers the matter in dispute before the court;[55] (iii) the applicant has made the application after entering an appearance but before delivering any pleading or taking any other step in the proceedings;[56] and (iv) the arbitration agreement is not null and void, inoperative or incapable of being performed,[57] or the subject matter is not arbitrable or is contrary to public policy.[58]

The burden lies initially with the applicant to show that an arbitration agreement exists to which he is a party and to which the subject matter in the legal proceeding relates. The burden then shifts to the party resisting a stay to show that the arbitration agreement is 'null and void, inoperative or incapable of being performed'. The power to grant a stay is mandatory such that a court must grant a stay if the conditions are fulfilled.[59] The court has, in addition, a duty to direct the parties to proceed to arbitration.[60]

The term 'null and void, inoperative or incapable of being performed' reflects common law concepts of void or voidable, unenforceable, and frustrated contracts. Singapore courts have yet to consider the ambit of the term, although it is generally given a very restrictive meaning in Model Law jurisdictions. The nullity or voidability must impact the arbitration agreement and not merely the underlying commercial contract.[61] In absence of indications to the contrary, parties' choice of the arbitral seat will be considered as their implied choice of the proper law to govern the arbitration agreement.[62] Whether a person is a party to an agreement to arbitrate has to be determined in accordance with the *lex arbitri* of the forum seized of the stay or joinder application.[63]

---

53. As defined under s. 5, *International Arbitration Act* (Cap. 143A, 2002 Rev Ed) (IAA), i.e., at least one of the parties to the arbitration agreement at the time of the conclusion of the agreement has its place of business outside Singapore; the place of arbitration is situated outside the State in which the parties have their place of business; the substantial part of the obligations or subject matter of the dispute are to be performed outside the State in which the parties have their places of business; or that the parties have expressly agreed that the subject matter of the arbitration agreement relates to more than one country.
54. Section 6(1), IAA.
55. *Ibid.*
56. *Ibid.*
57. Section 6(2), IAA.
58. Section 11, IAA.
59. Section 6(2), IAA. See e.g., *Dalian Hualiang Enterprise Group Co. Ltd. v. Louis Dreyfus Asia Pte Ltd.* [2005] 4 SLR(R) 646.
60. Article 8, UNCITRAL Model Law on International Commercial Arbitration ('Model Law').
61. Under the doctrine of separability, the arbitration agreement can survive a finding that the main contract is void.
62. *FirstLink Investments Corp. Ltd. v. GT Payment Pte Ltd.* [2013] SGHCR 28.
63. *The Titan Unity* [2014] SGHCR 12.

As for breach of an arbitration clause for a local arbitration,[64] the court has a discretionary power to grant a stay of court proceedings in favour of arbitration proceedings. Generally, the court is likely to stay judicial proceedings and uphold the parties' agreement to arbitrate. The applicant must show that (i) the applicant is a party to the arbitration agreement; (ii) the agreement covers the matter in dispute before the court; (iii) the applicant has made the application after entering an appearance but before delivering any pleading or taking any other step in the proceedings; and (iv) the applicant remains ready and willing to arbitrate.[65] The burden then shifts to the other party to 'show sufficient reason why the matter should not be referred to arbitration'.

Such 'sufficient reasons' may include:

(a) undue delay by the applicant in making application for stay;
(b) an allegation of fraud against the plaintiff;[66]
(c) the plaintiff's inability to finance the arbitration;
(d) the possible multiplicity of actions;[67] and
(e) the relief sought by the plaintiff was not one which was available in arbitration.[68]

Arbitration agreements may also be enforced by a prohibitory (anti-suit) injunction to prevent a breach of contract.

[C] Non-exercise of Jurisdiction

[1] Forum Non Conveniens

Moving away from the question of *existence* of the court's jurisdiction, the Singapore court has the power to stay proceedings on the ground that it is not the appropriate forum under the doctrine of forum non conveniens.

In proceedings commenced by service of process out of the jurisdiction, one of the critical steps which the plaintiff has to take to establish a proper case for the granting of leave is that Singapore is clearly the most appropriate forum to try the case (see below, at section 10.04[A][1]). The same legal principles govern both a stay

64. Defined as an arbitration where the place of arbitration is Singapore and where Part II of the IAA does not apply (s. 3 of the Arbitration Act (Cap 10, 2002 Rev Ed)) (AA).
65. Section 6, AA.
66. See *Anwar Siraj v. Teo Hee Lai Building Construction Pte Ltd.* [2007] 2 SLR(R) 500 at [48] where the court held that the allegation of fraud was not a separate justification for refusal of a stay. Nevertheless it should be a factor for the court to consider.
67. In *Steelcrete Construction and Engineering Pte Ltd. v. James Low Yao Chang* (unreported, July 2001; Suit No. 139/2001), the earlier arbitration proceedings were discontinued by order of court on the defendant's application on the ground that as the third party could not be compelled to participate, there was a risk of multiplicity of results.
68. *Four Pillars Enterprises Co. Ltd. v. Beiersdorf Aktiengesellschaft* [1999] 1 SLR(R) 382 (CA) – a sufficient reason for not granting a stay of winding up proceedings was that the relief sought was not one available in arbitration.

application and the application for service of process out of jurisdiction; the only difference is the party on whom the burden of proof lies.[69]

The basic principle of forum non conveniens established in *The Spiliada*[70] by the House of Lords is to identify the court which should adjudicate the dispute most suitably for the interests of all the parties and the ends of justice. The issue is whether the Singapore court is the natural or appropriate forum to adjudicate the dispute.

There is a difference in the burden of proof where the court's jurisdiction is obtained by service within jurisdiction as compared to service out of jurisdiction. In the former, the defendant applying to stay proceedings has the burden of proving that there is an available and clearly more appropriate forum elsewhere (commonly referred to as 'Stage One' of the *Spiliada* test).[71] If so, the legal burden shifts to the plaintiff to show that even though there is an available and clearly more appropriate forum elsewhere, there are circumstances for which justice requires that a stay of proceedings be refused ('Stage Two' of the *Spiliada* test). In contrast, where leave of court to serve process out of jurisdiction is sought, the burden lies on the plaintiff to show a 'good arguable case' that the Singapore court is the natural or appropriate forum to adjudicate the dispute.

Stage One of the *Spiliada* test requires the court to identify the forum which has the 'most real and substantial connection' with the matter at hand. This includes considering whether a trial held in this forum would result in the least inconvenience and expense to parties. The court is also entitled to consider other factors such as the law governing the transaction and places where parties reside or carry on business.

In Stage Two of the *Spiliada* test the court considers all other circumstances which may demonstrate that justice nevertheless dictates that a stay should be refused. These circumstances will include factors which go beyond those considered in Stage One. For this stage of the *Spiliada* test, the legal burden lies on the plaintiff to establish the existence of the said circumstances. The court's primary concern would be whether substantial justice can be obtained in the foreign prima facie natural forum. When considering these other circumstances, the court has to balance between justice to the parties and international comity. The court will not compare or pass judgment on the competence and independence of another country's judiciary.

Circumstances which may demonstrate that substantial justice cannot be obtained include: (a) a defective foreign legal system where the alternative forum operates a 'system of law that flies in the face of all accepted principles of justice acknowledged by courts in other jurisdictions';[72] (b) a forum where a plaintiff cannot obtain proper legal representation[73] or legal aid[74] which is available in the present

69. *Oriental Insurance Co. Ltd. v. Bhavani Stores Ltd.* [1997] 3 SLR(R) 363 at [21]-[22] (CA).
70. [1987] AC 460. *The Spiliada* continues to be applied and followed by the Singapore courts, see for example the Singapore Court of Appeal decision in *JIO Minerals FZC and others v. Mineral Enterprises Ltd.* [2011] 1 SLR 391 at [39][44].
71. See, e.g., *CIMB Bank Bhd v. Dresdner Kleinwort Ltd.* [2008] 4 SLR(R) 543 at [26] (CA).
72. *Q & M Enterprises Sdn Bhd v. Poh Kiat* [2005] 4 SLR 494 at [39]. Cf. *Deripaska v. Cherney* [2009] EWCA Civ 849 at [35]-[44].
73. *Oppenheimer v. Louis Rosenthal & Co. AG* [1937] 1 All ER 23 (CA) (Order 11). Cf. *Mohammed v. Bank of Kuwait and the Middle East KSC* [1996] 1 WLR 1483, [1996] ILPr 632 (CA) (where the issue was considered one of non-availability of an alternative forum).
74. *Lubbe v. Cape plc* [2000] 4 All ER 268, [2000] 1 WLR 1545 (HL).

forum; (c) a party being unable to join other parties in the foreign litigation;[75] or if (d) the plaintiff faces a real risk of bodily harm in the jurisdiction of the alternative forum.[76]

This is a discretionary exercise, though subject to a potential appeal.[77]

In a case brought in the SICC, the SICC must not decline to assume jurisdiction *solely* on the ground that the dispute between the parties is connected to a jurisdiction other than Singapore.[78]

[2] Lis alibi pendens

When a plaintiff seeks to sue the same defendant in two or more different jurisdictions over the same subject matter,[79] the defendant may invoke the doctrine of *lis alibi pendens* to compel the plaintiff to make an election as to which set of proceedings he wishes to pursue.[80] Apart from election, the defendant may seek a stay of local proceedings or a restraint of foreign proceedings.[81]

The court engages in a two stage inquiry. First, the defendant needs to demonstrate duplicity of actions in the different jurisdictions. Once this is established, the burden of proof then shifts to the plaintiff to justify the continuance of concurrent proceedings by showing 'very unusual circumstances'.[82] The Singapore courts have not yet examined what such 'very unusual circumstances' may be. English law on this issue will be persuasive.[83] Some examples of 'very unusual circumstances' include:

(a) Bringing parallel proceedings in order to prevent cross-border infringement of an intellectual property right.[84]

75. *Société Nationale Industrielle Aerospatiale v. Lee Kui Jak* [1987] AC 871 (PC Brunei) at 898-899.
76. *Oppenheimer v. Louis Rosenthal & Co. AG* [1937] 1 All ER 23 (CA) (Order 11); *Deripaska, supra* n. 57; *Ho Yuen Ki Winnie v. Ho Hung Sun Stanley* (CA, Hong Kong SAR, 23 May 2008); *Herbst Ehud v. Sampoerna Putera* [2005] 1 SLR 82 at [36].
77. In *BDA v BDB* [2013] 1 SLR 607, the Singapore High Court held that an appellate court could not interfere with the exercise of the discretion (even if the appellate court should disagree with the lower court's decision) unless 'the judge had misdirected himself on a matter of principle, or he had taken into account matters which he ought not to have taken into account or had failed to take into account matters which he ought to have taken into account, or his decision is plainly wrong': at [23].
78. Order 110 rule 18(2), Rules of Court.
79. The applicant need not show a total correspondence of issues, but the court will be more likely to find a *lis alibi pendens* where the issues are of a greater degree of similarity. *Virsagi Management (S) Pte Ltd v Welltech Construction Pte Ltd* [2013] 4 SLR 1097 at [47].
80. *Yusen Air & Sea Service (S) Pte Ltd. v. KLM Royal Dutch Airlines* [1999] 2 SLR(R) 955 at [27].
81. *Ibid.*, at [34].
82. *Ibid.*, at [27], applied in *Virsagi Management (S) Pte Ltd v Welltech Construction Pte Ltd* [2013] 4 SLR 1097 at [30].
83. Both *Yusen* (*supra* n. 62) and *Multi-Code Electronics Industries* (*supra* n. 64) cited *Australian Commercial Research and Development Ltd. v. ANZ McCaughan Merchant Bank Ltd.* [1989] 3 All ER 65 in applying the doctrine.
84. *Celltech R&D Ltd. v. MedImmune Inc.* [2004] EWCA Civ 1331.

(b) Where the proceedings in two jurisdictions are necessary to enforce both judgments locally and this appears to be the only way to obtain full satisfaction of the claim against the defendant.[85]
(c) Where there is a contractual agreement that parallel proceedings may be brought.[86]

In the event that the plaintiff elects to pursue foreign proceedings, local proceedings are generally discontinued.[87] Nevertheless, there may be situations where it would be more appropriate to grant a stay, such as where one of the actions is brought to obtain security by way of an attachment of assets. In *Multi-Code Electronics Industries (M) Bhd v. Toh Chun Toh Gordon*,[88] although the applicants only sought a stay of local proceedings, the High Court commented that even if a striking out was sought, it would have granted a stay in order to allow for the jurisdictional foundation of a *Mareva* or 'freezing' injunction in Singapore.

§10.03 APPLICABLE LAW

Issues that relate to the enforceability of a right are considered as 'procedural matters' and are governed by the law of the forum. On the contrary, issues related to the existence and content of a right are considered as 'substantive' and a foreign law can apply.
The distinction between procedure and substance may not always be clear. In *Shanghai Electric Group Co Ltd v PT Merak Energi Indonesia* [2010] 2 SLR 329, the crux of the matter was whether Singapore law (as the *lex fori*) or English law (as the proper law of the contract) governed an injunction to restrain the call on an on-demand bond. The court found that the English law applied as the injunction would have deprived the beneficiary of the substantive right to immediate payment upon demand.

[A] Choice of Law

The applicable or proper law of a contract is determined in three stages.[89] The first stage is to examine the contract itself to ascertain whether the contract expressly provides for what the governing law should be. In the absence of an express provision,

85. *Karafarin Bank v. Mansoury-Dara* [2009] EWHC 1217 (Comm.), [2009] 2 Lloyd's Rep. 289.
86. *Royal Bank of Canada v. Cooperatieve Centrale Raiffeisen-Boerenleenbank BA* [2004] EWCA Civ 7, [2004] 1 Lloyd's Rep. 471; *Deutsche Bank AG v. Highland Crusader Offshore Partners LP* [2009] EWCA Civ 725, [2010] 1 W.L.R. 1023.
87. *Yusen, supra* n. 62 at [32].
88. *Supra* n. 64 at [36].
89. *Pacific Recreation Pte Ltd. v. S Y Technolocy Inc.* [2008] 2 SLR 491 (CA) at [36]; *TQ v. TR* [2009] 2 SLR 961 (CA) at [32]; *Peh Teck Quee v. Bayerische Landesbank Gironzentrale* [2000] 1 SLR 148 (CA); *Overseas Union Insurance Ltd. v. Turegum Insurance Co.* [2001] 3 SLR 330 at [82]; *Las Vegas Hilton Corp. v. Khoo Teng Hock Sunny* [1997] 1 SLR 341; *Vita Food Products Inc. v. Unus Shipping Co. Ltd.* [1939] AC 277 (PC Nova Scotia); *Hang Lung Bank Ltd. v. Datuk Tan Kim Chua* [1986] SLR 441; *Amin Rasheed Shipping Corp. v. Kuwait Insurance Co.* [1984] AC 50; *The Komninos S* [1991] 1 Lloyd's Rep 271 (CA).

the second stage is to see whether the intention of parties can be inferred from the circumstances. If such inference is not possible, the third stage is to determine with which system of law the contract has its most close and real connection.

The law of the contract governs the validity, interpretation, requirement or not of consideration, content of the obligation, performance, and the discharge of the contract/obligation. Nevertheless, different parts of a contract may be governed by different laws.

[1] Express Stipulation

If an express provision is made in a contract for the law of a country, the principle of party autonomy in choosing the law to govern their contract will be accorded full effect.[90] The only qualification to this principle is that the application of foreign law should not be contrary to public policy, made bona fide and legal.[91]

Any uncertainty as to what system of law parties provided for will be determined by the law of the forum.[92] Parties' intentions as to what system of law they wanted to provide for will be objectively determined.[93]

It appears that courts are generally reluctant to interfere with parties' choice of law. It has been pointed out that 'an immeasurable volume of international business is transacted on the assumption that the choice of law by parties is supreme [and it would be] unwise to upset the apple cart'.[94]

In relation to legality, it appears that parties cannot pretend to contract under one law in order to validate an agreement that would be invalid under another law which the contract has the closest connection to.[95] Similarly, should parties contract under one law in order to avoid the application of another law otherwise applicable, this choice might not be construed as one made bona fide.[96] It is unclear what legal effect an illegal or non-bona fide express provision may have. It would be unduly harsh to

90. *Vita Food Products, supra* n. 71, at 290; *James Miller & Partners Ltd. v. Whitworth Street Estates (Manchester) Ltd.* [1970] 1 AC 583 at 603; *Peh Teck Quee, supra* n. 71, at [18]; *Pacific Electric Wire & Cable Co. Ltd. v. Neptune Orient Lines Ltd.* [1993] 3 SLR 60 at 67.
91. *Vita Food Products, supra* n. 71, at 290; *James Miller & Partners, supra* n. 72, at 603; *Peh Teck Quee, supra* n. 71, at [18]; *Pacific Electric Wire & Cable, supra* n. 72, at 67. Authorities in the middle of the twentieth century casting doubt whether the parties' choice is the connecting factor or merely a factor in the ascertainment of an objective proper law have generally not been influential (See *Boissevain v. Weil* [1949] 1 KB 482 (CA) at 491 – affirmed without reference to this point: [1950] AC 327; *Re Helbert Wagg & Co. Ltd.* [1956] Ch 323 at 341; *The Fehmarn* [1958] 1 WLR 159 at 162).
92. *Compagnie D'Armement Maritime SA v. Compagnie Tunisienne De Navigation SA* [1971] AC 572 at 603.
93. *Food Products Inc. v. Unus Shipping Co. Ltd.* [1939] AC 277 (PC Nova Scotia) at 290.
94. *Pacific Electric Wire & Cable Co. Ltd. v. Neptune Orient Lines Ltd. (Toko Kaiun Kaisha Ltd., third party and Prima Shipping Sdn Bhd, fourth party)* [1993] 2 SLR(R) 102 at [37].
95. *Re Nield* (1990) JLR N-12 (Royal Ct, Jersey, 1983).
96. *Peh Teck Quee, supra* n. 71, at [17]. See also *Re Nield* (1990) JLR N-12 (Royal Ct, Jersey, 1983).

conclude that there is no proper law provision and hence no contract. Viable alternatives include applying the law of the forum by default or objectively determining what system of law the contract should be governed by.[97]

[2] Implied Choice

If there is no express provision, an implied provision may be imputed into the contract. For an implied provision to be imputed there must be a real and not merely hypothetical common intention of the contracting parties, objectively ascertained from the terms of the contract and surrounding circumstances.[98] It will be the law of the forum which determines whether there is an implied provision and in such a determination, the normal rules of construction of contracts are applied.

The following non-exhaustive list of factors is usually considered when a court decides if an implied provision should be imputed:

(a) the country in which the contract is made;
(b) the country in which the contract is to be performed;
(c) if the contract relates to immovables, the country where they are situated;
(d) the country under whose flag a ship sails in which goods are contracted to be carried;
(e) whether there is an agreement to arbitrate in a particular forum;
(f) the language or terminology used in the contract;
(g) the form of the documents used in the contract;
(h) if there are other connected transactions or contracts;
(i) the place of residence of the parties; and
(j) the commercial purpose of the contract.

[B] Other Cases

If neither the express nor implied intention of contracting parties can be determined, the court will have to determine the governing law of the contract based on which law has the closest and most real connection with the contract.[99] The test may sometimes be formulated in terms of connections with systems of law[100] or a country of law.[101] It may also be that some factors are more closely connected to one than the other.[102] The common law test is one that is a combination of both.

---

97. This is the consequence if the express choice fails because it purports to deny the existence of a proper law (*The Iran Vojdan* [1984] 2 Lloyd's Rep 380) or because it purports to choose a non-national system of principles (*Shamil Bank of Bahrain EC v. Beximco Pharmaceuticals Ltd.* [2004] EWCA Civ 19, [2004] 1 WLR 1784 (CA)).
98. *Rex v. International Trustee for the Protection of Bondholders Aktiengesellschaft* [1937] AC 500 at 529; *Amin Rasheed Shipping Corp. v. Kuwait Insurance Co.* [1984] AC 50.
99. *Pacific Recreation, supra* n. 71, at [47].
100. *Bonython v. Commonwealth of Australia* [1951] AC 201 at 219.
101. *In Re United Railways of Havana and Regla Warehouses Ltd.* [1961] AC 1007 at 1068.
102. *James Miller & Partners, supra* n. 72, at 604.

It should be noted that the factors considered at this stage are almost the same as those used for determining an implied provision. The difference between the second and third stages of determination 'lies not in the factors to be taken into consideration, but the weight which is to be accorded to these factors'.[103]

The aim of this stage is to consider which law has the closest connection with the contract in question and the circumstances surrounding the creation of this contract.[104] Equal weight should to be accorded to all factors, even those which would not, under the second stage, have been strongly inferential of any intention as to the governing law.[105] The court will then have to look at all the circumstances and seek to find what just and reasonable persons ought to have intended if they had thought about the matter at the time when they made the contract.[106]

In case of torts, the double actionability rule still applies:[107] an action for an alleged tort committed in a foreign jurisdiction has to be actionable under both the laws of the home jurisdiction and the foreign jurisdiction.

[C] *Renvoi*

The extent to which *renvoi* is applicable in Singapore law is unclear.[108] It is therefore likely that the position in other common law countries will be persuasive. *Renvoi* is generally thought to be relevant in (at least some) issues of succession law,[109] family law, and issues involving immovable property. Its applicability in *inter vivos* transactions involving movable property has been more controversial.[110] It is unlikely to apply in the law of torts[111] and contracts,[112] although recent Australian cases have challenged this.

103. *Pacific Recreation*, *supra* n. 71, at [48].
104. *Ibid.*, at [48].
105. *Ibid.*
106. *Ibid.*, at [49].
107. *JIO Minerals FZC and others v Mineral Enterprises Ltd*, [2011] 1 SLR 391 at [88].
108. The only known authority applies it to an issue of succession to immovable property: *State of Johor v. Tunku Alam Shah ibni Tunku Abdul Rahman* [2005] 4 SLR 380 at [24].
109. *Collier v. Rivaz* (1841) 2 Curt 855, 163 ER 608 (formal validity of will); *Re Annesley* [1926] Ch 692 (essential validity of will).
110. *Glencore International AG v. Metro Trading International Inc.* [2001] 1 Lloyd's Rep 284, cf. *Iran (Islamic Republic of) v. Berend* [2007] EWHC 132 (QB); [2007] 2 All ER (Comm) 132. Locally, *Banque Indosuez v. Awal* [1998] SGHC 22 at [33] left the question open as regards rights in choses in action.
111. *M'Elroy v. McAllister* 1949 SC 110 at 126; *Private International Law: Choice of Law in Tort and Delict*, Law Commission No. 193 (1990) at [3.56]; but see *Neilson v. Overseas Projects Corporation of Victoria Ltd.* [2005] HCA 54, (2005) 223 CLR 331.
112. *Amin Rasheed Shipping Corp. v. Kuwait Insurance Co.* [1984] AC 50 at 61-62; but see *Vita Food Products*, *supra* n. 71, at 298; *O'Driscoll v. McDermott* [2006] WASCA 25 (CA, Western Australia); International Arbitration Act, Cap. 143A, 2002 Rev Ed), Sch. 1, Article 28(1).

[D] Mandatory Rules of the Forum and of Third States

Mandatory rules of the forum or other external mandatory rules are laws that will apply in the court of the forum even if there are foreign elements in the matter at hand or another system of foreign law is applicable. In Singapore, examples of these mandatory rules include certain provisions of the:

(a) Unfair Contract Terms Act.[113]
(b) Carriage by Air Act.[114]
(c) Carriage by Air (Montreal Convention, 1999) Act.[115]
(d) Carriage of Goods by Sea Act.[116]

[E] Proof of Foreign Law

Under Singapore law, foreign law is an issue of fact and must generally be proven and pleaded.[117]

Pursuant to the Evidence Act (Cap. 97, 1997 Rev Ed) (EA), statements of persons who 'give opinion as to public right or custom or matters of general interest' can be admitted into evidence.[118] Similarly, the opinions of experts expressed in any treatise commonly offered for sale and the grounds on which such opinions are held may be proved by the production of such treatise if the author is dead or cannot be found or has become incapable of giving evidence or cannot be called as a witness without an amount of delay or expense which the court regards as unreasonable.[119] Furthermore, Singapore courts, under the EA, are allowed to pay attention to any statement of law contained in books or reports printed or published under the authority of that country.[120]

The court may also take judicial notice of legislation passed in Commonwealth countries[121] and 'may resort for its aid to appropriate books or documents of reference'.[122]

It should be noted that as a general rule, the court will still require the opinion of an expert to assist it in interpreting materials relating to foreign law.[123] Usually, such an

113. Unfair Contract Terms Act (Cap. 396, 1994 Rev Ed), s. 27(2). See also *Brodin v. A/R Seljan* 1973 SLT 198.
114. Carriage by Air Act, Cap 32A, 2001 Rev Ed, s. 3(1).
115. Carriage by Air (Montreal Convention, 1999) Act, Cap. 32B, 2008 Rev Ed, s. 3(1).
116. Carriage of Goods by Sea Act, Cap 33, 1998 Rev Ed, s. 3(1).
117. *Rickshaw Investments Ltd. v. Nicolai Baron von Uexkull* [2007] 1 SLR 377 (CA) at [43]; *Multi-Code Electronics, supra* n. 62 at [49]-[50].
118. Section 32(1)(d), EA.
119. Section 62(2) EA.
120. Section 40 EA.
121. Section 59(1)(b) EA.
122. Section 59(2) EA.
123. *Pacific Recreation, supra* n. 71, at [60]. See also *Kuala Lumpur City Securities Sdn Bhd v. Boston Asset Management Pte Ltd.* [2006] SGHC 99 at [75]. For a succinct summary of the duties of an expert under Singaporean law, *Pacific Recreation* from [76] to [89].

opinion will be given by way of a written report signed by the expert,[124] with each party furnishing its own expert report to the court.[125] The expert's foremost duty is to assist the court, and this duty supersedes any obligations owed to the person instructing him or her.[126] It is the responsibility of the instructing solicitor, as an officer of the court, to draw the expert's attention to this.[127]

The expert's function can be summarised as follows: he is to

(a) inform the court of the relevant contents of the foreign law; identifying statutes or other legislation and explaining where necessary the foreign court's approach to their construction;
(b) identify judgments or other authorities, explaining what status they have as sources of the foreign law; and
(c) where there is no authority directly in point, to assist the court in making a finding as to what the foreign court's ruling would be if the issue was to arise for decision there.[128]

It is trite that the expert 'cannot merely present his conclusion on what the foreign law is without also presenting the underlying evidence and the analytical process by which he reached his conclusion'.[129]

As a general principle, if foreign law is not pleaded, the court will presume it to be the same as the relevant position under Singaporean law.[130] Presumably this will also be the position if a party is unable to prove that a particular foreign law applies to the matter at hand.

In the absence of proof, a court may refuse to presume that the foreign law in question is similar to the law of the forum where *inter alia:*

(a) it is not in the interests of justice;
(b) the foreign law is not based on common law;
(c) it is inherently improbable that the foreign law is the same; or
(d) fairness requires so.[131]

---

124. Order 40A rule 3(1), Rules of Court.
125. *Pacific Recreation, supra* n. 71, at [64].
126. Order 40A rule 2, Rules of Court. See *The H156* [1999] 3 SLR 756 at [27], *Vita Health Laboratories Pte Ltd. v. Pang Seng Meng* [2004] 4 SLR 162 at [82]-[83], cited with approval in *Pacific Recreation, supra* n. 71, at [69] and [70].
127. *Pacific Recreation, supra* n. 71, at [72].
128. *MCC Proceeds Inc. v. Bishopsgate Investment Trust plc* [1999] CLC 417 at [23], adopted in *Pacific Recreation, supra* n. 71, at [76].
129. *Pacific Recreation, supra* n. 71, at [85]. Without supporting legal arguments and justifications, bare assertions by opposing experts had been found singularly unhelpful to the court in *Wu Yang Construction Group Ltd. v. Zhejiang Jinyi Group Co. Ltd.* [2006] 4 SLR 451 at [14].
130. *Rickshaw Investments, supra* n. 98, at [43]; *Goh Chok Tong v. Tang Liang Hong* [1997] 2 SLR 641 at [79].
131. *Balmoral Group Ltd. v. Borealis (UK) Ltd.* (2006) EWHC Com 1900, [2006] 2 Lloyd's Rep 629 at [428]; *Damberg v. Damberg* [2001] 52 NSWLR 492.

In a case brought in by the SICC, the Court may, on the application of a party, make an order allowing any question of foreign law to be determined on the basis of submissions instead of proof.[132] The order would specify one or more persons to make such submissions.[133] If the person specified is a foreign lawyer, he or she must either be registered as a foreign lawyer or undertake to apply to be registered within seven days after the date on which the order is made.[134]

[F] Evasion of the Law

There appears to be no specific regulation governing evasion of the law. However, as set out above at section 10.03[A][2], should parties contract under one law in order to avoid the application of another law otherwise applicable, this choice might not be construed as one made bona fide.[135] Similar attempts to evade a mandatory rule of the forum may be regarded as one not made bona fide.[136]

§10.04 PROCEDURAL ISSUES

[A] Service of Summons and Judicial Orders Abroad

[1] Leave of Court

As explained at section 10.02[A][1] above, jurisdiction is founded by due service of originating process. Extra-territorial jurisdiction under section 16(1)(a)(ii), SCJA, requires the plaintiff to seek the leave of court in accordance with Order 11 of the Rules of Court.

The rules reflect the principle that the Singapore courts will only exercise jurisdiction if it is appropriate for the matter to be heard in Singapore. As such, leave of court to serve originating process out of Singapore will only be granted if:

(a) There is a 'good arguable case' that one or more of the limbs prescribed by Order 11 Rules 1(a) to 1(s) of the Rules of Court exist.[137]
(b) The case must be a proper one for service out of jurisdiction,[138] which means to say that:

132. Order 110 rule 25(1), Rules of Court.
133. Order 110 rule 25(3), Rules of Court.
134. Order 110 rule 28(2)(e), Rules of Court.
135. *Peh Teck Quee Peh Teck Quee, supra* n. 71, at [17]. See also *Re Nield* (1990) JLR N-12 (Royal Ct, Jersey, 1983).
136. *Golden Acres Ltd. v. Queensland Estates Pty Ltd.* [1969] Qd R 378, affirmed on appeal on the different reasoning of the application of local mandatory laws: *Golden Acres Pty Ltd. v. Queensland Estates Pty Ltd.* (1970) 123 CLR 418.
137. Order 11 rule 1(a)-(s), Rules of Court; *Transniko Pte Ltd. v. Communication Technology Sdn Bhd* [1995] 3 SLR(R) 941 at [7]-[9]; *Bradley Lomas Electroluk v. Colt Ventilation East Asia* [1999] 3 SLR(R) 1156.
138. Order 11 rule 2(2), Rules of Court.

(i) There is a serious issue to be tried; and
(ii) Singapore is the proper forum under the doctrine of forum non conveniens.

[a] Good Arguable Case

In order to first establish jurisdiction, the plaintiff must show that there is a 'good arguable case' that one of the following limbs is satisfied.[139] The Singapore Court of Appeal adopted the following explanation of a 'good arguable case':[140]

> It indicates that though the court will not at this stage require proof to its satisfaction, it will require something better than a mere prima facie case. The practice, where questions of fact are concerned, is to look primarily at the plaintiff's case and not to attempt to try disputes of fact on affidavit; it is of course open to the defendant to show that the evidence of the plaintiff is incomplete or plainly wrong. On questions of law, however, the court may go fully into the issues and will refuse leave if it considers that the plaintiff's case is bound to fail.

[b] Proper Case for Service

If the court is satisfied that the there is a good arguable case that one of the limbs of Order 11 rule 1(a)-(s) is met, it must nevertheless be satisfied that the case is 'a proper one for service out of jurisdiction'.[141] There are two aspects to this inquiry. First, the evidence must disclose that there is a serious issue to be tried as regards the merits of the action.[142] Second, the court must be satisfied that Singapore is the natural forum to hear the matter.

[c] Proper Case for Service: Forum Non Conveniens

As a matter of international comity, the Singapore court will not compel a foreigner to face local proceedings unless justice requires. Here, the Singapore courts have repeatedly endorsed the principles promulgated by the House of Lords in the *Spiliada*:[143]

(a) *Burden of proof*: The plaintiff has the burden to prove that he should be granted leave to serve process out of jurisdiction.[144]

139. Order 11 rule 1(a)-(s), Rules of Court.
140. *Bradley Lomas Electroluk v. Colt Ventilation East Asia* [1999] 3 SLR(R) 1156 at [15].
141. Order 11 rule 2(2), Rules of Court.
142. *Goodwill Enterprise (Malaysia) v. CT Nominees (in liquidation)* [1996] 1 SLR(R) 330 at [3].
143. *Supra* n. 55. See *Siemens AG v. Holdrich Investment Ltd.* [2010] 3 SLR 1007; *Murakami Takako, supra* n. 28; *CIMB Bank Bhd, supra* n. 56; *Good Earth Agricultural Co. Ltd. v. Novus International Pte Ltd.* [2008] 2 SLR(R) 711; *PT Hutan Domas Raya v. Ye Xiu Enterprises (Holdings) Ltd.* [2001] 1 SLR(R) 104.
144. The *Spiliada, supra* n. 55, at 479.

(b) *Principle*: The principle behind the inquiry is whether Singapore is *clearly*[145] the forum in which the case can be appropriately adjudicated in the interests of the parties and justice.[146] This is not a mere exercise in comparing the sheer number of connecting factors which point to different jurisdictions. What matters is the weight to be given to each connecting factor in the light of all the circumstances of the case. In a finely balanced case, a single connecting factor could well be decisive.[147]

(c) *Connecting factors*: The court will take into account all relevant factors, including 'the nature of the dispute, the legal and practical issues involved, such questions as local knowledge, availability of witnesses and their evidence and expense'.[148]

(d) Although the court may compare available juridical advantages available to parties across jurisdictions, this is not a decisive factor.[149]

[d] Formal Requirements

These requirements are reflected in the formal requirements for an application for leave to serve process overseas – it must be made by ex parte summons supported by an affidavit stating:[150]

(a) the grounds on which the application is made;
(b) that in the deponent's belief the plaintiff has a good cause of action;
(c) in what place or country the defendant is, or probably may be found;
(d) where the application is made under Rule 1(c), the grounds for the deponent's belief that there is between the plaintiff and the person on whom an originating process is to be served a real issue which the plaintiff may reasonably ask the court to try; and
(e) whether it is necessary to extend the validity of the writ.

[2] Service Abroad

There are different groups of countries that the Rules of Court provide for concerning service of process out of Singapore.

145. The Court of Appeal clarified that it was not necessary to show that Singapore is the most appropriate forum *by far*, only that it was the most appropriate forum on balance: *Siemens AG, supra* n. 121, at [8].
146. The *Spiliada, supra* n. 55, at 479; *Siemens AG, supra* n. 121, at [6]-[8].
147. *Ibid.*, at [19].
148. The *Spiliada, supra* n. 55, at 480.
149. *Ibid.*, at 482.
150. Order 11 rule 2(1), Rules of Court.

[a] Countries Where a Civil Procedure Convention Applies

A 'Civil Procedure Convention' is defined as including 'any convention, treaty or agreement of any description or any provision thereof between different States relating to civil procedure in the court'.[151] Currently, there are conventions[152] with Austria,[153] Italy,[154] and Germany[155] and a Judicial Assistance Treaty with the People's Republic of China.[156] It should be noted that the latter does not apply to service of process in Hong Kong.[157]

In these countries, the originating process may be served:[158]

(a) through the judicial authorities of that country; or
(b) through a Singapore consular authority in that country (subject to any provision of the convention as to the nationality of persons who may be so served).

[b] Countries Where No Civil Procedure Convention Applies

Where no civil procedure convention applies, the originating process may be served:[159]

(a) through the government of that country, where that government is willing to effect service;
(b) through a Singapore consular authority in that country, except where service through such an authority is contrary to the law of that country; or
(c) by a method of service authorised by the law of that country for service of any originating process issued by that country.

As such, the only common mode for service for convention and non-convention countries is through a Singapore consular authority in that country.

151. Order 1 rule 4, Rules of Court.
152. See conventions listed in Appendix C to the Rules of Court.
153. Convention between the United Kingdom and Austria regarding legal proceedings in civil and commercial matters, Gazette No. T2/1999.
154. Convention between the United Kingdom and Italy regarding legal proceedings in civil and commercial matters, Gazette No. T3/1999.
155. Convention between the United Kingdom and Germany regarding legal proceedings in civil and commercial matters, Gazette No. T4/1999.
156. Treaty on Judicial Assistance in civil and commercial matters between the Republic of Singapore and the People's Republic of China, Gazette No. T2/2001.
157. *Lee Hsien Loong v. Review Publishing Co. Ltd.* [2007] 2 SLR(R) 453.
158. Order 11 rule 4(1), Rules of Court.
159. Order 11 rule 4(2), Rules of Court.

[c] *Authorised by the Law of That Country for Service of Any Originating Process Issued by That Country*

Order 11 rule 4(2)(c) was introduced in 1991 and allowed any mode of service permitted by the foreign legal system with regard to its own domestic process. As such, as long as the foreign jurisdiction recognises service by a lawyer in that jurisdiction as a proper mode of service, Singapore plaintiffs may engage foreign lawyers to do so.[160]

[d] *Malaysia and Brunei Darussalam*

As for Malaysia and Brunei Darussalam, there is an additional method of service – the originating process may be sent by post or otherwise by the Registrar of the Singapore court to the Magistrate, Registrar or other appropriate officer of any court exercising civil jurisdiction in the area which the person to be served is said to be or to be carrying on business for service.[161]

[3] *Substituted Service Abroad*

The court has the power to order substituted service abroad,[162] which is governed by the following principles:

(a) Such substituted service will not be permitted in circumstances which would not justify leave to serve out of Singapore.[163]
(b) Personal service must be shown to be a 'practical impossibility'.[164]
(c) The proposed mode of service would 'in all reasonable probability' notify the defendant of the action.[165]
(d) The mode of substituted service is recognised by the law of the foreign jurisdiction.[166]

---

160. See, e.g., *Pacific Assets Management v. Chen Lip Keong* [2006] 1 SLR(R) 658, where service was properly made through a Malaysian law firm.
161. Order 11 rule 3(8)(b), Rules of Court.
162. Order 11 rule 3(1), Rules of Court.
163. Otherwise, this would amount to extending the categories for service out of jurisdiction. See *Myerson v. Martin* [1979] 1 WLR 1390.
164. See *Porter v. Freudenberg* [1915] 1 KB 857 at 889; *Lazard Bros & Co. v. Banque Industrielle de Moscou* (1932) 146 LT 240 (affirmed 148 LT 242).
165. *Porter v. Freudenberg* [1915] 1 KB 857 at 889.
166. Order 11 rule 3(2), Rules of Court. Therefore, in *Aw Chen v. Johannes Koplan* [1969] 2 MLJ 190, Austrian law did not recognise the posting of the notice of the order on an official notice board in the town hall of an Austrian city and a further application was made for the deletion of this part of the order.

[4] Specific Proceedings

Where leave has been obtained to serve an originating process on a State,[167] the following documents must be filed with the registry:

(a) a request for service to be arranged by the Permanent Secretary to the Ministry of Foreign Affairs;
(b) a sealed copy of the originating process; and
(c) a translation of the originating process in the official language of the State (unless it is English).

Except in case of proceedings by way of a counterclaim or actions in rem, service of any writ or originating process is done by transmission through the Singapore Ministry of Foreign Affairs to the Ministry of Foreign Affairs of the State concerned or in a manner agreed with the State concerned.

[5] Service of Other Documents

Leave of court is also required for the service abroad of 'any summons, notice or order issued, given or made',[168] unless leave for service of the originating process has already been granted. The modes of service of these documents are similar to that for the originating process.[169]

[B] Obtaining Evidence Abroad

As a common law system with an adversarial trial procedure, it is the responsibility of litigants in Singapore to obtain their own evidence and present it to the court.

In the event that evidence needs to be obtained abroad, the court may make an order:[170]

(a) for the issue of a letter of request to the judicial authorities of a foreign country for the taking of evidence by deposition;
(b) if the government of the foreign country allows, for a special examiner to be appointed to take such evidence; or
(c) if there is a Civil Procedure Convention[171] or where the Minister of Foreign Affairs consents, for the appointment of a Singapore consul as a special examiner.

167. See SIA, discussed above at s. 10.02[B][1].
168. Order 11 rule 8(1), Rules of Court.
169. Order 11 rule 8(3), Rules of Court.
170. Order 39 rule 2, Rules of Court.
171. See above, at s. 10.04[A][2].

An order for such deposition is not lightly given. First, Order 38 rule 9 of the Rules of Court provides that no deposition is to be received in evidence unless the deposition was taken pursuant to an order of court under Order 39 rule 1,[172] and 'either the party against whom the evidence is offered consents, or it is proved to the satisfaction of the court that the deponent is dead, or beyond the jurisdiction of the court, or unable from sickness or other infirmity to attend the trial'.[173]

The order will only be granted 'where it appears necessary for the purposes of justice'.[174] This will include considerations of whether: the expense and time of a deposition overseas is necessary;[175] the application had an ulterior motive to use the deposition process to delay proceedings;[176] the presence of the witness is necessary (e.g., if the demeanour of the witness is likely to be a significant factor);[177] the evidence is material and not covered by another witness.[178] Further, the order for the issuance of a letter of request will only be granted in view of considerations of international comity.[179]

The party intending to use any deposition in evidence at the trial must give notice of his intention to do so at a reasonable time before the trial.[180]

Where the foreign country is a signatory to the Hague Convention on the Taking of Evidence Abroad in Civil and Commercial Matters 1970, which provides for the taking of evidence (i) by means of letters of request, and (ii) by diplomatic or consular agents and commissioners, the procedure of the Convention will apply.[181]

On the other hand, the High Court of Singapore may make an order for the examination of witnesses and for the attendance and production of documents in relation to 'a matter pending before a court or tribunal in a place outside the jurisdiction'.[182]

172. Order 38 rule 9(1)(a), Rules of Court.
173. Order 38 rule 9(1)(b), Rules of Court. This echoes generally the position for the admissibility of hearsay evidence.
174. Order 39 rule 1(1), Rules of Court.
175. Pinsler ed., *Singapore Court Practice* (LexisNexis, Singapore), [39/2-3/2] (last accessed at www.lexisnexis.com/sg/legal/ on 31 Jul. 2013).
176. *Lewis v. Kingsbury* (1888) 4 TLR 626, at 639 – the court allowed the defendant's application but directed that the trial must not be delayed and that an amount which had been paid into court be paid out to the plaintiff.
177. *Napier v. Anthony & Co.* [1932] SSLR 82.
178. *Lawson v. Vacuum Brake* (1884) 27 Ch. D 137; *Armour v. Walker* (1883) 25 Ch D 673.
179. *Settebello Ltd. v. Banco Totta & Acores* [1985] 1 WLR 1050. Generally, the same principles to the exercise of discretion whether it is a case of giving effect to a foreign request, or making an order to issue a letter of request to a foreign authority: *Charman v. Charman* [2005] EWCA Civ 1606; [2006] 1 WLR1053 (CA).
180. Order 38 rule 9(2), Rules of Court.
181. http://www.hcch.net/index_en.php?act=conventions.text&cid=82 (last accessed on 4 Aug. 2014).
182. Order 66, Rules of Court.

[C] Restraint of Foreign Proceedings

The Singapore court may issue an injunction to compel the party subject to the order to refrain from instituting or continuing with proceedings abroad (commonly known as an 'anti-suit injunction').

The following legal principles are applicable:[183]

(a) the jurisdiction to grant the injunction is to be exercised when required by the ends of justice;
(b) the restraining order is not directed to the foreign court but against the party litigating (or threatening to litigate) abroad;
(c) the injunction will only be granted against a party who is amenable to the jurisdiction of the court (otherwise the injunction would not be effective); and
(d) as a matter of international comity, because such an order indirectly affects the foreign court, the jurisdiction must be exercised with caution.

The Court of Appeal has given the following further guidelines:[184]

(e) Whether the proceedings are vexatious and oppressive.
(f) Whether the injunction would be unjust to the party sought to be restrained; and
(g) Whether the foreign proceedings are in breach of an agreement between the parties.

An important consideration is whether the party is acting vexatiously or oppressively in foreign proceedings. These include situations in which the party is subjected to oppressive procedures in the foreign court, the commencement of foreign proceedings without justification, foreign proceedings motivated by bad faith, commencement of proceedings which are bound to fail, and foreign proceedings which cause extreme inconvenience.[185] To avoid improperly depriving a party of his right to pursue litigation in accordance with his rights, it is 'only in the clearest of circumstances' of vexation or oppression that an injunction is justified.[186]

Where foreign proceedings are brought in breach of contract, the court may grant an anti-suit injunction to enforce the contractual right.[187] International comity plays a reduced role because the basis of the injunction is to prevent a breach of contract.[188]

183. The Court of Appeal in *Bank of America National Trust and Savings Association* [1994] 2 SLR(R) 898 at [10]-[14], endorsing the principles formulated by the Privy Council in *Societe Nationale Industrielle Aerospatiale v. Lee Kui Jak* [1987] AC 871 at 892.
184. *John Reginald Stott Kirkham v. Trane US Inc.* [2009] 4 SLR(R) 248 at [28]-[29].
185. *Ibid.*, at [47]. See also *UBS AG v Telesto Investments Ltd* [2011] 4 SLR 503; *Beckkett Pte Ltd v Deutsche Bank AG* [2011] 1 SLR 524 (HC); [2011] 2 SLR 96 (CA).
186. *Ibid.*, at [46].
187. See, e.g., *WSG Nimbus Pte Ltd. v. Board of Control for Cricket in Sri Lanka*, [2002] 3 SLR 603.
188. *John Reginald Stott Kirkham v. Trane US Inc.* [2009] 4 SLR(R) 248 at [29].

The general rule is that the contract should be enforced. Generally, damages are an inadequate remedy in such situations.[189]

While anti-suit injunctions are generally interlocutory applications, it can also be an application for a permanent injunction.[190]

Where the application for an anti-suit injunction abroad is itself a breach of contract (such as an exclusive forum jurisdiction clause), an 'anti-anti-suit injunction' may be obtained to prevent such breach.[191]

[D] Proof of Foreign Public Documents

Public documents are defined as documents forming the acts or records of the acts of:[192]

(i) the sovereign authority;
(ii) official bodies and tribunals; and
(iii) public officers, legislative, judicial, and executive, whether of Singapore or of any part of the Commonwealth or of a foreign country.

Singapore is not a party to the Hague Convention Abolishing the Legalisation of Foreign Public Documents. Generally, foreign public documents must be proved by the original or a copy certified by its legal keeper, with a certificate under the seal of a notary public or of a consular officer of Singapore that the copy is duly certified by the officer having the legal custody of the original and upon proof of the character of the document according to the law of the foreign country.[193] Any document must be translated into English by a qualified translator before it will be accepted by the Singapore courts.

More specific rules apply to certain classes of documents and countries:

(i) The Acts of the Executive or the proceedings of the legislature of a foreign country: These may be proved by journals published by their authority or commonly received in that country as such, or by a copy certified under the seal of the country or sovereign, or by a recognition thereof in some public Act of Singapore.[194]
(ii) Malaysia: The Acts, orders or notifications of the Government of Malaysia or the proceedings of the Parliament of Malaysia may be proved by copies or

189. *Continental Bank NA v. Aeakos Cia Naviera SA* [1994] 2 All ER 540 (CA) at 551, [1994] 1 WLR 588 (CA). See also *The Angelic Grace* [1995] 1 Lloyd's Rep 87 (CA) at 96; *Petromin SA v. Secnav Marine Ltd.* [1995] 1 Lloyd's Rep 603; *National Westminster Bank v. Utrecht-America Finance Co.* [2001] EWCA Civ 658, [2001] 2 All ER 733 (CA); *OT Africa Line Ltd. v. Magic Sportswear Corp.* [2005] EWCACiv 710, [2005] 1 CLC 923 (CA) at [33].
190. *Ashlock William Grover v SetClear Pte Ltd* [2012] 2 SLR 625.
191. See, e.g., *Bankgesellschaft Berlin AG v. First International Shipping Corp. Ltd.* [2001] CP Rep. 62; *Sabah Shipyard (Pakistan) Ltd. v. Islamic Republic of Pakistan* [2003] 2 Lloyd's Rep 571 (CA).
192. Section 76, EA.
193. Section 80(g), EA.
194. Section 80(e), EA.

extracts contained in the Government Gazette of Malaysia or by the recognition thereof in any Act or Ordinance of Malaysia or any State thereof.[195] The proceedings of a municipal body, town board or other local authority in Malaysia may be proved by a copy of such proceedings certified by the legal keeper thereof, or by a printed book purporting to be published by the authority of such body.[196]

(iii) United Kingdom: Proclamations, orders or regulations issued by Her Majesty or by the Privy Council or by any department of Her Majesty's Government may be proved by copies or extracts contained in the London Gazette or the Gazette.[197]

(iv) Civil Procedure Convention Countries:[198] A document that has been drawn up or certified and duly sealed by a court or other competent authority of a Civil Procedure Convention country providing for the dispensation of the authentication of such documents may be received, filed or used in the court.[199] Any document not in the English language must be accompanied by a translation certified by a court interpreter or verified by the affidavit of a person qualified to translate it before it may be used in court.[200]

[E] Statute of Limitations

Traditionally, under the common law, limitation period laws were regarded as substantive if they had the effect of extinguishing the right (the existence of the right), but procedural if they only barred the remedy (the enforceability of the right).[201]

This has been legislatively clarified. Where a claim is governed by foreign law, it is the limitation period of that foreign law and not of Singapore law that will apply,[202] unless such an application would conflict with public policy[203] or cause undue hardship to a party or potential party.[204]

Where the foreign law provides that a limitation period is or may be extended or interrupted in respect of the absence of a party to the action or proceedings, so much of that law as provides for the extension or interruption shall be disregarded,[205] unless it conflicts with public policy or would cause undue hardship to a party or potential party.[206]

195. Section 80(c), EA.
196. Section 80(f), EA.
197. Section 80(d), EA.
198. See above, at s. 10.04[A][2].
199. Order 92 rule 1A, Rules of Court.
200. Order 92 rule 1, Rules of Court.
201. *Star City Pty Ltd. (fka Sydney Harbour Casino Pty Ltd.) v. Tan Hong Woon* [2002] 2 SLR 22 (CA) at [12].
202. Section 3(1), Foreign Limitation Periods Act 2012 (No. 13 of 2012).
203. *Ibid.*, s. 4(1).
204. *Ibid.*, s. 4(2).
205. *Ibid.*, s. 4(3).
206. *Ibid.*, s. 4(4).

Foreign judgments on limitation shall be deemed to have determined the matter on its merits.[207]

[F] Remedies and Damages

Generally, the availability of remedies is a question of procedure governed by the law of the forum[208] because a court can only give orders which it can enforce. However, a remedy of the forum will not be given if the effect is to distort the foreign right being enforced.[209]

As regards damages, the Court of Appeal has questioned the traditional approach of treating a head of claim for damages as relating to substantive law while the determination of the quantum for that head as relating to procedure (and therefore governed by the *lex fori*).[210] The Court of Appeal has suggested that quantification of damages for the wrong done was more akin to a substantive rather than procedural issue, although this was *obiter* dicta and the court made clear that it had not heard full argument.[211]

As regards equitable remedies, the discretionary nature of specific relief is historically a matter for the law of the forum, as it is closely tied to the administration of the remedy.[212] However, this blanket approach has been nuanced. In *Rickshaw Investments Ltd. v. Nicolai Baron von Uexkull,*[213] the Court of Appeal accepted the proposition that 'where equitable duties arise from a factual matrix where the legal foundation is premised on an independent established category such as contract or tort, the appropriate principle in so far as the choice of law is concerned ought to be centred on the established category concerned'.[214]

As such, courts have held that the applicable law for actions broadly categorised as 'equitable claims' (e.g., for a constructive trust,[215] breach of fiduciary duty,[216] confidentiality,[217] and claims in knowing receipt and dishonest assistance[218]) is the law of the place where the wrong was committed.

Tracing remains difficult to classify. It has been recognised as forming part of the law of evidence,[219] which is procedural. However, the law of tracing forms part and parcel of the plaintiff's substantive claim to beneficial title to the traced property. Its

207. *Ibid.*, s. 5.
208. *OBG Ltd. v. Allan* [2007] UKHL 21, [2008] 1 AC 1 at [126].
209. *Phrantzes v. Argenti* [1960] 2 QB 19 at 36.
210. *Goh Suan Hee v. Teo Cher Teck* [2010] 1 SLR 367 at [23].
211. *Ibid.*, at [22]-[23].
212. See, e.g., *Sumitomo Bank Ltd. v. Thahir Kartika Ratna and others and another matter*; [1992] 3 SLR(R) 638 at [140]-[172]; affirmed in *Thahir Kartika Ratna v. PT Pertambangan Minyak dan Gas Bumi Negara (Pertamina)* [1994] 3 SLR(R) 312, at [37].
213. *Supra* n. 98.
214. *Ibid.*, at [81].
215. *Manhattan Bank NV v. Israel British Bank (London) Ltd.* [1981] Ch. 105.
216. *Rickshaw Investments, supra* n. 98.
217. *OBG Ltd. v. Allan* [2008] 1 AC 1 at [126].
218. *OJSC Oil Co. Yugraneft v. Abramovich* [2008] EWHC Comm 2613.
219. *Foskett v. McKeown* [2001] 1 AC 102 at 113.

specific characterisation is likely to follow from the context in which it is said to arise.[220]

[G] Foreign Currency Obligations

The Singapore courts can enter judgments in foreign currency where that is the currency of claim. The judgment sum is converted to local currency at the date of execution of the judgment.

In a common law debt action,[221] where the foreign judgment is expressed in foreign currency, local judgment will be given in the foreign currency, to be converted to local currency at the time execution is authorised by the court. The judgment creditor does not have the right to elect another date for the conversion. The same principles apply where a registered foreign judgment under the Reciprocal Enforcement of Commonwealth Judgments Act (Cap 264, 1985 Rev Ed) (RECJA) or the Reciprocal Enforcement of Foreign Judgments Act (Cap 265, 2001 Rev Ed) (REFJA) is enforced with the same force and effect as if it were a local judgment expressed in foreign currency.

[H] Restraining Removal of Assets and Securing Evidence in Favour of a Foreign Arbitration/Judicial Process

Singapore courts have the power to grant a *Mareva* injunction against a defendant - an order to prevent the defendant from dissipating assets. The injunction operates in personam against the defendant and it is not unknown for injunctions to be granted in respect of foreign assets, and even for worldwide injunctions to be granted in exceptional circumstances. Similarly, Singapore courts can also grant an *Anton Piller Order*, subject to stringent requirements, for securing evidence in favour of foreign arbitral or judicial proceedings.

[1] **Mareva** *Injunction in Support of Foreign Judicial Processes*

A *Mareva* injunction is an ancillary relief to a substantive claim.[222] The Singapore courts clearly have the power to grant this type of asset-freezing order,[223] but can only do so in support of a justiciable cause of action before the Singapore court. A claim for a *Mareva* injunction is not itself a substantive cause of action.[224]

220. Yeo Tiong Min, *Choice of Law for Equitable Doctrines* (Oxford University Press, 2004), at [4.101]-[4.103], [5.30]-[5.34], [5.41], and [6.30].
221. Commencing a common law action for a debt owed pursuant to the foreign judgment.
222. *The Siskina* [1979] AC 210; *Mercedes Benz AG v. Leiduck* [1996] 1 AC 284; *Karaha Bodas Co LLC v. Pertamina Energy Trading Ltd.* [2006] 1 SLR 112 (CA); *Swift-Fortune Ltd. v. Magnifica Marine SA* [2007] 1 SLR 629 (CA).
223. Supreme Court of Judicature Act (Cap 322, 1999 Rev Ed), s. 18(2), Sch. 1, para. (5). See also Civil Law Act (Cap 43, 1999 Rev Ed), s. 4(10); *Art Trend Ltd.* v. *Blue Dolphin (Pte) Ltd.* [1983] 1 MLJ 25, 29.
224. *The Siskina*, *supra* n. 199.

Thus, where a Singapore court obtains jurisdiction as of right (presence or submission), and an action is stayed by reason only of a foreign court being more appropriate as a forum, the court remains seized of proceedings and continues to have in personam jurisdiction over the defendant.[225] In such a context the substantive cause of action remains justiciable, and a *Mareva* injunction can be awarded in support of the foreign proceedings.

The position is different if jurisdiction over the defendant can be obtained only by leave of court for service of process out of the jurisdiction. Until such leave is granted, the substantive cause of action will not be justiciable before Singapore courts,[226] and a *Mareva* injunction cannot be awarded until the cause of action crystallises into a foreign judgment capable of enforcement in Singapore.[227]

[2] **Mareva** ***Injunction in Support of Foreign Arbitral Processes***

The statutory framework in Singapore gives its courts power to grant *Mareva* injunctions in support of foreign arbitral processes. Section 12A of the International Arbitration Act (Cap. 143A, 2002 Rev Ed) (IAA), in particular, sets out the power of the Singapore High Court to order interim measures in support of arbitrations conducted both inside and outside Singapore for the purpose of preserving evidence or assets.[228] In a recent decision, the Court of Appeal considered that the assets to be preserved could include those contractual rights 'which, if lost, would not adequately be remediable by an award of damages'.[229]

Where an arbitrating party has a cause of action against a defendant subject to the personal jurisdiction of Singapore courts, the court also has power under section 4(10) of the Civil Law Act (Cap. 43, 1999 Rev Ed) to grant a *Mareva* injunction in aid of the foreign arbitration.[230]

In the event that the court grants a stay of court proceedings in favour of foreign arbitral processes, the court retains the power to make interim or supplementary orders, including a *Mareva* injunction if it is appropriate to do so.[231]

225. *House of Spring Gardens Ltd. v. Waite* [1984] FSR 277, 283.
226. *The Siskina, supra* n. 199; *Mercedes Benz v. Leiduck* [1996] 2 AC 284.
227. *Baidini v. Baidini* [1987] FLR 463; *A/A D/S Svendborg v. Maxim Brand*, Unreported, 23 Jan. 1989.
228. Cap 143A, 2002 Rev Ed, s. 12A; *Equinox Offshore Accommodation Ltd. v. Richshore Marine Supplies Pte Ltd.* [2010] SGHC 122, [21]; *Maldives Airports Co. Ltd. and another v. GMR Malé International Airport Pte Ltd.* [2013] 2 SLR 449, [33]-[34]; See also Cap 143A, 2002 Rev Ed, Sch. 1, Art. 9.
229. *Maldives* Airports, *supra* n. 25.
230. *Front Carriers Ltd. v. Atlantic & Orient Shipping Corp.* [2006] 3 SLR(R) 854, referred to in *Swift-Fortune Ltd. v. Magnifica Marine SA* [2007] 1 SLR(R) 629 (CA), [69]-[70]; *Multi-Code Electronics, supra* n. 62, [116]-[117].
231. Section 6(2) and 6(3) of the *IAA*, (Cap. 143A, 2002 Rev Ed); *Channel Tunnel Group Ltd. v. Balfour Beatty Construction Ltd.* [1993] AC 334.

§10.05 RECOGNITION AND ENFORCEMENT OF FOREIGN DECISIONS

[A] Judicial Decisions: Requirements and Limitations

[1] In Personam Judgments

A foreign judgment in personam for a sum of money may be enforced by action under the common law ('common law debt action'); registered under the RECJA; or the REFJA. The RECJA and REFJA provide efficient and effective means of enforcement, but the statutes are applicable only if the foreign judgment originates from a court gazetted under them.

[a] Suing Afresh on the Underlying Cause of Action

A successful judgment creditor may choose to ignore the foreign judgment and sue afresh on the underlying cause of action in Singapore court, provided it is not an abuse of process to do so, and provided that the foreign judgment does not create a cause of action or issue estoppel[232] in relation to the earlier litigation between parties.

[b] Enforcement and Recognition of Judgments

[i] Common Law Action

A final and conclusive in personam foreign judgment for a definite or ascertainable sum of money is enforceable by common law debt action in Singapore courts[233] if:

(a) the foreign court had been internally competent;
(b) had international jurisdiction over the party sought to be bound; and
(c) no defences apply under the private international law of Singapore.

A foreign judgment meeting these requirements creates a fresh obligation on the part of the debtor to pay the judgment debt,[234] although from the perspective of the

232. *Lee Tat Development Pte Ltd. v. MCST Plan No 301* [2005] 3 SLR(R) 157; *Wing Joo Loong Ginseng Hong (Singapore) Co. Pte Ltd. v. Qinghai Xinyuan Foreign Trade Co. Ltd.* [2009] 2 SLR(R) 814; *Motor Image Enterprises Pte Ltd. v. SCDA Architects Pte Ltd.* [2011] 1 SLR 497.

233. In *Poh Soon Kiat v. Desert Palace Inc. (trading as Caesars Palace)* [2009] SGCA 60, a foreign judgment was unenforceable under Singapore law because the court held it to be a judgment setting aside the appellant's fraudulent transfer of foreign property, instead of a foreign money judgment enforceable by a common law action.

234. *Ralli v. Angullia* (1917) 15 SSLR 33 at 76, 91, 94; *In the Matter of the Marriage Settlement of Tan Tian Neo* [1926] SSLR 120, 126; *Ho Hong Bank Ltd. v. Ho Kai Neo* [1932] MLJ 76 at [77]; *Hong Pian Tee v. Les Placements Germain Gauthier Inc.* [2002] 2 SLR 81 (CA) at [30]; *Re Cheah Theam Swee* [1996] 2 SLR 76 at 82-83.

enforcing forum it is a simple debt and not a judgment debt.[235] This simple debt is often sued on via summary judgment procedures.[236]

[ii] Enforcement by Registration

A foreign judgment from a country gazetted under the RECJA[237] or REFJA[238] becomes enforceable with the same legal force as a local judgment after successful registration in Singapore. The rules of registration under the RECJA or REFJA closely resemble the common law requirements for enforcement of foreign judgments and the defences to enforcement,[239] although they are not identical (in particular, a judgment creditor seeking enforcement by registration can serve notice of registration without leave of court). The statutory provisions of each regime must be interpreted according to its own terms, and be given effect even if the meaning of one provision differs from a corresponding provision in the other, or if the meaning deviates from the position under common law.[240]

RECJA judgments - registration is discretionary - are enforceable under common law as well, although a judgment creditor cannot recover costs arising from this means of enforcement unless a previous application to register was refused, or otherwise ordered by the court.[241] In contrast, foreign judgments to which the REFJA applies - registration is compulsory - cannot be enforced at common law[242] (precluding the creditor from obtaining pre-judgment relief).

The application for registration must be made within twelve months (RECJA judgments) or six years (REFJA judgments) after the date of the judgment.

Neither RECJA nor REFJA apply to foreign insolvency orders. Since the law of the place of incorporation of a company governs its existence and status,[243] a Singapore court will recognise the foreign winding-up order issued in the jurisdiction where the company is incorporated.

[iii] International Jurisdiction

In general, international jurisdiction is established over a party if the party was resident or possibly present in the foreign country when proceedings commenced, or if the party voluntarily submitted to the jurisdiction of the foreign court.

235. *Hawksford v. Giffard* (1866) 12 App Cas 122 (PC Jersey) at 126-127.
236. Order 14, Rules of Court. See, e.g., *Hong Pian Tee, supra* n. 211; *Wu Shun Foods Co. Ltd. v. Ken Ken Food Manufacturing Pte Ltd.* [2002] 4 SLR 877.
237. The federal jurisdiction of Australia, the states of New South Wales, Queensland, South Australia, Tasmania, Victoria, Western Australia, Australian Capital Territories, Norfolk Island, and Northern Territory; New Zealand, Sri Lanka, Malaysia, Windward Islands, Pakistan, Brunei Darussalam, Papua New Guinea, and India (except Jammu and Kashmir).
238. Hong Kong SAR.
239. *Re Patrick Tan* [1994] 2 SLR 728 at 732.
240. *Harrisons Trading (Peninsular) Sdn Bhd v. Juta Perkara Sdn Bhd* [1997] 2 SLR 496 at [32].
241. Section 3(5), RECJA.
242. Section 7(1), REFJA.
243. *Banque International de Commerce de Petrograd v. Gouskassow* [1923] 2 KB 682.

[iv] Severability

If a foreign judgment is regarded as severable, unobjectionable parts may be recognised or enforced.[244]

[c] Defences under Private International Law

Generally, a foreign judgment will not be recognised or enforced if doing so would be contrary to the fundamental public policy of the forum,[245] or lead to conflict with an earlier judgment decided or recognised under private international law. Foreign judgments will also not be given effect if they had been obtained by fraud,[246] or in breach of principles of natural justice,[247] or if recognition or enforcement amounts to direct or indirect enforcement of foreign penal, revenue or other public laws[248] (the award of exemplary damages by a foreign court is not considered penal).

Outside these recognised exceptions, the common law takes a restrictive view of the defences available against recognition or enforcement of foreign judgments, in the interests of preserving international comity. In particular, it is not considered relevant whether or not the underlying cause of action is known in the forum.

Furthermore, there is a unique defence to registration under the REFJA - in case the foreign proceedings had been brought in breach of an agreement between the parties. Under highly exceptional circumstances, the court has the power to issue an anti-enforcement injunction against the reliance on a foreign judgment outside Singapore.

[2] Recognition of In Rem Judgments

A judgment in rem from a foreign court may be recognised in Singapore courts as binding on all parties if the foreign court is found to have had international jurisdiction on the matter, and had necessarily decided on the status of the *res*.[249]

244. *Yong tet Miaw v. MBf Finance Bhd* [1992] 2 SLR 761.
245. *Loucks v. Standard Oil Co. of New York* 224 NY 99 (1918) at 111, adopted in *Liao Eng Kiat v. Burswood Nominees Ltd.* [2004] 4 SLR 690 (CA) at [29]; REFJA, s. 5(1)(a)(v).v.
246. *Price v. Dewhurst* (1837) 8 Sim 279; 41 ER 30; *Ralli v. Angullia, supra* n. 211, at [85]; *Hong Pian Tee, supra* n. 211; RECJA, s. 3(2)(d); REFJA, s. 5(1)(a)(iv).
247. *Jacobson v. Frachon* (1928) 138 LT 386 at 392; RECJA, s. 3(2)(c).
248. A Briggs, *The Revenue Rule in the Conflict of Laws: Time for Makeover*, SJLS 280, at 285 (2001); s. 3(2)(f), RECJA; s. 3(2)(b), REFJA.
249. *Pattni v. Ali* [2007] 2 AC 85, [2007] 2 WLR 102, [2006] UKPC 51 (PC Isle of Man) at [21]; *Trans-World (Aluminium) Ltd. v. Cornelder China (Singapore)* [2003] 3 SLR 501 at [17]; *Payna Chettiar v. Maimoon bte Ismail* [1997] 3 SLR 387 at [12]; JJ Fawcett and JM Carruthers, *Cheshire, North and Fawcett: Private International Law* (14th Ed, 2008) at 532-533.

[B] Arbitral Awards (Including ICSID Awards): Requirements and Limitations

The laws governing private international commercial arbitration in Singapore are laid out in the International Arbitration Act (IAA)[250] and the Arbitration (International Investment Disputes) Act (Cap 11, 2012 Rev Ed) (AIIDA).

Foreign arbitral awards may, by leave of the Singapore High Court, be enforced in the same manner as a High Court judgment or an order to the same effect.[251] Applications may be made ex parte, but must be supported by an affidavit: (1) exhibiting originals or certified copies of the arbitration agreement and original award; (2) stating the names and places of residence or business of the creditors and debtors; (3) stating the extent to which the arbitral award has not been complied with at the date of the application.[252] When registering a foreign award for enforcement, a certified English translation of the award must also be provided.[253] After leave is given by the High Court, judgment may be entered in favour of the creditor according to the terms of the original arbitral award.

The party against whom the enforcement is sought may request that the enforcement be refused on similar grounds as contained in the 1958 Convention on the Recognition and Enforcement of Foreign Arbitral Awards (to which Malaysia is party). In addition, the court may refuse enforcement if (i) the subject matter of the difference between the parties to the award is not capable of settlement by arbitration under the law of Singapore; or (ii) enforcement of the award would be contrary to the public policy of Singapore.

By virtue of Singapore's ratification of the Convention on the Settlement of Investment Disputes between States and Nationals of Other States ('ICSID Convention') and incorporation of the ICSID Convention in The Schedule of the AIIDA, Singapore's courts are also obligated to recognise and enforce pecuniary obligations imposed by arbitral awards rendered pursuant to the ICSID Convention.[254] All that is required is simple presentation of a copy of the award to the Singapore High Court, pursuant to Article 54(2) of the ICSID Convention. Similarly, Singapore is also a party to the 2009 ASEAN Comprehensive Investment Agreement.

§10.06 RECOGNITION OF OTHER FOREIGN PUBLIC DOCUMENTS

Foreign documents or certificates are only recognised by the authorities of a state if their authenticity and evidentiary value had been previously determined by an

250. The IAA governs international arbitration seated in Singapore – unless parties opt out in favour of the Arbitration Act–, and is based on the Model Law, which gives effect to the New York Convention on the Recognition and Enforcement of Foreign Arbitration Awards.
251. Section 19, IAA; s. 46, AA.
252. Order 69, rule 14(1), Rules of Court for AA awards; Order 69A rule 6(1), Rules of Court for IAA awards.
253. Section 30, IAA.
254. Cap 11, 2012 Rev Ed., Article 54(1), the Schedule.

internationally accepted procedure. Since Singapore is not a party to The Hague Convention on Abolishing the Requirement of Legalisation for Foreign Public Documents, foreign public documents must be 'legalised' before the documents can be recognised in Singapore, either at the administration issuing the document or an Embassy of Singapore in the foreign state.

§10.07 TREATIES FOR JUDICIAL COOPERATION

Singapore is a party to the 1970 Hague Convention on the Taking of Evidence Abroad in Civil and Commercial Matters, but has excluded the application of Chapter II of the Convention. Therefore, although depositions may be taken pursuant to letters of request submitted directly to the Singapore High Court,[255] consular depositions and depositions conducted pursuant to a commission are not permitted in Singapore. Singapore is also a party to the 1980 Hague Convention on Civil Aspects of International Child Abduction. Aside from the Evidence Convention, Singapore is also a party to several bilateral treaties that provide rules for the taking of evidence abroad in criminal matters.

Uniquely, the Court of Appeal of Singapore referred a question of foreign law to the High Court of Justice of England and Wales,[256] which was answered by the Commercial Court in London.[257] Following from this, the Supreme Courts of Singapore and New South Wales have entered into a Memorandum of Understanding to work closely and expeditiously on issues arising under foreign law.[258]

With respect to service of process, Singapore is not a party to the 1965 Hague Convention on the Service Abroad of Judicial and Extrajudicial Documents in Civil and Commercial Matters.[259] Foreign courts serving documents on Singapore are thus still required to do so via consular or diplomatic channels. Service abroad may nevertheless be effected pursuant to bilateral Civil Procedure Conventions entered into between Singapore and a foreign country,[260] such as the Treaty on Judicial Assistance in civil and commercial matters between the Republic of Singapore and the People's Republic of China.[261]

255. Designated as the Central Authority for Singapore for the purposes of the Convention. See http://www.hcch.net/index_en.php?act = authorities.details&aid = 532 and Article 2 of the Hague Evidence Convention.
256. *Westacre Investments Inc. v. The State-Owned Company Yugoimport SDPR* (also known as Jugoimport-SDPR) [2009] 2 SLR(R) 166.
257. *Westacre Investments Inc. v. Yugoimport SDPR* [2008] EWHC 801 (Comm.).
258. See http://www.supremecourt.lawlink.nsw.gov.au/supremecourt/sco2_internationaljudicial cooperation/SCO2_agreement_singapore.html (last accessed on 4 Aug. 2014).
259. See http://www.hcch.net/index_en.php?act = conventions.status&cid = 17 (last accessed on 4 Aug. 2014).
260. Order 11 rule 4, Rules of Court; see Appendix C for the list of countries.
261. Appendix C, Rules of Court.

CHAPTER 11

Taiwan

Yao-Ming Hsu[*]

§11.01 CODIFICATION OF PRIVATE INTERNATIONAL LAW AND RELEVANCE OF CASE LAW

[A] Codification and Case Law

Taiwan codified in 1953 its conflict of laws rules in a single statute, i.e., the 'Law Concerning the Application of Laws for Civil Matters Involving Foreign Elements' (hereinafter Code of Private International Law or 'PIL Code').[1] In May 2011, following a trend in the region, the first amendment to the PIL Code entered into force. The amendment changed some out dated provisions (the national and social conditions in Taiwan had dramatically changed since 1953) and incorporated some of the principles contained in several Conventions developed by the Hague Conference on Private International Law ('Hague Conventions'). Nevertheless, the 1953 PIL Code still applies to legal relations or facts that happened before the entering into force of the amendment.[2]

Although several drafts were produced by experts in private international law at the request of the 'Judicial Yuan' (the supreme organ for judicial affairs in Taiwan),[3] it

* Associate Professor, College of Law, National Cheng-Chi University, Taipei, Taiwan; Double Bachelors in Political Science and LLB in National Taiwan University (NTU), Taipei, Taiwan; LLM in Chinese Philosophy of Law in NTU; DEA (LLM) in International Law and European Community Law in Université Aix-Marseille, France; DEA (LLM) in Legal Theory in Université Aix-Marseille, France; Doctor of Law also in International Law and European Community Law in Université Aix-Marseille, France. Email: ymhsu@nccu.edu.tw.

1. http://jirs.judicial.gov.tw/eng/FLAW/FLAWDAT10.asp?lsid = FL001357.
2. Supreme Court Decision No. Tai-Shang 1913 of 2011.
3. For the process, see Tieh-Jhen Liu, *Comments on the Amendment of 'Application Law of Civil Matters Involving Foreign Element'*, The Law Monthly 3 (1995). The first version (1999) had a total of 144 articles, then 67 articles in 2001 and finally 60 articles in the third edition (2003). For

is a pity that the relevant propositions on international jurisdiction and on recognition/enforcement of foreign judgments remained in blank. In addition, the structure of the PIL Code has been criticised by one of the drafters[4] for ignoring the most appropriate framework and for lacking logical consistency. For example, while Chapter 1 is supposed to contain 'General Provisions', Articles 2-5 only regulate issues related to *lex personalis* (conflicts of nationality, conflicts of residence, and multiple laws in a nation). Furthermore, from Chapter 2 to Chapter 6, the PIL Code imitates the legislative framework of the Civil Code instead of stressing its independence from the substantial regulations.

In Taiwan, the relevance of case law is relatively minor because Taiwan belongs to the civil law tradition and there are not that many cases relating to private international law. However, some pioneering cases for interpreting ambiguities in legal texts or for filling the gaps in normative structure do exist. For example, regarding the application of public order; exceptional criteria for denying the res judicata effect of judgments rendered by Chinese courts.

[B] Multilateral Conventions Providing Uniform Substantive Law and/or International Jurisdictional Rules

Although the Constitution contains no specific provision regarding the relation between international treaties and domestic legislation, the Judicial Yuan Interpretation No. 329[5] considers that treaties that have been passed by the domestic legislation procedures hold the same status as laws. Taiwan is a party to neither the UN Convention on Contracts for the International Sale of Goods (CISG), nor the Conventions for the International Carriage of Goods. Taiwan is not party to any of the multilateral treaties administered by the World Intellectual Property Organization (WIPO). However, being a Member of the World Trade Organisation (WTO), some articles of the Paris and Berne Conventions will be indirectly applicable in Taiwan through the Agreement on Trade-Related Aspects of Intellectual Property Rights (TRIPs).

a detailed comparison of each version, see Jhih-Wen Wang, *Review of the Amendment of 'Application Law of Civil Matters Involving Foreign Element'*, Hwa Kang Law Review 1, 5-12 (2004). The final draft (2007) was submitted to the 'Legislative Yuan' (the Taiwanese Parliament). The amendment was passed by the Legislative Yuan on 30 Apr. 2010 and entered into force on 26 May 2011.

4. Yuan-Hua Li, *Comment on the Draft 'Application Law of Civil Matters Involving Foreign Element' of October 28, 2003*, Taiwan Law Review 25, 26-28 (2003).
5. http://www.judicial.gov.tw/constitutionalcourt/en/p03_01.asp?expno=329.

§11.02 JURISDICTION OF LOCAL COURTS IN FOREIGN-RELATED CASES

[A] Grounds for Jurisdiction

[1] General

Until now, neither the Code of Civil Procedure (CCP),[6] nor the PIL Code contained specific grounds of international jurisdiction. Only Article 53(1) of the Act of Family Disputes prescribed that if one of the parties has the Taiwanese nationality, Taiwanese courts have jurisdiction.

Basically, we could do nothing but to use some legal reasoning of analogy, by referring to similar clauses in the CCP. Consequently, by analogical application of Article 1 of the CCP, general rules for setting international jurisdiction lie also in the court of the defendant's domicile or – when that court cannot exercise jurisdiction or for a claim arising from transactions or events taking place within the jurisdiction of the court in the defendant's residence – in the court of the defendant's residence. Similarly, applying by analogy Article 2 of the CCP, private legal persons or unincorporated association may be sued in the court where its principal office or principal place of business in Taiwan is located.

Similarly, some *special jurisdictions* (which are not exclusively exercised) are set by the place of action (Articles 3-17 of the CCP). For example:

- In matters relating to *proprietary rights*, in the court for the location of the defendant's attachable property or the subject matter of the claim (if it is a creditor's right, then either the place of the debtor's domicile or the location of the subject matter of a security).
- In matters relating to a *debt arising from or secured by a ship*, an action may be initiated in the court for the location of the ship.
- In *salvage matters*, an action may be initiated in the court for the location where the salvage took place, or where the salvaged ship first arrived.
- In matters relating to *torts*, an action may be initiated in the court for the location where the tortious act occurred.
- In *contract matters*, an action may be initiated in the court for the place agreed to by the parties as the place of performance of the contract.
- In matters relating to *debts or rights in rem* of any real property provided as a security for such debt, an action may be initiated against the same defendant in the court for the place where the real property is located.

[2] Exclusive Jurisdiction

The real exclusive jurisdiction is the litigation concerning immovable, in which the court of the place where the immovable is located has exclusive jurisdiction.

6. http://law.moj.gov.tw/Eng/LawClass/LawContent.aspx?PCODE=B0010001.

[B] Exclusion of Jurisdiction

[1] Immunity

[a] Sovereign Immunity

There is no specific provision within the CCP or reported case law concerning the sovereign immunity of foreign states. Even though Taiwan rarely participates in multilateral international treaties, based on international comity and international customary law, Taiwanese courts would apply immunity from jurisdiction. Taiwan adopts a restrictive approach, in which pure commercial transaction could not be immune from Taiwanese jurisdiction.

[b] Diplomatic and Consular Immunity

Taiwan is not a party to the 1961 Vienna Convention on Diplomatic Relations and the 1963 Vienna Convention on Consular Relations.

Article 144 of the CCP states that when service is to be effectuated in the domicile or residence or office of a person who enjoys immunity, the Ministry of Foreign Affairs may be requested to effect service.

[c] Other Immunities

Taiwan is not a party to the 1961 Convention on the Privileges and Immunities of the United Nations and the 1947 Convention on the Privileges and Immunities of the Specialised Agencies.

[2] Non-justiciable Claims

There is no specific provision regarding non-justiciable claims.

[3] Forum Agreements in Favour of Foreign Courts

According to the CCP, absent any exclusive jurisdiction of the Taiwanese courts, parties are free to choose any foreign jurisdiction to resolve their contract disputes. Its validity is based on the principle of party autonomy. However, it seems to be unfair to the weaker party.

[4] Arbitration Clause

According to Article 4 of the Arbitration Law (amended in 1998 and 2002 to conform its legal framework to the UNCITRAL Model Law), written agreements to arbitrate are given binding effect by the courts. If a legal action is initiated in conflict with a valid arbitral agreement, the court shall, upon petition by the adverse party, suspend the legal action and order the plaintiff to submit to arbitration within a specified time, unless the defendant proceeds to respond to the legal action. After the suspension, the legal action shall be deemed to have been withdrawn when an arbitral award is made.

[C] Non-exercise of Jurisdiction

[1] Forum Non Conveniens

Before 2003, the Supreme Court did not discuss the possibility for Taiwanese courts to apply the principle of forum non conveniens; some lower courts admitted the possible application of this principle.[7] Nevertheless, doctrinal discussions tended to accept it and finally a new Article 182-2 was added in the CCP in 2003.

[2] Lis alibi pendens

According to Article 182-2 of the CCP, when a party initiates an action with regard to a subject matter for which an action is pending in a foreign court, if:

(i) reasons exist for the court reasonably to believe that the foreign court's judgment on the action may be recognised in Taiwan; and
(ii) it is not substantially inconvenient for the defendant to litigate in such foreign country;

then the court by a ruling may stay the proceeding until the entry of a final and binding judgment on the action in that foreign country, except where the parties have otherwise consented to have the subject matter adjudicated by the Taiwanese court.

Before deciding on the ruling provided in the preceding paragraph, the court shall accord the parties an opportunity to be heard.

§11.03 APPLICABLE LAW

[A] Choice of Law

During the drafting period, discussions emerged about the choice between a detailed or summarised legislative formality.[8] For example, the detailed forms of contract can be divided into four categories: real estate and movable property contract, auction and bid contract, employment contract, and consumer contract. The PIL Code chose the simplified formality and marked specific regulations for torts.

Article 20(1) of the PIL Code should be the most important rule among all the amendments regarding obligations. It adopts the principle of party autonomy (similar

7. For example, Taipei District Court Procedural Decision Su-Zi N. 1756 of 1996.
8. Jhih-Wen Wang, *The Amendment of Choice-of-Law of Foreign Contract*, Taiwan Law Review 5, 6-8 (2008).

to the EU Regulation Rome I).[9] Consent requires a valid agreement in an express form (validity is to be determined under the law contained in the choice of law clause). Therefore, floating choice of law clauses are not included since they are not specific enough to determine whether the agreement is valid or not.[10]

[B] Other Cases

According to Article 20(2) of the PIL Code, if there is no choice of law agreement between the parties, or if it is void, the formation and effect of the juridical act are governed by the law which is most closely connected with it.

To prevent the flaw of varied discretions of judges that might be unfair and unpredictable, the new rule incorporates the characteristic performance principle originated from EU Regulation Rome I and presumes the *lex rei sitae* as the most significant law for the legal act of real estate. Article 20(3) of the PIL Code also contains the presumption that the law of the domicile of the party obliged under the most characteristic obligation at the time he/she undertook the juridical act is presumed to be the most closely connected law.

Nevertheless, it must be reminded that (i) usually the payment of money does not constitute the characteristic performance, except in specific contracts such as loan agreements;[11] and (ii) the presumptions of characteristic performance are rebuttable.[12]

The *legal capacity of a person* is governed by his/her national law (Article 9 of the PIL Code). According to Articles 13 and 14 of the PIL Code, the national law of a *legal person* is the law under which it was incorporated and governs the internal affairs of such legal person. However, if a foreign legal person establishes a branch in Taiwan, the internal affairs of that branch are governed by the laws of Taiwan.

Article 16 of the PIL Code states that the *formal requisites of a juridical act* are governed by the law applicable to the act. Nevertheless, it will also be effective if it complies with the formal requisites of the place where the act was undertaken; where a juridical act is undertaken at different places, it is effective if it complies with the formal requisites of any one of the places.

Negotiorum gestio is governed by the law of the place where the management was undertaken (Article 23 of the PIL Code), while *unjust enrichment* is governed by the law of the place of the enrichment (Article 24 of the PIL Code).

According to Article 25 of the PIL Code, *torts* are governed by the law of the place where the tort was committed unless another law is most closely connected with the tort. Articles 26 and 28 of the PIL Code contain specific rules for product liability and torts committed by means of communication. Article 29 of the PIL Code regulates that the existence of a direct claim of an injured person against the insurer of the person

9. Regulation No. 593/2008 of 17 Jun. 2008 on the law applicable to contractual obligations (Rome I).
10. Rong-Chuan Chen, *The New Autonomy of Private International Law – Party Autonomy principle of New Law in the 100th year of Republic Era*, Taiwan Law Review 151-152 (2010).
11. Jhih-Wen Wang, *supra* n. 8, at 18.
12. Rong-Chuan Chen, *supra* n. 10, at 155.

liable for the tort is governed by the law applicable to the insurance contract but the injured person also may assert a direct claim if the law applicable to the obligation permits its assertion. Besides, according to Article 31 of the PIL Code, where the parties with respect to an *obligation which arises otherwise than from a juridical act* agree to the application of the law of Taiwan after a suit has been brought in a Taiwanese court, the law of Taiwan is applied.

[C] *Renvoi*

According to Article 6 of the PIL Code, when the applicable national law of a party indicates that another law should govern the legal relation in question, such other law should be applied. However, if the national law of the party or the other law indicates, in turn, the law of Taiwan as applicable, the later will apply.

Former Article 29 of the PIL Code adopted jointly the remission, transmission, and indirect remission. Given that the international legislations gradually limit the scope of *renvoi* in order to simplify the application of law, the amendment introduced in current Article 6 of the PIL Code eliminates the original middle paragraph 'if according to the applicable law, the foreign-related matter shall apply other law, then other law shall be applied'. Besides, new Article 6 added 'if according to the *lex patriae* of the parties or other laws, the law of Republic of China shall be applied, shall the law of Republic of China be applied to the foreign-related matter' to the original article.

Although according to the recitals of this amendment its original aim is to simplify the sorts of *renvoi*,[13] the amended paragraph does not seem to achieve the aim set ahead. As we could see, the main text of amended Article 6 'when according to this law, *lex patriae* of the parties should be applied, and if according to the *lex patriae* the foreign subject matter shall be determined by other laws, then the other law should be applied' seems to be the transmission. Further, the proviso 'according to the *lex patriae* of the parties or other laws, the law of Republic of China shall be applied, shall the law of Republic of China be applied to the foreign-related matter' appears to be the remission. Nevertheless, if we read the proviso with the main text, indirect remission is also possible. Although the amendment deleted the contested middle paragraph of the former Article 29, the sorts of *renvoi*, especially the indirect remission that is only taken by few countries, was not simplified as planned. Thus, the amended wordings do not fit with the amended purpose. In fact, most counties merely regulate remission and transmission, so I recommend that if this new law would like to follow the international trend for simplifying the sorts of *renvoi*, the wording 'or other laws' in the proviso should be deleted for designating only the remission. This further clarification will be much more appropriate.[14]

13. Also in favour of this aim, see Yuan-Hua Li, *supra* n. 4, at 32.
14. Yao-Ming Hsu, *Comment on the Amendment Draft of Application Law of Civil Matters Involving Foreign Element of Taiwan in 2007*, in *Latest Issues of Private International Law and EU Private International Law* 221, 235-236 (2010).

[D] Mandatory Rules of the Forum and of Third States

According to Article 8 of the PIL Code, the application of the law of a foreign state is excluded if such application leads to a violation of the public order or *boni mores* of Taiwan.

Former Article 25 of the PIL Code had set up the clause of public policy to exclude the application of foreign law in certain circumstances, but it used the wording '*provisions*' ('...according to the law, if the *provisions* of foreign laws will violate the public policy of Republic of China, this foreign law shall be excluded'). The term '*provision*' seems to adopt the approach of 'provisions of foreign laws' as an exclusion basis, and it apparently goes against the international trend which prefers the approach of 'application result of foreign law',[15] so the new Article 8 of the PIL Code changed the wording to: '...if the *result* of application of foreign law will violate the public policy of Republic of China, this foreign law shall be excluded'. Professor Rong-Chuan Chen takes this position as well. Since the new law abundantly adopts the applicable law of the closest relation, the situations that need to be excluded by the public policy provision should be manifestly reduced.[16]

Besides, no clear indication exists in the PIL Code regarding the mandatory rules of a third state. Theoretically, if the court decides to apply some foreign law, its mandatory rules should be included.

[E] Proof of Foreign Law

According to Article 283 of the CCP, a party has the burden of proof with regard to foreign laws which are unknown to the court. Nevertheless, the court may investigate on its own initiative. There is no specific regulation providing for the effects of the lack of proof. In practice, the *lex fori* would be applied for convenience.

[F] Evasion of the Law

According to Article 7 of the PIL Code, where a party to a civil matter involving foreign elements evades a compulsory provision or a prohibition of the Taiwanese law, that compulsory provision or prohibition is nevertheless applied.

This amendment prevents the parties from applying the 'false' applicable law, which violates the mandatory or prohibited rules of Taiwan, by changing connecting factors on purpose. Scholar Li[17] deems it as an improper provision, since it limits its effect to cases of evasion of the *lex fori*. In fact, all applicable laws that are mandatory or prohibited rules shall not be evaded by the parties, no matter whether they are *lex fori* or the laws of other nations. The second possible shortcoming of this amendment

15. *See* Jin-Ying Tsai, *Restriction of Application of Foreign Law*, Cross-Strait Law 137 (2006).
16. Rong-Chuan Chen, *supra* n. 10, at 31.
17. Yuan-Hua Li, *supra* n. 4, at 31.

is that it does not regulate the effects of the acts for changing connecting factors.[18] If the 'ground act' of changing connecting factors is legal, e.g., the alteration of nationality, how could we rationalise that the 'result act' should be bound to the law of Taiwan? For instance, if a national of Taiwan had already changed the nationality to Japan, then it is undoubted that his *lex patriae* shall be the law of Japan; otherwise, the principle of 'certain connecting factor points to certain applicable law' will be ruined. According to the doctrinal discussions, the proposition of 'validating the ground act, but invalidating the result act' usually confronts the criticism of logical contradiction. If we favour this proposition, much stronger reasoning shall be provided. Professor Rong-Chuan Chen considers that 'the parties can legally change any connecting factor, and such a legal act is valid',[19] and 'what the new law limits is only the functioning of the connecting factor for designating the applicable law'. But if so, could we say that the new regulation of evasion of law seems to create the exception of the maxim of 'certain connecting factor points to certain applicable law'?

§11.04 PROCEDURAL ISSUES

Taiwanese law applies to procedural issues.

[A] Service of Summons and Judicial Orders Abroad

According to Article 123 of the CCP, except as otherwise provided, service of process will be administered by the court clerk on his/her own authority. Article 128 of the CCP states that service upon a foreign juridical person or unincorporated association which has set up an office or a place of business in Taiwan shall be effectuated upon its representative or administrator in Taiwan.

If service is to be made in a foreign country, Article 145 of the CCP requires it to be done by the competent authorities of the country requested, or the relevant authorised institution by Taiwan in that country. Where service cannot be effectuated in that way, it may be done by registered mail. Counsel or agent duly authorised may accept service abroad if such service is done in accordance with the laws of the foreign country.[20]

The court may, on motion, allow service by constructive notice where service in a foreign country cannot be done in accordance with Article 145, or it is foreseeable to be futile. In such a case, service shall take effect sixty days thereafter.

Since Taiwan is not party to any international agreement for judicial cooperation, requests for assistance from foreign courts will be governed, based on the principle of reciprocity, by Article 5 of the 1963 Law in Supporting Foreign Courts Consigned Cases.[21] It requires translation into Chinese of the request and documents to be served

18. See Jhih-Wen Wang, *supra* n. 3, at 20.
19. Rong-Chuan Chen, *supra* n. 10, at 30.
20. Supreme Court Decision Tai-Shang-Zi N. 109 of 2008.
21. http://law.moj.gov.tw/Eng/LawClass/LawAll.aspx?PCode=B0010014.

as well as a certification issued by the requesting country stating it would render similar assistance to Taiwanese courts if needed.

[B] Obtaining Evidence Abroad

Taiwan is not party to the 1970 Hague Convention on the Taking of Evidence Abroad in Civil and Commercial Matters. According to Article 295 of the CCP, if evidence is to be taken in a foreign country, the evidence-taking shall be entrusted to be conducted by the competent jurisdictional authorities of such country or the relevant ambassador/minister/envoy/consul or other institution or organisation of Taiwan in that country authorised to do so. The evidence-taking conducted by a foreign authority shall take effect insofar as it is not contrary to the laws of Taiwan irrespective of the contravention, if any, with the laws of the country of such foreign authority.

Requests for assistance from foreign courts will be governed, based on the principle of reciprocity, by Article 6 of the 1963 Law in Supporting Foreign Courts Consigned Cases.

[C] Restraint of Foreign Proceedings

There is no specific provision regarding restraint of foreign proceedings.

[D] Proof of Foreign Public Documents

Taiwan is not a party to the Hague Convention Abolishing the Legalisation of Foreign Public Documents. Therefore, it is for Article 356 of the CPP to govern the proof of foreign public documents. A document, which by formality and tenor may be considered a public document, is presumed to be authentic. In case of doubt, the court may request the government agency or public officer who issued such document to make a statement. If the document has been certified by the ambassador/minister/envoy/consul or other authorised institution of Taiwan in the foreign country, it shall be presumed to be authentic.

[E] Statute of Limitations

According to Articles 36 and 37 of the PIL Code, the time limitation of action for a claim is governed by the law applicable to the legal relationship from which the claim arose. And the extinction of an obligation is governed by the law applicable to the formation and effect of the obligation.

[F] Remedies and Damages

Remedies and damages are determined by the law applicable to the dispute. Nevertheless, there could be some exceptions imposed by Article 8 of the PIL Code (public order).

For example, in case of product liability, Article 51 of the Taiwan Code of Consumers Protection[22] allows to claim punitive damages up to three times the amount of actual damages as a result of injuries caused by the wilful act of misconduct of business operators. If a foreign applicable law allows for a higher amount of punitive damages, the court may decide not to overpass the limit of three times the actual damages; and if the foreign law does not allow punitive damages and the claimant is a Taiwanese, the court may consider Article 51 of the Code of Consumers Protection as mandatory.

[G] Foreign Currency Obligations

Article 202 of the Civil Code provides that when the object of the obligation is expressed in a foreign currency, the debtor may pay in the Taiwanese currency at the market rate of the place and time of performance, except if it has been agreed upon by the parties that payment shall be made in the foreign currency.

[H] Restraining Removal of Assets and Securing Evidence in Favour of a Foreign Arbitration/Judicial Process

There is no specific provision regarding restraining removal of assets in favour of a foreign process.

§11.05 RECOGNITION AND ENFORCEMENT OF FOREIGN DECISIONS

[A] Judicial Decisions: Requirements and Limitations

Taiwan has not entered into any bilateral treaty providing for the recognition and enforcement of judicial decisions. Therefore, the only applicable regime is contained in Article 402 of the CCP. Taiwanese courts will recognise foreign civil/commercial judgments unless:

(1) The foreign court lacked jurisdiction pursuant to the laws of Taiwan; nevertheless, according to scholars, this paragraph should be interpreted as 'pursuant to international customs'.
(2) A default judgment is rendered against the losing defendant, except in the case where the notice or summons of the initiation of action had been legally

22. http://law.moj.gov.tw/Eng/LawClass/LawContent.aspx?PCODE=J0170001.

served in a reasonable time in the foreign country or had been served through judicial assistance provided under the laws of Taiwan.

(3) The performance ordered by such judgment is contrary to the public policy or morals of Taiwan. The Supreme Court has stated that foreign decisions awarding punitive damages are recognisable and not contrary to the public order of Taiwan.[23]

(4) There exists no mutual recognition between the foreign country and Taiwan. This requirement is considered fulfilled if an expectation of future reciprocity exists.[24]

Taiwanese courts have recognised judicial decisions rendered in Australia, Belgium, Hong Kong, Japan, South Korea, Malaysia, New Zealand, the Philippines, Singapore, South Africa, United Kingdom, the United States of America, and Vietnam.

Appeal is possible within twenty days of receiving the judgment denying recognition. Appeals may be made first to the High Court and then to the Supreme Court. Article 4-1 of the Code of Enforcement regulates that, upon requests of parties, recognised foreign decisions could be enforced in name of exequatur issued by Taiwanese courts.

According to the 1997 'Act Governing Relations with Hong Kong and Macau',[25] judgments rendered by the courts of Hong Kong and Macau fall under the general regime contained in Article 402 of the CCP.

Article 74 of the 'Act Governing Relations Between Peoples Of The Taiwan Area and The Mainland Area'[26] states that an application for 'recognition' of a final and irrevocable civil judgment or ruling rendered in Mainland China may be filed before a Taiwanese court in so far as it is not contrary to the public order or good morals of Taiwan. In addition, Article 74 requires that Mainland China grants similar recognition. In 1998, the Supreme People's Court of Mainland China promulgated the 'Regulation for Recognition of Civil Judgments of the Courts of the Taiwan Region' (effective since 26 May 1998), recognising judgments of a court of Taiwan. Furthermore, some 'Additional regulations for Recognition of Civil Judgments of the Courts of the Taiwan Region' also announced by the Supreme People's Court was also promulgated since 14 May 2009. Following these announcements, Taiwan restored its recognition of judgments rendered in Mainland China.

[B] Arbitral Awards (Including ICSID Awards): Requirements and Limitations

Taiwan is not a signatory to the New York Convention, so it is for the Arbitration Law to regulate the mechanism of recognition and enforcement of both domestic and

23. Supreme Court Decisions Tai-Shang Tzu N. 835 of 2008 and No. 2193 of 2010.
24. Supreme Court Decision Tai-Shang Tzu N. 1943 of 2004.
25. http://law.moj.gov.tw/Eng/LawClass/LawContent.aspx?PCODE=Q0010003.
26. http://law.moj.gov.tw/Eng/LawClass/LawContent.aspx?PCODE=Q0010001.

foreign arbitration awards. The Arbitration Law considers as foreign any arbitral award rendered outside Taiwan or rendered in Taiwan with foreign arbitration rules.

In order for foreign arbitral awards to be enforceable in Taiwan they have to be previously recognised by the court (Article 47 of the Arbitration Law). Any application shall be submitted to the court and accompanied by the following documents (and its translation into Chinese):

(1) The original arbitral award or an authenticated copy.[27]
(2) The original arbitration agreement or an authenticated copy.
(3) The full text of the foreign arbitration law and regulation, the rules of the foreign arbitration institution or the rules of the international arbitration institution which applied to the foreign arbitral award.

In accordance with Article 49 of the Arbitration Law, the court shall dismiss an application for recognition of a foreign arbitral award if (a) the recognition or enforcement would be contrary to the public order or good morals of Taiwan, or (b) if the subject matter of the dispute was not subject to arbitration under Taiwanese law. The court may also refuse recognition if the state where the arbitral award is made, or whose laws govern the arbitral award, does not recognise and enforce Taiwanese arbitral awards.[28] Furthermore, Article 50 provides for a mechanism similar to Article V of the New York Convention, by which the respondent may request the court to dismiss the application for recognition.

Taiwanese courts have recognised awards issued, amongst others, in France, Hong Kong, South Korea, Switzerland, United Kingdom, and Vietnam.

Article 42 of the 1997 'Act Governing Relations with Hong Kong and Macau' applies the general regime contained in the Arbitration Law to 'the validity, petition for court recognition, and suspension of execution proceedings in cases involving civil arbitral awards made in Hong Kong or Macau'.

Similar to what happens with the recognition and enforcement of judicial decisions, Article 74 of the 1992 'Act Governing Relations Between Peoples Of The Taiwan Area and The Mainland Area', allows for recognition and enforcement of a final and irrevocable arbitral award rendered in Mainland China (unless the arbitral award is contrary to the public order or good morals of Taiwan). Above-mentioned Articles 49 and 50 of the Arbitration Law would apply to control the recognition application. However, it requires reciprocity by the courts of Mainland China.

Although Taiwan is not a party to the 1965 Washington Convention on the Settlement of Investment Disputes, it has entered into some bilateral investment treaties providing for investment arbitration.[29]

27. Authenticated by the embassies, consulates, representative offices, liaison offices or any other organisations authorised by Taiwan.
28. The Supreme Court Tai-Kang Tzu N. 335 of 1986 has confirmed the court's discretionary power and the need of enhancing international judicial cooperation.
29. http://investmentpolicyhub.unctad.org/IIA/CountryBits/205.

§11.06 TREATIES FOR JUDICIAL COOPERATION

Because of the sui generis nature of Taiwan's international status, Taiwan has not entered into any international agreement regarding issues of judicial cooperation of a civil or commercial nature. Furthermore, Taiwan is not a party to any of the Hague Conventions on Private International Law issues (though some of their principles have been embodied in the PIL Code).

CHAPTER 12
Thailand

Chinnawat Thongpackdee & Vanina Sucharitkul[*]

§12.01 CODIFICATION OF PRIVATE INTERNATIONAL LAW AND RELEVANCE OF CASE LAW

[A] Codification and Case Law

In Thailand, the supreme law of the land is the Constitution. The Thai legal system is based on the codified civil law approach, with the content of the legal codes (which were largely written early in the twentieth century) being influenced substantially by international sources and both civil (mainly France and Germany) and common law systems. Acts, which at times supplement Codes, make detailed provisions for particular issues or industries, and which are themselves supplemented by subordinate legislation (Royal Decrees, Ministerial Regulations, Notifications, etc.).

Private international law rules were codified in 1938 in the Conflict of Laws Act B.E. 2481. Its section 3 provides that 'wherever there is no provision in the Act or in any other laws of Thailand to govern a case of conflict of laws, the general principles of private international law shall apply'.

In Thailand, there is no system of case law as is normally understood in common law countries and judge-made precedents only exist in the form of final decisions of the Supreme Dika Court. Most decisions of the Court of First Instance and Court of Appeals are not publically reported.

* Chinnawat Thongpackdee, Partner, Herbert Smith Freehills (Thailand) Limited. Vanina Sucharitkul, Attorney at Herbert Smith Freehills (Thailand) Limited.

[B] Multilateral Conventions Providing Uniform Substantive Law and/or International Jurisdictional Rules

International treaties have to be transposed into domestic legislation in order for them to be binding in Thailand. Thailand is a party to neither the UN Convention on Contracts for the International Sale of Goods (CISG), nor the Conventions for the International Carriage of Goods by Air and by Sea.

Thailand is a party to four multilateral treaties administered by the World Intellectual Property Organization (WIPO).[1]

§12.02 JURISDICTION OF LOCAL COURTS IN FOREIGN-RELATED CASES

Apart from the civil courts, Thailand counts with specialised judges sitting in the Central Intellectual Property and Intellectual Trade Court, located in Bangkok, to deal with intellectual property and international trade law. In addition, this Court has jurisdiction over civil and criminal cases related to some international transactions. The Court has special procedures

[A] Grounds for Jurisdiction

[1] General

According to section 4 of the Civil Procedure Code, a case can be filed before the courts of Thailand if it is the country in which (a) *lex domicilii*, either of the parties is domiciled, (b) *locus contractus* or *locus delicti commissi*, the cause of action arises, (c) *lex situs*, the defendant has property, or (d) *lex patriae*, the plaintiff has citizenship (nationality).

If the defendant is not domiciled within Thailand, but operates or used to operate either in whole or in part a commercial activity within Thailand (by himself or his agent or his contact person carrying out such commercial activities in Thailand), the place used by himself, his agent, or his contact person for operating commercial activities or the place of residence of his agent or his contact person on the date of submitting the plaint or within the previous two years, is regarded a domicile of the defendant (section 3 of the Civil Procedure Code).

Thai courts also have in rem jurisdiction. Ship arrest in Thailand is governed by the Arrest of Ships Act B.E. 2534 (1991), which adopts the general principles in the Brussels Convention on the Arrest of Sea-Going Ships of 1952, with some differences. Irrespective of the domicile of the defendant, a creditor domiciled in Thailand may apply to the court for an order to arrest (i) any sea-going ship, irrespective of the flag, of which a debtor is in possession (if the maritime claim arises out of the ship or its business activities and if the debtor was in possession of the ship at the time the maritime claim arises and the arrest is applied for) or (ii) the sea-going ship,

1. http://www.wipo.int/treaties/en/ShowResults.jsp?country_id = 168C.

irrespective of the flag, owned or in possession by the debtor and giving raise to disputes of ownership, possession between co-owners, employment, earnings, or disputes over the mortgage of that ship. If the debtor is not in Thailand, the court may, before enforcing such order, direct the creditor to furnish security to cover potential damages arising out of the arrest. Within thirty days after the warrant of arrest has been posted, the creditor must initiate an action based on a maritime claim before (i) the court issuing the arrest order or (ii) any other court competent to deal with such action in accordance with the Civil Procedure Code. The Act also contains express provisions for service of the pleading to the debtor not domiciled in Thailand. Additionally, foreign ships can be seized or arrested by Thai war ships in the High Seas.[2]

[2] Exclusive Jurisdiction

Thai law is silent on the issue of exclusive jurisdiction.

[B] Exclusion of Jurisdiction

[1] Immunity

[a] Sovereign Immunity

There is no specific Act or reported case concerning the sovereign immunity of foreign states. However, it can be assumed that a court will apply general international customary law regarding sovereign immunity.

[b] Diplomatic and Consular Immunity

Specific statutes dealing with immunities from jurisdiction include the Consular Immunities and Privileges Act B.E. 2541 (1998) and the Diplomatic Immunities and Privileges Act B.E. 2527 (1984) which accord foreign consuls and diplomats accredited in Thailand immunity from the jurisdiction of Thai courts. The Acts serve to implement the 1961 Vienna Convention on Diplomatic Relations, the 1963 Vienna Convention on Consular Relations[3] to which Thailand is a party. Prior to the enactment of such Acts, Thai courts accepted the principles and practice of diplomatic immunity based on customary international law.

2. Article 19 of the Convention on the High Seas 1958.
3. 'The Government of the Kingdom of Thailand declares that the term "competent judicial authority" under Article 41(1) of the Convention means all competent officials under Thai criminal procedure.'

[c] Other Immunities

Thailand is a party to the 1946 Convention on the Privileges and Immunities of the United Nations, though excluding immunity for UN officials of Thai nationality, and the 1947 Convention on the Privileges and Immunities of the Specialised Agencies.

[2] Non-justiciable Claims

Thai courts only have jurisdiction over land and immovable property located in Thailand.

[3] Forum Agreements in Favour of Foreign Courts

Agreements to exclude the jurisdiction of the Thai court in favour of a foreign court are valid insofar as they do not limit the Thai court's jurisdiction to hear the case.[4]

Section 150 of the Civil and Commercial Code provides that 'an act is void if its object is expressly prohibited by law or is impossible, or is contrary to public order or good morals'. An act will not be deemed void if it deviates from a provision of law unless the law relates to public order or good morals.[5] As the Civil Procedure Code is a law governing public order, parties cannot derogate from such legal obligations (e.g., section 4 governing jurisdiction).[6]

Therefore, a clause providing for the exclusive jurisdiction of a foreign court is not enforceable and does not prevent Thai courts from hearing the case if they have jurisdiction according to section 4 of the Civil Procedure Code. In a case where parties contracted that any dispute that arises shall be submitted to the London Courts, the court found such clause to be contrary to section 4(1) of the Civil Procedure Code and therefore void.[7]

[4] Arbitration Clause

If a party to an arbitration agreement commences proceedings in court against the other party to the agreement without submitting the dispute to arbitration, the party against whom the case is commenced may apply to the court to strike out the case. The application must be made no later than the date of filing the defence or within the period allowed by law for filing the defence.[8] If the court is satisfied that an arbitration

---

4. Supreme Court Decision No. 951/2539 (1996).
5. Section 151 of the Civil and Commercial Code states, 'An act is not void on account of its differing from a provision of any law if such law does not relate to public order or good morals'.
6. Supreme Court Decision No. 951/2539 (1996).
7. *Ibid.*
8. Section 14 of the Arbitration Act states: In case where any party to the arbitration agreement commences any legal proceedings in court against the other party thereto without submitting such dispute to arbitration pursuant to the arbitration agreement, the party against whom the legal proceedings are commenced may file with the competent court, no later than the date of filing the statement of defence or within the period for filing the statement of defence in

agreement exists and there are no grounds for finding it void or unenforceable or incapable of being performed, the court must issue an order striking out the case.

In order for an arbitration agreement to be enforceable under the Thai Arbitration Act of 2002, there must be a clear agreement by the contractual parties to submit all or some of their present or future disputes to arbitration. Furthermore, the arbitration agreement must be in writing, whether in the form of a contract or exchange of information, letters, telegrams, facsimiles or other documents of a similar nature and bear the signatures of the parties (electronic signature is acceptable). In practice, Thai courts do uphold and enforce arbitration agreements and dismiss litigation brought in breach of such an agreement. Contracts between a government agency and a private party may contain a binding arbitration clause (section 15 of the Arbitration Act) unless the agreement is void, unenforceable, or impossible to be performed. Nevertheless, in 2004, the cabinet passed some resolutions inhibiting government agencies from agreeing on arbitration clauses in new concession contracts unless approved by the cabinet on a case-by-case basis.

[C] Non-exercise of Jurisdiction

[1] Forum Non Conveniens

The doctrine of forum non conveniens, which is prominent in common law jurisdictions, is little known in the Thai legal system. There is no provision in the Code that compels the court to hear or not to hear a case under its jurisdiction. If the case is within the court's jurisdiction, the court will hear the case.

[2] **Lis alibi pendens**

Under the Civil Procedure Code, in domestic cases, a plaintiff is prohibited from filing the same plaint with the same court or other courts in Thailand. Section 173 paragraph 2(1) of the Civil Procedure Code states that from the date of filing a law suit, the case has been pending in the trial and in consequence the plaintiff cannot file the same plaint with the same Court or other Courts. Nevertheless, there is no similar rule in relation to foreign proceedings.

---

accordance with the law, a motion requesting the court to issue an order striking out the case, so that the parties may proceed with the arbitral proceedings. Upon the court having completed the inquiry and finding that there are no grounds for rendering the arbitration agreement void or unenforceable or incapable of being performed, the court shall issue an order striking out the case.

§12.03 APPLICABLE LAW

[A] Choice of Law

The expression 'choice of law' as used in this context means the choice of applicable law to the case in dispute.

[1] Express Stipulation

The Thai legal system recognises the parties' autonomy to negotiate any terms of the contract, including the choice of law. This principle of freedom of contract is clearly embodied in section 13 of the Thai Conflict of Laws Act, which stipulates that '[t]he question as to what law is applicable in regard to the essential elements or effects of a contract is determined by the intention of the parties thereof'.

The Conflict of Laws Act acknowledges both the parties' expressed and inferred choice to select any law as the proper law of their contract even though there may be no connection between the substance of the obligations and the law chosen. Nevertheless, according to section 5 of the Conflict of Laws Act, the choice of law will apply only insofar as it is not contrary to public order and good morals of the people.[9] Furthermore, according to Article 4 of the Act on the Carriage of Goods by Sea (B.E.2534), the law stated in the bill of lading will be applicable unless one of the parties has Thai nationality or is a company registered in Thailand.

It is not clear from the Conflict of Laws Act and there is no judgment of the Thai Supreme Court as to whether or not *depeçage* is allowed.

[2] Implied Choice

As mentioned before, the Conflict of Laws Act also acknowledges inferred choice of law. Some of the factors considered by the Thai Supreme Court for ascertaining an inferred choice of law are: (i) a clause in a charter party providing for arbitration in the United Kingdom;[10] and (ii) the fact that a maritime insurance contract was made in English.[11]

[B] Other Cases

In case of obligations, the Conflict of Laws Act sets out rules for determining the governing law where the parties have not made a choice. In the absence of choice, section 13 provides:

9. 'Whenever the law of a foreign country is to govern, it shall be applied in so far as it is not contrary to the public order or good morals of Siam [Thailand]'.
10. Judgment No. 1645/2538 (B.E.).
11. Judgment No. 996/2496 (B.E.).

> If such intention, expressed or implied, cannot be ascertained, the law applicable is the law common to the parties when they are of the same nationality, or, if they are not of the same nationality, the law of the place where the contract has been made.
> When the contract is made between persons at a distance, the place where the contract is deemed to have been made is the place where notice of acceptance reaches the offeror. If such place cannot be ascertained the law of the place where the contract is to be performed shall govern.

Based on Thai conflict rules, the following laws shall be applied in the following order, if the parties have failed to choose the law applicable to their contract:

(1) *lex patriae*, the law of the country where the party have common nationality;
(2) *lex loci contractus* (execution), the law of the place where the contract was made;
(3) *lex loci contractus* (performance), the law of the country where the contract is to be performed.

In its judgment No. 3223/2525, in a case where a contract entered into in Singapore by two Americans had been breached in Thailand, the Supreme Court reviewed a decision of the Thai Labour Court and considered that the place where the contract was made could not be considered as an implied choice of law and that the common nationality of both parties should determine the applicable law.

[1] Formal Validity

As a general rule, the formal validity of a juristic act is governed by the law of the country where the act is made (section 9 of the Conflict of Laws Act). A contract shall not be void when made in accordance with the formalities prescribed by the law applicable to the contract (section 13). Regarding immovable property, the law of the country where it is located governs the form required for the validity of a contract, document, or other juristic acts relating to immovable property.

[2] Negotiorum Gestio and Unjust Enrichment

Regarding obligations arising out of management of affairs without mandate (*negotiorum gestio*) or of undue enrichment, the law of the place where the facts from which such obligation has arisen shall be applied.

[3] Torts

Under section 15 of the Conflict of Laws Act, an obligation arising out of a wrongful act is governed by the law of the place where the facts constituting such wrongful act have taken place. Nevertheless, the double actionability rule applies (the act has to be considered wrongful also according to Thai law).

[4] *Property*

Movable and immovable property is governed by the law of the place where the property is located, even for issues of succession. Movable property in transit continues to be subject to the law of the place where such property was located at the institution of the action.

[5] *Law of Nationality*

The law of nationality governs: (i) the capacity for affecting a betrothal, (ii) conditions of marriage, (iii) the validity of divorce by mutual consent, (iv) the relationship and property between husband and wife (if different nationality, the one of the husband will be considered), (v) the capacity for entering into a pre-nuptial agreement, (vi) the effects of such agreement (if different nationality, the presumed law chosen by the parties or of the first matrimonial domicile will be applicable), and (vii) obligations of maintenance.

[6] *Succession*

Succession by statutory right or by will is governed by the law of domicile of the deceased at the time of his death. The capacity of a person to make a will is governed by the law of his nationality at the time when the will is made. The will has to comply with the form prescribed by the law of his nationality and of the country where the will is made. Revocation of a will and effects/interpretation of the will (as well as nullity) are governed by the law of his domicile (i) at the time of the revocation or (ii) his death, respectively.

[C] *Renvoi*

Section 4 of the Conflict of Laws Act provides for the application of single *renvoi*:

> Whenever the law of a foreign country is to govern and under that law it is the law of Siam[12] which shall be applied, the internal law of Siam governs and not the Siamese rules on conflict of laws.

[D] Mandatory Rules of the Forum and of Third States

Thai mandatory rules of law will apply to a dispute irrespective of the private parties' exercise of their autonomy in choosing a foreign applicable law. These are provisions that are overriding and the respect for which is crucial for safeguarding the public interests, such as its political, social, or economic organisation, to such an extent that they are applicable to any situation (e.g., statute of limitations).

12. Thailand was formerly known as Siam.

Thai courts also have discretion to apply mandatory rules of a third State provided there is a close connection between the subject matter of the parties' contract and the State promulgating the mandatory rules. There is no strict guidance or factors on what constitute a close connection and the matter is entirely within the court's discretion.

[E] Proof of Foreign Law

The party seeking to apply foreign law bears the burden of proof of the law claimed to be applicable. That party must satisfy the court that there is an agreement specifying a foreign law as the governing law and prove the content of that foreign law. Section 8 of the Conflicts of Laws Act provides that where an applicable foreign law is not proven to the satisfaction of the court, the domestic law of Thailand shall be applied. A foreign lawyer may present testimony as an expert witness on foreign law.

[F] Evasion of the Law

There is no specific regulation on evasion of the law. Nevertheless, if parties attempting to evade the application of Thai internal law, Thai courts will likely disregard the content of foreign law and apply Thai law.

§12.04 PROCEDURAL ISSUES

[A] Service of Summons and Judicial Orders Abroad

Thailand is not a signatory to the 1965 Hague Convention on the Service Abroad of Judicial and Extrajudicial Documents in Civil or Commercial Matters. Accordingly, the service of summons and judicial orders can be complex and will largely depend on where the case originates. Nevertheless, Thailand does maintain treaties addressing issues of service of summons and judicial orders with certain nations such as Australia, China, and Laos.

Judicial cooperation agreements are designed to reduce diplomatic channels by establishing direct contact between the Office of the Judiciary and the relevant entity in the contracting State. When permitted by a relevant treaty, the service of summons may be addressed directly through the Office of the Judiciary instead of through the Ministry of Foreign Affairs.

[B] Obtaining Evidence Abroad

Thailand is a party neither to the 1970 Hague Convention on the taking of Evidence Abroad in Civil or Commercial Matters nor to the 1963 Vienna Convention on Consular

Relations. For a Thai court procedure, obtaining evidence abroad is governed by the Civil Procedure Code or any relevant bilateral or multilateral treaties in place.[13]

Absent a judicial cooperation treaty, the Thai court can make a request via diplomatic channels, which will consider the request based on the theory of reciprocity and comity. If the request is granted, the evidence shall be governed by the requested country's domestic law. Any documentary evidence in the Thai court must be provided with Thai translation.

On the other hand, the court may order a party in Thailand to preserve and produce documents, permit inspection of things...

[C] Restraint of Foreign Proceedings

Under Thai law, the court has no power to issue anti-suit injunctions or an order restraining a person from commencing or continuing proceedings in a foreign court.

[D] Proof of Foreign Public Documents

Thailand is not a signatory to the 1961 Hague Convention Abolishing the Requirement for Legalisation for Foreign Public Documents.

Although there is no specific regulation on proof of foreign public documents, any foreign documents submitted must be originals or certified true copies and must be translated into Thai.

[E] Statute of Limitations

Section 5 of the Conflict of Laws Act allows the application of foreign law insofar as that foreign law is not contrary to the public order or good morals. Under Thai law, the statute of limitations is considered a law that relates to the public order.[14] Therefore, the statute of limitations under the agreed applicable law which is different to what is provided under Thai law cannot be enforceable, in the event that the defendant has raised the issue on statute of limitation in court.[15]

Claims for personal injury and other wrongful acts (torts) are barred after one year from the day when both the wrongful act and the identity of the defendant became known to the injured person. The maximum time limit is ten years from the date when the wrongful act was committed. For many contractual disputes, the prescription period is either two or five years, depending on the nature of claim. Other prescription

---

13. See the list of Agreements on judicial cooperation at the end of the chapter.
14. Supreme Court Decision No. 1583/2511 (1968).
15. Section 193/29 of the CCC: 'When prescription has not been set up as a defense, the Court cannot dismiss the claim on the ground of prescription.'

periods apply in particular circumstances (e.g., annulment of a shareholders' resolution). A ten-year period applies where no other time period is specified. Prescription periods fixed by law cannot be extended or reduced by agreement of the parties.[16]

[F] Remedies and Damages

The law applicable to the dispute will apply to remedies and damages. Nevertheless, in relation to torts, the injured party cannot claim compensation or remedies other than those allowed by Thai law (section 15 of the Conflict of Laws Act).

Under Thai law, the court has the power to grant a wide range of remedies on application by a party or, where permitted by law, as it sees fit. Those remedies include final injunctive relief, declarations, orders for an account of profits, and the transfer of property and, most commonly, a monetary award of damages to compensate for loss suffered. Non-compensatory (punitive or exemplary) damages are rarely awarded.[17]

[G] Foreign Currency Obligations

Claims in a Thai court can be made in foreign currency. However, according to section 196 of the Civil and Commercial Code, the other party may make the payment in Thai currency.[18] In that case, the commutation is made according to the rate of exchange current in the place of payment at the time of payment.

---

16. Section 193/11 of the CCC states: 'The periods of prescription fixed by law cannot be extended or reduced.'
17. Section 42 of the Consumer Case Procedure Act B.E. 2551 (2008) states:

> If the act upon which the complaint is based arises from the operator's wilful act to unfairly take advantage of the consumer or intent to cause damage to the consumer or, with gross negligence, indifference to damage to be caused to the consumer, or act in breach of responsibility as a professional businessman who is usually trusted by the public, when the court adjudicates that the business operator pay damages to the consumer, the court shall have the power to order the business operator to pay damages as punishment in addition to the amount of the actual damages fixed by the court as may be deemed appropriate, taking into account such circumstances as damage suffered by the plaintiff, benefit received by the business operator, financial condition of the business operator, relief by the business operator from the damage, and the consumer's contribution to the damage.
>
> In fixing damages for punishment under paragraph one, the court shall have the power to fix the damages by not more than two times the actual damages fixed by the court. However, if the actual damage[s] fixed by the court is not more than Baht 50,000, the court shall have the power to fix the damages for punishment by not more than five times the actual damages fixed by the court.

18. Supreme Court Decision No. 4751/2553 (2010).

[H] Restraining Removal of Assets and Securing Evidence in Favour of a Foreign Arbitration/Judicial Process

A plaintiff before the Thai court may file an application requesting the court to order a temporary injunction restraining the defendant from removing assets (or preventing the transfer, sale or disposal of such assets) until final judgment. Similarly, a plaintiff can file an ex parte application for the seizure or attachment of assets before the judgment is rendered.

In Thailand, prior to the IP&IT Court regime in 1997, there were no provisions similar to an Anton Piller Order. Since then, just a few such applications have been granted. One of the very few reported cases is *GSI Group Inc. v. Almin Enterprise Co. Ltd et al.* The requirements for issuing such Order are contained in sections 28-29 of the Act for the Establishment and Procedure of the IP&IT Court.

Absent judicial cooperation agreements, Thai courts lack jurisdiction to grant such interim measures in favour of foreign arbitration or judicial processes.

§12.05 RECOGNITION AND ENFORCEMENT OF FOREIGN DECISIONS

[A] Judicial Decisions: Requirements and Limitations

There are no provisions for recognition or enforcement of foreign judgments. Moreover, Thailand has not entered into any international treaty or convention in this regard. Thailand has no tradition of recognising or enforcing foreign judgments. Therefore, the Thai court has no authority to recognise or enforce a foreign judgment and the foreign judgment creditor must commence proceedings afresh.

Nevertheless, a foreign court judgment can be relied on as admissible evidence in a new case re-instituted in Thailand. This principle is mainly derived from an old Supreme Court case from 1918, which is in fact the only precedent reported to date.[19] However, it should be noted that since Thailand does not recognise the common law principle of binding judicial precedent, this case is regarded as merely persuasive.

In that case, the plaintiff and defendant, both Vietnamese citizens, entered into a contract whereby the defendant sold the plaintiff fifteen rickshaws and two bicycles. The contract was made in Saigon. According to the plaintiff's claim, he paid the price of the goods to the defendant but the defendant failed to deliver the goods to him. The plaintiff then filed a legal action against the defendant in the Saigon Civil Court. The court rendered a judgment in favour of the plaintiff. The defendant fled to Bangkok where the plaintiff sought enforcement of the Saigon Civil Court judgment against him.

This attempted enforcement was unsuccessful. The Supreme Court of Siam held that the Vietnamese judgment was a default judgment. It was not a final and conclusive judgment on the merits of the case possible to be enforced, and the plaintiff did not adduce any evidence to support his argument on the defendant's breach of contract.

19. Supreme Court Decision No. 585/2461.

Hence, the case was dismissed. However, in the ruling of the court, the Supreme Court formulated guidelines in relation to foreign judgments as follows:

- According to principles of private international law, the courts in one country may give effect to a judgment made in the courts of another country by treating the judgment debt as an ordinary debt that can be pursued through normal litigation processes.
- The foreign court whose judgment is being relied on must be a competent court with jurisdiction over the parties and the claim.
- In order to carry any weight in the Thai courts, the foreign judgment must be final and conclusive on the merits.

[B] Arbitral Awards (Including ICSID Awards): Requirements and Limitations

Thailand is a party to the New York Convention on the Recognition and Enforcement of Foreign Arbitral Awards 1958 (New York Convention), and no reservations were entered on accession. Recognition and enforcement of foreign awards may therefore only be refused on the grounds permitted by the New York Convention, as implemented by the Arbitration Act. Moreover, Thailand is a party to the 1923 Geneva Protocol on Arbitration Clauses (Geneva Convention).

Thai law does not distinguish between awards made in Thailand and awards made outside of Thailand for purposes of applications to court for recognition and enforcement.[20] In respect of both types of awards, a party seeking to enforce any award will have three years within which to file its application with the court, and the grounds for denying enforcement will essentially be those set out in Article V of domestic as well as foreign awards of the New York Convention.

Appeal is only allowed when:[21]

(1) The recognition or enforcement of the award is contrary to public order or good morals.
(2) The order or judgment is contrary to the provisions of law relating to public order or good morals.
(3) The order or judgment is not in accordance with the arbitral award.
(4) The judge who has tried the case gave a dissenting opinion in the judgment.

20. Section 41 of the Arbitration Act states:

> Subject to Section 42, Section 43 and Section 44, an arbitral award, irrespective of the country in which it was made, shall be recognized as binding on the parties, and upon petition to the competent Court, shall be enforced. In the case where an arbitral award was made in a foreign country, the award shall be enforced by the competent court only if it is subject to an international convention, treaty, or agreement to which Thailand is a party. Such award shall be applicable only to the extent that Thailand commits to be bound.

21. Section 45 of the Arbitration Act.

(5) It is an order on provisional measure under section 16. An appeal against an order or judgment under this Act shall be made to the Supreme Court or the Supreme Administrative Court, as the case may be.

Conservatory measures are in principle available pending enforcement of an award, subject to the same limitations that apply to this kind of measures generally. A party seeking enforcement must file the request within three years from the date upon which an award may be enforced. The court shall examine the application without delay.[22]

Thailand has signed the Convention on the Settlement of Investment Disputes between States and Nationals of Other States ('ICSID Convention'), but has not ratified it and is not expected to do so soon. On the contrary, Thailand is a party to the 2009 ASEAN Comprehensive Investment Agreement, according to which has to provide for the enforcement in its territory of the awards rendered under its investment dispute settlement mechanism.

§12.06 RECOGNITION OF OTHER FOREIGN PUBLIC DOCUMENTS

Thai law is silent on requirements of recognition of foreign public documents. In practice, however, Thai courts will recognise foreign public documents such as a notarised and legalised document. However, as Thailand is not a party to the Hague Convention Abolishing the Requirement for Legalisation for Foreign Public Documents 1961 (or the Apostille Convention), the Ministry of Foreign Affairs is the department that has an authority to authenticate a document that originated outside of Thailand or a document from Thailand that will be used in another country.

§12.07 TREATIES FOR JUDICIAL COOPERATION

Thailand has entered into an agreement or Memorandum of Understanding (MoU) on judicial cooperation (focused on access to courts, taking of evidence and service of judicial documents) with the following countries:[23]

(a) The Republic of Indonesia (it is the first bilateral agreement entered into in order to implement the provisions of the ASEAN Declaration on Concord on Judicial Co-Operation).
(b) The Socialist Republic of Vietnam.
(c) The People's Republic of China: includes an article on recognition and enforcement of arbitral awards in accordance with the New York Convention of 1958.
(d) The Kingdom of Spain.
(e) Australia.

22. Section 42 of the Arbitration Act.
23. http://www.jla.coj.go.th/info.php?cid = 15.

(f) The Socialist Republic of Vietnam.
(g) (MoU) the Republic of Korea.
(h) (MoU) the Republic of Singapore.

In addition, there is an Agreement between the Supreme Courts of Thailand and the Russian Federation on judicial cooperation; and a MoU between the Office of the Judiciary of Thailand and the Supreme People's Court of Laos

Thailand is also a party to the 1980 Hague Convention on Civil Aspects of International Child Abduction and the 1993 Hague Convention on Protection of Children and Co-operation in Respect of Intercountry Adoption.

CHAPTER 13
Timor-Leste (East-Timor)

*Miguel de Lemos**

§13.01 CODIFICATION OF PRIVATE INTERNATIONAL LAW AND RELEVANCE OF CASE LAW

[A] Codification and Case Law

The legal system of Timor-Leste[1] is the result of various contributions from foreign or former legal orders, namely those of Portugal and Indonesia, with an additional peculiarity: at the time of the UN Transitional Administration (UNTAET) it received a number of elements difficult to classify systematically. Over time, pragmatic ad hoc solutions, which may be classified as mixed or hybrid, were sought without concern for systematic coherence in relation to traditional classifications.[2]

Even so, following its independence, Timor-Leste has been taking definite steps to consolidate its legal system within the legal family of civil law systems. By way of example, we may refer to the primacy of written law over case law and customary law, as well as to the codification process. The rules of Private International Law (PIL),[3] and

* Legal Consultant, Timor-Leste. Former Legal Adviser to the National Parliament and the Ministry of Justice of Timor-Leste.

1. Timor-Leste is a small state in South East Asia which was recognised as being independent by the United Nations on 20 May 2002. The legislation in force in Timor-Leste is partially available, in Portuguese, on the Internet. For the statutes cited in this article, see the website of the Court of Appeal which includes consolidated versions or the website of the *Jornal da República*: http://www.tribunais.tl/; http://www.jornal.gov.tl/. The Court of Appeal Rulings are also available for consultation online, on the respective website.
2. Examples are the combination of law-making from the Anglo-Saxon system – Common Law – and the Civil Law system, whilst maintaining Indonesian legislation, together with the promissory and embryonic legislation of UNTAET, among others.
3. The Timor-Leste code, with regard to PIL, like the Portuguese one, covers not only the Law of Conflicts, but also the Law of Recognition (of foreign decisions) and the Law of International Judicial Jurisdiction, the latter being governed by the Code of Civil Procedure, as will be shown.

more specifically the Law of Conflicts, are codified in the Civil Code (CC). The Civil Code[4] revoked the Indonesian Civil Code, which had been adopted and was in force in the Timorese legal system, pursuant to the provisions in Article 1 of Law 10/2003, of 7 August.[5]

The new Timorese Civil Code corresponds to adoption or transplantation of the Portuguese Civil Code,[6] with only a few occasional novelties, namely regarding family law. Additionally, the rules on proof set out in the Portuguese Civil Code were not adopted by the Timorese one, but rather by the Code of Civil Procedure (CCP), which predates it.

The rules on the Law of Conflicts are thus to be found in Chapter III, Title I of Book I of the Civil Code, under the heading: the rights of foreigners and conflicts of law. It aims to cover all the private international law issues governed by the Civil Code.

Notwithstanding the civil law nature of the Timorese legal order and despite not being a direct source of law, case law plays a special role regarding PIL (i) due to its role in developing and clarifying the codified rules and (ii) because it increases the solutions to new problems. Even so, issues relating to PIL have not yet been dealt with in the courts in a manner which corresponds to their importance.[7]

[B] Multilateral Conventions Providing Uniform Substantive Law and/or International Jurisdictional Rules

According to Article 9(2) of the Constitution, the provisions of international treaties shall prevail unless they contradict the Timorese Constitution.

Timor-Leste is a party to neither the UN Convention on Contracts for the International Sale of Goods (CISG), nor the Conventions for the International Carriage of Goods by Air. Timor-Leste is a party to the 1910 International Convention for the Unification of Certain Rules of Law Relating to Collision between Vessels, the 1910 International Convention for the Unification of Certain Rules of Law Relating to Assistance and Salvage at Sea, and the 1924 International Convention for the Unification of Certain Rules of Law Relating to Bills of Lading (Hague Rules). Timor-Leste is not party to any of the multilateral treaties administered by the World Intellectual Property Organization (WIPO).

4. Approved by Law 10/2011, of 14 September and published in *Jornal da República*, Series I, no. 34, at 1 et seq.
5. Upon restoration of independence and the consequent international recognition and transfer of sovereign powers, it became necessary to clarify the law in force in the country. The Constitution of the Republic itself states that the law previously in force in the country is applicable while the laws and regulations in force in Timor-Leste are not amended or revoked, in all that does not prove to be contrary to the Constitution and the principles enshrined in it.
6. Approved by Decree-Law 47344, of 25 Nov. 1966, with the subsequent amendments. For more detail, see João Baptista Machado, *Lições de Direito Internacional Privado* (3rd Updated ed., Reprint, 2006), at 422.
7. In the context of Timor-Leste, PIL is an area of law with great potential for expansion, given, in particular, the occurrence of many multiple location situations, as a result of the heavy migration, multinational families and growing international trade, among others.

§13.02 JURISDICTION OF LOCAL COURTS IN FOREIGN-RELATED CASES

[A] Grounds for Jurisdiction

[1] General

In order for a Timorese court to have international jurisdiction, the case must be linked to Timor or to its legal order by means of a certain relevant connection, which may be related to the parties or to the facts. This is the understanding which is legally enshrined in the CCP, approved by Decree-Law 1/2006, of 21 February.[8]

Pursuant to Article 48(1) of the CCP, the international jurisdiction of the Timorese courts is dependent on confirmation of one of the following circumstances:[9]

- *Defendant's domicile criterion*, according to which the Timorese courts have jurisdiction when the defendant, or one of the defendants, is domiciled in Timorese territory, with an exception being laid down regarding cases concerning real or personal rights of enjoyment of real estate located in foreign countries. For the purposes of this article, the domicile is calculated using the combined rules of Articles 79 et seq. of the CC. In the case of legal persons, Article 152 of the CC lays down that the 'domicile' is that which is established in the company's articles of association or, where there is no mention in the articles of association, the place where key management functions are normally carried on. It should also be noted, however, referring to Article 48(2) of the CCP, that international jurisdiction is not only given to the Timorese courts in cases where the legal person has its registered or main head office in the country. It is sufficient to have an organised centre of activity there.[10]
- The *coincidence criterion*, which establishes a parallel between the rules of international jurisdiction and the rules of territorial jurisdiction. Thus, the Timorese courts have international jurisdiction when the case must be brought in national territory, in line with the rules of territorial jurisdiction established in Articles 50-63 of the CCP. This criterion is based on the presumption that if the connecting elements used to determine the domestic jurisdiction 'point to a place located in [Timorese] territory the [Timorese] courts have international jurisdiction'.[11]

---

8. Published in *Jornal da República*, Series I, no. 4, at 1134 et seq.
9. As José Lebre de Freitas states in *Código de Processo Civil anotado* (2nd ed., volume 1, Coimbra Editora), at 137, each of the designated factors granting jurisdiction have value in their own right, so that it is sufficient to confirm one of them for the courts to be considered competent.
10. The current trend in the various systems which receive Portuguese legal solutions, is towards restricting the jurisdiction of the State of the forum when the case relates to a branch, agency, subsidiary or delegation. The reasonableness of this solution is based on the fact that cases of exorbitant jurisdiction can thus be overcome. It therefore seems reasonable, in the case of Timor-Leste, to adopt the same solution.
11. Luís Lima Pinheiro, *Direito Internacional Privado, Volume III – Competência Internacional e Reconhecimento de Decisões Estrangeiras* (Almedina, 2nd ed., 2012), at 280.

- The *criterion of causality*, which indicates that the Timorese courts have jurisdiction when the act which gives rise to the cause of action, or one of the acts included in it, has been practised in Timorese territory. It should be noted that the *tout court* application of this criterion may lead to situations of exorbitant jurisdiction. Regarding this issue we may see the considerations below on the theory of forum non conveniens.
- Lastly, Article 48(1)(d) of the CCP lays down the *criterion of necessity*, which implies international jurisdiction of the Timorese courts when the right being invoked can only be protected by means of bringing a case in the Timorese courts or, on the other hand, when it is not possible to require the claimant, without considerable difficulty, to initiate proceedings in the foreign country. In both cases there must be a substantial element of real or personal connection between the object of the litigation and the Timorese legal system.[12] The aim of this criterion is to exclude from the Timorese legal system the possibility of denying justice due to lack of a competent court, a situation which is inadmissible in the light of the Timorese legal order under Article 26(2) of the Constitution.

[2] Submitted to Jurisdiction

The Timorese law also allows the competence of the courts to be decided by agreement. This possibility is enshrined in Article 67 of the CCP, under the heading 'jurisdiction agreements'. The admissibility, the specific requirements for validity and the efficacy of the jurisdiction agreement depend on the legal order of the designated court.[13] Thus, when assessing the validity of the jurisdiction agreement, whether exclusive or not, it will be necessary to consider paragraph 3 of the aforementioned article, which requires that the five requirements set out therein are confirmed cumulatively, namely:

(i) that the dispute relates to available rights;
(ii) it is accepted by the designated court;
(iii) there is a serious interest of the parties or for one of them provided this does not involve a serious inconvenience for the other;
(iv) it does not relate to subject matter which is the exclusive competence of the Timorese courts;
(v) it is a written agreement or is confirmed in writing with express mention of the competent jurisdiction.

[3] Exclusive Jurisdiction

Timorese legislation sets out exhaustive provisions on exclusive jurisdiction. This *reservation of jurisdiction* 'prevents the courts of foreign legal orders from learning,

12. José Lebre de Freitas, *Supra* n. 9, at 140: '... the requirement which has the aim of preventing this factor granting jurisdiction from being converted into a "lesson in judicial altruism"'.
13. Luís Lima Pinheiro, *supra* n. 11, at 305.

with efficacy before the [Timorese] jurisdiction, of cases the object of which is considered to be a matter of public interest…'.[14]

This is achieved via Article 49 of the CCP:

- In subparagraph (a), Timor-Leste claims exclusive competence for its courts regarding real or personal rights of enjoyment of real estate located in Timorese territory.
- In subparagraph (b), it lays down the special procedures for corporate recovery and for bankruptcy concerning persons domiciled in Timor-Leste or legal persons or companies whose head offices are located in Timorese territory.
- Furthermore, subparagraph (c) rules on the appreciation of cases concerning the validity of the act of incorporation or the decree of dissolution of legal persons or companies which have their head office in Timorese territory, and on the appreciation of the validity of the resolutions of their respective bodies.
- Cases whose main object is appreciation of the validity of registration in public records of any rights which are subject to registration in Timor-Leste are dealt with exclusively by the Timorese courts, in line with subparagraph (d).
- Lastly, subparagraph (e) rules on executions against goods which exist in Timorese territory.[15]

[B] Exclusion of Jurisdiction

[1] Immunity

[a] Sovereign Immunity

The Timorese legal system, like its Portuguese source, does not set out a legal solution for this issue. Nevertheless, international customary law with its updated content and meaning applies, via Article 9 of the Constitution, and it can be assumed that, following the dominant trend, a restrictive concept of immunity from jurisdiction will be followed by Timorese courts.

Hence, it is only in cases where they are acting in *ius imperii* that a foreign entity may not be sued in the Timorese courts. However, there is the possibility to sue in all acts of a commercial or private nature, so-called *iure gestionis* (in which States, diplomatic agents and international organisations function as private parties, and the

14. José Lebre de Freitas, *supra* n. 9, at 142.
15. The Timorese CCP is widely influenced by the Portuguese one, with a large number of solutions being common to both systems. Accordingly, the Timorese legislator opted, in this article, to follow the wording of the Portuguese statute given by Decree-Law 329-A/95 in which there is no provision on cases referring to employment relations (since these are dealt with specifically in separate legislation). This subject matter is not dealt with in Timorese law.

actions are beyond the exercise of their sovereignty),[16] since the Timorese courts apply the international rules of jurisdiction as their local rules.

It can therefore be concluded that, although the Timorese legal system has not laid down internal rules on immunity from jurisdiction and there is not, so far, a case law solution which satisfies or helps to clarify the issue, the jurisdiction of the Timorese courts applies to all entities to which, by means of international customary law, immunity from jurisdiction is awarded, whenever they act in *iure gestionis*.

[b] Diplomatic and Consular Immunity

Timor-Leste is a party to the 1961 Vienna Convention on Diplomatic Relations and the 1963 Vienna Convention on Consular Relations. It is common practice to deny immunity to diplomatic representatives when what is at issue are cases concerning immovable property or succession cases and they act in a private capacity.

[c] Other Immunities

Timor-Leste is a party neither to the 1961 Convention on the Privileges and Immunities of the United Nations nor to the 1947 Convention on the Privileges and Immunities of the Specialised Agencies.

[2] Non-justiciable Claims

There is no specific provision regarding non-justiciable claims.

[3] Forum Agreements in Favour of Foreign Courts

Article 67 of the CCP allows the parties to agree to refer disputes arising out of their legal relationship to the court of a different forum, provided that those disputes relate to multiple locations and Timor-Leste courts have no exclusive jurisdiction.

According to paragraph 2 of the aforementioned article, the agreement may involve granting exclusive jurisdiction or merely alternative jurisdiction to that of the Timorese courts, when this exists, with alternative jurisdiction being assumed in cases of doubt.

Paragraph 3(a) requires the availability of the subject matter – that is, jurisdiction agreements are only accepted in relation to available rights – and the acceptance by the courts named in the choice of court clause. Furthermore, it must be justified by the serious interest of both parties or of one of them, provided that, in the latter case, it

16. Regarding the distinction between *iure imperii* and *iure gestionis*, it has been mooted that it would be possible to 'distinguish between intentions which relate to the exercise of powers of authority and intentions of content and foundation, similar to those that we would classify without hesitation as legal-private'. (Luís Lima Pinheiro, *Direito Internacional Privado, Volume I – Introdução e Direito de Conflitos, Parte Geral* (Almedina, 2001), at 20).

does not involve serious inconvenience for the other party. Lastly, the agreement must arise out of a written agreement or be confirmed in writing, and must include express mention of the competent jurisdiction.

It should be added that an agreement is deemed to be in written form if it is set out in a document signed by the parties, or results from an exchange of letters, telexes, telegrams, or other means of communication of which written proof remains, whether those instruments contain the agreement directly, or whether they contain a clause referring to any document in which it is contained – as set out in Article 67(4) of the CCP.

[4] Arbitration Clause

The CCP, in Article 372, lays down exceptions which prevent the court from discussing the merits of the case and give rise to dismissal of the proceedings (or to the case being referred to another court). These are the so-called dilatory exceptions (paragraph 2). Although not exhaustively, Article 373 of the CCP lists the main dilatory exceptions, and does not include breach of an arbitration agreement.

As such, and given that Timor-Leste does not have ordinary regulations on the subject of arbitration,[17, 18] the indication is that an arbitration clause will not be an impediment to what the Timorese courts may discover regarding the dispute, in line with the rules of international jurisdiction.[19]

17. Regarding alternative dispute resolution, the Timorese legal order provides solutions which, in our opinion, are not adequate for modern international legal trade, with a lack, in particular, of any law on arbitration. In the light of Law 2/2002, of 7 August, it might be accepted that the Indonesian Law on Arbitration and Alternative Dispute Resolution (Law 30/1999, of 12 August) is in force in Timor. However, under Law 10/2003, of 20 November, which provides an interpretation of Article 1 of Law 2/2002 and Sources of Law, Indonesian law is applicable in Timor only if that law was applicable and in force de facto before 25 Oct. 1999. Since the Indonesian Arbitration law was approved weeks after the referendum, it is unrealistic to think that in such a short space of time the law could have had any real relevance in Timor, and it should not therefore be considered part of the Timorese legal order.
18. Timor-Leste is a party to the Convention on the Settlement of Investment Disputes between States and Citizens of Other States ('ICSID Convention'). The Law on External Investment, Law 5/2005 of 7 July, referred to the ICSID Convention on the subject matter of dispute resolution and arbitration (Article 23). Law 5/2005 was revoked by the Law on Private Investment, Law 14 /2011, of 28 September, which provides that disputes between the State and the Investor must, additionally, 'be resolved by means of arbitration, in line with the rules of the International Chamber of Commerce, unless otherwise agreed'.
19. In the equivalent article, the Portuguese legislator provided expressly for breach of an arbitration agreement as a dilatory exception. This rule was intentionally removed from the Timorese CCP, which, combined with the absence of rules on arbitration, can only lead to the conclusion suggested, unless a better understanding can be found.

[C] Non-exercise of Jurisdiction

[1] Forum Non Conveniens

In Timor-Leste there is no legal provision that allows the courts to refuse jurisdiction when there is another competent jurisdiction. Thus, the figure of forum non coveniens or *demarche*, with similar reach, is not accepted.

Notwithstanding, some Portuguese legal theory has been warning of problems that arise from strict application of the *criterion of causality*; in particular, the exorbitant jurisdiction of the courts of the forum which is deemed competent when the act that gives rise to the cause of action has been practised in Timor, or one of the acts included in it. In this sense, it would be important, that:

> this criterion be combined with an exception clause based on the theory of forum non conveniens: it would be necessary to check whether the link between the case and the [Timorese] legal order is strong enough to justify the jurisdiction of our courts.[20,21]

[2] Lis alibi pendens

As a general rule, the Timorese courts do not refuse jurisdiction when a foreign court is already appreciating a case which is identical to that of the forum in terms of the subjects, the claim, and the cause of action. Article 376(3) of the CCP lays down that the fact that the claim is pending in a foreign jurisdiction is irrelevant, unless otherwise established in international conventions.

In light of this, and bearing in mind the lack of international conventions on the matter in force in Timor-Leste, it can be concluded that foreign *lis pendens* is irrelevant and does not have the effect of paralysing the action in the courts. There is nothing therefore to prevent a case from being brought in a Timorese court, despite a simultaneous case, with the aforementioned elements, or a res judicata decision given in a similar case (although not subject to internal adoption) having been dealt with in a foreign court.

---

20. Luís Lima Pinheiro (Vol. III), *supra* n. 11, at 279. Similarly, J.P. Remédio Marques in *A acção declarativa à luz do Código Revisto* (2nd ed., Coimbra Editora), at 288: 'It seems to us that the application of this criterion may lead to excesses when the fact included in a complex cause of action confirmed in Portugal is irrelevant to the consideration of the intended legal purpose ... It would therefore be particularly useful to provide in Portuguese law for the possibility of the Portuguese courts stepping aside from their jurisdiction in those situations (which are part of a complex cause of action), based on the idea of "forum non conveniens" – grounds for refusing the granting of international jurisdiction provided for essentially in the Common Law systems.'
21. It would therefore be appropriate in Timor-Leste, in a similar way to the practise of Portuguese courts, to require that when the assessment of the international jurisdiction of the Timorese courts is being made, that the material facts located in national territory are relevant to justify a strong connection of the case with the State of Timor-Leste.

§13.03 APPLICABLE LAW[22]

[A] Choice of Law

[1] *Express Stipulation*

The principle of party autonomy 'will come up against mandatory rules which establish the limit of its action'.[23] The principle of party autonomy in choice of law is laid down in Articles 33 and 40 of the CC.[24]

Article 40 of the CC, which is the legal source of the rule on conflicts regarding obligations arising from legal transactions, establishes in paragraph 1 that these obligations, and the actual substance of the transaction that gives rise to them, are governed by the law that the respective subjects have stated or that they had in mind.

Article 33 of the CC, on the personal law of international legal persons, lays down the principle of private autonomy and allows the founders of the entity to designate the law which regulates it. Hence, the personal law of international legal persons is that which is designated in the agreement which established the legal person or in the respective articles of association.

[2] *Implied Choice*

Moreover, the choice of applicable law may be express or tacit, as a result of the wording 'that they had in mind'. In order to determine the tacit choice of the law, the specific circumstances of the transaction in question must be considered.

[B] Other Cases

In line with the scheme of the code, following the general provisions, the legislator provides specific rules governing the choice of law in matters of private law set out in the Code.

[1] *Personal Law*

The status of individuals, the capacity of persons, family relationships, and successions on death are governed by the personal law of the respective subjects, subject to some restrictions.

---

22. For a summary of the main rules of conflicts see, *mutatis mutandis*, João Baptista Machado, *supra*, n. 6 at 339-452.
23. Isabel Maria Tello de Magalhães Collaço, *Da compra e venda em Direito Internacional Privado – Aspectos fundamentais, vol. I* (Lisbon, 1954), at 33-34; Marques dos Santos, *Algumas considerações sobre a autonomia da vontade no Direito Internacional Privado em Portugal e no Brasil*, in *Estudos em Homenagem à Professora Doutora Isabel de Magalhães Collaço*, volume I (Coimbra, Almedina, 2002), at 379-429.
24. It is an issue of debate in legal theory if Articles 52(3) and 61(a) of the CC also enshrine the principle or a mere material autonomy.

The capacity to effect transactions is also governed by the personal law, by means of Articles 24 and 27 of the CC. The same law regulates the age of majority and emancipation, and also (Article 29 of the CC) guardianship and similar figures which protect incapacitated persons. The legal representation of incapacitated persons is subject to the law regulating the legal relationship from which the power of representation stems (Article 36 of the CC). Thus, 'the representation of the parents is... subject to the law which, pursuant to Art. [56], has competence to regulate their relations with the children, and that of the guardians and curators to the personal law of the incapacitated persons, pursuant to Art. [29]'.[25]

Article 27 of the CC sets out that a legal transaction effected in Timor-Leste by a person who is incapacitated according to the competent personal law may not be annulled on the basis of incapacity if the Timorese internal law, when applied, would consider that person to be capable. Hence, we have an exception to the rule in Article 24, which is not applicable when the other party was aware of the incapacity or when the legal transaction is unilateral, or belongs to the domain of family law or successions or is related to the disposal of real estate located abroad. Lastly, paragraph 3 establishes the condition of remission to the law of the country where the transaction was effected, if that law enshrines rules which are identical to those established in the previous paragraphs.

Article 26 of the CC applies the personal law also to the existence and protection of rights of personality (name, personal portrayal, privacy). However, foreigners or stateless persons are not afforded any legal protection that is not recognised in Timorese law.

With regard to legal persons, the decisive connecting element in assessing the law or the personal status, as set out in Article 32(1) of the CC, is the law of the State where the head office and effective seat of administration is located. It should be noted that the connecting element is not only the registered head office but rather the *operational headquarters*, which may not be the same. The applicable law will have competence to govern the capacity of the legal person; the constitution, functioning and competence of its bodies; the means of acquiring and losing the status of member and the corresponding rights and duties; the liability of the legal person, and of the respective bodies and members, in relation to third parties; and the conversion, dissolution and winding up of the legal person. Paragraph 3 states that in case of transfer of the head office to a new country, the legal personality is not extinguished if there is agreement between the laws of both places. Lastly, paragraph 4 rules that merger of entities with different personal laws is permitted if both personal laws so allow.[26]

25. Pires de Lima and Antunes Varela, *Código Civil Anotado, Volume I (Artigos 1.° a 761.°)*, (4th Revised and Updated ed., Coimbra Editora, 1987), at 77.
26. It should be noted, as Baptista Machado states (*supra*, n. 6 at 349), that the solutions set out in Article 32 must be applied by analogy to organisations of persons or property which do not have legal personality.

[2] Law Governing Legal Transactions

Article 34(1) of the CC stipulates that the perfection, interpretation and integration of the declaration of negotiations are governed by the law applicable to the substance of the transaction, which also applies to lack of will and defects of will. It may be noted that the law applicable to the substance of the transaction varies according to its object. The legislator also established the value of conduct as a declaration of negotiations (paragraph 2) and the value of silence as a means of declaration (paragraph 3). In the former case it is determined by the law of the common habitual residence of the declarant and the consignee and, in the absence of this, by the law of the place where the conduct occurred. In the latter case, the value of silence as a means of declaration is also determined by the law of the common habitual residence and, in the absence of this, by the law of the place where the offer was received.

According to Article 35(1) of the CC, the form of the declaration is governed by the law applicable to the substance of the transaction; it is, therefore, sufficient to observe the law in force in the place where the declaration is made, unless the law governing the substance of the transaction requires, for it not to be void or ineffective, that a certain form is observed, even if the transaction is concluded abroad. In this case, it is accepted that the law governing the form of the declaration may be different from that which governs the substance of the transaction. Paragraph 2 establishes that the declaration of negotiations is also formally valid if, rather than it being in the form set out in the local law, the form which has been observed is that laid down by the State to which the rule of conflicts of that law refers, without prejudice to the provisions of the last part of the previous paragraph. It sets out a solution of remission by reason of *favor negotii*, as will be explained below.

In line with Article 36 of the CC, legal representation is subject to the law governing the legal relationship from which the representative power stems. Representation of the legal person through its bodies (organic representation) is governed by the respective personal law (Article 37 of the CC). Voluntary representation is governed, regarding its existence, extent, modification, effects, and extinction of the representative powers, by the law of the State where the powers are exercised (Article 38 of the CC). As a rule we have the law of the State where the powers of voluntary representation are exercised, thus protecting the interests of legal trading. However, paragraph 2 states that, if the representative exercises the powers of representation in a country other than the one indicated by the represented party, and the third party with whom he contracts is aware of this, the law of the country where the represented party habitually resides is the applicable one. Paragraph 3 presents the applicable law as that of the professional domicile if the representative exercises the representation in a professional capacity and the third party with whom he contracts is aware of this. Lastly, paragraph 4 sets out that when the representation relates to the disposal or administration of real estate, the law of the country where this property is located is the applicable law.[27]

27. As Baptista Machado states (*supra*, n. 6 at 357), 'we must distinguish... the representation, which, like any other contract, is governed by the law of autonomy [Art. 40 et seq.]'.

[3] Obligations

Article 40 of the CC provides that the principle of private autonomy will rule. Article 41 establishes an additional criterion for the choice of law, i.e.:[28]

> a) for unilateral legal transactions, the law of the habitual residence of the declarant; b) for contracts, the law of the common habitual residence of the parties and, where there is no common residence: i) for gratuitous contracts, the law of the habitual residence of the party providing the benefit; ii) for other contracts, the law of the place where the contracts are concluded.

According to Articles 42 and 43 of the CC, in the case of *negotiorum gestio* the applicable law is that of the place where the *gestor* carries on his main activity, while unjust enrichment is governed by the law which formed the basis for the transfer of the financial asset to the enriched party.

[4] Torts

Article 44(1) of the CC lays down the rule of the *lex loci delicti*: non-contractual liability, based either on an illicit act or on risk or on any legal conduct, is governed by the law of the State where the main activity which caused the harm occurred; in case of liability due to omission, the applicable law is that of the place where the liable person should have acted.

In case of cross-border delicts, Article 44(2) of the CC states that if the law of the State where the harmful effect is produced considers the agent liable, but the law of the country where his activity took place does not consider him to be so, the former law is applicable, provided that the agent should have foreseen the production of harm in that country as a consequence of his act or omission.

Article 44(3) of the CC provides a deviation from the general rule, by applying the law of the nationality or of the common habitual residence if the agent and the injured party have the same nationality or, in the absence of this, the same habitual residence, and if they happen to meet in a foreign country, without prejudice to the provisions of the local State law which must be applied indiscriminately to all persons.[29]

[5] Rights In Rem

Regarding rights in rem, the general rule applied by Article 45(1) of the CC is the *lex rei sitae*: The rules on possession, ownership and other rights in rem are defined by the law of the State in whose territory those things are located. Nevertheless, Article 45(2) and (3) lay down two special rules:

---

28. *Ibid.*, at 358.
29. These provisions are 'rules of strictly territorial application, like those that govern the traffic, civil construction, etc. If the local law considers a certain fact or certain conduct to be an infraction, the personal law of the agent or the injured party is no longer of interest; there is an illicit act according to the local law and it is important to draw all the consequences from it.' (Pires de Lima and Antunes Varela, *supra* n. 25 at 82).

- for things which are the object of transnational transportation (*res in transitu*), these are deemed to be located in the country of their destination, which law applies in relation to the constitution or transfer of rights;
- The constitution and transfer of rights over means of transportation subject to a system of registration are governed by the law of the country where the registration has been made.

Article 46 of the CC, on the capacity to constitute rights in rem over immovable assets or dispose of them, sets out a deviation from the rule of the personal law in matters relating to capacity, indicating a condition for remission to the *lex rei sitae*, and applying the law of the location of the thing, provided that that law so determines.[30]

According to Article 47 of the CC, copyright is regulated by the law of the place of the first publication of the work and, when it has not been published, by the personal law of the author, without prejudice to any provisions in special legislation.[31] Industrial property is governed by the law of the country of its creation.

[6] Family Relations

Article 48 of the CC establishes that the *capacity* to marry or to enter into a prenuptial agreement is governed, in relation to each intended spouse, by the respective personal law, which is also responsible for defining the lack of will and defects of will of the contracting parties.

Regarding the *formal validity* of the marriage, Article 49 rules that:

> the general principle on the form of the marriage is not in line with the general principle regarding the form of the declaration of negotiations expressed in Art. [35]. As a rule, the principle of *locus regit actum* is followed with marriage, bearing in mind the solemnity of the act and the variety of forms that it takes in different countries.[32]

However, Article 50(1) of the CC establishes that the marriage of two foreigners in Timor-Leste may be celebrated in accordance with the form provided for in the national law of either of the contracting parties, before the respective diplomatic agents, although on the condition that there is reciprocity. For their part, paragraphs 2 and 3 establish the rules for the marriage abroad of two Timorese persons or a Timorese and a foreigner.

30. As Pires de Lima and Antunes Varela state (in *Ibid.*), the CC does not contain 'rules in this sense and, consequently, the personal law, in general terms, must be applied to things located in [Timorese] territory, regarding capacity'.
31. Without prejudice to Article 60 of the Constitution, on 'programming' content, by means of which the State commits itself to guaranteeing and protecting the creation, production and trading of literary, scientific and artistic work, including the legal protection of copyright, the legal order of Timor-Leste does not contain any special legislation on this matter. What results from the letter of the base law is *only* that the State is charged with the 'duty to legislate to realize and ensure those rights'. AAVV, *Constituição Anotada – República Democrática de Timor-Leste* (Direitos Humanos-Centro de Investigação Interdisciplinar – Escola de Direito da Universidade do Minho), at 218.
32. Pires de Lima and Antunes Varela, *supra* n. 25, at 85.

Article 51(1) of the CC determines that *relations between spouses* (effects of marriage) are governed by the common national law, or alternatively (paragraph 2), where the spouses do not have the same nationality, the law of their common habitual residence is applicable or, in the absence of this, the law of the country with which the family life is deemed to be more closely connected.

Regarding *property relations* of spouses and prenuptial agreements (Article 52 of the CC), the 'rules..., for the purpose of conflict of laws, are of a mixed nature, simultaneously institutional and contractual'.[33] Thus, the substance and effects of prenuptial agreements and of the rules on property, by law or convention, are defined by the national law of the spouses at the time of celebration of the marriage. Where the spouses do not have the same nationality, the law of their common habitual residence on the date of the marriage will apply and, where this is also absent, the law of the first conjugal residence. Lastly, if the applicable law is a foreign one and one of the spouses has his or her habitual residence in Timorese territory, an agreement may be made in favour of one of the regimes admitted in the CC. There is some debate in Portuguese legal theory as to whether the equivalent rule in the Portuguese CC truly lays down the principle of private autonomy.[34]

It may be noted that, by means of Article 53(1) of the CC, the property rules may be altered, if the competent law so authorises, that is, if the common national law allows it, provided that the limit imposed by paragraph 2 is observed (namely, the fact that the new agreement may not have retroactive effect to the detriment of a third party). Pursuant to the previously mentioned Article 51, alternatively the law of the common habitual residence or the law of the country with which the family life is deemed to be most closely connected is applied.

Determination of the law which applies to situations of legal separation of persons and property and divorce is performed in line with Article 54 of the CC, by the common national law, the law of the common habitual residence and the law of the country with which the family life is deemed to be most closely connected, following the provisions of Article 51. It may be noted that, if during the course of marriage there is a change in the competent law, only a relevant fact may provide grounds for separation or divorce at the time this change occurs. Given the above, it may be stated, following Baptista Machado's line, that 'not every consequence of separation or divorce is governed by the law to which Art. [54] refers: several of them are nothing more than simple repercussions of the divorce (or separation) on other relations or legal situations'.[35]

33. João Baptista Machado, *supra*, n. 6 at 406.
34. See Marques dos Santos (*supra* n. 23, at 379-429) who, taking part in the legal debate, in the sense of considering that the legislator effectively enshrined the principle of private autonomy, lists the various positions in summary form: 'According to Luís de Lima Pinheiro we have here only a material reference to the [Timorese] law, which has to respect the injunctive rules of the competent foreign law, while Rui Moura Ramos understands that the choice of one of the regimes of property allowed by the [Timorese] law is valid even if this goes against the provisions in the imperative rules of the competent law and sees in this provision a limited manifestation of conflicting autonomy'.
35. João Baptista Machado, *supra*, n. 6 at 418.

With regard to establishing parentage, Article 55 of the CC applies the personal law of the progenitor at the time the relationship is established. However, in case of a child of a married woman, the establishment of parentage in relation to the father is governed by the common national law of the mother and the husband, and in the absence of this, the law of the common habitual residence of the spouses and, where this is also absent, the personal law of the child. When determining which of the laws is applicable attention is paid to the time of the birth of the child or to the time of dissolution of the marriage, if the latter occurs before the birth.

According to Article 57 of the CC, the personal law of the adopting person is applicable to establishment of parentage by adoption. However, if the adoption is performed by a husband and wife or the adopted child is the child of the spouse of the adopting person, the common national law of the spouses is competent and, in the absence of this, the law of their common habitual residence; if this is also absent, the law of the country with which the family life of the adopting persons is deemed to be most closely connected will be applied. A parallel can thus be drawn with the provisions of Article 55 (parentage). Article 57(3) makes the provisions of Article 56 applicable to relations between the adopting person and the adopted child, and between the latter and the birth family, with these being subject to the personal law of the adopted child. Lastly, Article 57(4) cumulatively requires that not only the personal law of the adopting person is taken into account (paragraph 1) but also the law which governs the relations between the adopted child and its progenitors. Thus, if the competent law for regulating the relations between the adopted child and its progenitors does not recognise the figure of adoption, or does not allow it in relation to whoever is in the family situation of the adopted child, the adoption is not permitted.

In relations between parents and children, the applicable law is, via Article 56 of the CC, the common national law of the parents or, alternatively, the law of their common habitual residence and, if the parents also do not have a common habitual residence, the personal law of the child. In the cases referred to in paragraph 2, if the parentage is only deemed to be established in relation to one of the progenitors, the personal law of the latter is applied; if one of the progenitors is deceased, the personal law of the surviving progenitor is the competent law.

[7] Successions

By means of Article 59 of the CC, succession is governed by the personal law of the deceased at the time of his or her death, and this is also the competent law to define the powers of the administrator of the inheritance or the executor of the will. In this sense it is said that 'the personal law of the deceased is responsible for regulating… everything that relates to the succession phenomenon',[36] notwithstanding the specific articles which we will consider below.

Article 60(1) of the CC establishes that the capacity of disposal *mortis causa* is governed by the personal law on the date of the declaration of negotiations. In the case

36. Pires de Lima and Antunes Varela, *supra* n. 25, at 99.

of interpretations of disposals *mortis causa*, Article 61 of the CC establishes that the applicable law will be the personal law on the date of the declaration. Subparagraph (a) introduces an exception in the event that there is an express or implicit reference to another law. Marques dos Santos notes that:

> it is therefore possible for the deceased to opt for a law which is not his personal law at the time of the declaration... the interpretation of its clauses and disposals *mortis causa*, so that the law designated by the will of the interested party prevails, therefore, over the personal law... there being, here, consequently, as I understand it, yet another case of true autonomy of conflicting will.[37]

Article 61(b) of the CC also introduces a deviation from Article 34, since, regarding the lack of will or defects or will, the personal law will also apply. Subparagraph (c) also requires the application of the personal law to joint wills and agreements as to future successions, subject to the provisions of Article 52. As Baptista Machado states 'this exception can only mean that the admissibility of the agreement as to future successions inserted in the prenuptial agreement does not depend on the personal law or laws of the institutors, but on the law designated by Art. [52] to govern prenuptial agreements',[38] that is, the personal law of the intended spouses at the time the marriage is celebrated.

Lastly, Article 62 of the CC regulates the form of the disposals *mortis causa*. This article follows the general rule set out in paragraphs 1 and 2 of Article 35 of the CC regarding the form of the declaration of negotiations. Thus, disposals on death, and their revocation or modification, will be valid, regarding the form, if they correspond to the provisions of the law of the place where the act is concluded, or those of the personal law of the owner of the inheritance, either at the time of the declaration or at the time of death, or even the provisions of the law to which the rules of conflict of laws of local law refer. Paragraph 2 establishes that, if the personal law of the owner of the inheritance at the time of the declaration requires a certain form to be observed, in order for it not to be void or ineffective, even if the act is performed abroad, this requirement will be respected.

It may be noted that paragraph 1 operates *renvoi* by reason of *favor negotii*, as referred to for Article 35(2) of the CC, in the terms which will be explained below.

[C] *Renvoi*

According to Article 15 of the Timorese CC, in the absence of a provision to the contrary, reference to foreign law determines only the application of the internal law of that legal order. However, *renvoi* is allowed when:

- The rules of Private International Law of the law referred by the Timorese rule on conflicts estipulate the application of another foreign law and that law is

37. Marques dos Santos, *supra* n. 23, at 379-429. See, in the opposite sense, quoted by the author, Lima Pinheiro and Moura Ramos.
38. João Baptista Machado, *supra* n. 6, at 444.

considered competent. Nevertheless, Article 16(2) of the CC provides the cessation of the *renvoi* if the law referred by the Timorese rules on conflict is personal law and the interested party is normally resident in Timorese territory or in a country whose rules of conflict consider the internal law of the State of his nationality to be competent. Although this exception exists for matters of personal status, such as capacity, family relationships and succession on death, it also applies to cases of guardianship and curatorship, property relations between spouses, parental responsibility, relations between adopter and adoptee and succession on death, if the national law indicated by the rule on conflicts returns to the law of the location of the immovable property and if this is deemed competent.

- If the provisions of Private International Law of the law referred by the Timorese rule of conflicts determine the application of Timorese substantive law. We have the so-called return of jurisdiction, by means of Article 17(1) of the CC, which is based on the sole assumption that the foreign law applies Timorese substantive Law. Nevertheless, Article 17(2) functions as a limitation in matters of personal status, stipulating that Timorese law is only applicable if the interested party has his habitual residence in Timorese territory or if the law of the country of this residence considers Timorese internal law to be equally competent.

Notwithstanding the above, and under Article 18(1) of the CC, in the situations referred to in the aforementioned Articles 16 and 17, return ceases when the result of its application is the invalidity or ineffectiveness of a legal transaction which would be valid or effective according to the rule set out in Article 15 or the illegitimacy of a status would otherwise be legitimate. The principle of *favor negotii* is thus established as a limitation on return.

In parallel, the CC sets out additional provisions which contain special rules of return, based on the principle of *favor negotii*. As stated by Lima Pinheiro 'it is favouring the formal validity of the business rather than international harmony of the solutions which is pursued by the admissibility of return in these cases'.[39] Thus, Articles 35(2) and 62(1) *in fine*, allow for return, without requiring, as Article 16(1) does, that the law to where the case is returned is deemed competent.

[D] Mandatory Rules of the Forum and of Third States

The Timorese codes, along the lines of the Portuguese ones, do not adopt the concept of rules of immediate or necessary application, also known as *lois de police*. However, Portuguese legal theory has shown itself to be favourable to the application of spatially self-limiting rules of the *lex causae*, except when their application results in an attack on the International Public Order clause of the forum or when those self-limiting rules

39. Luís Lima Pinheiro (Vol. I), *supra*, n. 16, at 380-381.

are at the same time spatially self-limiting rules and their spatial scope of application is not complied with.

It may be noted that where the law of a third State includes spatially self-limiting rules, the legal theory is ready to accept the need/possibility of the court attributing effects to it when in the law of the forum there is a legal entitlement of being heard: e.g., Articles 35(1), 44(3), and 62(2) of the CC. Even where this entitlement does not come from a legal source, some legal theory has shown itself to be favourable to accepting that the spatially self-limiting rules of the 3rd state may be accepted based on making an ad hoc unilateral rule on conflicts of the forum bilateral.[40]

One should add that, within the current framework of Timorese case law, clarification of this issue is somewhat delicate. Firstly, this is because rules of necessary application have an indefinite character, with the judge being responsible for deciding whether or not a given rule is in fact of necessary application (*lois de police*). As has been mentioned, there are not as yet a substantial number of court decisions to allow us to unravel a solution for the issue presented, which will largely depend on how the courts operate.

[E] Proof of Foreign Law

The Timorese legal order treats foreign law as *law* rather than as *fact*.[41] In line with the principle of presenting evidence, the facts have to be alleged and proven by the parties. On the other hand, as a result of the principle of officiousness, the law must be known by the court, and researched and determined on its own initiative. On this issue Article 412 of the CCP states that the judge is not subject to the allegations of the parties regarding the investigation, interpretation, and application of the rules of law, but may only employ the facts presented by the parties, except as otherwise provided for in Articles 391 and 413 of the CCP.

Therefore, despite not establishing a burden of proof regarding the foreign law, Article 516 of the CCP sets out a duty on the parties to cooperate with the court. Whoever relies on local or foreign customary law is responsible for proving its existence. However, the court must seek to obtain the respective knowledge of its own accord. Furthermore, discovery is also the responsibility of the court whenever it has to make a decision based on local or foreign customary law and neither of the parties has invoked it, or the opposing party has accepted its existence and content or has not opposed this.

By not establishing a burden, there is no need to reject the claim of the parties if the content of the right invoked cannot be proven. For the parties, as Ferrer Correia states, it is 'a pure and simple obligation of means, and the task may prove to be impossible or extremely difficult'.[42]

40. *Ibid.*, at 212 et seq.
41. 'Foreign Law is applied among us *as law*': Ferrer Correia, *Lições de Direito Internacional Privado – I* (3rd Reprint of the October 2000 ed., Almedina), at 427.
42. *Ibid.*, at 428.

Article 22(1) of the CC determines that the foreign law is interpreted within the system to which it belongs and in line with the rules of interpretation established within it. The person interpreting it, in this case a foreigner, therefore has a special duty of care in assessing the interpretation criteria, the case law and the legal theory of the country from which the applicable foreign law originates.

We may note, particularly bearing in mind that the Timorese CC corresponds to transplantation of the Portuguese CC, that:

> the fact that the same rule is simultaneously in force in several legal orders – as happens, for example, with the vast majority of the rules of the Portuguese Civil Code of 1966 which is in force in Portugal and in the Portuguese-speaking countries [currently including Timor-Leste] – does not prevent the respective interpretation from being different.[43]

When it is not possible to determine the reach and content of the applicable foreign law, Article 22(2) of the CC orders application of the law which is additionally competent. Only in the absence of this, via Article 516(3) of the CCP, will Timorese common law be applied.

[F] Evasion of the Law

Article 20 of the CC states that, when applying the rules on conflicts, situations of fact or of law are irrelevant if have been created with the fraudulent intention of avoiding the applicability of the law which would be competent in other circumstances. Thus the figure of abuse of law 'constitutes an instrument of the fairness of the connection and an ethical limit placed on private autonomy in structuring the specific content of the elements of connection'.[44]

From the wording of Article 20 of the CC, we may highlight two elements which constitute abuse: one objective and the other subjective. The first is the fictitious internationalisation of a purely internal situation or manipulation of the element of connection, assuming that 'the relevant connections in conflict law (can) be framed, "located" or "relocated" by the parties' actions'.[45] The second, *animus fraudandi*, takes the form of a desire of the parties to set aside the application of the mandatory rule which would normally be applied.

As a consequence of abuse of law, in the Timorese system situations of fact or of law created with fraudulent intent must be considered irrelevant. Hence, the rule which it was sought to set aside shall be applied, and the legal transactions carried out and the rights acquired as a result of the abuse will be considered ineffective.

43. Luís Lima Pinheiro (Vol. I), *Supra* n. 16, at 455.
44. *Ibid.*, at 385.
45. João Baptista Machado, *supra*, n. 6 at 275.

§13.04 PROCEDURAL ISSUES

[A] Service of Summons and Judicial Orders Abroad

Timor-Leste is not a signatory to the 1965 Hague Convention on the Service Abroad of Judicial and Extrajudicial Documents in Civil or Commercial Matters.

Both the serving of summons and judicial orders abroad and the obtaining of proof abroad follow the out-dated method of the letter rogatory, the rules on which are set out in Articles 141 et seq. of the CCP. The letter rogatory, by definition, transmits a request for judicial assistance, formulated by a national judicial authority to a foreign judicial authority, seeking the performance of diligences with a view to enabling the investigation or the trial of certain facts. Article 146(2) of the CCP lays down that letters rogatory, whatever the purpose for which they are intended, are sent by the secretary and directly addressed to the foreign authority or court, unless there is a treaty or provision to the contrary. Dispatch is by diplomatic or consular means when this is the form by which the State receives the letters. If the letter rogatory is not received by official means it is delivered to the interested party. *Démarches* of dispatch by diplomatic or consular means are the responsibility of Public Prosecutor's Office.

[B] Obtaining Evidence Abroad

Timor-Leste is not a party to the 1970 Hague Convention on the taking of Evidence Abroad in Civil or Commercial Matters. There is no specific provision on this matter. The considerations presented in the previous section would be applicable.

[C] Restraint of Foreign Proceedings

So-called anti-suit injunctions are a procedural technique of a preventive nature which many civil law countries are unfamiliar with and which does not therefore exist in the legal order of Timor-Leste. Their aim is to give rise to a court decision which prevents one of the parties from beginning or pursuing given court or arbitral proceedings. This injunction is aimed at the party which has brought or will bring a case in a foreign court rather than at the foreign court itself (in the context of jurisdiction in personam, of some Common Law systems).

In relation to Timor-Leste, this issue has never been placed before the courts. It seems to us, however, that the issuing of an injunction with the aim of inhibiting or preventing a party from having his constitutional right to access to justice (access to the courts), as set out in Article 26 of the Constitution, is not admissible on the grounds that it is unconstitutional.

[D] Proof of Foreign Public Documents

Since Timor-Leste has not yet ratified any international instrument on this subject, or with relevance for PIL, the rules to be followed here will also be the internal rules set out in the ordinary law. Thus, in line with Article 579(1) of the CCP, proof of authentic or private documents issued in a foreign country, in accordance with the respective law, is made in the same way as for documents of the same nature drawn up in Timor-Leste. The aforementioned documents may be legalised by means of paragraph 2 of the same article, if the document is not legalised, under the terms of the procedural law, and if there are grounds for doubts as to its authenticity, or the authenticity of its recognition, its legalisation may be required.

[E] Statutes of Limitations

The issue of limitation and prescription in the context of conflict of laws is provided for in Article 39 of the CC, which sets out that the law applicable to these is the law to which they refer, i.e., the law regulating the substance and not the *lex fori*. As Baptista Machado states: 'if a right is subject to a particular law it means precisely that the content of that right, its modification, extinction, etc., is regulated by that law'.[46]

[F] Remedies and Damages

The law applicable to the dispute, not the *lex fori*, determines the type and amount of remedies.

[G] Foreign Currency Obligations

Obligations in a foreign currency, are monetary obligations and follow the rules laid down in Articles 484 et seq. of the CC. As this obligation is to be fulfilled in a foreign currency, it is said to be improper or impure when the debtor may opt to comply in the national currency, according to the exchange rate of the day of compliance and the place established for such. This is the solution which is specifically contained in Article 492(1) of the CC, unless that possibility has been excluded by the interested parties.

[H] Restraining Removal of Assets and Securing Evidence in Favour of a Foreign Arbitration/Judicial Process

A request for restraining removal of assets and/or securing evidence will not be granted in support of foreign arbitral or judicial proceedings.

§13.05 RECOGNITION AND ENFORCEMENT OF FOREIGN DECISIONS

[A] Judicial Decisions: Requirements and Limitations

A system of formal review or deliberation is laid down in Timor-Leste. The internal rules for reviewing foreign decisions are a special regime (Article 790 of the CCP) and are set out in Articles 838-845 of the CCP.

46. *Ibid.*, at 357.

Article 838(1) of the CCP stipulates that, notwithstanding treaties, conventions and special laws, no decision on private rights rendered by a foreign court or by foreign arbitrators shall be effective in Timor-Leste, regardless of the nationality of the parties, without being reviewed and confirmed. A need is therefore established to review and confirm the res judicata decision.[47]

Article 672 of the CCP, which concerns the *enforceability of decisions*, lays down that, notwithstanding treaties, conventions and special laws, the decisions rendered by courts or by arbitrators in a foreign country may only serve as the basis for enforcement after they have been reviewed and confirmed by the Supreme Court of Justice.[48] The enforceability of foreign decisions also depends, therefore, on a process of review and confirmation. It is assumed for the decision to be enforceable that it 'has content, determined according to the Law of the State of origin, capable of being enforced'.[49]

With regard to the constitutive effectiveness of the decisions (those which constitute, modify, or extinguish legal situations), it is understood that for these to produce effects they must be subject to a review procedure. On the other hand, the incidental effects are not dependent on review, since the decision on those effects is taken by the national law of the recognising state, Timor-Leste.

Article 840 of the CCP establishes the requirements needed in order to confirm foreign decisions. It is necessary:

(a) that there is no doubt as to the authenticity of the document containing the decision nor regarding the intelligence of the decision;
(b) that it has become res judicata according to the law of the country in which it was rendered;
(c) that it comes from a foreign court whose jurisdiction has not been brought about by abuse of law and that it does not rule on matters which are the exclusive jurisdiction of the Timorese courts;
(d) that the exception of *lis pendens* or res judicata on the grounds of a case in a Timorese court cannot be invoked, unless it was the foreign court which prevented the jurisdiction;
(e) that the defendant has been correctly summoned for the action, pursuant to the law of the country of the court of origin, and that the *inter partes* and equality of the parties principles have been observed in the proceedings;
(f) that it does not contain a decision the recognition of which leads to a result which is clearly incompatible with the principles of international public order of the state of Timor-Leste.[50]

47. 'To confirm a foreign decision, after it has been reviewed, is to recognize, in the State of the forum, the effects it would have in the State of origin, as a jurisdictional act, according to the law of that same State'. (Marques dos Santos *supra* n. 23, at 105).
48. To date, since the Supreme Court of Justice has not yet been set up, and in line with Article 164 of the Constitution, these duties have been assigned to the Court of Appeal, the highest level of court in Timor-Leste.
49. See Luís Lima Pinheiro (Vol. III), *supra* n. 11, at 478; and notes.
50. For more detail on the requirements set out, see: Ferrer Correia, *supra* n. 41, at 476-483.

The material nature of the review is present in the article which lays down the grounds for challenging the request, Article 844 of the CCP, more precisely in paragraph 2, as follows: if the decision has been rendered against a legal or natural person of Timorese nationality, the challenge may also be based on the notion that the result of the case would have been more favourable to him if the foreign court had applied the material law of Timor-Leste, when the issue should be resolved by the latter according to the Timorese conflict of law rules.

[B] Arbitral Awards (Including ICSID Awards): Requirements and Limitations

Timor-Leste is not a party to the 1958 Convention on the Recognition and Enforcement of Foreign Arbitral Awards 1958 (New York Convention).

The CCP lays down, in Articles 671, 672 and 841, a regime identical to that for the recognition of judicial decisions – a system of assimilation –[51] with the latter article stating in particular that Article 840 (dealing with judicial decisions) is applicable to the arbitral decision, as far as it may be. 'The effectiveness of the foreign arbitral decision in the legal order of the forum generally depends on its prior review and confirmation....'[52]

Accordingly, the material effects of the arbitral decision are comparable to those mentioned with regard to foreign judicial decisions, although there is a lack of Timorese case law which would allow for an assessment of the reach and consequences of the legal solutions provided for, and the general principles of law are resorted to in order to fill the gaps.

The relevance of the above is clear insofar as Timor-Leste is a party to the ICSID Convention. It is necessary to make this instrument operational and in line with the internal rules, which have been non-existent until now; although it is understood that the impositions presented within the internal rules of recognition will apply.

§13.06 RECOGNITION OF OTHER FOREIGN PUBLIC DOCUMENTS

The question of enforceability of the decisions and deeds drawn up in a foreign country are laid down in Article 49 of the Portuguese CCP, which is at the root of Article 672 of the Timorese CCP. Despite the heading, Article 672 of the Timorese CCP contains only a single paragraph on decisions, and does not lay down the Portuguese solution in paragraph 2 of the enforceability of the deed, regardless of the review procedure, without a judicial declaration of enforceability being required.[53] Thus, the Timorese

51. For greater detail, see Luís Lima Pinheiro (Vol. III), *supra* n. 11, at 565 et seq.
52. Dário Moura Vicente, *Da Arbitragem Comercial Internacional – Direito aplicável ao mérito da causa* (Coimbra Editora, 1990), at 51.
53. As Abílio Neto states in *Código de Processo Civil Anotado* (14th ed., Ediforum, 1997), at 117: 'Regarding the enforceability of deeds drawn up in a foreign country, the law gives them the same value as a decision rendered by a foreign court which has been reviewed and confirmed'.

system is lacking with regard to the solution to be given to the enforceability of deeds drawn up in foreign countries.

In the light of the above, in our view, the solution to be given to the issue should be to make this deed equivalent to the foreign extra-judicial deed, that is, legalising it so that it may be enforceable, and it does not seem reasonable to us to subject an extra-judicial deed to a review procedure identical to that for decisions.[54] Thus, an enforcement action may be brought with the foreign deed. In the event that this is contested, the validity shall be assessed in the light of the substantive provisions of the law the application of which is determined by the rules of PIL. In this article the 'legislator' simplifies the Portuguese regime, perhaps not entirely intentionally, but *a fortiori* it cannot have wished to remove the enforceability of foreign deeds.

§13.07 TREATIES FOR JUDICIAL COOPERATION

As mentioned before, to date the Timorese legal order does not contain any type of conventional instrument regarding issues of judicial cooperation of a civil or commercial nature.[55] Furthermore, Timor-Leste is not a party to any of the Hague Conventions on Private International Law issues.

54. The following comment on Article 49 of the Portuguese CCP (by Abílio Neto, *Ibid.*) therefore becomes relevant: 'The internal structure of an extra-judicial deed is governed by the law of the country in which the document is issued, although it must be legalized to become enforceable...; the enforceability is determined exclusively by the *lex fori*, that is, by Art. [*669.*] and by the provisions that complement it (3rd ed., Lopes Cardoso, Manual, p. 94)'.
55. The internal legislation, treaties and international conventions in force in Timor-Leste must be published in the *Jornal da República*. *Jornal da República* can be consulted at: http://www.jornal.gov.tl/.

CHAPTER 14

Vietnam

Nguyen Thi Xuan Trinh & Konrad Hull[*]

§14.01 CODIFICATION OF PRIVATE INTERNATIONAL LAW AND RELEVANCE OF CASE LAW

[A] Codification and Case Law

Private international law in Vietnam is in the process of development. It has not been codified in a comprehensive code or law but it is partly governed in several laws. Basic principles or provisions of private international law are mainly stipulated in the Civil Code (2005) in the title of 'Civil relations involving a foreign element' and Decree No. 138/2006/ND-CP dated 15 November 2006 providing details for implementation of provisions of the Civil Code on civil relations involving a foreign element.

Pursuant to the Civil Code, a civil relation involving a foreign element is defined as a civil relation in which at least one of the participating parties is a foreign body, organisation or individual or is a Vietnamese residing overseas, or a civil relation between participating parties being Vietnamese citizens or organisations but the basis for the establishment, modification, or termination of such relation was the law of a foreign country, or such basis arose in a foreign country, or the assets involved in the relation are located in a foreign country.

The Vietnamese legal system follows civil law, with some influence from the French civil law. Vietnam does not recognise case law, which does not have any legal value in Vietnam. Furthermore, there is no centralised court judgment depository or any other means to search case law in Vietnam. In practice, the People's Supreme Court of Vietnam has organised annual meetings to summarise hearing issues during the year. In summary documents, the People's Supreme Court raises certain cases as

* Nguyen Thi Xuan Trinh, Partner, VNA Legal. Konrad Hull, Partner, VNA Legal.

examples to point out legal mistakes in hearings, in judgments or violation of litigation laws. Such examples are references for lower courts in resolution of cases, but are not 'case law'.

[B] Multilateral Conventions Providing Uniform Substantive Law and/or International Jurisdictional Rules

According to Article 759 of the Civil Code, where an international treaty of which Vietnam is a member contains provisions different from those in the Civil Code, such international treaty will prevail.

Vietnam is a party to neither the UN Convention on Contracts for the International Sale of Goods (CISG), nor the Conventions for the International Carriage of Goods by Air and by Sea. However, Vietnam is a party to the Agreement on International Goods Transport by Rail (SGMS), as well as to ten multilateral agreements and protocols administered by the World Intellectual Property Organization (WIPO).[1]

§14.02 JURISDICTION OF LOCAL COURTS IN FOREIGN-RELATED CASES

[A] Grounds for Jurisdiction

[1] General

Pursuant to the Civil Procedure Code, which entered into force on 1 January 2005, a civil affair involving foreign elements is a civil affair in which at least one concerned party is a foreigner or Vietnamese residing in a foreign country or a civil relation between concerned parties being Vietnamese citizens, bodies or organisations in which the ground for establishment, alteration, or termination is subject to the laws of a foreign country or which arises in a foreign country or which relates to assets located in a foreign country.

The Vietnamese courts will resolve civil affairs involving foreign elements in the following cases:

(a) The defendant is a foreign body or organisation whose head office is situated in Vietnam or the defendant whose managing body, branch, or representative office is situated in Vietnam.
(b) The defendant is a foreign citizen or person without nationality who resides, works, or lives permanently in Vietnam or has assets in the territory of Vietnam.
(c) The plaintiff is a foreign citizen or person without nationality who resides, works, or lives permanently in Vietnam in respect of civil affairs in relation to a petition for support or identification of parent.

1. http://www.wipo.int/treaties/en/ShowResults.jsp?country_id=185C.

(d) A civil affair in relation to a civil relation the basis for establishment, alteration, or termination of which is subject to the law of Vietnam or which arises in the territory of Vietnam but in which at least one party is a foreign individual, body, or organisation.
(e) A civil affair in relation to a civil relation the basis for establishment, alteration, or termination of which is subject to the law of a foreign country or which arises in a foreign country in which all of the parties are Vietnamese citizens, bodies, or organisations and the plaintiff or defendant resides in Vietnam.
(f) A dispute arising from a contract all or part of which is performed in the territory of Vietnam.
(g) A divorce proceeding in which the plaintiff or defendant is a Vietnamese citizen.

[a] Maritime Activities

Regarding *maritime activities*, the Maritime Code provides that:

(a) Where the parties to a maritime dispute are all foreign organisations or individuals and they have agreed in writing to refer their dispute to a Vietnamese arbitrator, the Vietnamese arbitrator shall have the right to resolve such dispute notwithstanding that it occurred outside the territory of Vietnam.[2]
(b) A maritime dispute stipulated in point (a) above may also be resolved by a Vietnamese court if the grounds for establishment, modification or termination of the relations between the parties to such dispute comply with the law of Vietnam or if the property connected with such relations is located in Vietnam.[3]

[b] Civil Aviation Activities

Regarding *civil aviation* activities, the Civil Aviation Law[4] provides that:

(a) Vietnamese courts have jurisdiction to resolve disputes arising from international aviation carriage contracts in respect of passengers, luggage, goods at the choice of claimants in the following cases:
    (i) The carrier has its head office or main business location in Vietnam.
    (ii) The carrier has its business location and executes carriage contracts in Vietnam.
    (iii) Vietnam is the destination of the carriage journey.

2. Clause 2 of Article 260 of the Maritime Code of Vietnam No. 40/2005/QH11 dated 14 Jun. 2005.
3. *Ibid.*, Clause 3.
4. No. 66/2006/QH11. Revised in November 2014.

International carriage contracts mean carriage contracts which, according to agreements of parties in the contracts, places of departure and destination situate in the territories of two countries or in the territory of one country but the agreed stop place situates in the territory of another country, regardless of interruption in the carriage or load transfer.

(b) In respect of disputes on damages occurring in cases where passengers die or are injured, in addition to the provisions of point (a) above, the Vietnamese courts have jurisdiction to resolve such disputes if passengers have their main and regular residence in Vietnam at the time of the accident causing death or injury occurring provided that:
   (i) The carrier has activities of exploitation of passenger carriage directly by the carrier's airplanes or by airplanes of other carriers under a contract executed between carriers regarding joint venture in exploitation of passenger carriage flights.
   (ii) The carrier using its office or office of other carriers who have a joint venture contract signed with the carrier to conduct business in passenger carriage by aviation in Vietnam.

(c) The court where damages have been occurred has jurisdiction to resolve compensation for damages requested by third person in land, except otherwise regulated by international treaties which Vietnam is a signatory.

[2] Exclusive Jurisdiction

Vietnamese courts will have exclusive jurisdiction for the following civil cases involving foreign elements:

(a) Any civil case relating to the rights with respect to assets being immovable property in the territory of Vietnam.
(b) Any dispute arising from a transport contract and the head office or branch of the carrier being situated in Vietnam.
(c) Any divorce case between a Vietnamese citizen and a foreign citizen or person without nationality if both husband and wife reside, work or live in Vietnam.

Vietnamese courts will have exclusive jurisdiction for the following civil matters involving foreign elements:

(a) Determination of a legal event if such event occurs in the territory of Vietnam.
(b) Declaration that a foreign citizen or person without nationality has restricted capacity for civil acts or has lost the capacity for civil acts if he or she resides, works or lives in Vietnam and such declaration relates to the establishment of his or her rights or obligations in the territory of Vietnam.
(c) Declaration that a foreign citizen or person without nationality is missing or dead if she or he is present in Vietnam at the time of occurrence of an event which is a ground for declaration that a person is missing or dead and such

declaration relates to the establishment of his or her rights or obligations in the territory of Vietnam.

(d) Petition to a Vietnamese court for a declaration that a Vietnamese citizen is missing or dead if such declaration relates to the establishment of his or her rights or obligations in the territory of Vietnam.

(e) Recognition that property existing in the territory of Vietnam has been abandoned or recognition of the ownership rights of a person who currently controls an abandoned property in the territory of Vietnam.

Vietnamese law also provides that any civil affair which has been accepted by a Vietnamese court for resolution in accordance with the provisions on jurisdiction set out above must continue to be resolved by such court even if there is a change of nationality, place of residence, or address of any party or fresh evidence which results in such civil affair falling under the jurisdiction of another Vietnamese court or of a foreign court.

[B] Exclusion of Jurisdiction

[1] Immunity

[a] Sovereign Immunity

Vietnam has no specific law dealing with immunity of jurisdiction, except for some provisions relating to diplomatic agencies and officials.

[b] Diplomatic and Consular Immunity

Pursuant to the Civil Procedure Code, civil affairs relating to foreign organisations, bodies, and individuals entitled to diplomatic or consular immunities and privileges in accordance with international treaties which Vietnam has signed or acceded to will be settled via diplomatic channels.

Pursuant to the Ordinance on privileges and immunities for diplomatic representative bodies, consular bodies and representative bodies of international organisations in Vietnam, dated 23 August 1993, diplomatic officials are entitled to immunity from criminal jurisdiction in Vietnam. They are also entitled to immunity from civil jurisdiction and administrative penalties, except in cases where they participate into the following disputes in a personal capacity:

(a) private real estates situated in the territory of Vietnam;
(b) inheritance;
(c) commercial or occupational activities conducted by them in Vietnam beyond their official function.

Similarly, consular officials and staff when performing their functions are entitled to immunity from criminal jurisdiction, unless they commit serious offences.[5] They are also entitled to immunity from civil and administrative jurisdiction, except for civil cases:

(a) regarding a contract signed by them not in the capacity of a person authorised by the appointing country;
(b) regarding a traffic accident that occurred in Vietnam for which there is a compensation claim made by a third party.

It appears from the above provision that the immunity applicable to diplomatic officials or consular officials in Vietnam is restrictive and not absolute.

[c] Other Immunities

Vietnam is a party to the 1961 Convention on the Privileges and Immunities of the United Nations, but not to the 1947 Convention on the Privileges and Immunities of the Specialised Agencies.

[2] Forum Agreements in Favour of Foreign Courts

Except for a provision in the Maritime Code which provides that parties to contracts relating to maritime activities of which at least one party is a foreign organisation or individual can agree to choose foreign courts to resolve disputes,[6] it appears that this issue has not clearly been provided in Vietnamese laws. Whilst Vietnamese law in other circumstances is silent on the choice of foreign courts, it is generally assumed that because pursuant to various laws (such as the Civil Code and Commercial Law) civil relations or agreements between parties with a foreign elements can choose foreign law as the governing law, foreign courts by implication can hear such matters provided they are not subject to exclusive jurisdiction of Vietnamese courts.

[3] Arbitration Clause

A valid arbitration clause will impede Vietnamese courts to accept and hear the case, unless the arbitration agreement is unable to be performed.[7] There is no clarification under Vietnamese law as to when an arbitration agreement is considered to be unable to be performed.

5. The term 'serious offence' is defined by the Criminal Code of Vietnam as an offence causing great harm to society and the maximum penalty bracket for such offence is up to seven years of imprisonment.
6. Article 4(2) and Article 260 of the Maritime Code of Vietnam No. 40/2005/QH11 dated 14 Jun. 2005.
7. Article 6 of the Law on Commercial Arbitration No. 54/2010/QH12 dated 17 Jun. 2010.

[C] Non-exercise of Jurisdiction

[1] Forum Non Conveniens

The doctrine of forum non conveniens is not applied in Vietnam.

[2] **Lis alibi pendens**

Pursuant to Article 413 of the Civil Procedure Code, in cases where a civil affair involving foreign elements has been *issued with a judgment by a foreign court* in a country with which Vietnam has an international treaty in force on recognition and execution of civil judgments and decisions, an application for a legal action or petition in Vietnam shall be returned or such civil affair shall be suspended by a Vietnamese court.

In addition, when a civil affair involving foreign elements has been *accepted by a foreign court* and the judgment or decision of such foreign court in relation to such civil affair is *recognised and executed in Vietnam*, an application for a legal action or petition in Vietnam shall be returned or such civil affair shall be suspended by a Vietnamese court.

§14.03 APPLICABLE LAW

Procedural issues are governed by the *lex fori*.

[A] Choice of Law

[1] Express Stipulation

Generally, in respect of civil relations involving foreign elements, the civil law of Vietnam will apply. However, Article 759 of the Civil Code also allows parties to contracts to agree on the application of foreign laws if such agreement does not conflict with provisions of the Code or any other legal instruments of Vietnam. In addition, parties can agree on the law applicable to the ownership of movable assets in transit.[8] This concept has also been expressed in some other laws as follows:

(1) In commercial activities, the Commercial Law allows parties to transactions involving foreign elements to agree on the application of foreign laws and international commercial practices if such foreign laws or international commercial practices are not contrary to the basic principles of the laws of Vietnam.

8. Article 766 of the Civil Code. If parties do not choose the law applicable to the ownership of movable assets in transit, the law of the country of destination will apply.

(2) Vietnamese law[9] provides that for foreign exchange activities which have not been regulated by Vietnamese law, parties can agree to apply foreign laws or international practices if such application is not contrary to the basic principles of the laws of Vietnam.
(3) In maritime activities, the Maritime Code of Vietnam allows parties participating in a contract relating to maritime activities, where at least one is a foreign organisation or individual, to agree to the application of foreign laws or international maritime custom for their contractual relations. In addition, if the Maritime Code so stipulates or if it is agreed by the parties in their contracts, foreign laws may be applied in Vietnam to contractual relations relating to maritime activities provided that such laws do not contravene the fundamental principles of the laws of Vietnam.
(4) In foreign investment activities in Vietnam, the Investment Law of Vietnam allows parties to agree in contracts the application of foreign laws or international investment practice if such activities have not been regulated by Vietnamese laws and such application is not contrary to the basic principles of the laws of Vietnam.[10]
(5) In disputes involved foreign elements to be resolved by a Vietnamese arbitral institution or a foreign arbitral institution licensed to operate in Vietnam, the board of arbitrators will apply the law chosen by the parties. If the parties fail to choose the applicable law, the board of arbitrators will decide the applicable law which the council thinks most appropriate.

Please note that there is no clarification under Vietnamese law as to what the 'basic principles of the laws of Vietnam' are. In practice, it is completely subject to the interpretation of the Vietnamese courts.

Current Vietnamese laws allow parties to make a choice of law in limited cases, mostly related to contracts.

[2] Implied Choice

Vietnamese law is silent on implied choice of law.

[B] Other Cases

If no law is chosen by the parties, the following general rules will apply:

(a) The civil law of Vietnam will apply to civil relations involving foreign elements, unless otherwise provided by the Civil Code.

9. Ordinance and Decree 70/2014/ND-CP dated 17 Jul. 2014 on foreign exchange.
10. Article 5 of the Investment Law No. 59/2005/QH11 dated 29 Nov. 2005.

(b) Where an international treaty of which Vietnam is a member contains provisions different from those in the Civil Code, such international treaty will apply.

(c) In the case where the Civil Code, another legal instrument of Vietnam, or an international treaty of which Vietnam is a member provides for the application of foreign law, the law of such foreign country will apply if its application or the consequences of its application are not inconsistent with the fundamental principles of the law of Vietnam.

(d) Where civil relations involving foreign elements are not governed by the Civil Code, any other legal instrument of Vietnam, any international treaty of which Vietnam is a member or any civil contract signed between the parties, international customary practices shall be applied provided that such application, or the consequence thereof, is not contrary to the basic principles of the laws of Vietnam.

[1] Civil Subjects

The civil legal capacity of a foreigner shall be determined according to the law of his/her nationality. In cases where a foreigner establishes and/or performs civil transactions in Vietnam, his/her civil act capacity shall be determined according to the law of the Socialist Republic of Vietnam.

In respect of a stateless person, the law applicable to him/her will be the law of the country of residence of such person or, if such person has no place of residence, the laws of Vietnam. In respect of a foreigner with multiple foreign nationalities, the law applicable to such person will be the law of the country of which he or she holds nationality and where he or she resided at the time when the civil relations were established. If such foreigner is not resident in any of the countries of which he or she holds nationality, the applicable law shall be the law of the country of which he or she holds nationality and with which he or she maintains the closest ties regarding civil rights and obligations.

The civil legal capacity of a foreign legal person shall be determined according to the law of the country where such foreign legal person has been established except when such company establishes and/or performs civil transactions in Vietnam (the law of Vietnam will apply).

[2] Property Rights

Regarding property rights, the Civil Code provides that:

(a) The establishment, implementation, alteration and termination of property ownership rights and the contents of such rights shall be determined according to the law of the country where such property is located, except:
   - in case of movable property being transported, the law of the country of destination applies, unless otherwise agreed upon;

- in case of determination of the ownership rights to civil aircraft and seagoing vessels in Vietnam, the law on civil aviation and the maritime law of Vietnam shall be respected.

(b) The differentiation between movable and immovable property shall be determined in accordance with the law of the country where such property is located.

[3] Succession

Regarding succession:

(a) The inheritance at law must comply with the laws of the nationality of the deceased before their death. Nevertheless, inheritance rights to immovables must comply with the laws of the countries where such immovables are located.
(b) The capacity to make, change and cancel testaments must comply with the laws of the countries where the testators are citizens. Forms of testament must comply with the laws of the countries where the testaments are made.

[4] Contractual Obligations

In respect of civil contracts, the following rules will apply:

(a) The laws of the country in which the contract is performed will apply to determine the rights and obligations of parties to a civil contract.
(b) The law of Vietnam will apply for a civil contract which is entered into in Vietnam and performed entirely in Vietnam.
(c) Where a civil contract does not state the place of performance, the place of performance of the contract shall be determined in accordance with the laws of Vietnam.
(d) Contracts relating to immovable property located in Vietnam must comply with the laws of Vietnam.
(e) The form of a contract must comply with the law of the country where the contract was entered into. In the case where a contract is entered into in a foreign country and breaches the provisions on the form of a contract pursuant to the laws of that country, but is not contrary to the provisions on the form of such contract pursuant to the law of Vietnam, the form of such contract entered into in the foreign country shall, nevertheless, be recognised in Vietnam.
(f) The form of a contract relating to the formation or transfer of ownership rights to structures, residential housing or other immovable property within the territory of Vietnam must comply with the laws of Vietnam.
(g) In the case of entering into a contract in absentia, the determination of the place where the contract was entered into must comply with the law of the

country of residence of the individual being the party requesting the contract to be entered into, or of the country where the head office of the legal entity is located where the party requesting the contract to be entered into is a legal entity.

(h) The point of time of entering into a contract in absentia shall be determined in accordance with the law of the country of the person requesting that the contract be entered into if such party receives an answer agreeing to the proposal of the such party that the contract be entered into.

[5] Maritime and Civil Aviation Activities

Regarding maritime activities, the Maritime Code of Vietnam provides that:

(a) The law of the flag State shall apply to cases of legal relations relating to ownership of property aboard seagoing ships, charter contracts, contracts hiring crew, contracts for carriage of passengers and luggage by sea, distribution of salvage awards between the owner of a rescuer ship and the crew of the rescuer ship, recovery of property sunk on the high seas, and incidents occurring aboard seagoing ships on the high seas.

(b) The law of the place where a seagoing ship docks immediately after general average occurs shall apply to cases of legal relations relating to general average.

(c) The law of the relevant country where a collision, salvage remuneration, or recovery of property sunk in the internal waters or territorial sea of a country occurs shall apply to such cases.
The law of the relevant country where an arbitrator or a court is the first to deal with the dispute shall apply to cases of legal relations relating to collisions or salvage operations performed on the high seas.
The law of the flag State shall apply to cases of collisions occurring on the high seas or the internal waters or territorial sea of another country between seagoing ships of the same nationality.

(d) The law of the relevant country where cargo is delivered pursuant to a contract shall apply to cases of legal relations relating to carriage of cargo.

Regarding civil aviation activities, the Civil Aviation Law of Vietnam provides that:

(a) The law of the country registering nationality of airplanes shall apply for social relationships arising in flying planes and for determining rights to airplanes.

(b) The law of the country where contracts relevant to rights to airplanes are signed shall apply to determine the form of contracts.

(c) The law of the country where salvage or preservation of airplanes is performed shall apply for payment of salvage remuneration or remuneration for preservation of airplanes.
(d) The law of the country where accidents from airplane collisions or obstruction or from flying airplanes causing damages to third persons on land occurs shall apply for compensation of damages.

[6] Torts

Regarding torts, the law to be applied is the one of the country where the act causing damage takes place or where the actual consequences of such act arise. In cases where the act causing damage occurs outside the territory of Vietnam and the person who causes the damage and the victim are both Vietnamese citizens or legal persons, the law of Vietnam shall apply.[11]

[7] Unilateral Transactions

In case of unilateral civil transactions, the rights and obligations of the party that voluntarily performs the unilateral civil transaction shall be determined in accordance with the law of his/her residence or principal place of business.[12]

[C] *Renvoi*

According to Article 759 of the Civil Code, if the applicable foreign law refers back to the law of Vietnam, the law of Vietnam will apply.

[D] Mandatory Rules of the Forum and of Third States

Vietnamese law does not provide a clear and specific provision on this issue. Nevertheless, Article 759 of the Civil Code states that in case the Civil Code of Vietnam, another legal instrument of Vietnam, or an international treaty of which Vietnam is a member provides for the application of a foreign law, the law of such foreign country will apply if its application or the consequences of its application are not inconsistent with the fundamental principles of the law of Vietnam.

[E] Proof of Foreign Law

Vietnamese law is silent on this issue. However, there is a principle under the Civil Procedure Code of Vietnam stating that concerned parties have rights and obligations to provide evidence to the court and to prove that their requests have grounds and are

11. Article 773 of the Civil Code.
12. Article 772 of the Civil Code.

lawful. The court will only conduct the verification and collection of evidence in certain cases stipulated by the Civil Procedure Code, through one or a number of the following measures:[13]

(a) Taking the testimony of a concerned party or witness.
(b) Cross-examination between concerned parties or between concerned parties and witnesses.
(c) Seeking the opinion of an expert.
(d) Deciding on valuation of assets, requesting for evaluation of price of assets.
(e) Conducting on inspection or evaluation on-the-spot.
(f) Authorising the taking, verification of evidence, documents.
(g) Requesting individuals, bodies or organisations to provide readable, audible or visible materials or other objects relating to the resolution of the civil affairs.

[F] Evasion of the Law

There is no Vietnamese written statutory provision governing this issue. However, as noted above, even if a foreign law is chosen by the parties, such law can only be recognised by Vietnamese courts if the application of such law is not contrary to the basic principles of the laws of Vietnam. In practice, if the court of Vietnam thinks that there may be an evasion of the Vietnamese law, it can rule that the application of such foreign laws is contrary to the basic principles of the laws of Vietnam and therefore defeat its application.

§14.04 PROCEDURAL ISSUES

[A] Service of Summons and Judicial Orders Abroad

Vietnam is not a signatory to the 1965 Hague Convention on the Service Abroad of Judicial and Extrajudicial Documents in Civil or Commercial Matters.

The service of summons and judicial orders abroad in civil cases involving foreign elements when there is a relevant international treaty or the foreign country applied the reciprocal principle will be conducted in accordance with a judicial mandate procedure as follows:

(a) Provincial People's Courts or Appeal Courts of the Supreme People's Court have the authority to request for judicial mutual assistance regarding civil matters ('Authorised Courts'). In resolving civil matters, if District People's Courts have a need of judicial mutual assistance, they can prepare a judicial mandate dossier to be sent to the Provincial People's Court for the Provincial People's Courts to act in their authority.

13. Article 85 of the Civil Procedure Code.

(b) A judicial mandate dossier will include the following documents:
   (i) Request form for implementation of a judicial mandate in prescribed form.
   (ii) A Judicial mandate form.
   (iii) Other documents as requested by the competent authorities of the requested country.
   (iv) Other documents and materials serving the implementation of the judicial mandate such as notices on acceptance of cases, judgments or decisions of the courts, etc.

(c) Authorised Courts will send the judicial mandate dossier to the Ministry of Justice of Vietnam.

(d) If Vietnam and the requested foreign country have signed a relevant international treaty, then:
   (i) Within ten working days from the date of receipt of the dossier from the Authorised Courts, for complete and valid dossiers, the Ministry of Justice will transfer the dossier to the competent authorities of the foreign country or to the Ministry of Foreign Affairs of Vietnam.
   (ii) Within five working days from the date of receipt of the dossier from the Ministry of Justice, the Ministry of Foreign Affairs will transfer the dossier to Vietnamese Representative Bodies in the foreign country.
   (iii) Within five working days from the date of receipt of the dossier from the Ministry of Foreign Affairs, the Vietnamese Representative Bodies have to transfer the dossier to the competent authorities of the foreign country.

(e) If Vietnam and the requested foreign country have not signed an international treaty on mutual judicial assistance for civil matters or agreements or there is no precedent practice in application of the reciprocal principle, the Ministry of Justice will transfer the dossier to the Ministry of Foreign Affairs. Within ten working days from the date of receipt of the dossier (or twenty working days if opinion of the Ministry of Justice and/or the Supreme People's Court is needed), the Ministry of Foreign Affairs will consider and decide whether or not the reciprocal principle should be applied.

   Where the Ministry of Foreign Affairs decides to request the competent authority of a foreign country to apply the reciprocal principle, then:
   (i) It will send the judicial mandate dossier to the Vietnamese Representative Body in the foreign country attaching to it a diplomatic note requesting the competent authority of the foreign country to apply the reciprocal principle.
   (ii) Within five working days from the date of receipt of the dossier from the Ministry of Foreign Affairs, the Vietnamese Representative Body shall send the dossier requesting for application of the reciprocal principle to the competent authority of the foreign country.
   (iii) Within five working days from the date of receipt of official reply of the foreign competent authority, the Vietnamese Representative Body will send a written notification to the Ministry of Foreign Affairs.

(iv) Within five working days from the date of receipt of written notification of the Vietnamese Representative Body, the Ministry of Foreign Affairs shall notify the result to the Ministry of Justice and the Supreme People's Court for knowledge and coordination.

If the competent authority of a foreign country agrees to apply the reciprocal principle with conditions, the Ministry of Foreign Affairs shall consider and decide after consulting the Ministry of Justice and the Supreme People's Court.

(f) Within five working days from the date of fulfilment of the judicial mandate or from the date of receipt of written result notice regarding the implementation of the judicial mandate from the competent authorities of a foreign country, the Vietnamese Representative Body in the foreign country shall send a written notice of result of implementation, minutes of transfer of the judicial mandate dossier together with attached materials, and evidence to the Ministry of Foreign Affairs.

(g) Within three months from the date of receipt of the judicial mandate dossier from the Ministry of Foreign Affairs or the Ministry of Justice, the Vietnamese Representative Body must notify the Ministry of Foreign Affairs if the foreign competent authorities do not notify the result of the judicial mandate or do not reply to the request of Vietnam for the application of the reciprocal principle;

(h) Within five working days from the date of receipt of written result notice from the Vietnamese Representative Body, the Ministry of Foreign Affairs will send such notice to the Ministry of Justice to transfer it to the court.

In cases where the judicial mandate cannot be conducted because Vietnam and the foreign country have not signed an international treaty or do not apply reciprocity, the Vietnamese courts still need to make judicial mandate dossiers. The service of summons and judicial orders will be performed as follows:

(a) Publicly post the judicial mandate dossier in the head office of the court, the people's committee of the commune of the last residence of the concerned party within six months.

(b) Publish in nationwide daily newspapers within three consecutive issues.

(c) Broadcast in nationwide radio station or television station in the channel for foreigners three times in three consecutive days.

[B] Obtaining Evidence Abroad

Vietnam is not a party to the 1970 Hague Convention on the taking of Evidence Abroad in Civil or Commercial Matters. Obtaining evidence abroad in civil cases involving foreign elements will be implemented in accordance with the procedures for judicial mandate as mentioned in section 14.04[A] above.

[C] Restraint of Foreign Proceedings

Vietnamese law is silent on whether or not a local court can be asked to stop a foreign arbitral or judicial proceeding on the same matter. Given this, it appears that restraint of foreign proceedings by local Vietnamese court is not possible or would be highly unlikely.

[D] Proof of Foreign Public Documents

Vietnam is not a signatory to the 1961 Hague Convention Abolishing the Requirement for Legalisation for Foreign Public Documents.

Any papers or documents which are prepared, issued or authenticated by foreign competent bodies in accordance with the law of a foreign country or outside the territory of Vietnam shall be recognised by Vietnamese courts if such papers or documents have been consularised, unless otherwise provided by an international treaty which Vietnam has signed or acceded to.

Vietnam has signed mutual legal assistance treaties or consular treaties with certain countries for exemption of legalisation for certain documents such as Algeria, Poland, Bulgaria, Belarus, Cambodia, Cuba, Taiwan, Denmark, Hungary, Iraq, Italy, Lao, Mongolia, Russia, Japan, France, Rumania, Czech, Switzerland, China, Ukraine, and Slovakia.

Any paper or document which is prepared in a foreign language and submitted to a Vietnamese court must be accompanied by a Vietnamese translation duly notarised and consularised.

[E] Statute of Limitations

Statutes of limitations for a civil relation involving a foreign element will be governed by the law applicable to the dispute.[14]

[F] Remedies and Damages

Compensation for contractual remedies and damages:

(a) Remedies and damages shall be determined pursuant to the governing law chosen by parties to the contract. If no choice of law is made in the contract, the rights and obligations of the parties to a civil contract shall be determined in accordance with the laws of the country in which the contract is performed.

(b) A civil contract which is entered into in Vietnam and performed entirely in Vietnam must comply with the laws of the Socialist Republic of Vietnam.

14. Article 777 of the Civil Code.

(c) Where a civil contract does not state the place of performance, the place of performance of the contract shall be determined in accordance with the laws of the Socialist Republic of Vietnam.
(d) Contracts relating to immovable property located in Vietnam must comply with the laws of the Socialist Republic of Vietnam.

Compensation for non-contractual damages:

(a) Compensation for non-contractual damages shall be determined in accordance with the law of the country in which the act causing damage occurred or in which the actual consequences of such act arise.
(b) Compensation for any damage caused by an aircraft flying in international airspace or by a ship sailing at sea shall be determined in accordance with the law of the country of nationality of the aircraft or ship, except where otherwise provided by the law on civil aviation and the maritime law of the Socialist Republic of Vietnam.
(c) Where the act causing damage occurs outside the territory of the Socialist Republic of Vietnam and both the person causing such damage and the victim of such damage are Vietnamese citizens or Vietnamese legal entities, the laws of the Socialist Republic of Vietnam shall apply.

[G] Foreign Currency Obligations

Pursuant to Vietnamese laws on foreign exchange, in the territory of Vietnam, all transactions, payments, displaying, advertising, quotations, setting/fixing prices, and recording of prices in contracts and agreements and other similar forms made by residents are not permitted to be made in foreign currency, except for certain specified exceptions. However, foreign currency is allowed to be used in transactions between residents and non-residents. Given this, it appears that claims between residents and non-residents can be in a foreign currency as stipulated in their transaction documents.

Residents include:

(1) Credit institutions and branches of foreign banks established and carrying on business in Vietnam.
(2) Economic institutions established and carrying on business in Vietnam.
(3) State bodies, units of the people's armed forces, political organisations, socio-political organisations, socio-political-professional organisations, social organisations, socio-professional organisations and social funds, and charitable funds of Vietnam operating in Vietnam.
(4) Diplomatic representative offices and consulate representative offices of Vietnam in foreign countries, as well as representative offices in international organisations.
(5) Representative offices in foreign countries of the institutions stipulated in sub-clauses (1), (2), (3).

(6) Vietnamese citizens residing in Vietnam; Vietnamese citizens residing overseas for a duration of less than twelve months; and Vietnamese citizens working for any of the organisations stipulated in sub-clauses (4) and (5) above and the individuals accompanying such citizens.

(7) Vietnamese citizens travelling overseas for purposes of tourism, study, medical treatment, or visits.

(8) Foreigners permitted to reside in Vietnam for a duration of twelve months or more. In the case of foreigners staying in Vietnam for study, medical treatment, tourism, or working for diplomatic representative offices, consulates or representative offices of foreign organisations in Vietnam, such duration shall exclude any period of ineligibility as resident;

(9) Branches in Vietnam of foreign economic institutions and forms of presence in Vietnam of foreign parties participating in investment activities in accordance with the provisions of the law on investment, and operating offices of foreign contractors in Vietnam.

Non-residents means entities other than those included above.

[H] Restraining Removal of Assets and Securing Evidence in Favour of a Foreign Arbitration/Judicial Process

It appears that interim measures, including restraining removal of assets, can only be applied for cases which Vietnamese courts are in the process of resolving. It is not possible to request for restraining removal of assets in Vietnam in favour of a foreign arbitration or judicial process.

§14.05 RECOGNITION AND ENFORCEMENT OF FOREIGN DECISIONS

[A] Judicial Decisions: Requirements and Limitations

Pursuant to the Civil Procedure Code of Vietnam, a foreign civil judgment or order will be recognised and enforced in Vietnam only if such country has signed an agreement with Vietnam regarding enforcement of foreign court judgments, or is a co-signatory with Vietnam to a multilateral treaty on the recognition and enforcement of foreign court judgments. Until now, Vietnam has only signed agreements with certain COMECON[15] countries on the enforcement of foreign court judgments. However, it is doubtful that a Vietnamese Court would enforce judgments from these countries as a matter of practice. Except for the above, no other agreements exist, and Vietnam is not yet a signatory to any multilateral treaty on the recognition and enforcement of foreign judgments.

15. The Council for Mutual Economic Assistance (COMECON) was an economic organization under the leadership of the former Soviet Union.

If there is no applicable international treaty on the recognition and enforcement of foreign court judgments, a civil judgment or order issued by a foreign court can also be considered, recognised and enforced in Vietnam by Vietnamese courts on a reciprocal basis.

In order for a foreign judgment or order to be recognised and enforced in Vietnam, an application must be sent to the Ministry of Justice of Vietnam. Attached to the application, the applicant must also send documents or materials as required in an international treaty of which Vietnam is a signatory or participant. If the international treaty does not have such requirement or in the absence of any international treaty, the applicant must provide a valid copy of the judgment or decision of the foreign court; a document certifying that such judgment or decision is in force, the time-limit for enforcement has not expired and such judgment or decision should be enforced in Vietnam, unless such items have been specified in the judgment or decision; and a document certifying that a copy of such judgment or decision has been served to the person against whom an enforcement is sought. If the person against whom an enforcement is sought or his/her legal representative was absent at the trial of the foreign court, a document certifying that such person was duly summoned is required.

Within seven days from the date of receipt of the application and attached documents, the Ministry of Justice must transfer the dossier to the competent court, which within three working days from the date of receipt, must accept and notify the Prosecution Office at the same level; Within four to six months from the date of acceptance, the court can decide to suspend its consideration of the application or suspend its consideration of the application and return the dossier to the Ministry of Justice or commence a court meeting to consider the application; Within one month from the date of issuance of decision to commence a court meeting, the court must commence a court meeting to consider the application and to decide whether or not to recognise and enforce such judgment or decision of the foreign court in Vietnam.[16]

Vietnamese courts will not recognise the following civil judgments or decisions of foreign courts for enforcement in Vietnam:[17]

(a) The judgment or decision is not yet legally enforceable in accordance with the laws of the country in which the court has made such judgment or decision.
(b) The person against whom an enforcement is sought or his/her legal representative was absent at the trial of the foreign court because such person was not properly summoned.
(c) The case falls under the exclusive jurisdiction of Vietnamese courts.
(d) The case has been resolved by a legally enforceable judgment of a Vietnamese court or by a legally enforceable foreign judgment which has been recognised by Vietnamese courts or a Vietnamese court has accepted and is resolving the case before the foreign tribunal accepted to hear the case.

16. Articles 350–354 of the Civil Procedure Code.
17. Article 356 of the Civil Procedure Code.

(e) The time-limit for enforcement of the judgment has expired in accordance with the law of the country in which the court has made such civil judgment or decision, or in accordance with the laws of Vietnam.
(f) The recognition and enforcement in Vietnam of the civil judgment or decision of the foreign court is contrary to the basic principles of the laws of Vietnam.

In principle, a Vietnamese court will not review the case but only check and verify the judgment or decision of the foreign court and documents attached to the application against the provisions of the Civil Procedure Code, other provisions of Vietnamese laws and of the relevant international treaties in force in Vietnam. Nevertheless, in practice, there can be a re-hearing of the case by the Vietnamese court and the likelihood of the success of any such application is limited.

Within fifteen days as from the date the court decided on the recognition or non-recognition, the involved parties or their lawful representatives are entitled to appeal against such decision.[18] Also the procuracies of the same level or the Supreme People's Procuracy shall be entitled to protest against such court decision.

[B] Arbitral Awards (Including ICSID Awards): Requirements and Limitations

Like foreign civil judgments, Article 343 of the CPC provides that a foreign arbitral award will be recognised in Vietnam if the award is issued in a country or by an arbitrator of a country that has signed an agreement with Vietnam regarding enforcement of foreign arbitral awards, or is a co-signatory with Vietnam to a multilateral treaty on the recognition and enforcement of foreign arbitral awards.

Vietnam is a party to the 1958 New York Convention on the Recognition and Enforcement of Foreign Arbitral Awards (although with the reciprocity and commercial reservations). In addition, foreign arbitral awards can also be recognised and enforced in Vietnam on a reciprocal basis. Pursuant to Vietnamese law, a party wishing to enforce a foreign arbitral award in Vietnam can only do so if it submits an application to the Ministry of Justice for a review of the award by the relevant Vietnamese Court and such application is accepted. However, Vietnamese courts will not recognise and enforce a foreign arbitral award that is contrary to Vietnamese law principles. Therefore, there can be a re-hearing in the Vietnamese courts of any foreign arbitral award, and this has been the practice to date. Very few foreign arbitral awards have been successfully enforced in Vietnam.

In order for a foreign arbitral award to be recognised and enforced in Vietnam, an application must be sent to the Ministry of Justice of Vietnam. Attached to the application, the applicant must also send documents or materials as required in an international treaty of which Vietnam is a party. If the international treaty does not have such requirement, or in the absence of any international treaty, the applicant must provide a valid copy of the foreign arbitral award and a valid copy of the

18. Article 358 of the Civil Procedure Code.

arbitration agreement entered into by the parties. Applications may be filed if: (i) the defendant has its principal office or residence in Vietnam, or (ii) where assets related to the enforcement are located in Vietnam at the time of filing the application.[19]

Within seven days from the date of receipt of the application and attached documents, the Ministry of Justice must transfer the dossier to the competent court, who within three working days must accept and notify the Prosecution Office at the same level; Within two to four months from the date of acceptance, the court can decide to temporarily suspend its consideration of the application or suspend its consideration of the application or commence a court meeting to consider the application; Within twenty days from the date of issuance of decision to commence a court meeting, the court must commence a court meeting to consider the application and to decide whether or not to recognise and enforce such foreign arbitral award in Vietnam.[20]

Vietnamese courts will not recognise foreign arbitral awards on grounds similar to those set out in Article V of the 1958 New York Convention.[21] Article 348 of the Civil Procedure Code ensures that any proceeds or assets realised from the enforcement of a foreign arbitral award may be transferred abroad. Within fifteen days as from the date the courts issue the decision on recognition or non-recognition, the involved parties or their lawful representatives may lodge appeals against such decisions.[22] Also the procuracies of the same level or the Supreme People's Procuracy shall be entitled to protest against such court decision.

Vietnam is not a party to the Convention on the Settlement of Investment Disputes Between States and Nationals of Other States ('ICSID Convention'), but has ratified the 2009 ASEAN Comprehensive Investment Agreement, according to which Vietnam has to provide for the enforcement in its territory of the awards rendered under its investment dispute settlement mechanism.

§14.06 RECOGNITION OF OTHER FOREIGN PUBLIC DOCUMENTS

In order to be recognised and used in Vietnam, foreign documents must be consularised by the Ministry of Foreign Affairs, its authorised bodies or Vietnamese diplomatic representative offices, consular agencies or other bodies authorised to perform consular functions of Vietnam in foreign countries,[23] except for the following documents which are exempted from consularisation:

(a) Documents exempted from consularisation in accordance with international treaties to which Vietnam and relevant foreign countries are participants or in accordance with the reciprocal principle.

19. Article 344 of the Civil Procedure Code.
20. Articles 366, 367 and 368 of the Civil Procedure Code.
21. Article 370 of the Civil Procedure Code.
22. Article 372 of the Civil Procedure Code.
23. Decree No. 111/2011/ND-CP of the Government of Vietnam dated 5 Dec. 2011 regarding consular certification and consularisation.

(b) Documents transferred directly or via diplomatic way between competent authorities of Vietnam and competent authorities of foreign countries.
(c) Documents exempted from consularisation in accordance with the provisions of Vietnamese law.
(d) Documents which the receiving bodies of Vietnam do not request for consularisation in accordance with provisions of Vietnamese law.

Regarding Point (a) above, Vietnam has signed mutual legal assistance treaties or consular treaties with certain countries for exemption of consularisation for certain documents such as Algeria, Poland, Bulgaria, Belarus, Cambodia, Cuba, Taiwan, Denmark, Hungary, Iraq, Italy, Lao, Mongolia, Russia, Japan, France, Rumania, Czech, Switzerland, China, Ukraine, and Slovakia.

For certain documents, relevant Vietnamese authorities will not perform the consularisation, including:

(a) Documents repaired, erased, and not yet corrected in accordance with the law.
(b) Documents in the dossiers requested for legalisation that have inconsistent details.
(c) Forged documents or documents issued or certified not in accordance with the authority provided by law.
(d) Documents with signatures or seals which are not original.
(e) Documents with contents breaching rights and interests of the State of Vietnam or not in conformity with guidelines or policies of the State of Vietnam, or other cases which may cause adverse impact to the State of Vietnam.

In order to be legalised by the Vietnamese competent authorities, foreign documents must firstly be certified by the diplomatic representative bodies, consular bodies, or other competent bodies of the foreign country.

§14.07 TREATIES FOR JUDICIAL COOPERATION

Vietnam has signed the following judicial assistance treaties with Algeria, Belarus, Bulgaria, China, Cuba, Czech Republic, France, Hungary, Lao, Mongolia, Poland, Russia, Taiwan, and Ukraine. Vietnam is also a party to the 1993 Convention on Protection of Children and Co-operation in Respect of Intercountry Adoption.

Index

M

N

P

S

T

U